T0200478

Software Design for Flexibility

Software Design for Flexibility

How to Avoid Programming Yourself into a Corner

Chris Hanson and Gerald Jay Sussman

foreword by Guy L. Steele Jr.

The MIT Press
Cambridge, Massachusetts
London, England

This book was set in Computer Modern by the authors with the LaTeX typesetting system and was printed and bound in the United States of America.

Library of Congress Cataloging-in-Publication Data

Names: Hanson, Chris (Christopher P.), author. | Sussman, Gerald Jay, author.
Title: Software design for flexibility : how to avoid programming yourself into a corner / Chris Hanson and Gerald Jay Sussman ; foreword by Guy L. Steele Jr.
Description: Cambridge, Massachusetts : The MIT Press, [2021] | Includes bibliographical references and index.
Identifiers: LCCN 2020040688 | ISBN 9780262045490 (hardcover)
Subjects: LCSH: Software architecture. | Software patterns.
Classification: LCC QA76.76.D47 H35 2021 | DDC 005.1/112–dc23
LC record available at https://lccn.loc.gov/2020040688

10   9   8   7   6   5   4

A computer is like a violin. You can imagine a novice trying first a phonograph and then a violin. The latter, he says, sounds terrible. That is the argument we have heard from our humanists and most of our computer scientists. Computer programs are good, they say, for particular purposes, but they aren't flexible. Neither is a violin, or a typewriter, until you learn how to use it.

Marvin Minsky, "Why Programming Is a Good Medium for Expressing Poorly-Understood and Sloppily-Formulated Ideas" in *Design and Planning*, (1967)

Contents

Foreword

Sometimes when you're writing a program, you get stuck. Maybe it's because you realize you didn't appreciate some aspect of the problem, but all too often it's because you made some decision early in the program design process, about a choice of data structure or a way of organizing the code, that has turned out to be too limiting, and also to be difficult to undo.

This book is a master class in specific program organization strategies that maintain flexibility. We all know by now that while it is very easy to declare an array of fixed size to hold data to be processed, such a design decision can turn out to be an unpleasant limitation that may make it impossible to handle input lines longer than a certain length, or to handle more than a fixed number of records. Many security bugs, especially in the code for the Internet, have been consequences of allocating a fixed-size memory buffer and then failing to check whether the data to be processed would fit in the buffer. Dynamically allocated storage (whether provided by a C-style `malloc` library or by an automatic garbage collector), while more complicated, is much more flexible and, as an extra benefit, less error-prone (especially when the programming language always checks array references to make sure the index is within bounds). That's just a very simple example.

A number of early programming language designs in effect made a design commitment to reflect the style of hardware organization called the *Harvard architecture*: the code is *here*, the data is *there*, and the job of the code is to massage the data. But an inflexible, arm's-length separation between code and data turns out to be a significant limitation on program organization. Well before the end of the twentieth century, we learned from functional programming languages (such as ML, Scheme, and Haskell) and from object-oriented programming languages (such as Simula, Smalltalk, C++, and Java) that there are advantages to being able to treat code as data, to treat data as code, and to bundle smallish amounts of code and related data together rather than organizing code and data separately as monolithic chunks. The most flexible kind of data is a record structure that can contain not only "primitive data items" such as numbers and characters but also references to executable code, such as a function. The most powerful kind of code constructs other code that has been bundled with just the right amount of curated data; such a bundle is not just a "function pointer" but a *closure* (in a functional language) or an *object* (in an object-oriented language).

Jerry Sussman and Chris Hanson draw on their collective century of programming experience to present a set of techniques, developed and tested during decades of teaching at MIT, that further extend this basic strategy for flexibility. Don't just use functions; use *generic* functions, which are open-ended in a way that plain functions are not. Keep functions small. Often the best thing for a function to return is another function (that has been customized with curated data). Be prepared to treat data as code, perhaps even to the extreme of creating a new embedded programming language within your application if necessary. (That is one view of how the Scheme language got its start: the MacLisp dialect of Lisp did not support a completely general form of function closure, so Jerry and I simply used MacLisp to code an embedded dialect of Lisp that did support the kind of function closure we needed.) Be prepared to replace a data structure with a more general data structure that subsumes the original and extends its capabilities. Use automatic constraint propagation to avoid a premature commitment to which data items are inputs and which are outputs.

This book is not a survey, or a tutorial—as I said before, it is a master class. In each chapter, watch as two experts demonstrate an advanced technique by incrementally developing a chunk of working code, explaining the strategy as they go, occasionally pausing to point out a pitfall or to remove a limitation. Then be prepared, when called on, to demonstrate the technique yourself, by extending a data structure or writing additional code—and then to use your imagination and creativity to go beyond what they have demonstrated. The ideas in this book are rich and deep; close attention to both the prose and the code will be rewarded.

Guy L. Steele Jr.
Lexington, Massachusetts
August 2020

Preface

We have all spent too much time trying to deform an old piece
of code so that it could be used in a way that we didn't realize
would be needed when we wrote it. This is a terrible waste of
time and effort. Unfortunately, there are many pressures on us to
write code that works very well for a very specific purpose, with
few reusable parts. But we think that this is not necessary.

It is hard to build systems that have acceptable behavior over a
larger class of situations than was anticipated by their designers.
The best systems are evolvable: they can be adapted to new situations with only minor modification. How can we design systems
that are flexible in this way?

It would be nice if all we had to do to add a new feature to a
program was to add some code, without changing the existing code
base. We can often do this by using certain organizing principles
in the construction of the code base and incorporating appropriate
hooks at that time.

Observations of biological systems tell us a great deal about how
to make flexible and evolvable systems. Techniques originally developed in support of symbolic artificial intelligence can be viewed
as ways of enhancing flexibility and adaptability in programs and
other engineered systems. By contrast, common practice of computer science actively discourages the construction of systems that
are easily modified for use in novel settings.

We have often programmed ourselves into corners and had to
expend great effort refactoring code to escape from those corners.
We have now accumulated enough experience to feel that we can
identify, isolate, and demonstrate strategies and techniques that
we have found to be effective for building large systems that can
be adapted for purposes that were not anticipated in the original design. In this book we share some of the fruits of our over
100 years of programming experience.

This book

This book was developed as the result of teaching computer programming at MIT. We started this class many years ago, intending
to expose advanced undergraduate students and graduate students
to techniques and technologies that are useful in the construction
of programs that are central to artificial intelligence applications,
such as mathematical symbolic manipulation and rule-based sys-

tems. We wanted the students to be able to build these systems flexibly, so that it would be easier to combine such systems to make even more powerful systems. We also wanted to teach students about dependencies—how they can be tracked, and how they can be used for explanation and to control backtracking.

Although the class was and is successful, it turned out that in the beginning we did not have as much understanding of the material as we originally believed. So we put a great deal of effort into sharpening our tools and making our ideas more precise. We now realize that these techniques are not just for artificial intelligence applications. We think that anyone who is building complex systems, such as computer-language compilers and integrated development environments, will benefit from our experience. This book is built on the lectures and problem sets that are now used in our class.

The contents

There is much more material in this book than can be covered in a single-semester class. So each time we offer the class we pick and choose what to present. Chapter 1 is an introduction to our programming philosophy. Here we show *flexibility* in the grand context of nature and of engineering. We try to make the point that flexibility is as important an issue as efficiency and correctness. In each subsequent chapter we introduce techniques and illustrate them with sets of exercises. This is an important organizing principle for the book.

In chapter 2 we explore some universally applicable ways of building systems with room to grow. A powerful way to organize a flexible system is to build it as an assembly of domain-specific languages, each appropriate for easily expressing the construction of a subsystem. Here we develop basic tools for the development of domain-specific languages: we show how subsystems can be organized around mix-and-match parts, how they can be flexibly combined with *combinators*, how *wrappers* can be used to generalize parts, and how we can often simplify a program by abstracting out a domain model.

In chapter 3 we introduce the extremely powerful but potentially dangerous flexibility technique of predicate-dispatched *generic procedures*. We start by generalizing arithmetic to deal with symbolic algebraic expressions. We then show how such a generalization can be made efficient by using type tags for data, and we demonstrate the power of the technique with the design of a simple, but easy to elaborate, adventure game.

In chapter 4 we introduce symbolic *pattern matching*, first to enable term-rewriting systems, and later, with *unification*, to show how type inference can easily be made to work. Here we encounter the need for *backtracking* because of segment variables. Unification is the first place where we see the power of representing and combining *partial-information* structures. We end the chapter with extending the idea to matching general graphs.

In chapter 5 we explore the power of *interpretation* and *compilation*. We believe that programmers should know how to escape the confines of whatever programming language they must use by making an interpreter for a language that is more appropriate for expressing the solution to the current problem. We also show how to naturally incorporate backtracking search by implementing nondeterministic `amb` in an interpreter/compiler system, and how to use *continuations*.

In chapter 6 we show how to make systems of *layered data* and *layered procedures*, where each data item can be annotated with a variety of metadata. The processing of the underlying data is not affected by the metadata, and the code for processing the underlying data does not even know about or reference the metadata. However, the metadata is processed by its own procedures, effectively in parallel with the data. We illustrate this by attaching units to numerical quantities and by showing how to carry dependency information, giving the provenance of data, as derived from the primitive sources.

This is all brought together in chapter 7, where we introduce *propagation* to escape from the expression-oriented paradigm of computer languages. Here we have a wiring-diagram vision of connecting modules together. This allows the flexible incorporation of multiple sources of partial information. Using layered data to support tracking of dependencies enables the implementation of *dependency-directed backtracking*, which greatly reduces the search space in large and complex systems.

This book can be used to make a variety of advanced classes. We use the combinator idea introduced in chapter 2 and the generic procedures introduced in chapter 3 in all subsequent chapters. But patterns and pattern matching from chapter 4 and evaluators from chapter 5 are not used in later chapters. The only material from chapter 5 that is needed later is the introduction to `amb` in sections 5.4 and 5.4.1. The layering idea in chapter 6 is closely related to the idea of generic procedures, but with a new twist. The use of layering to implement dependency tracking, introduced as an example in chapter 6, becomes an essential ingredient in propagation (chapter 7), where we use the dependencies to optimize backtracking search.

Scheme

The code in this book is written in Scheme, a mostly functional language that is a variant of Lisp. Although Scheme is not a popular language, or widely used in an industrial context, it is the right choice for this book.[1]

The purpose of this book is the presentation and explanation of programming ideas. The presentation of example code to elucidate these ideas is shorter and simpler in Scheme than in more popular languages, for many reasons. And some of the ideas would be nearly impossible to demonstrate using other languages.

Languages other than those in the Lisp family require lots of ceremony to say simple things. The only thing that makes our code long-winded is that we tend to use long descriptive names for computational objects.

The fact that Scheme syntax is extremely simple—it is just a representation of the natural parse tree, requiring minimal parsing—makes it easy to write programs that manipulate program texts, such as interpreters, compilers, and algebraic expression manipulators.

It is important that Scheme is a permissive rather than a normative language. It does not try to prevent a programmer from doing something "stupid." This allows us to play powerful games, like dynamically modulating the meanings of arithmetic operators. We would not be able to do this in a language that imposes more restrictive rules.

Scheme allows assignment but encourages functional programming. Scheme does not have static types, but it has very strong dynamic typing that allows safe dynamic storage allocation and garbage collection: a user program cannot manufacture a pointer or access an arbitrary memory location. It is not that we think static types are not a good idea. They certainly are useful for the early exorcism of a large class of bugs. And Haskell-like type systems can be helpful in thinking out strategies. But for this book

---

[1] We provide a short introduction to Scheme in Appendix B.

the intellectual overhead of static types would inhibit consideration of potentially dangerous strategies of flexibility.

Also Scheme provides special features, such as reified continuations and dynamic binding, that are not available in most other
languages. These features allow us to implement such powerful
mechanisms as nondeterministic `amb` in the native language (without a second layer of interpretation).

Acknowledgments

This book would not have been possible without the help of a great number of MIT students who have been in our classes. They actually worked the problems and often told us about bad choices we made and things we did wrong! We are especially indebted to those students who served as teaching assistants over the years. Michael Blair, Alexey Radul, Pavel Panchekha, Robert L. McIntyre, Lars E. Johnson, Eli Davis, Micah Brodsky, Manushaqe Muco, Kenny Chen, and Leilani Hendrina Gilpin have been especially helpful.

Many of the ideas presented here were developed with the help of friends and former students. Richard Stallman, Jon Doyle, David McAllester, Ramin Zabih, Johan deKleer, Ken Forbus, and Jeff Siskind all contributed to our understanding of dependency-directed backtracking. And our understanding of propagation, in chapter 7, is the result of years of work with Richard Stallman, Guy Lewis Steele Jr., and Alexey Radul.

We are especially grateful for the help and support of the functional-programming community, and especially of the Scheme Team. Guy Steele coinvented Scheme with Gerald Jay Sussman back in the 1970s, and he has given a guest lecture in our class almost every year. Arthur Gleckler, Guillermo Juan Rozas, Joe Marshall, James S. Miller, and Henry Manyan Wu were instrumental in the development of MIT/GNU Scheme. Taylor Campbell and Matt Birkholz have made major contributions to that venerable system. We also want to thank Will Byrd and Michael Ballantyne for their help with understanding unification with segment variables.

Hal Abelson and Julie Sussman, coauthors with Gerald Jay Sussman of *Structure and Interpretation of Computer Programs*, helped form our ideas for this book. In many ways this book is an advanced sequel to SICP. Dan Friedman, with his many wonderful students and friends, has made deep contributions to our understanding of programming. We have had many conversations about the art of programming with some of the greatest wizards, such as William Kahan, Richard Stallman, Richard Greenblatt, Bill Gosper, and Tom Knight. Working with Jack Wisdom for many years on mathematical dynamics helped clarify many of the issues that we address in this book.

Sussman wants to especially acknowledge the contributions of his teachers: ideas from discussions with Marvin Minsky, Seymour Papert, Jerome Lettvin, Joel Moses, Paul Penfield, and Edward Fredkin appear prominently in this text. Ideas from Carl Hewitt, David Waltz, and Patrick Winston, who were contemporaneous students of Minsky and Papert, are also featured here. Jeff Siskind and Alexey Radul pointed out and helped with the extermination of some very subtle bugs.

Chris learned a great deal about large-scale programming while working at Google and later at Datera; this experience has influenced parts of this book. Arthur Gleckler provided useful feedback on the book in biweekly lunches. Mike Salisbury was always excited to hear about the latest developments during our regular meetings at Google. Hongtao Huang and Piyush Janawadkar read early drafts of the book. A special thanks goes to Rick Dukes, the classmate at MIT who introduced Chris to the lambda papers and set him on the long road towards this book.

We thank the MIT Department of Electrical Engineering and Computer Science and the MIT Computer Science and Artificial Intelligence Laboratory (CSAIL) for their hospitality and logistical support. We acknowledge the Panasonic Corporation (formerly the Matsushita Electric Industrial Corporation) for support of Gerald Jay Sussman through an endowed chair. Chris Hanson was also partially supported by CSAIL and later by Google for this work.

Julie Sussman, PPA, provided careful reading and serious criticism that forced us to reorganize and rewrite major parts of the text. She has also developed and maintained Gerald Jay Sussman over these many years.

Elizabeth Vickers, spouse of many years, provided a supporting and stable environment for both Chris and their children, Alan and Erica. Elizabeth also cooked many excellent meals for both authors during the long work sessions in Maine. Alan was an occasional but enthusiastic reader of early drafts.

Chris Hanson and Gerald Jay Sussman

Software Design for Flexibility

1

Flexibility in Nature and in Design

It is difficult to design a mechanism of general utility that does any particular job very well, so most engineered systems are designed to perform a specific job. General-purpose inventions, such as the screw fastener, are rare and of great significance. The digital computer is a breakthrough of this kind, because it is a universal machine that can simulate any other information-processing machine.[1] We write software that configures our computers to effect this simulation for the specific jobs that we need done.

We have been designing software to do particular jobs very well, as an extension of past engineering practice. Each piece of software is designed to do a relatively narrow job. As the problem to be solved changes, the software must be changed. But small changes to the problem do not often entail only small changes to the software. Software is designed too tightly for there to be much flexibility. As a consequence, systems cannot evolve gracefully. They are brittle and must be replaced with entirely new designs as the problem domain changes.[2] This is slow and expensive.

Our engineered systems do not have to be brittle. The Internet has been extended from a small system to one of global scale. Our cities evolve organically, to accommodate new business models, life styles, and means of transportation and communication. Indeed, from observation of biological systems we see that it is possible to build systems that can be adapted to changes in the environment, both individually and as an evolutionary ensemble. Why is this not the way we design and build most software? There are histor-

---

[1] The discovery of the existence of universal machines by Alan Turing [124], and the fact that the set of functions that can be computed by Turing machines is equivalent to both the set of functions representable in Alonzo Church's λ calculus [17, 18, 16] and the general recursive functions of Kurt Gödel [45] and Jacques Herbrand [55], ranks among the greatest intellectual achievements of the twentieth century.

[2] Of course, there are some wonderful exceptions. For example, Emacs [113] is an extensible editor that has evolved gracefully to adapt to changes in the computing environment and to changes in its users' expectations. The computing world is just beginning to explore "engineered frameworks," for example, Microsoft's .net and Sun's Java. These are intended to be infrastructures to support evolvable systems.

ical reasons, but the main reason is that we don't know how to do this generally. At this moment it is an accident if a system turns out to be robust in the face of changes in requirements.

Additive programming

Our goal in this book is to investigate how to construct computational systems so that they can be easily adapted to changing requirements. One should not have to modify a working program. One should be able to add to it to implement new functionality or to adjust old functions for new requirements. We call this *additive programming*. We explore techniques to add functionality to an existing program without breaking it. Our techniques do not guarantee that the additions are correct: the additions must themselves be debugged; but they should not damage existing functionality accidentally.

Many of the techniques we explore in this book are not novel: some of them date back to the early days of computing! They are also not a comprehensive set, but simply some that we have found useful. Our intention is not to promote the use of these techniques, but to encourage a style of thinking that is focused on flexibility.

In order for additive programming to be possible, it is necessary to minimize the assumptions about how a program works and how it will be used. Assumptions made during the design and construction of a program may reduce the possible future extensions of the program. Instead of making such assumptions, we build our programs to make just-in-time decisions based on the environment that the program is running in. We will explore several techniques that support this kind of design.

We can always combine programs to get the union of the behaviors that each supports. But we want the whole to be more than the sum of its parts; we want the parts of the combined system to cooperate to give the system capabilities that no one part can provide by itself. But there are tradeoffs here: the parts that we combine to make a system must sharply separate concerns. If a part does one thing extremely well, it is easier to reuse, and also easier to debug, than one that combines several disparate capabilities. If we want to build additively, it is important that the individual pieces combine with minimal unintended interactions.

To facilitate additive programming, it is necessary that the parts we build be as simple and general as we can make them.

For example, a part that accepts a wider range of inputs than is
strictly necessary for the problem at hand will have a wider applicability than one that doesn't. And families of parts that are
built around a standardized interface specification can be mixed
and matched to make a great variety of systems. It is important
to choose the right abstraction level for our parts, by identifying
the domain of discourse for the family and then building the family for that domain. We start consideration of these requirements
in chapter 2.

For maximum flexibility the range of outputs of a part should
be quite small and well defined—much smaller than the range of
acceptable inputs for any part that might receive that output.
This is analogous to the static discipline in the digital abstraction that we teach to students in introductory computer systems
subjects [126]. The essence of the digital abstraction is that the
outputs are always better than the acceptable inputs of the next
stage, so that noise is suppressed.

In software engineering this principle is enshrined as "Postel's
law" in honor of Internet pioneer Jon Postel. In RFC760 [97],
describing the Internet protocol, he wrote: "The implementation
of a protocol must be robust. Each implementation must expect
to interoperate with others created by different individuals. While
the goal of this specification is to be explicit about the protocol,
there is the possibility of differing interpretations. In general, an
implementation should be conservative in its sending behavior,
and liberal in its receiving behavior." This is usually summarized
as "Be conservative in what you do, be liberal in what you accept
from others."

Using more general parts than appear to be necessary builds a
degree of flexibility into the entire structure of our systems. Small
perturbations of the requirements can be tolerated, because every
component is built to accept perturbed (noisy) inputs.

A family of mix-and-match parts for a particular domain of
discourse is the foundation of a *domain-specific language*. Often
the best way to attack a family of hard problems is to make a
language—a set of primitives, means of combination, and means
of abstraction—that makes the solutions for those problems easy
to express. So we want to be able to erect appropriate domain-
specific languages as needed, and to combine such languages flexibly. We start thinking about domain-specific languages in chap-

ter 2. More powerfully, we can implement such languages by direct
evaluation. We expand on this idea in chapter 5.

One strategy for enhancing flexibility, which should be familiar
to many programmers, is *generic dispatch*. We will explore this
extensively in chapter 3. Generic dispatch is often a useful way
to extend the applicability of a procedure by adding additional
handlers (methods) based on details of the arguments passed to
the procedure. By requiring handlers to respond to disjoint sets
of arguments, we can avoid breaking an existing program when
a new handler is added. However, unlike the generic dispatch in
the typical object-oriented programming context, our generic dispatch doesn't involve ideas like classes, instances, and inheritance.
These weaken the separation of concerns by introducing spurious
ontological commitments.

A quite different strategy, to be explored in chapter 6, is to
layer both data and procedures. This exploits the idea that data
usually has associated metadata that can be processed alongside
the data. For example, numerical data often has associated units.
We will show how providing the flexibility of adding layers after
the fact can enhance a program with new functionality, without
any change to the original program.

We can also build systems that combine multiple sources of
partial information to obtain more complete answers. This is most
powerful when the contributions come from independent sources of
information. In chapter 4 we will see how type inference is really
a matter of combining multiple sources of partial information.
Locally deducible clues about the type of a value, for example that
a numerical comparison requires numerical inputs and produces a
boolean output, can be combined with other local type constraints
to produce nonlocal type constraints.

In chapter 7 we will see a different way to combine partial information. The distance to a nearby star can be estimated geomet-
rically, by parallax: measuring the angle by which the star image
shifts against the background sky as the Earth revolves around the
Sun. The distance to the star can also be estimated by consideration of its brightness and its spectrum, using our understanding
of stellar structure and evolution. Such estimates can be combined to get estimates that are more accurate than the individual
contributions.

A dual idea is the use of *degeneracy*: having multiple ways
to compute something, which can be combined or modulated as

needed. There are many valuable uses for degeneracy, including error detection, performance management, and intrusion detection. Importantly, degeneracy is also additive: each contributing part is self-contained and can produce a result by itself. One interesting use of degeneracy is to dynamically select from different implementations of an algorithm depending on context. This avoids the need to make assumptions about how the implementation will be used.

Design and construction for flexibility has definite costs. A procedure that can take a greater variety of inputs than are necessary for solving the current problem will have more code than absolutely necessary and will take more thinking by the programmer than absolutely necessary. The same goes for generic dispatch, layering, and degeneracy, each of which involves constant overheads in memory space, compute time, and/or programmer time.

But the principal cost of software is the time spent by programmers over the lifetime of the product, including maintenance and adaptations that are needed for changing requirements. Designs that minimize rewriting and refactoring reduce the overall costs to the incremental additions rather than complete rewrites. In other words, long-term costs are additive rather than multiplicative.

1.1 Architecture of computation

A metaphor from architecture may be illuminating for the kind of system that we contemplate. After understanding the nature of the site to be built on and the requirements for the structure to be constructed, the design process starts with a *parti*: an organizing principle for the design.[3] The *parti* is usually a sketch of the geometric arrangement of parts. The *parti* may also embody abstract ideas, such as the division into "served spaces" and "servant spaces," as in the work of Louis Isadore Kahn [130]. This decomposition is intended to divide the architectural problem into parts by separating out infrastructural support, such as the hallways, the restrooms, the mechanical rooms, and the elevators, from the

---

[3]A *parti* (pronounced parTEE) is the central idea of an architectural work: it is "the [architectural] composition being conceived as a whole, with the detail being filled in later." [62]

spaces to be supported, such as the laboratories, classrooms, and offices in an academic building.

The *parti* is a model, but it is usually not a completely workable structure. It must be elaborated with functional elements. How do we fit in the staircases and elevators? Where do the HVAC ducts, the plumbing, the electrical and communications distribution systems go? How will we run a road to accommodate the delivery patterns of service vehicles? These elaborations may cause modifications of the *parti*, but the *parti* continues to serve as a scaffold around which these elaborations are developed.

In programming, the *parti* is the abstract plan for the computations to be performed. At small scale the *parti* may be an abstract algorithm and data-structure description. In larger systems it is an abstract composition of phases and parallel branches of a computation. In even larger systems it is an allocation of capabilities to logical (or even physical) locales.

Traditionally, programmmers have not been able to design as architects. In very elaborate languages, such as Java, the *parti* is tightly mixed with the elaborations. The "served spaces," the expressions that actually describe the desired behavior, are horribly conflated with the "servant spaces," such as the type declarations, the class declarations, and the library imports and exports.[4] More spare languages, such as Lisp or Python, leave almost no room for the servant spaces, and attempts to add declarations, even advisory ones, are shunned because they impede the beauty of the exposed *parti*.

The architectural *parti* should be sufficiently complete to allow the creation of models that can be used for analysis and criticism. The skeleton plan of a program should be adequate for analysis and criticism, but it should also be executable, for experiment and for debugging. Just as an architect must fill in the *parti* to realize the structure being designed, a programmer must elaborate the plan to realize the computational system required. Layering (introduced in chapter 6) is one way to build systems that allow this kind of elaboration.

---

[4]Java *does* support interfaces, which could be considered a kind of *parti*, in that they are an abstract representation of the program. But a *parti* combines both abstract and concrete components, while a Java interface is wholly abstract. Not to mention that over-use of interfaces is considered a "code smell" by many programmers.

1.2 Smart parts for flexibility

Large systems are composed of many smaller components, each
of which contributes to the function of the whole either by directly providing a part of that function or by cooperating with
other components to which it is interconnected in some pattern
specified by the system architect to establish a required function.
A central problem in system engineering is the establishment of
interfaces that allow the interconnection of components so that
the functions of those components can be combined to build compound functions.

For relatively simple systems the system architect may make
formal specifications for the various interfaces that must be satisfied by the implementers of the components to be interconnected.
Indeed, the amazing success of electronics is based on the fact that
it is feasible to make such specifications and to meet them. High-
frequency analog equipment is interconnected with coaxial cable
with standardized impedance characteristics, and with standardized families of connectors [4]. Both the function of a component
and its interface behavior can usually be specified with only a
few parameters [60]. In digital systems things are even clearer:
there are static specifications of the meanings of signals (the digital abstraction); there are dynamic specifications of the timing of
signals [126]; and there are mechanical specifications of the form
factors of components.[5]

Unfortunately, this kind of a priori specification becomes pro-
gressively more difficult as the complexity of the system increases.
We could specify that a chess-playing program plays a *legal* game—
that it doesn't cheat—but how would one begin to specify that
it plays a *good* game of chess? Our software systems are built

---

[5] *The TTL Data Book for Design Engineers* [123] is a classic example of a
successful set of specifications for digital-system components. TTL specifies several internally consistent "families" of small-scale and medium-scale
integrated-circuit components. The families differ in such characteristics as
speed and power dissipation, but not in function. The specification describes
the static and dynamic characteristics of each family, the functions available in
each family, and the physical packaging for the components. The families are
cross-consistent as well as internally consistent in that each function is available in each family, with the same packaging and a consistent nomenclature
for description. Thus a designer may design a compound function and later
choose the family for implementation. Every good engineer (and biologist!)
should be familiar with the lessons of TTL.

with large numbers of custom-made highly specialized parts. The difficulty of specifying software components is exacerbated by the individualized nature of the components.

By contrast, biology constructs systems of enormous complexity without very large specifications (considering the problem to be solved!). Every cell in our bodies is a descendant of a single zygote. All the cells have exactly the same genetic endowment (about 1 GByte of ROM!). However, there are skin cells, neurons, muscle cells, etc. The cells organize themselves to be discrete tissues, organs, and organ systems. Indeed, the 1 GByte of ROM specifies how to build the enormously complex machine (the human) from a huge number of failure-prone parts. It specifies how to operate those basic parts and how to configure them. It also specifies how to operate that compound machine reliably, over a great range of hostile conditions, for a very long life span, and how to defend that machine from others that would love to eat it!

If our software components were simpler or more general they would have simpler specifications. If the components were able to adapt themselves to their surroundings, the precision of their specification would be less important. Biological systems exploit both of these strategies to build robust complex organisms. The difference is that the biological cells are dynamically configurable, and able to adapt themselves to their context. This is possible because the way a cell differentiates and specializes depends on its environment. Our software doesn't usually have this ability, and consequently we must adapt each part by hand. How could biology possibly work?

Consider another example. We know that the various components of the brain are hooked together with enormous bundles of neurons, and there is nowhere near enough information in the genome to specify that interconnect in any detail. It is likely that the various parts of the brain learn to communicate with each other, based on the fact that they share important experiences.[6] So the interfaces must be self-configuring, based on some rules of consistency, information from the environment, and extensive exploratory behavior. This is pretty expensive in boot-up time (it

---

[6]An elementary version of this self-configuring behavior has been demonstrated by Jacob Beal in his S.M. thesis [9].

takes some years to configure a working human), but it provides a kind of robustness that is not found in our engineered entities to date.

One idea is that biological systems use contextual signals that are informative rather than imperative.[7] There is no master commander saying what each part must do; instead the parts choose their roles based on their surroundings. The behaviors of cells are not encoded in the signals; they are separately expressed in the genome. Combinations of signals just enable some behaviors and disable others. This weak linkage allows variation in the implementation of the behaviors that are enabled in various locales without modification of the mechanism that defines the locales. So systems organized in this way are evolvable in that they can accommodate adaptive variation in some locales without changing the behavior of subsystems in other locales.

Traditionally, software systems are built around an imperative model, in which there is a hierarchy of control built into the structure. The individual pieces are assumed to be dumb actors that do what they are told. This makes adaptation very difficult, since all changes must be reflected in the entire control structure. In social systems, we are well aware of the problems with strict power structures and centralized command. But our software follows this flawed model. We can do better: making the parts smarter and individually responsible streamlines adaptation, since only those parts directly affected by a change need to respond.

Body plans

All vertebrates have essentially the same body plan, yet the variation in details is enormous. Indeed, all animals with bilateral symmetry share homeobox genes, such as the Hox complex. Such genes produce an approximate coordinate system in the developing animal, separating the developing animal into distinct locales.[8] The locales provide context for a cell to differentiate. And information derived from contact with its neighbors produces more context that selects particular behaviors from the possible behav-

---

[7]Kirschner and Gerhart examine this [70].

[8]This is a very vague description of a complex process involving gradients of morphogens. We do not intend to get more precise here, as this is not about biology, but rather about how biology can inform engineering.

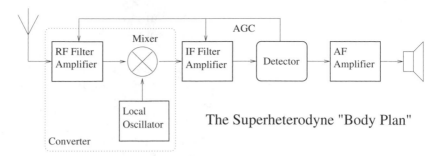

Figure 1.1   The superheterodyne plan, invented by Major Edwin Armstrong in 1918, is still the dominant "body plan" for radio receivers.

iors that are available in the cell's genetic program.[9] Even the methods of construction are shared—the morphogenesis of ducted glands, and organs such as lungs and kidneys, is based on one embryological trick: the invagination of epithelium into mesenchyme automagically[10] produces a branching maze of blind-end tubules surrounded by differentiating mesenchyme.[11]

Good engineering has a similar flavor, in that good designs are modular. Consider the design of a radio receiver. There are several grand "body plans" that have been discovered, such as direct conversion, TRF (tuned radio frequency), and superheterodyne. Each has a sequence of locales, defined by the engineering equivalent of a Hox complex, that patterns the system from the antenna to the output transducer. For example, a superheterodyne receiver (figure 1.1) has a standard set of locales (from nose to tail).

The modules identified in this plan each decompose into yet other modules, such as oscillators, mixers, filters, and amplifiers, and so on down to the individual electronic components. Additionally, each module can be instantiated in many possible ways: the RF section may be just a filter, or it may be an elaborate filter and amplifier combination. Indeed, in an analog television

[9]We have investigated some of the programming issues involved in this kind of development in our Amorphous Computing project [2].

[10]Automagically: "Automatically, but in a way which, for some reason (typically because it is too complicated, or too ugly, or perhaps even too trivial), the speaker doesn't feel like explaining." From *The Hacker's Dictionary* [117, 101]

[11]One well-studied example of this kind of mechanism is the formation of the submandibular gland of the mouse. See, for example, the treatment in [11] or the summary in [7] section 3.4.3.

receiver part of the output of the mixer is processed as AM by the video chain and another part is processed as FM to produce the audio. And some sections, such as the converter, may be recursively elaborated (as if parts of the Hox complex were duplicated!) to obtain multiple-conversion receivers.

In biological systems this structure of compartments is also supported at higher levels of organization. There are tissues that are specialized to become boundaries of compartments, and tubes that interconnect them. Organs are bounded by such tissues and interconnected by such tubes, and the entire structure is packaged to fit into coeloms, which are cavities lined with specialized tissues in higher organisms.

Similar techniques can be used in software. A body plan is just a wrapper that combines partially specified components. This is a kind of *combinator*: a thing that combines subparts together into a larger part. It is possible to create *combinator languages*, in which the components and the composite all have the same interface specification. In a combinator language, it is possible to build arbitrarily large composites from small numbers of mix-and-match components. The self-similar structures make combination easy. In chapter 2 we will begin to build combinator-based software, and this theme will run through all of the rest of the book.

Something similar can be done with domain-specific languages. By making an abstraction of the domain, we can use the same domain-independent code in different domains. For example, numerical integrators are useful in any domain that has numerical aspects, regardless of the domain. Another example is pattern matching in chapter 4, which can be applied to a wide variety of domains.

Biological mechanisms are universal in that each component can, in principle, act as any other component. Analog electronics components are not universal in that sense. They do not adapt themselves to their surroundings based on local signaling. But there are universal electrical building blocks (a programmable computer with analog interfaces, for example!).[12] For low-frequency applications one can build analog systems from such blocks. If each block had all of the code required to be any block in the system, but was specialized by interactions with its neigh-

---

[12]Piotr Mitros has developed a novel design strategy for building analog circuits from potentially universal building blocks. See [92].

bors, and if there were extra unspecialized "stem cells" in the package, then we could imagine building self-reconfiguring and self-repairing analog systems. But for now we still design and build these parts individually.

In programming we do have the idea of a universal element: the *evaluator*. An evaluator takes a description of some computation to be performed and inputs to that computation. It produces the outputs that would arise if we passed the inputs to a bespoke component that implemented the desired computation. In computation we have a chance to pursue the powerfully flexible strategy of embryonic development. We will elaborate on the use of evaluator technology in chapter 5.

1.3   Redundancy and degeneracy

Biological systems have evolved a great deal of robustness. One of the characteristics of biological systems is that they are redundant. Organs such as the liver and kidney are highly *redundant*: there is vastly more capacity than is necessary to do the job, so a person missing a kidney or part of a liver suffers no obvious incapacity. Biological systems are also highly *degenerate*: there are usually many ways to satisfy a given requirement.[13] For example, if a finger is damaged, there are ways that the other fingers may be configured to pick up an object. We can obtain the necessary energy for life from a great variety of sources: we can metabolize carbohydrates, fats, and proteins, even though the mechanisms for digestion and for extraction of energy from each of these sources is quite distinct.

The genetic code is itself degenerate, in that the map from codons (triples of nucleotides) to amino acids is not one-to-one: there are 64 possible codons to specify only about 20 possible amino acids [86, 54]. As a consequence, many point mutations (changes of a single nucleotide) do not change the protein specified by a coding region. Also, quite often the substitution of one amino acid with a similar one does not impair the biological activity of a protein. These degeneracies provide ways that variation

---

[13]Although clear in extreme cases, the distinction biologists make between redundancy and degeneracy is fuzzy at the boundary. For more information see [32].

can accumulate without obvious phenotypic consequences. Furthermore, if a gene is duplicated (not an uncommon occurrence), the copies may diverge silently, allowing the development of variants that may become valuable in the future, without interfering with current viability. In addition, the copies can be placed under different transcriptional controls.

Degeneracy is a product of evolution, and it certainly enables evolution. Probably degeneracy is itself selected for, because only creatures that have significant amounts of degeneracy are sufficiently adaptable to allow survival as the environment changes.[14] For example, suppose we have some creature (or engineered system) that is degenerate in that there are several very different independent mechanisms to achieve some essential function. If the environment changes (or the requirements change) so that one of the ways of achieving an essential function becomes untenable, the creature will continue to live and reproduce (the system will continue to satisfy its specifications). But the subsystem that has become inoperative is now open to mutation (or repair), without impinging on the viability (or current operation) of the system as a whole.

The theoretical structure of physics is deeply degenerate. For example, problems in classical mechanics can be approached in multiple ways. There is the Newtonian formulation of vectoral mechanics and the Lagrangian and Hamiltonian formulations of variational mechanics. If both vectoral mechanics and either form of variational mechanics are applicable, they produce equivalent equations of motion. For analysis of systems with dissipative forces like friction, vectoral mechanics is effective; variational methods are not well suited for that kind of system. Lagrangian mechanics is far better than vectoral mechanics for dealing with systems with rigid constraints, and Hamiltonian mechanics provides the power of canonical transformations to help understand systems using the structure of phase space. Both the Lagrangian and Hamiltonian formulations help us with deep insights into the role of symmetries and conserved quantities. The fact that there are three overlapping ways of describing a mechanical system, which agree when they are all applicable, gives us multiple avenues of attack on any problem [121].

---

[14]Some computer scientists have used simulation to investigate the evolution of evolvability [3].

Engineered systems may incorporate some redundancy, in critical systems where the cost of failure is extreme. But they almost never intentionally incorporate degeneracy of the kind found in biological systems, except as a side effect of designs that are not optimal.[15]

Degeneracy can add value to our systems: as with redundancy, we can cross-check the answers of degenerate computations to improve robustness. But degenerate computations are not just redundant but *different* from one another, meaning that a bug in one is unlikely to affect the others. This is a positive characteristic not only for reliability but also for security, as a successful attack must compromise multiple degenerate parts.

When degenerate parts generate partial information, the result of their combination can be better than any individual result. Some navigation systems use this idea to combine several positional estimates to generate a highly accurate result. We will explore the idea of combining partial information in chapter 7.

1.4   Exploratory behavior

One of the most powerful mechanisms of robustness in biological systems is exploratory behavior.[16] The idea is that the desired outcome is produced by a generate-and-test mechanism (see figure 1.2). This organization allows the generator mechanism to be general and to work independently of the testing mechanism that accepts or rejects a particular generated result.

For example, an important component of the rigid skeleton that supports the shape of a cell is an array of microtubules. Each microtubule is made up of protein units that aggregate to form it. Microtubules are continually created and destroyed in a living cell; they are created growing out in all directions. However, only microtubules that encounter a kinetochore or other stabilizer in the cell membrane are stable, thus supporting the shape determined

---

[15]Indeed, one often hears arguments against building degeneracy into an engineered system. For example, in the philosophy of the computer language Python it is claimed: "There should be one—and preferably only one—obvious way to do it." [95]

[16]This thesis is nicely explored in the book of Kirschner and Gerhart [70].

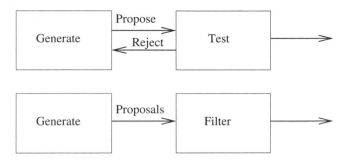

Figure 1.2 Exploratory behavior can be accomplished in two ways. In one way a generator proposes an action (or a result), which may be explicitly rejected by a tester. The generator then must propose an alternative. Another way is that the generator produces all of the alternatives, without feedback, and a filter selects one or more that are acceptable.

by the positions of the stabilizers [71]. So the mechanism for growing and maintaining a shape is relatively independent of the mechanism for specifying the shape. This mechanism partly determines the shapes of many types of cells in a complex organism, and it is almost universal in animals.

Exploratory behavior appears at all levels of detail in biological systems. The nervous system of a growing embryo produces a vastly larger number of neurons than will persist in the adult. Those neurons that find appropriate targets in other neurons, sensory organs, or muscles will survive, and those that find no targets kill themselves. The hand is fashioned by production of a pad and deletion, by apoptosis (programmed cell death), of the material between the fingers [131]. Our bones are continually being remodeled by osteoblasts (which build bone) and osteoclasts (which destroy bone). The shape and size of the bones is determined by constraints determined by their environment: the parts that they must be associated with, such as muscles, ligaments, tendons, and other bones.

Because the generator need not know about how the tester accepts or rejects its proposals, and the tester need not know how the generator makes its proposals, the two parts can be independently developed. This makes adaptation and evolution more efficient, because a mutation to one or the other of these two subsystems need not be accompanied by a complementary mutation to the other. However, this isolation can be expensive because of the wasted effort of generation and rejection of failed proposals.[17]

Indeed, generate and test is a metaphor for all of evolution. The mechanisms of biological variation are random mutations: modifications of the genetic instructions. Most mutations are neutral in that they do not directly affect fitness because of degeneracy in the systems. Natural selection is the test phase. It does not depend on the method of variation, and the method of variation does not anticipate the effect of selection.

There are even more striking phenomena: even in closely related creatures some components that end up almost identical in the adult are constructed by entirely different mechanisms in the embryo.[18] For distant relationships, divergent mechanisms for constructing common structures may be attributed to "convergent evolution," but for close relatives it is more likely evidence for separation of levels of detail, in which the result is specified in a way that is somewhat independent of the way it is accomplished.

Engineered systems may show similar structure. We try to separate specification from implementation: there are often multiple ways to satisfy a specification, and designs may choose different implementations. The best method to use to sort a data set depends on the expected size of the data set, as well as the computational cost of comparing elements. The appropriate representation of a polynomial depends on whether it is sparse or dense. But if choices like these are made dynamically (an unusual system) they are deterministic: we do not see many systems that simultaneously try several ways to solve a problem and use the one that converges first (what are all those cores for, anyway?). It is even rare to find systems that try multiple methods sequentially: if one method fails try another. We will examine use of backtracking

---

[17]This expense can be greatly reduced if there is sufficient information present to quickly reduce the number of candidates that must be tested. We will examine a very nice example of this optimization in chapter 7.

[18]The cornea of a chick and the cornea of a mouse are almost identical, but the morphogenesis of these two are not at all similar: the order of the morphogenetic events is not even the same. Bard [7] section 3.6.1 reports that having divergent methods of forming the same structures in different species is common. He quotes a number of examples. One spectacular case is that the frog *Gastrotheca riobambae* (see del Pino and Elinson [28]) develops ordinary frog morphology from an embryonic disk, whereas other frogs develop from an approximately spherical embryo.

to implement generate-and-test mechanisms in pattern matching in chapter 4. We will learn how to build automatic backtracking into languages in chapter 5. And we will learn how to build a dependency-directed backtracking mechanism that extracts as much information as possible from failures in chapter 7.

1.5   The cost of flexibility

> Lisp programmers know the value of everything but the cost of nothing.
>
> Alan Perlis paraphrasing Oscar Wilde

We have noted that generality and evolvability are enhanced in systems that use generics, layers, redundancy, degeneracy, and exploratory behavior. Each of these is expensive, when looked at in isolation. A mechanism that works over a wide range of inputs must do more to get the same result than a mechanism specialized to a particular input. A redundant mechanism has more parts than an equivalent nonredundant mechanism. A degenerate mechanism appears even more extravagant. And a mechanism that explores by generate-and-test methods can easily get into an infeasible exponential search. Yet these are key ingredients in evolvable systems. Perhaps to make truly robust systems we must be willing to pay for what appears to be a rather elaborate and expensive infrastructure.

Part of the problem is that we are thinking about cost in the wrong terms. Use of time and space matters, but our intuition about where those costs come from is poor. Every engineer knows that evaluating the real performance of a system involves extensive and careful measurements that often show that the cost is in surprising places. As complexity increases, this will only get harder. But we persist in doing premature optimization at all levels of our programs without knowing its real value.

Suppose we separate the parts of a system that have to be fast from the parts that have to be smart. Under this policy, the cost of generality and evolvability can be confined to the parts that have to be smart. This is an unusual perspective in computing systems, yet it is ubiquitous in our life experience. When we try to learn a new skill, for example to play a musical instrument, the initial stages involve conscious activity to connect the intended effect to the physical movements required to produce it. But as the skill is mastered, most of the work is done without conscious attention. This is essential to being able to play at speed, because the conscious activity is too slow.

A similar argument is found in the distinction between hardware and software. Hardware is designed for efficiency, at the cost of having a fixed interface. One can then build software on top of that interface—in effect creating a virtual machine—using software. That extra layer of abstraction incurs a well-known cost, but the tradeoff is well worth the generality that is gained. (Otherwise we'd still be programming in assembly language!) The point here is that this layered structure provides a way to have both efficiency and flexibility. We believe that requiring an entire system to be implemented in the most efficient possible way is counterproductive, preventing the flexibility for adapting to future needs.

The real cost of a system is the time spent by programmers—in designing, understanding, maintaining, modifying, and debugging the system. So the value of enhanced adaptability may be even more extreme. A system that is easily adapted and maintained eliminates one of the largest costs: teaching new programmers how the existing system works, in all its gory detail, so that they know where to reach in and modify the code. Indeed, the cost of our brittle infrastructure probably greatly exceeds the cost of flexible design, both in the cost of disasters and in the lost opportunity costs due to the time of redesign and rebuilding. And if a significant fraction of the time spent reprogramming a system for a new requirement is replaced by having that system adapt itself to the new situation, that can be an even bigger win.

The problem with correctness

> To the optimist, the glass is half full. To the pessimist, the glass is half empty. To the engineer, the glass is twice as big as it needs to be.
>
> author unknown

But there may be an even bigger cost to building systems in a way that gives them a range of applicability greater than the set of situations that we have considered at design time. Because we intend to be willing to apply our systems in contexts for which they were not designed, we cannot be sure that they work correctly!

In computer science we are taught that the "correctness" of software is paramount, and that correctness is to be achieved by establishing formal specification of components and systems of components and by providing proofs that the specifications of a combination of components are met by the specifications of the components and the pattern by which they are combined.[19] We assert that this discipline makes systems more brittle. In fact, to make truly robust systems we must discard such a tight discipline.

The problem with requiring proofs is that it is usually harder to prove general properties of general mechanisms than it is to prove special properties of special mechanisms used in constrained circumstances. This encourages us to make our parts and combinations as special as possible so we can simplify our proofs. But the combination of tightly specialized parts is brittle—there is no room for variation![20]

We are not arguing against proofs. They are wonderful when available. Indeed, they are essential for critical system components, such as garbage collectors (or ribosomes).[21] However, even for safety-critical systems, such as autopilots, the restriction of applicability to situations for which the system is provably correct as specified may actually contribute to unnecessary failure. Indeed, we want an autopilot to make a good-faith attempt to safely fly an airplane that is damaged in a way not anticipated by the designer!

We are arguing against the discipline of *requiring* proofs: the requirement that everything must be proved to be applicable in a situation before it is allowed to be used in that situation ex-

---

[19]It is hard, and perhaps impossible, to specify a complex system. As noted on page 7, it is easy to specify that a chess player must play legal chess, but how would we specify that it plays well? And unlike chess, whose rules do not change, the specifications of most systems are dynamically changing as the conditions of their usage change. How do we specify an accounting system in the light of rapidly changing tax codes?

[20]Indeed, Postel's Law (on page 3) is directly in opposition to the practice of building systems from precisely and narrowly specified parts: Postel's law instructs us to make each part more generally applicable than absolutely necessary for any particular application.

[21]A subtle bug in a primitive storage management subsystem, like a garbage collector, is extremely difficult to debug—especially in a system with concurrent processes! But if we keep such subsystems simple and small they can be specified and even proved "correct" with a tractable amount of work.

cessively inhibits the use of techniques that could enhance the robustness of designs. This is especially true of techniques that allow a method to be used, on a tight leash, outside of its proven domain, and techniques that provide for future expansion without putting limits on the ways things can be extended.

Unfortunately, many of the techniques we advocate make the problem of proof much more difficult, if not practically impossible. On the other hand, sometimes the best way to attack a problem is to generalize it until the proof becomes simple.

2
Domain-Specific Languages

One powerful strategy for building flexibility into a programming project is to create a *domain-specific language* that captures the conceptual structure of the subject matter of the programs to be developed. A domain-specific language is an abstraction in which the nouns and verbs of the language are directly related to the problem domain. Such a language allows an application program to be written directly in terms of the domain. By its nature, a domain-specific language implements a fairly complete model of the domain, in excess of what is needed for a particular application.[1] Although this may seem like extra work that is not essential to the particular problem at hand, it is often less work than writing a monolithic program, and the resulting program is much easier to modify, debug, and extend.

So a domain-specific language layer is built to support more than just the development of a particular program. It provides a general framework for the construction of a variety of related programs that share the domain of discourse. It simplifies the process of extending an existing application in that domain. And it provides a substrate that allows related applications to cooperate.

In this chapter we first introduce systems of combinators, a powerful organizational strategy for the erection of domain-specific language layers. We will demonstrate the effectiveness of this strategy by showing how to reformulate the ugly mess of regular expressions for string matching into a pretty combinator-based domain-specific language embedded in Scheme. But sometimes we have components that do not easily fit into a clean system— sometimes we need a system of adapters. We illustrate this with a domain-specific language for making unit-conversion wrappers for procedures, allowing procedures written assuming one unit system to be used with a different unit system. Finally, we consider the broad domain of board games. We see how it is possible to abstract the details of the domain by building an interpreter for the rules of the game.

---

[1]The generality of the domain model is an example of "Postel's law"—see page 3.

2.1   Combinators

Biological systems achieve much of their adaptability through the use of very general parts (cells) that are dynamically configured and consequently able to adjust as their environment changes. Computational systems usually do not use this strategy, instead relying on a hierarchy of custom parts and combinations. In recent years, large libraries of well-specified higher-level parts have raised the abstraction level of this activity. But the means of combination are rarely abstracted or shared, other than as "patterns."[2]

In some situations we can improve on this practice by simple strategies that promote the use of shared combination mechanisms. If the systems we build are made up from members of a family of "mix-and-match" components that combine to make new members of the family, perturbations of the requirements can sometimes be addressed by rearrangement of components.

A *system of combinators* is a set of primitive parts and a set of means of combining parts such that the interface specifications of the combinations are the same as those of the primitives. This enables construction without accidental interactions between the parts. A classic example of a combinator-like system is TTL [123], which is a historic library of standard parts and combinations for building complex digital systems.

Combinator systems provide a design strategy for domain-specific languages. The elements of the system are words in the language, and the combinators are used to combine them into phrases. Combinator systems have the significant advantage that they are easy to build and to reason about, but they have limitations, which we will discuss in section 3.1.5. When they fit the domain, they are an excellent strategic choice.

But how do we arrange to build our systems by combining elements of a family of mix-and-match components? We must identify a set of primitive components and a set of *combinators* that combine components so as to make compound components with the same interface as the primitive components. Such sets of combinators are sometimes explicit, but more often implicit, in mathematical notation.

---

[2]There are some notable exceptions: the functional programming extensions introduced by Java 8 directly capture useful combinations. Functional programming languages, such as Lisp and Haskell, have libraries of useful combination mechanisms.

2.1.1 Function combinators

The use of functional notation in mathematics is a combinator discipline. A function has a domain, from which its arguments are selected, and a range (or codomain) of its possible values. There are combinators that produce new functions as combinations of others. For example, the composition $f \circ g$ of functions f and g is a new function that takes arguments in the domain of g and produces values in the codomain of f. If two functions have the same domain and codomain, and if arithmetic is defined on their common codomain, then we can define the sum (or product) of the functions as the function that when given an argument in their common domain, is the sum (or product) of the values of the two functions at that argument. Languages that allow first-class procedures provide a mechanism to support this means of combination, but what really matters is a good family of pieces.

Organizing a system around combinators has several advantages. The parts that are made can be arbitrarily mixed and matched. Any combination yields a legal program, whose behavior transparently depends only on the behaviors of the parts and the ways that they are combined. The context in which a part appears does not change the behavior of the part: it is always acceptable to pick up a compound part to use it in a new context, without worry about its behavior in that context. Thus such programs are easy to write, easy to read, and easy to verify. A program built on combinators is extensible, because introduction of new parts or new combinators does not affect the behavior of existing programs.

We can think of function combinators as implementing wiring diagrams that specify how a function is built by combining its parts. For example, functional composition represents a box made of two subboxes so that the output of the first feeds the input of the second, as shown in figure 2.1. A program that implements this idea is straightforward:

```
(define (compose f g)
  (lambda args
    (f (apply g args))))
```

(It gets more exciting if we want to check that the arities match: that the function represented by procedure f takes only one argument, to match the output of g. It gets even more fun if g can

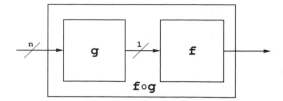

Figure 2.1   The composition $f \circ g$ of functions f and g is a new function that is defined by this "wiring diagram." The input to $f \circ g$ is given to g. The output of g is then passed to f, and it produces the output of $f \circ g$.

return multiple values and f must take those arguments. We may also want to check that the arguments passed to the composition are the right number for g. But these are fine points that we will deal with later.)

We can demonstrate composition with a simple example:

```
((compose (lambda (x) (list 'foo x))
          (lambda (x) (list 'bar x)))
 'z)
(foo (bar z))
```

It is sometimes nicer to name the procedure that is being returned by a combinator. For example, we could write compose as

```
(define (compose f g)
  (define (the-composition . args)
    (f (apply g args)))
  the-composition)
```

The name the-composition is not defined outside of the scope of the definition of compose, so there is no obvious advantage to this way of writing the compose procedure. We often use anonymous procedures defined by lambda expressions in our programs, as in the first version of compose above. So the choice of how to write the program is mostly a matter of style.[3]

Even with just this compose combinator we can write some rather elegant code. Consider the problem of computing the nth

---

[3]Here things are simple, but in complex programs with many internal procedures, descriptive names can make things easier to read and understand. In MIT/GNU Scheme there is a minor advantage to naming the procedure being returned here, because the debugger can show this name for a procedure that would otherwise be anonymous.

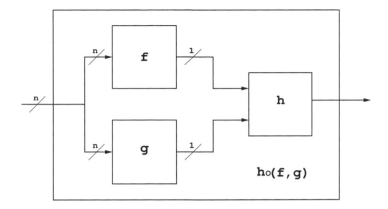

Figure 2.2   In `parallel-combine` the functions f and g take the same number of arguments. The input to the "parallel combination" is passed to both of them. Their outputs are then combined by the function h, of two arguments.

iterate of a function $f^n(x) = f(f^{n-1}(x))$. We can write this elegantly as a program:

```
(define ((iterate n) f)
  (if (= n 0)
      identity
      (compose f ((iterate (- n 1)) f))))

(define (identity x) x)
```

The result of `((iterate n) f)` is a new function, of the same type as `f`. It can be used wherever `f` can be used. So `(iterate n)` is itself a function combinator. Now we can use this to determine the result of repeatedly squaring a number:

```
(((iterate 3) square) 5)
```
390625

Notice the analogy: function composition is like multiplication, so function iteration is like exponentiation.

There are many simple combinators that are generally useful in programming. We will present just a few here to give a feeling for the range of possibilities.

We can arrange to use two functions in parallel, then combine their results with a specified combiner function (see figure 2.2). This parallel combination is implemented with the procedure

```
(define (parallel-combine h f g)
  (define (the-combination . args)
    (h (apply f args) (apply g args)))
  the-combination)

((parallel-combine list
                   (lambda (x y z) (list 'foo x y z))
                   (lambda (u v w) (list 'bar u v w)))
 'a 'b 'c)
((foo a b c) (bar a b c))
```

The `parallel-combine` combinator can be useful in organizing a complex process. For example, suppose we have a source of images of pieces of vegetable. We may have one procedure that given the image can estimate the color of the vegetable, and another that can give a description of the shape (leaf, root, stalk, ...). We may have a third procedure that can combine these descriptions to identify the vegetable. These can be neatly composed with `parallel-combine`.

Arity

There are entire families of combinators that we can use in programming that we don't normally think of. Many of these appear in common mathematical contexts. For example, tensors are an extension of linear algebra to linear operators with multiple arguments. But the idea is more general than that: the "tensor combination" of two procedures is just a new procedure that takes a data structure combining arguments for the two procedures. It distributes those arguments to the two procedures, producing a data structure that combines the values of the two procedures. The need to unbundle a data structure, operate on the parts separately, and rebundle the results is ubiquitous in programming. The wiring diagram in figure 2.3 shows `spread-combine`. It is a generalization of the tensor product in multilinear algebra. In the mathematical tensor product, f and g are linear functions of their inputs, and h is a trace over some shared indices; but tensors are just the special case that inspired this combinator.

The program to implement `spread-combine` is a bit more complicated than `parallel-combine`, because it must distribute the correct arguments to `f` and `g`. Here is a first draft of that code:

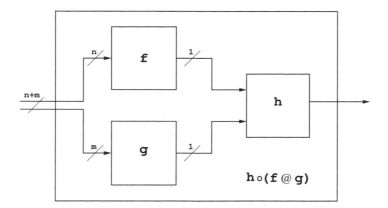

Figure 2.3   In `spread-combine` the $n+m$ arguments are split between the functions f and g. The first n arguments go to f and the m other arguments go to g. The resulting outputs are then combined by the function h, of two arguments.

```
(define (spread-combine h f g)
  (let ((n (get-arity f)))
    (define (the-combination . args)
      (h (apply f (list-head args n))
         (apply g (list-tail args n)))))
    the-combination))
```

This code requires a way of determining how many arguments a procedure takes (its *arity*), because it has to pick out the arguments for f and then pass the rest to g.

This version of `spread-combine` is not very good. The most egregious problem is that `the-combination` takes any number of arguments, so it does not have a well-defined numerical arity, and thus it cannot be passed to another combinator that needs its arity. For example, the result of a `spread-combine` cannot be passed as the second argument f to another `spread-combine`. So, somehow, we have to decorate `the-combination` with an appropriate arity. Here is a second draft:

```
(define (spread-combine h f g)
  (let ((n (get-arity f)) (m (get-arity g)))
    (let ((t (+ n m)))
      (define (the-combination . args)
        (h (apply f (list-head args n))
           (apply g (list-tail args n))))
      (restrict-arity the-combination t))))
```

Here, the procedure `the-combination` that is returned has its arity specified, so it can be the input to some other combinator that requires an arity. The `restrict-arity` procedure takes a procedure, annotates it so that its arity can be obtained by `get-arity`, and returns the annotated procedure.

This is pretty good, but the best programs are written by paranoids! We want to catch errors as early as possible, before they become hard to locate or cause serious trouble. So let's annotate this code with an *assertion* in *Paranoid Programming Style*, to check that we have the right number of arguments to our combination.

```
(define (spread-combine h f g)
  (let ((n (get-arity f)) (m (get-arity g)))
    (let ((t (+ n m)))
      (define (the-combination . args)
        (assert (= (length args) t))
        (h (apply f (list-head args n))
           (apply g (list-tail args n))))
      (restrict-arity the-combination t))))

((spread-combine list
                 (lambda (x y) (list 'foo x y))
                 (lambda (u v w) (list 'bar u v w)))
 'a 'b 'c 'd 'e)
((foo a b) (bar c d e))
```

The special form `assert` is just a convenient way to signal an error if its argument does not have a true value.

One way to write `restrict-arity` and `get-arity` is as follows:

```
(define (restrict-arity proc nargs)
  (hash-table-set! arity-table proc nargs)
  proc)

(define (get-arity proc)
  (or (hash-table-ref/default arity-table proc #f)
      (let ((a (procedure-arity proc))) ;arity not in table
        (assert (eqv? (procedure-arity-min a)
                      (procedure-arity-max a)))
        (procedure-arity-min a))))

(define arity-table (make-key-weak-eqv-hash-table))
```

Here we are using a hash table to attach a "sticky note" to the procedure.[4] This is a simple trick for adding information to an existing object, but it depends on the uniqueness of the object being annotated, so it should be used carefully.

If the procedure `get-arity` is unable to find an explicit value in `arity-table`, it computes one using primitives from the underlying MIT/GNU Scheme system. This involves some hair, because those primitives support a more general idea of arity: that a procedure requires a minimum number of arguments, and may have an optional maximum number of arguments. Our arity code expects an arity to be a fixed number of arguments, and so `get-arity` cannot work with any other kind of procedure. Unfortunately, this excludes procedures like + that take any number of arguments. Changing the arity code to use a more general notion of arity would complicate it, and our goal here is to have a clear exposition rather than a general solution (see exercise 2.2).

Exercise 2.1: Arity repair

The procedures `compose` and `parallel-combine` that we have introduced do not obey the requirement that they advertise the arity of the combination. Thus they would not be good citizens of our family of combinators. Fix the implementations of `compose` and `parallel-combine` shown above, so that

- they check their components to make sure that the arities are compatible;
- the combination they construct checks that it is given the correct number of arguments when it is called;
- the combination advertises its arity correctly for `get-arity`.

Exercise 2.2: Arity extension

Our exposition of useful combinators is flawed in that the arity mechanism we displayed cannot handle the more general arity mechanism used by MIT/GNU Scheme. For example, the addition procedure, which is the value of +, can take any number of arguments:

```
(procedure-arity-min (procedure-arity +)) = 0
(procedure-arity-max (procedure-arity +)) = #f
```

and the arctangent procedure can take either 1 or 2 arguments:

---

[4]Documentation of hash table procedures in MIT/GNU Scheme can be found in [51].

```
(procedure-arity-min (procedure-arity atan)) = 1
(procedure-arity-max (procedure-arity atan)) = 2
```

It is useful to extend the handling of arities so that combinators can
work with these more complex situations.

a. Sketch a plan for how to extend the combinators to use the more
general arities. Note that you may not always be able to use arithmetic
on the arities. What choices will you have to make in reformulating
`spread-combine`? For example, what kinds of restrictions will be needed
on the procedures `f`, `g`, and `h` in `spread-combine`?

b. Apply your plan and make it all work!

   For any language there are primitives, means of combination,
and means of abstraction. A *combinator language* defines primitives and means of combination, inheriting its means of abstraction from the underlying programming language. In our example,
the primitives are functions, and the means of combination are the
combinators `compose`, `parallel-combine`, `spread-combine`, and
others we may introduce.

Multiple values
Notice that `parallel-combine` and `spread-combine` are similar in
that each is the application of a combiner `h` to the results of `f`
and `g`. But we did not use `compose` to construct these combinators. To abstract this pattern we need to be able to return multiple
values from the combination of `f` and `g` and then use those multiple values as arguments for `h`. We could do this by returning a
compound data structure, but a better way is to use the Scheme
multiple-value return mechanism. Given multiple values we can
define `spread-combine` as a composition of two parts, `h` and this
combination of `f` and `g`:[5]

```
(define (spread-apply f g)
  (let ((n (get-arity f)) (m (get-arity g)))
    (let ((t (+ n m)))
      (define (the-combination . args)
        (assert (= (length args) t))
        (values (apply f (list-head args n))
                (apply g (list-tail args n))))
      (restrict-arity the-combination t))))
```

---

[5] We thank Guy L. Steele Jr. for suggesting that we show this decomposition.

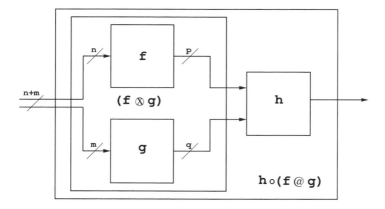

Figure 2.4   The combinator `spread-combine` is really a composition of two parts. The first part, `spread-apply`, is the combination of the functions f and g with the correct arguments routed to them. The second part is the combiner h, which is just composed with the first part. This decomposition is enabled by use of the multiple-values mechanism of Scheme.

The Scheme procedure `values` returns the results of applying both `f` and `g`.[6]

Below we will generalize `compose` so that we can directly implement the abstraction shown in figure 2.4 as follows:

```
(define (spread-combine h f g)
  (compose h (spread-apply f g)))
```

This has the same behavior as our original version:

```
((spread-combine list
                 (lambda (x y) (list 'foo x y))
                 (lambda (u v w) (list 'bar u v w)))
 'a 'b 'c 'd 'e)
((foo a b) (bar c d e))
```

To make this work, we generalize `compose` to allow multiple values to pass between the composed procedures:

---

[6]Documentation of `values`, `call-with-values`, and `let-values` can be found in [51] and [109].

```
(define (compose f g)
  (define (the-composition . args)
    (call-with-values (lambda () (apply g args))
      f))
  (restrict-arity the-composition (get-arity g)))
```

Here the second argument to compose returns two values:

```
((compose (lambda (a b)
            (list 'foo a b))
          (lambda (x)
            (values (list 'bar x)
                    (list 'baz x))))
 'z)
```
(foo (bar z) (baz z))

Now we can generalize even further. We can allow all of the functions we are combining to return multiple values. If f and g both return multiple values we can combine those values into multiple values that the-combination can return:

```
(define (spread-apply f g)
  (let ((n (get-arity f)) (m (get-arity g)))
    (let ((t (+ n m)))
      (define (the-combination . args)
        (assert (= (length args) t))
        (let-values ((fv (apply f (list-head args n)))
                     (gv (apply g (list-tail args n))))
          (apply values (append fv gv))))
      (restrict-arity the-combination t))))

((spread-combine list
                 (lambda (x y) (values x y))
                 (lambda (u v w) (values w v u)))
 'a 'b 'c 'd 'e)
```
(a b e d c)

The only restriction is that the total number of values returned must be appropriate for the arity of h.

Exercise 2.3: A quickie

Reformulate parallel-combine to be a composition of two parts and to allow the parts to return multiple values.

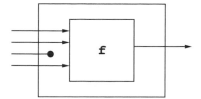

Figure 2.5   The combinator (`discard-argument` 2) takes a three-argument function f and makes a new function of four arguments that ignores its third argument (i=2) and passes the remaining arguments to f.

A small library

Many common patterns of usage can be captured as combinators, and very pretty programs are often constructed using such techniques. It is to our advantage to expose and abstract such common patterns. Here are a few more to think about.

Often we have an interface that is more general than necessary in a particular situation. In such a case we may want to preserve the interface, but call some more specialized procedure that does not need all of the parameters we can supply in the general case; so we choose to make a version of our specialized procedure that ignores some arguments.

The procedure `discard-argument` takes the index, i, of the argument to be discarded and returns a combinator. The combinator takes a function, f, of n arguments and returns a new function `the-combination` of $n + 1$ arguments that applies f to the n arguments resulting from deleting the ith argument from the $n + 1$ given arguments. Figure 2.5 illustrates this idea. The code for this combinator is:

```
(define (discard-argument i)
  (assert (exact-nonnegative-integer? i))
  (lambda (f)
    (let ((m (+ (get-arity f) 1)))
      (define (the-combination . args)
        (assert (= (length args) m))
        (apply f (list-remove args i)))
      (assert (< i m))
      (restrict-arity the-combination m))))
```

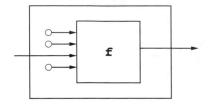

Figure 2.6   The combinator ((curry-argument 2) 'a 'b 'c) specifies three of the arguments to the four-argument function f, leaving
the third argument (i=2) to be supplied in the call to the resulting
one-argument function.

```
(define (list-remove lst index)
  (let lp ((lst lst) (index index))
    (if (= index 0)
        (cdr lst)
        (cons (car lst) (lp (cdr lst) (- index 1))))))

(((discard-argument 2)
  (lambda (x y z) (list 'foo x y z)))
 'a 'b 'c 'd)
(foo a b d)
```

One can generalize this combinator to discard multiple arguments.

The opposite of the situation of discard-argument also commonly occurs. In figure 2.6 we see a wiring diagram for special-
izing a procedure by specifying all but one argument in advance,
leaving one to be passed in the call. This is traditionally called
currying in honor of the logician Haskell Curry, who was an early
investigator of combinatory logic.[7]

The code for curry-argument poses no surprises:

```
(define ((curry-argument i) . args)
  (lambda (f)
    (assert (= (length args) (- (get-arity f) 1)))
    (lambda (x)
      (apply f (list-insert args i x)))))
```

---

[7]Combinatory logic was invented by Moses Schönfinkel [108] and developed
by Haskell Curry [26] in the early 20th century. Their goal had nothing to do
with computation, but rather to simplify the foundations of mathematics by
eliminating the need for quantified variables.

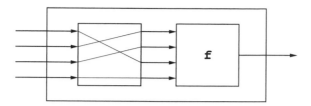

Figure 2.7   The combinator (`permute-arguments` 1 2 0 3) takes a function f of four arguments and produces a new function of four arguments that permutes its arguments according to the supplied permutation before passing them to f.

```
(define (list-insert lst index value)
  (let lp ((lst lst) (index index))
    (if (= index 0)
        (cons value lst)
        (cons (car lst) (lp (cdr lst) (- index 1)))))))

((((curry-argument 2) 'a 'b 'c)
  (lambda (x y z w) (list 'foo x y z w)))
 'd)
(foo a b d c)
```

Note that here we do not need to use `restrict-arity` because the returned procedure has exactly one argument.[8] In exercise 2.5 we generalize this combinator for currying, to leave multiple arguments to be supplied.

Sometimes we want to use a library procedure that has a different order of arguments than the standard that we are using in the current application. Rather than make a special interface for that procedure, we can use a general permutation procedure to rearrange things, as in figure 2.7. This program is also simple, but notice that the procedure `the-combination` that is returned from the combinator and actually runs on `args` does not have to interpret the permutation specification—this is done once in the `let` surrounding `the-combination` and referred to within. In general, writing code this way allows some deep optimizations by early computation, even in the light of very late binding!

---

[8]The MIT/GNU Scheme `procedure-arity`, used in `get-arity`, will produce a numerical arity for the procedure returned, so we do not need to put a sticky note on it.

```
(define (permute-arguments . permspec)
  (let ((permute (make-permutation permspec)))
    (lambda (f)
      (define (the-combination . args)
        (apply f (permute args)))
      (let ((n (get-arity f)))
        (assert (= n (length permspec)))
        (restrict-arity the-combination n)))))

(((permute-arguments 1 2 0 3)
  (lambda (x y z w) (list 'foo x y z w)))
 'a 'b 'c 'd)
(foo b c a d)
```

The procedure `make-permutation` is simple, but it is not efficient:

```
(define (make-permutation permspec)
  (define (the-permuter lst)
    (map (lambda (p) (list-ref lst p))
         permspec))
  the-permuter)
```

2.1.2   Combinators and body plans

A moral of this story is that a structure composed of combinations of combinators is a body plan, much like the body plans
of animals or engineering patterns like the superheterodyne radio
receiver (figure 1.1 on page 10). Consider the `compose` combinator. It provides an arrangement of locales, the procedures f and
g. The locales are connected by a standard interconnect, but that
is all that is required of f and g. Indeed, these components may
be anything that can take the right number of arguments and can
return the right number of values. So the combinators are organizing principles, like Hox genes: they specify locales and their
relationship without mandating what happens inside each locale.

Exercise 2.4: As compositions?

You may have noticed that the combinators made by `discard-argument`,
`curry-argument`, and `permute-arguments` can each be thought of as a
composition of an argument manipulation and a procedure. Rebuild
these combinators as compositions using the multiple-value return mechanism.

Exercise 2.5: Useful combinators

It is time to fill out this small library a bit more.

a. The combinators `discard-argument` and `curry-argument` could be generalized to allow ignoring or prespecializing on more than one argument. The method of specifying the permutation for `permute-arguments` seems to be a pretty general way to specify arguments by their order in a call (zero-based). Build generalized versions of these procedures that have such an interface. Name them `discard-arguments` and `curry-arguments`. Make your code compatible with the code in the text: your `(curry-arguments 2)` should do exactly what `(curry-argument 2)` does.

b. What other combinators would you find useful? Make up a list, with appropriate use cases that you might encounter in actual code. Write implementations of them for your library.

c. Further generalize `compose` so that it can take any number of functional aguments. The expression `(compose f g h)` is equivalent to `(compose f (compose g h))`. Note that it should also be equivalent to `(compose (compose f g) h)`. Be careful: what is the composition of zero arguments?

2.2 Regular expressions

Regular expressions are widely used for string matching. Although regular-expression systems are derived from a perfectly good mathematical formalism, the particular choices made by implementers to expand the formalism into useful software systems are often disastrous: the quotation conventions adopted are highly irregular; the egregious misuse of parentheses, both for grouping and for backward reference, is a miracle to behold. In addition, attempts to increase the expressive power and address shortcomings of earlier designs have led to a proliferation of incompatible derivative languages.

On the surface, regular expressions look like a combinator language, because expression fragments can be combined to make more complex expressions. But the meaning of a fragment is highly dependent on the expression it is embedded in. For example, if we want a caret, ^, in a bracket expression, [...], the caret must not be in the first character position, because if the caret appears after the first character it is just an ordinary character, but if it appears as the first character it negates the meaning of the bracket expression. Thus a bracket expression may not contain just a caret.

So the syntax of the regular-expression language is awful; there are various incompatible forms of the language; and the quotation conventions are *baroquen* [sic]. While regular expression languages are domain-specific languages, they are bad ones. Part of the value of examining regular expressions is to experience how bad things can be.

Nevertheless, there is a great deal of useful software, for example `grep`, that uses regular expressions to specify the desired behavior. We will invent a better domain-specific combinator language for specifying regular expressions and a means of translating this language to conventional regular-expression syntax. We will use the POSIX Basic Regular Expression (BRE) syntax as a target for our translator [96], since it is a subset of most other regular-expression syntaxes. POSIX also defines a more powerful Extended Regular Expression (ERE) syntax, which we will consider in an exercise.

With this machinery we will be able to use the capabilities of systems like `grep` from inside the Scheme environment. We will have all the advantages of a combinator language. It will have a clean, modular description while retaining the ability to use existing tools. Users of this language will have nothing to *grep* about, unless they value concise expression over readability.

As with any language there are primitives, means of combination, and means of abstraction. Our language allows the construction of patterns that utilities like `grep` can match against character-string data. Because this language is embedded in Scheme, we inherit Scheme's power: we can use Scheme constructs to combine patterns and use Scheme procedures to abstract them.

2.2.1   A regular expression combinator language

Patterns are built out of these primitive patterns:

(`r:dot`) matches any character except newline

(`r:bol`) matches only the beginning of a line

(`r:eol`) matches only the end of a line

(`r:quote` *string*) matches the *string*

(`r:char-from` *string*) matches one character that is in the *string* (`r:char-not-from` *string*) matches one character that is not in the *string*

Patterns can be combined to make compound patterns:

(`r:seq` *pattern* ...)
This pattern matches each argument *pattern* in sequence, from left to right.

(`r:alt` *pattern* ...)
This pattern tries each argument *pattern* from left to right, until one of these alternatives matches. If none matches then this pattern does not match.

(`r:repeat` *min max pattern*)
This pattern tries to match the argument *pattern* a minimum of *min* times but no more than a maximum of *max* times. If *max* is given as `#f` then no maximum is specified. If *max* equals *min* the given pattern must be matched exactly that many times.

Here are some example patterns:

(`r:seq` (`r:quote` `"a"`) (`r:dot`) (`r:quote` `"c"`))
matches any three-character string beginning with a and ending with c. For example, it will match abc and aac and acc.

(`r:alt` (`r:quote` `"foo"`) (`r:quote` `"bar"`) (`r:quote` `"baz"`))
matches either foo, bar, or baz.

(`r:repeat` 3 5 (`r:alt` (`r:quote` `"cat"`) (`r:quote` `"dog"`)))
matches catdogcat and catcatdogdog and dogdogcatdogdog but not catcatcatcatdogdogdog.

We will implement patterns as Scheme expressions. Thus we can freely mix them with any Scheme code, giving us all the power of the programming language.

2.2.2 Implementation of the translator

Let's look at how this language is implemented. Regular expressions will be represented as strings in the POSIX Basic Regular Expression syntax.

```
(define (r:dot) ".")
(define (r:bol) "^")
(define (r:eol) "$")
```

These directly correspond to regular-expression syntax.

Next, `r:seq` implements a way to treat a given set of regular-expression fragments as a self-contained element:

```
(define (r:seq . exprs)
  (string-append "\\(" (apply string-append exprs) "\\)"))
```

The use of parentheses in the result isolates the content of the given expression fragments from the surrounding context. Unfortunately, the use of \ in the translated output is necessary. In basic regular expressions, the parenthesis characters are treated as self-quoting characters. Here we need them to act as grouping operations, which is done by preceding each with a backslash. Adding insult to injury, when this regular expression is put into a Scheme string, it is necessary to quote each backslash character with *another backslash*. So our example `(r:seq (r:quote "a")` `(r:dot) (r:quote "c"))` translates to \(\(a\).\(c\)\), or as a Scheme string `"\\(\\(a\\).\\(c\\)\\)"`. Ugh.

The implementation of `r:quote` is a bit harder. In a regular expression, most characters are self-quoting. However, some characters are regular-expression operators and must be explicitly quoted. We wrap the result using `r:seq` to guarantee that the quoted string is self-contained.

```
(define (r:quote string)
  (r:seq
   (list->string
    (append-map (lambda (char)
                  (if (memv char chars-needing-quoting)
                      (list #\\ char)
                      (list char)))
                (string->list string)))))

(define chars-needing-quoting
  '(#\. #\[ #\\ #\^ #\$ #\*))
```

To implement alternative subexpressions, we interpolate a vertical bar between subexpressions and wrap the result using `r:seq`:

```
(define (r:alt . exprs)
  (if (pair? exprs)
      (apply r:seq
             (cons (car exprs)
                   (append-map (lambda (expr)
                                 (list "\\|" expr))
                               (cdr exprs))))
      (r:seq)))
```

```
(r:alt (r:quote "foo") (r:quote "bar") (r:quote "baz"))
```
translates to \(\(\(foo\)\|\(bar\)\|\(baz\)\). In addition to
quoting the parenthesis characters, we must also quote the vertical bar character, which is otherwise a self-quoting character in
this syntax. Note that alternative expressions, unlike the rest of
the regular expressions supported here, are not supported by BRE
syntax: they are an extension defined by GNU grep that is supported by many implementations. (Alternatives *are* supported by
ERE syntax.)

It is straightforward to implement repetition by using copies of
the given regular expression:

```
(define (r:repeat min max expr)
  (apply r:seq
        (append (make-list min expr)
                (cond ((not max) (list expr "*"))
                      ((= max min) '())
                      (else
                        (make-list (- max min)
                                   (r:alt expr "")))))))
```

This makes min copies of expr, followed by (- max min) optional
copies, where each optional copy is an alternative of the expression and an empty expression. If there is no maximum,[9] the expression is followed by an asterisk to match any number of times.
So (r:repeat 3 5 (r:alt (r:quote "cat") (r:quote "dog")))
translates to something large that might cause seizures in the
reader.

The implementation of r:char-from and r:char-not-from is
complicated by the need for baroque quotation. This is best organized in two parts, the first to handle the differences between
them, and the second for the quotation handling that they have
in common:

```
(define (r:char-from string)
  (case (string-length string)
    ((0) (r:seq))
    ((1) (r:quote string))
    (else
      (bracket string
               (lambda (members)
                 (if (lset= eqv? '(#\- #\^) members)
                     '(#\- #\^)
                     (quote-bracketed-contents members)))))))
```

---

[9]We indicate that there is no maximum by calling r:repeat with #f for max.

```
(define (r:char-not-from string)
  (bracket string
           (lambda (members)
             (cons #\^ (quote-bracketed-contents members)))))))

(define (bracket string procedure)
  (list->string
    (append '(#\[)
            (procedure (string->list string))
            '(#\]))))
```

The special cases for r:char-from handle empty and singleton sets
of characters specially, which simplifies the general case. There is
also a special case for a set containing only caret and hyphen. But
r:char-not-from has no such special cases.

The general case handles the quotation of the three characters
that have special meaning inside a bracket by placing them in
positions where they are not operators. (We told you this was
ugly!)

```
(define (quote-bracketed-contents members)
  (define (optional char)
    (if (memv char members) (list char) '()))
  (append (optional #\])
          (remove
            (lambda (c)
              (memv c chars-needing-quoting-in-brackets))
            members)
          (optional #\^)
          (optional #\-)))

(define chars-needing-quoting-in-brackets
  '(#\] #\^ #\-))
```

In order to test this code, we can print the corresponding grep
command and use cut and paste to run it in a shell. Because
different shells use different quoting conventions, we need to not
only quote the regular expression, but also choose which shell to
use. The Bourne shell is ubiquitous, and has a relatively simple
quoting convention.

```
(define (write-bourne-shell-grep-command expr filename)
  (display (bourne-shell-grep-command-string expr filename)))
```

```
(define (bourne-shell-grep-command-string expr filename)
  (string-append "grep -e "
                 (bourne-shell-quote-string expr)
                 " "
                 filename))
```

The Bourne quoting convention uses single-quote characters surrounding a string, which quotes anything in the string other than a single-quote, which ends the quoted string. So, to quote a single-quote character, we must end the string, quote the single quote explicitly using backslash, and then start another quoted string. The shell interprets this concatenation as a single token. (Are we having fun yet?)

```
(define (bourne-shell-quote-string string)
  (list->string
   (append (list #\')
           (append-map (lambda (char)
                         (if (char=? char #\')
                             (list #\' #\\ char #\')
                             (list char)))
                       (string->list string))
           (list #\'))))
```

The moral of this story

Our translator is very complicated because most regular expressions are not composable to make larger regular expressions unless extreme measures are taken to isolate the parts. Our translator does this work, but consequently the regular expressions that it generates have much unnecessary boilerplate. Humans don't write regular expressions this way, because they use boilerplate only where necessary—but they often miss instances where it is necessary, causing hard-to-find bugs.

The moral of this story is that regular expressions are a beautiful example of how *not* to build a system. Using composable parts and combinators to make new parts by combining others leads to simpler and more robust implementations.

Exercise 2.6: Adding * and + to regular expressions

In the traditional regular expression language the asterisk (*) operator following a subpattern means zero or more copies of the subpattern. A common extension to the language adds the plus-sign (+) operator. A plus sign following a subpattern means one or more copies of the subpattern.

Define Scheme procedures `r:*` and `r:+` to take a pattern and iterate it as necessary. This can be done in terms of `r:repeat`.

Demonstrate your procedures on real data in complex patterns.

Exercise 2.7: A bug, one bad joke, two tweaks, and a revelation

Ben Bitdiddle has noticed a problem with our implementation of (`r:repeat` *min max expr*).

The use of (`r:alt expr` `""`) at the end of the `r:repeat` procedure is a bit dodgy. This code fragment translates to \(*expr*\|\), where *expr* is the value of `expr`. This relies on the fact that alternation with something and nothing is the equivalent of saying "one or none." (We will omit the required but confusing backslashes in the rest of this explanation.) That is: (*expr*|) denotes one or no instances of *expr*. Unfortunately, this depends on an undocumented GNU extension to the formal POSIX standard for REs.

Specifically, section 9.4.3 of the POSIX standard[10] states that a vertical line appearing immediately before a close parenthesis (or immediately after an open parenthesis) produces undefined behavior. In essence, an RE must not be a null sequence.

GNU `grep` just happens to "do the right thing" when presented with (*x*|). Not all `grep` implementations are as tolerant.

Therefore, Ben asks his team of three code hackers (Louis, Alyssa, and Eva) to propose alternative workarounds. Ultimately, he proposes his own patch, which you will implement.

- Louis Reasoner suggests that a simple, elegant fix would be to replace the code fragment (`r:alt expr` `""`) with a straightforward call to (`r:repeat 0 1 expr`).

- Alyssa P. Hacker proposes to rewrite the else clause of `r:repeat` to translate (`r:repeat 3 5` *x*) into the equivalent of (*xxx*|*xxxx*|*xxxxx*) instead of the naughty *xxx*(*x*|)(*x*|) non-POSIX-compliant undefined regular expression that our code produces. She refers to section 9.4.7 of the POSIX regular expression documentation.[11]

- Eva Lu Ator points to the question mark (?) operator in section 9.4.6.4[12] and proposes that a better fix would be to implement an `r:?` operator and replace (`r:alt expr` `""`) with (`r:? expr`).

- Meanwhile, Ben looks closely at the RE spec and has a revelation. He proposes that `r:repeat` be reimplemented to emit Interval Expressions. See section 9.3.6.5 of the POSIX documentation.[13] Please try not to get sick.

---

[10] ERE Special Characters, [96] #tag_09_04_03

[11] ERE Alternation, [96] #tag_09_04_07

[12] EREs Matching Multiple Characters, [96] #tag_09_04_06

[13] BREs Matching Multiple Characters, [96] #tag_09_03_06

Let's consider each proposal:

a. Everyone giggles at Louis's silly joke. What's so funny about it? That is, what's wrong with this idea?

A one-sentence punchline will do.

b. What advantages does Eva's proposal have over Alyssa's in terms of both code and data?

A concise yet convincing few sentences suffice.

c. What advantage does Ben's proposal have over all the others? Specifically, ponder which section of the POSIX document he cites versus which sections the others cite, then take a quick peek at exercise 2.10 below and consider the implications. Also, consider the size of the output strings in this new code as well as the overall clarity of the code.

Again, a brief sentence or two is sufficient.

d. Following Ben's proposal, reimplement `r:repeat` to emit Interval Expressions. Hint: Scheme's `number->string` procedure should be handy. Caveat: Beware the backslashes.

Show the output generated by `r:repeat` on a few well-chosen sample inputs. Demonstrate your procedure on real data in some complex patterns.

Exercise 2.8: Too much nesting

Our program produces excessively nested regular expressions: it makes groups even when they are not necessary. For example, the following simple pattern leads to an overly complex regular expression:

```
(display (r:seq (r:quote "a") (r:dot) (r:quote "c")))
\(\(a\).\(c\)\)
```

Another problem is that BREs may involve back-references. (See section 9.3.6.3 of the POSIX regular expression documentation.[14]) A back-reference refers to a preceding parenthesized subexpression. So it is important that the parenthesized subexpressions be ones explicitly placed by the author of the pattern. (Aargh! This is one of the worst ideas we have ever heard of—grouping, which is necessary for iteration, was confused with naming for later reference!)

To do: Edit our program to eliminate as much of the unnecessary nesting as you can. Caution: There are subtle cases here that you have to watch out for. What is such a case? Demonstrate your better version of our program and show how it handles the subtleties.

Hint: Our program uses strings as its intermediate representation as well as its result. You might consider using a different intermediate representation.

---

[14]BREs Matching Multiple Characters, [96] `#tag_09_03_06`

Exercise 2.9: Back-references

Add a procedure for constructing back-references. (See exercise 2.8.) Have fun getting confused about BREs.

Exercise 2.10: Standards?

> The best thing about standards is that there are so many to choose from.
>
> Andrew S. Tannenbaum

In addition to Basic Regular Expressions (BREs), there are Extended Regular Expressions (EREs) defined in the POSIX regular expression documentation [96]. Some software, such as `egrep`, uses this version of regular expressions. Unfortunately EREs are not a conservative extension of BREs: ERE syntax is actually inconsistent with BRE syntax! It is an interesting project to extend our Scheme pattern language so that the target can be either BREs or EREs.

a. What are the significant differences between BREs and EREs that make this a pain? List the differences that must be addressed.

b. How can our translator be factored so that our language can translate into either kind of regular expression, depending on what is needed? How can we maintain the abstract layer that is independent of the target regular expression language? Explain your strategy.

c. Implement the strategy you devised in part **b**. Demonstrate your work by making sure that you can run `egrep` as well as `grep`, with equivalent results in cases that test the differences you found in part **a**.

2.3   Wrappers

Sometimes we can repurpose an existing program by wrapping it rather than rewriting it. Consider the problem of computing how the radius of a sphere of gas varies with the temperature, keeping the pressure constant. The ideal gas law is

$$PV = nRT, \tag{2.1}$$

where P is the pressure, V is the volume, n is the amount of the gas, R is the gas constant, and T is the temperature. So the volume is computed by

```
(define (gas-law-volume pressure temperature amount)
  (/ (* amount gas-constant temperature) pressure))

(define gas-constant 8.3144621)          ;J/(K*mol)
```

and the radius of a sphere is computed by

```
(define (sphere-radius volume)
  (expt (/ volume (* 4/3 pi)) 1/3))

(define pi (* 4 (atan 1 1)))
```

(Note: 4/3 and 1/3 are rational constants—the slash is not an infix division operator.) The choice of gas constant makes this program use SI units, so the pressure is in newtons per square meter, the temperature is in kelvins, the amount is in moles, the volume is in cubic meters, and the radius is in meters.

This looks straightforward, but use of other units can make things complicated. Suppose we want to measure the temperature in degrees Fahrenheit, the pressure in pounds per square inch, and the radius in inches. Determining the correct formula is more complicated than computing the numerical answer. We could modify the simple formula to account for the units, but this obscures the idea of the program and specializes it to the particular problem. Alternatively, we could arrange to have a modular way to convert the units.

A unit conversion is a procedure that is linked to its inverse. We can write temperature conversions between conventional units, such as Fahrenheit and Celsius temperatures, and between SI and conventional units.

```
(define fahrenheit-to-celsius
  (make-unit-conversion (lambda (f) (* 5/9 (- f 32)))
                        (lambda (c) (+ (* c 9/5) 32))))

(define celsius-to-kelvin
  (let ((zero-celsius 273.15)) ;kelvins
    (make-unit-conversion (lambda (c) (+ c zero-celsius))
                          (lambda (k) (- k zero-celsius)))))
```

We can access the inverse procedure using unit:invert. For example,

```
(fahrenheit-to-celsius -40)
```
-40

```
(fahrenheit-to-celsius 32)
```
0

```
((unit:invert fahrenheit-to-celsius) 20)
```
68

We can compose unit conversions:

```
((compose celsius-to-kelvin fahrenheit-to-celsius) 80)
299.81666666666666
```

And we can define compound unit conversions. For example, pressure can be expressed in in pounds per square inch or newtons per square meter.[15]

```
(define psi-to-nsm
  (compose pound-to-newton
           (unit:invert inch-to-meter)
           (unit:invert inch-to-meter)))
```

So now we can compute, in inches, the radius of a sphere occupied by 1 mole of an ideal gas at 68°F and 14.7 psi.

```
((unit:invert inch-to-meter)
 (sphere-radius
  (gas-law-volume
   (psi-to-nsm 14.7)
   ((compose celsius-to-kelvin fahrenheit-to-celsius) 68)
   1)))
7.049624635839811
```

This is a mess! This implementation of unit conversions, while simple to program, is hard to read and hard to use. On the other hand, it nicely separates several concerns. The physics of the gas law is separated from the geometry of the sphere and the units of measurement. The physical and geometric descriptions are uncluttered and each is easy to read.

We can do better. We can build a small domain-specific language, where the domain is units. This will simplify the job of constructing new converters, and make the resulting converters more readable.

---

[15]Note that the composition of two instances of meter-to-inch is a sensible way to convert square meters to square inches. There are unit conversions for which this is not true. For example, taking the square of a kelvin-to-Celsius conversion doesn't make sense, even though the numerical computation produces consistent results. This is a consequence of the fact that Celsius temperature has an offset from the physically meaningful kelvin temperature. Indeed, the square of a Celsius temperature has no physical meaning.

2.3.1 Specialization wrappers

One way to proceed is to make a general family of wrappers that can take a procedure like `gas-law-volume` and produce a version of that procedure specialized by unit conversions for its output and inputs. Although we will show how to do this for unit conversions, the code will be general enough to build wrappers for arbitrary transformations of data.

For the problem at hand we can construct a specializer for the `gas-law-volume` procedure that knows its native units (SI). The specializer is defined by a simple language that is compiled into the appropriate combinations of primitive unit conversions. This is somewhat like a combinator system except that the combinators are generated by the compiler according to a high-level specification. We will see this technique again in chapter 4, where we use it to compile combinations of pattern-matching procedures from patterns.

```
(define make-specialized-gas-law-volume
  (unit-specializer
    gas-law-volume
    '(expt meter 3)                     ; output (volume)
    '(/ newton (expt meter 2))          ; pressure
    'kelvin                             ; temperature
    'mole))                             ; amount
```

To make a version of the `gas-law-volume` procedure that uses other units we supply the units that we want to use:

```
(define conventional-gas-law-volume
  (make-specialized-gas-law-volume
    '(expt inch 3)                      ; output (volume)
    '(/ pound (expt inch 2))            ; pressure
    'fahrenheit                         ; temperature
    'mole))                             ; amount
```

This procedure can then be used to produce the volume in cubic inches, and therefore we can get the radius in inches.

```
(sphere-radius (conventional-gas-law-volume 14.7 68 1))
7.04962463583981
```

2.3.2   Implementing specializers

How can we make this work? There are two parts: a procedure
`unit-specializer` that wraps a given procedure with the necessary unit conversions, and a means of translating the given unit
expressions into the appropriate unit conversion. The first part is

```
(define (unit-specializer procedure implicit-output-unit
                          . implicit-input-units)
  (define (specializer specific-output-unit
                       . specific-input-units)
    (let ((output-converter
           (make-converter implicit-output-unit
                           specific-output-unit))
          (input-converters
           (map make-converter
                specific-input-units
                implicit-input-units)))
      (define (specialized-procedure . arguments)
        (output-converter
         (apply procedure
                (map (lambda (converter argument)
                       (converter argument))
                     input-converters
                     arguments))))
      specialized-procedure))
  specializer)
```

The procedure `unit-specializer` takes a procedure to be specialized and its implicit native units, and returns a specializer that
takes specific units and creates a specialized version of the given
procedure. The only tricky part is making sure that unit expressions are passed to `make-converter` in the correct order.

The second part of the solution is `make-converter`, which takes
two unit expressions, and returns a converter procedure that converts data in the first unit to the second unit. For this problem,
we will make a version of `make-converter` that's really dumb: it
treats the unit expressions as literal constants that can be compared with `equal?`. With that simplification, `make-converter` can
use a table lookup to find the appropriate converter, which means
we have to explicitly provide every necessary conversion rather

than deriving them from primitive unit conversions. Here's an example of how the table is created:

```
(register-unit-conversion 'fahrenheit 'celsius
                          fahrenheit-to-celsius)

(register-unit-conversion 'celsius 'kelvin
                          celsius-to-kelvin)
```

This registers the conversions we defined earlier. Once these conversions are registered, we can look up either conversion direction by the order of arguments passed to `make-converter`.

However, what we need isn't either of these conversions, but instead the conversion from `fahrenheit` to `kelvin`. Since we don't want to infer this from the existing definitions—an interesting but much more complex implementation—we will have to build compound conversions from the existing ones. To make that easy, we will introduce an "algebra" of unit conversions, as follows:

```
(define (unit:* u1 u2)
  (make-unit-conversion (compose u2 u1)
                        (compose (unit:invert u1)
                                 (unit:invert u2))))
```

The procedure `unit:*`, combined with `unit:invert`, provides us with a general ability to combine unit conversions. For convenience, we will add the following, which are easily derived from `unit:*` and `unit:invert`:

```
(unit:/ u1 u2)
(unit:expt u n)
```

With this algebra, we can write the conversions we want:

```
(register-unit-conversion 'fahrenheit 'kelvin
   (unit:* fahrenheit-to-celsius celsius-to-kelvin))

(register-unit-conversion '(/ pound (expt inch 2))
                          '(/ newton (expt meter 2))
   (unit:/ pound-to-newton
           (unit:expt inch-to-meter 2)))

(register-unit-conversion '(expt inch 3) '(expt meter 3)
   (unit:expt inch-to-meter 3))
```

2.3.3 Adapters

What we have shown here is one possible technique for taking an existing program and broadening its applicability without changing the original program. The resulting "adapter" mechanism is itself extensible and can be used to generalize many other kinds of programs.

This is an important principle: rather than rewriting a program to adapt it to a new purpose, it's preferable to start with a simple and general base program and wrap it to specialize it for a particular purpose. The program doesn't know anything about the wrappers, and the wrappers make few assumptions about the underlying program. And the `unit-specializer` procedure knows very little about either. Because these parts are so loosely coupled, they can each be generalized for many purposes, including those we aren't thinking about here. This is a kind of layering strategy, which we will expand upon in chapter 6.

Exercise 2.11: Implementing unit conversions

Here we ask you to fill in the details that make this system work.

a. As a warmup, write the procedures `register-unit-conversion`, and `make-converter`.

b. Write the procedures `unit:/` and `unit:expt`.

c. Fill out a library of conversions for conventional units to SI units. This requires conversions for mass and length. (Time is in seconds in both systems. However, you may be interested in minutes, hours, days, weeks, years, etc. Don't get stuck trying to make this universal.)

d. Make some useful compounds, like velocity and acceleration.

e. For a real project, extend this specializer system for some other data conversion of some other program, having nothing to do with units.

f. Another big extension is to build `make-converter` so that it can derive compound conversions, as required, from previously registered conversions. This will require a graph search.

2.4 Abstracting a domain

Let's look at how a domain-specific language layer can be created as a basis for software about board games. There are many common features of board games; each game combines some of those features. A *domain model* can be built that captures the common structure of a class of board games, in terms of the abstract concepts that describe board games, such as pieces, potential locations, and primitive behaviors such as moving and capturing.

A particular board game program may be constructed entirely in terms of the domain model. If the domain model is sufficiently general, it will support future variation without change to the model itself.

Let's consider board games such as chess and checkers. They are both two-person games played on a board that is a rectangular grid. The players have pieces that are arrayed on the board. There is never more than one piece at any position on the board. The players alternate moves. On each move a player chooses a piece and moves it to some other location on the board. Sometimes an opponent's piece is captured. This is an informal description of a domain model for a class of board games.

Based on this kind of domain model we will construct a *referee* for checkers that will compute all legal moves for a player at a given state of play. The domain model's implementation is fairly complex, providing implementations of pieces, coordinates, and the board. In order to simplify our presentation we will restrict ourselves to just what is needed by the referee.

The general organization of the referee is that it will generate all the legal moves for each piece separately and then aggregate them. In order to do this, it's helpful to have an abstraction that keeps track of the effects of moving a piece. For example, one effect might change a piece's position, another might change its type (e.g., "kinging" in checkers), and yet another might capture an opponent's piece. Each legal move consists of a sequence of such changes applied to the initial state of the move.

A good program must be written many times. This is true of the programs we show. The first draft may not clearly separate out the concerns, but by making that draft the programmer learns the structure of the problem. We will show two different implementations, which will reveal the evolution of the program as we identify shortcomings in our draft.

2.4.1 A monolithic implementation

Let's start with a simple version of the referee that one might write to understand what really has to be done.

A checkers domain model

The first implementation will be built on a domain model that is specific to checkers and fairly simple. In the later implementation we will abstract away the checkers-specific parts and hide many of the details of the domain model. The final domain model will support other similar board games, and perhaps other domains.

The domain model we will use has three abstract types. A *board* tracks the live pieces and the color of the player to move next (the *current* player). It can be asked what piece, if any, is in a particular position. A *piece* has a color, a position, and whether it is a king. A *position* is specified by *coordinates* that are relative to the player to move. Here are the operations on boards:

(current-pieces *board*)
gets a list of the pieces belonging to the current player.

(is-position-on-board? *coords board*)
tests whether the given *coords* specify a position on *board*. Coordinates that do not satisfy this predicate will cause errors when used with other operations.

(board-get *coords board*)
gets the piece that is at the position specified by *coords*. If there is no piece in that position it returns #f.

(position-info *coords board*)
describes what occupies the position *coords* in *board*. If the position is empty the value is unoccupied; if it contains one of the current player's pieces the value is occupied-by-self; if it contains an opponent's piece the value is occupied-by-opponent.

(is-position-unoccupied? *coords board*)
is equivalent to position-info returning unoccupied.

(is-position-occupied-by-self? *coords board*)
is equivalent to position-info returning occupied-by-self.

(is-position-occupied-by-opponent? *coords board*)
is equivalent to position-info returning occupied-by-opponent.

There is a similarly small set of operations on pieces:

(piece-coords *piece*)
gets the coordinates of *piece*.

(`should-be-crowned?` *piece*)
tests whether *piece* should be crowned—specifically, if it is not already a king and is on the opponent's home row.

(`crown-piece` *piece*)
gets a new piece identical to *piece* except that it is a king.

(`possible-directions` *piece*)
gets a list of directions that *piece* may consider for a move. This does not take into account whether moving in that direction is permissible.

The coordinate system is simple: just row and column integers. When we refer to *coordinates* or *coords*, we mean absolute coordinates on the board. We use the term *offset* for relative coordinates. An offset can be added to some coordinates to produce new coordinates, or inversely two coordinates can be subtracted to produce an offset. A *direction* is an offset in which the row and column are 0, 1, or −1; For checkers, the possible directions are the two forward diagonals, with the row 1 and the column either −1 or 1. Once a piece becomes a king, it can additionally use the backward diagonals, with row −1. In chess, the possible moves use additional directions, depending on the piece, while a knight move needs a more complex definition. We won't define the procedures for manipulating coordinates; they should be self-explanatory.

A checkers referee

We need a data structure to represent each move. Since any given move may require changing a piece's position multiple times, we will use a list of *step* objects, each of which specifies the piece prior to the step, the piece after the step, the board after the step, and whether the step is a jump. Such a list, which we will call a *path*, is ordered from newest step to oldest. This ordering facilitates sharing of common subpaths that may occur when a move can be continued in multiple ways.

(`step-to` *step*)
gets the piece after *step* is taken.

(`step-board` *step*)
gets the board after *step* is taken.

(`make-simple-move` *new-coords piece board*)
gets a step that moves *piece* to *new-coords* on *board*.

(make-jump *new-coords jumped-coords piece board*)
gets a step that moves *piece* to *new-coords* on *board* and removes
the opponent's piece at *jumped-coords*.

(replace-piece *new-piece old-piece board*)
gets a step that replaces *old-piece* with *new-piece* on *board*.

(path-contains-jumps? *path*)
tests whether any of the steps in *path* are jumps.

Let's build our referee. We will start by describing what simple
steps are possible from a given starting point in a given direction.
The try-step procedure identifies a potential next step, augmenting the given path. If there is no such step, it returns #f.

```
(define (try-step piece board direction path)
  (let ((new-coords
         (coords+ (piece-coords piece) direction)))
    (and (is-position-on-board? new-coords board)
         (case (position-info new-coords board)
           ((unoccupied)
            (and (not (path-contains-jumps? path))
                 (cons (make-simple-move new-coords
                                         piece
                                         board)
                       path)))
           ((occupied-by-opponent)
            (let ((landing (coords+ new-coords direction)))
              (and (is-position-on-board? landing board)
                   (is-position-unoccupied? landing board)
                   (cons (make-jump landing
                                    new-coords
                                    piece
                                    board)
                         path))))
           ((occupied-by-self) #f)
           (else (error "Unknown position info"))))))
```

The procedure looks at the position one step along the given direction; if it's unoccupied, then it's possible to move there. (We
explicitly test whether this is a continuation of a jump, as that
is not allowed in checkers.) If the position is occupied by one of
the player's pieces, no move is possible. But if the position is
occupied by an opponent's piece, and the next position in that
direction is unoccupied, then we can jump over the opponent's
piece and capture it.

We must try each possible direction for the piece. The procedure `compute-next-steps` returns a list of possible next paths by augmenting an existing path by one step.

```
(define (compute-next-steps piece board path)
  ;; filter-map drops false values
  (filter-map (lambda (direction)
                (try-step piece board direction path))
              (possible-directions piece)))
```

The rules of checkers mandate choosing a jump when one or more is possible:

```
(define (evolve-paths piece board)
  (let ((paths (compute-next-steps piece board '())))
    (let ((jumps (filter path-contains-jumps? paths)))
      (if (null? jumps)
          paths
          (evolve-jumps jumps)))))
```

And after an initial jump, we must test for other possible jumps:

```
(define (evolve-jumps paths)
  (append-map (lambda (path)
                (let ((paths
                       (let ((step (car path)))
                         (compute-next-steps (step-to step)
                                             (step-board step)
                                             path))))
                  (if (null? paths)
                      (list path)
                      ;; continue jumping if possible
                      (evolve-jumps paths))))
              paths))
```

That is the logic for generating the moves for a single piece. The referee must do this for every piece and aggregate the results:

```
(define (generate-moves board)
  (crown-kings
   (mandate-jumps
    (append-map (lambda (piece)
                  (evolve-paths piece board))
                (current-pieces board)))))
```

This procedure does two things in addition to generating the moves. First, the aggregated moves may contain jumps for some

pieces and ordinary moves for others, in which case only the jumps
are legal moves.

```
(define (mandate-jumps paths)
  (let ((jumps (filter path-contains-jumps? paths)))
    (if (null? jumps)
        paths
        jumps)))
```

Second, if any piece reaches the opponent's home row, it must be
made a king.

```
(define (crown-kings paths)
  (map (lambda (path)
         (let ((piece (step-to (car path))))
           (if (should-be-crowned? piece)
               (cons (replace-piece (crown-piece piece)
                                    piece
                                    (step-board (car path)))
                     path)
               path)))
       paths))
```

Critique

This code is quite nice; it is surprisingly compact, and it is written
in terms of the domain model. However, the rules of checkers are
distributed throughout the code. The availability of a jump is
discovered in the procedure `try-step`, but the fact that jumps
may chain is in `evolve-jumps`. Also, the rule that if a jump is
available a jump must be taken is split between the procedures
`evolve-paths` and `mandate-jumps`. A more subtle problem is that
the control structure of the referee is interwoven with the rules.
For example, the accumulation of changes (steps in the path) is
built into the control structure, as is chaining of a multiple jump.
The reason why the logic for mandating jumps is in two places is
that it is required by the distribution of the control structure.

2.4.2   Factoring out the domain

Let's try to ameliorate the problems noted in the previous implementation. Can we separate the domain model and control
structure from the rules of checkers?

A domain model

We can reuse the coordinates, pieces, and board from our monolithic implementation, since they are largely unchanged. However, we will eliminate the specific idea of king and non-king pieces, instead using a symbolic type. This introduces two new operations:

(`piece-type` *piece*)
gets the type of *piece*.

(`piece-new-type` *piece type*)
gets a new piece identical to *piece* except that it has the given *type*.

We redefine `should-be-crowned?` and `crown-piece` to use the piece type, so they behave the same as before, but they are no longer part of the core domain model.

Although the procedure `possible-directions` is specific to checkers, we will use it here, but only when defining the rules of checkers. It is not part of the new domain model.

The step data structure is also specific to checkers, because it specifies whether a step is a jump. We will replace it with a more general structure called a *change*:

(`make-change` *board piece flags*)
creates a new change object. The *flags* argument is a list of symbols that we can use to indicate changes of state such as capture of a piece. The selectors `get-board`, `get-piece`, and `get-flags` can be used to get the corresponding parts of a change.

Like the piece type, the change flags provide a way to add game-specific features to the domain model without baking them in.

We will replace the path idea with a more abstract notion called a *partial move*. A partial move consists of an initial board and piece, together with zero or more changes. Our code uses the identifier `pmove` for a partial move.

(`initial-pmove` *board piece*)
creates a pmove with no changes and no flags.

(`is-pmove-empty?` *pmove*)
tests whether *pmove* is empty: in other words, if it has no changes.

(`is-pmove-finished?` *pmove*)
tests whether *pmove* has been flagged as finished.

(`current-board` *pmove*)
returns the board from the most recent change in *pmove*; if there
are no changes, it returns the board passed as an argument to
`initial-pmove`.

(`current-piece` *pmove*)
returns the piece from the most recent change in the *pmove*; if
there are no changes, it returns the piece passed as an argument
to `initial-pmove`.

The next operations extend a pmove in different ways. When we
say "extends *pmove* by *foo*" we mean "extends *pmove* by adding
a change object that does *foo*."

(`new-piece-position` *coords pmove*)
extends *pmove* by moving its piece to *coords*.

(`update-piece` *procedure pmove*)
extends *pmove* by replacing its piece with the result of calling
procedure on its piece.

(`finish-move` *pmove*)
extends *pmove* by adding a change object with a flag that specifies that the move is complete. The result always satisfies the
predicate `is-pmove-finished?`.

In the implementation of section 2.4.1, we used the terms *jumping* and *capturing* interchangeably. But capturing is a more general idea: for example, in chess, capturing is done by displacing
a piece rather than jumping over it. We use a change flag to en-
code the act of capturing a piece, and the following procedures to
manage that flag:

(`captures-pieces?` *pmove*)
tests whether any pieces are captured by *pmove*.

(`capture-piece-at` *coords pmove*)
extends *pmove* by removing the piece at *coords*. The position specified by *coords* must contain an opponent's piece. The operation
also sets a flag in the new change object saying that a piece was
captured; the resulting pmove always satisfies `captures-pieces?`.

An executive
To help separate the control structure from the rules of checkers we
build a rule executive that captures the control structure without
incorporating the specific content of the rules. In this kind of

game there are two kinds of rule. One kind, which we will call an *evolution rule*, augments a pmove, possibly returning multiple derived pmoves. The other kind, an *aggregate rule*, acts on a set of pmoves, eliminating some that are not allowed or extending some to incorporate changes, such as crowning a king.

Here is an executive that starts with some empty pmoves, one for each of the player's pieces, and evolves these into a collection of pmoves that represent finished moves. It then applies the aggregate rules to the collection of finished pmoves, ultimately returning a collection of the legal moves.

An evolution rule is implemented as a procedure that transforms a given pmove into a collection of new pmoves, some of which may be finished (satisfy is-pmove-finished?). The executive recursively applies all of the evolution rules to the collection of pmoves until all of them are finished.

An aggregate rule is implemented as a procedure that accepts a collection of finished pmoves and produces a new collection. Each aggregate rule is applied once, and there are no ordering constraints between aggregate rules, so the executive can compose them together into a single procedure that is the composite aggregate rule. If there are no aggregate rules, then the composite simply returns its argument.

```
(define (execute-rules initial-pmoves evolution-rules
                       aggregate-rules)
  ((reduce compose (lambda (x) x) aggregate-rules)
   (append-map (lambda (pmove)
                 (evolve-pmove pmove evolution-rules))
               initial-pmoves)))

(define (evolve-pmove pmove evolution-rules)
  (append-map (lambda (new-pmove)
                (if (is-pmove-finished? new-pmove)
                    (list new-pmove)
                    (evolve-pmove new-pmove evolution-rules)))
              (append-map (lambda (evolution-rule)
                            (evolution-rule pmove))
                          evolution-rules)))
```

An evolution rule is registered for use in the executive by the procedure define-evolution-rule and an aggregate rule is registered by the procedure define-aggregate-rule. Each rule has a name, the game that it is registered in, and a procedure implementing its behavior.

Rules of checkers

Here is a rule for simple moves. This looks for any unoccupied adjacent position in a possible direction, and extends the pmove to include a move to that position. After such a move, it is not legal to continue moving, so we mark that pmove as finished.

```
(define-evolution-rule 'simple-move checkers
  (lambda (pmove)
    (if (is-pmove-empty? pmove)
        (get-simple-moves pmove)
        '())))

(define (get-simple-moves pmove)
  (filter-map
   (lambda (direction)
     (let ((landing (compute-new-position direction 1 pmove))
           (board (current-board pmove)))
       (and (is-position-on-board? landing board)
            (is-position-unoccupied? landing board)
            (finish-move (new-piece-position landing pmove)))))
   (possible-directions (current-piece pmove))))
```

In `get-simple-moves`, the procedure `compute-new-position` gets the proposed landing site of the piece possibly being moved, given the `direction` and `distance` for the move. The procedure `offset*` multiplies an offset and a number to get a new offset scaled by the number.

```
(define (compute-new-position direction distance pmove)
  (coords+ (piece-coords (current-piece pmove))
           (offset* direction distance)))
```

The rule for jumps is similar, except that it must look for an occupied position followed by an unoccupied position in a given direction. When no jumps are possible, a pmove is finished.

```
(define-evolution-rule 'jump checkers
  (lambda (pmove)
    (let ((jumps (get-jumps pmove)))
      (cond ((not (null? jumps))
             jumps)
            ((is-pmove-empty? pmove)
             '())   ; abandon this pmove
            (else
             (list (finish-move pmove)))))))
```

```
(define (get-jumps pmove)
  (filter-map
   (lambda (direction)
     (let ((possible-jump
            (compute-new-position direction 1 pmove))
           (landing (compute-new-position direction 2 pmove))
           (board (current-board pmove)))
       (and (is-position-on-board? landing board)
            (is-position-unoccupied? landing board)
            (is-position-occupied-by-opponent? possible-jump
                                                board)
            (capture-piece-at possible-jump
                              (new-piece-position landing
                                                  pmove)))))
   (possible-directions (current-piece pmove))))
```

Making kings is independent of other rules: just look at all the completed moves and crown any non-king that is on the opponent's home row.

```
(define-aggregate-rule 'coronation checkers
  (lambda (pmoves)
    (map (lambda (pmove)
           (let ((piece (current-piece pmove)))
             (if (should-be-crowned? piece)
                 (update-piece crown-piece pmove)
                 pmove)))
         pmoves)))
```

And finally, the rule mandating that a jump be taken when one or more is available is done at the end by detecting that case and throwing away all the non-jump moves.

```
(define-aggregate-rule 'require-jumps checkers
  (lambda (pmoves)
    (let ((jumps (filter captures-pieces? pmoves)))
      (if (null? jumps)
          pmoves
          jumps))))
```

Critique
The rule-based implementation of our referee solves the problems we identified earlier. It removes the control structure from our program and localizes it in the executive. As a consequence, the rules are specific: each checkers rule is expressed by a single pro-

cedural rule. The rules are not diffused as they were in the earlier implementation.

However, this comes at a cost: we must add applicability conditions to each rule to prevent it being applied to pmoves for which it is inappropriate.[16] For example, the `simple-move` rule must exclude any nonempty pmoves that it is given, because a nonempty pmove might include one or more jumps, which cannot be continued with a simple move. This is a general mis-feature of rule-based systems: every rule must be able to accept the output of any rule; this is normally handled by encoding the control state in the data the rules are applied to.

Exercise 2.12: A bit of chess

Using the same domain model we used for checkers, it is possible to capture the rules of chess. There are several important differences, besides the fact that chess involves many types of pieces. One difference is that the range of motion of rooks, bishops, and queens is limited only by obstruction. Another difference is that capture is by displacement rather than jump. In this exercise we will consider only rooks and knights; the remaining pieces are addressed in exercise 2.13.

a. Construct an analogous referee to generate the legal moves for a rook. Don't try to implement the castling rule.

b. Augment your referee to model the behavior of a knight.

Exercise 2.13: More chess

Make a full implementation of the rules of chess.

Exercise 2.14: An advanced project

Choose some other domain, not a board game, and build an implementation of the rules of some process using the rule executive and a domain model of your design. This is not easy.

2.5   Summary

The techniques displayed and elaborated on in this chapter can be helpful in the design and development of every large-scale system. It is almost always to our advantage to build our systems using mix-and-match interchangeable parts with well-defined interfaces.

---

[16]However, because the rule executive explicitly handles finished pmoves, we don't need to test for those in the rules.

In languages with higher-order procedures and lexical scoping, like Scheme or Java, it is easy to make systems of combinators—standard means of combination, such as `compose`—for a library of interchangeable parts. And it is convenient to make parametric parts that share a common interface specification. For example, if our interface specification is procedures that take one argument and return one value, then

```
(define (make-incrementer dx)
  (lambda (x) (+ x dx)))
```

defines a set of interchangeable incrementers. It is much harder to make systems of combinators and libraries of combinable parts with languages like C that do not have lexically scoped higher-order procedures. But with careful planning and some effort it can be done.

When we are confronted with a system based on parts that do not compose cleanly, such as regular expressions, it is often possible to ameliorate the difficulties by metaprogramming. In that case we built a new combinator-based language that we compiled to the regular expression language, making a pleasant but long-winded alternative. Our regular-expressions combinator language is a fine domain-specific intermediate language for programs that need to match strings, but it is not so nice as a scripting language for a user to type. For that purpose we would want to design a clean and more concise syntax for matching strings that can be compiled to a combinator-based intermediate language.[17]

Wrappers are a common strategy for making old code useful in a new context. We showed how programs that assumed a particular unit system could be used with other unit systems, by building a system of wrappers that automatically did the necessary unit conversions. To do this we made a small domain-specific language for expressing unit conversions that compiled into the appropriate wrapper.

But wrappers can be used for more than just adapters for old code. We can wrap a procedure with a wrapper that checks input arguments for reasonableness and checks that the output is a plausible result given the inputs. If such checks fail, the wrapper can raise an error signal. This "paranoid programming style" is

---

[17]SRFI 115 [110] is an interesting example.

a very powerful tool for protecting a system from misuse and for debugging.

As illustrated with regular expressions and with unit conversions, often the best way to attack a class of problems is to invent a domain-specific language in which the solutions are easy to express. To explore this strategy we divided the problem of generating the legal moves for a board game into three individually extensible pieces: a domain model, a control-structure executive, and the specific rules of the game. The domain model provides a set of primitives that are combined to make the rules, giving us a language for expressing the rules. The application of the rules is sequenced by the control-structure executive. This combination forms the essence of a domain-specific language for expressing the rules of checkers-like board games.

Every good language has primitives, means of combination of those primitives, and means of abstraction for the combinations. The examples shown in this chapter are embedded in Scheme, and thus are able to use Scheme's powerful means of combination and abstraction. But this is only the start. In chapter 5 we will transcend this embedding strategy, using the powerful idea of metalinguistic abstraction.

3
Variations on an Arithmetic Theme

In this chapter we introduce the extremely powerful but potentially dangerous flexibility technique of predicate-dispatched *generic procedures*. We start out in the relatively calm waters of arithmetic, modulating the meanings of the operator symbols. We first generalize arithmetic to deal with symbolic algebraic expressions, and then to functions. We use a combinator system where the elements being combined are packages of arithmetic operations.

But soon we want even more flexibility. So we invent dynamically extensible generic procedures, where the applicability of a handler is determined by predicates on the supplied arguments. This is very powerful and great fun. Using generic procedures to extend the arithmetic to operate on "differential objects," we get automatic differentiation with very little work!

Predicate dispatch is pretty expensive, so we investigate ways to ameliorate that expense. In the process we invent a kind of tagged data, where a tag is just a way of memoizing the value of a predicate. To finish the chapter we demonstrate the power of generic procedures with the design of a simple, but easy to elaborate, adventure game.

3.1   Combining arithmetics

Suppose we have a program that computes some useful numerical results. It depends on the meanings of the arithmetic operators that are referenced by the program text. These operators can be extended to work on things other than the numbers that were expected by the program. With these extensions the program may do useful things that were not anticipated when the program was written. A common pattern is a program that takes numerical weights and other arguments and makes a linear combination by adding up the weighted arguments. If the addition and multiplication operators are extended to operate on tuples of numbers as well as on the original numbers, the program can make linear combinations of vectors. This kind of extension can work because the

set of arithmetic operators is a well-specified and coherent entity.
Extensions of numerical programs with more powerful arithmetic
can work, unless the new quantities do not obey the constraints
that were assumed by the author of the program. For example,
multiplication of matrices does not commute, so extension of a
numerical program that depends on the fact that multiplication
of numbers is commutative will not work. We will ignore this
problem for now.

3.1.1   A simple ODE integrator

A differential equation is a description of how the state of a system
changes as an independent variable is varied; this is called the *evolution* of the system's state.[1] We can approximate the evolution of
a system's state by sampling the independent variable at various
points and approximating the state change at each sample point.
This process of approximation is called *numerical integration.*

Let's investigate the generality of numerical operations in a numerical integrator for second-order ordinary differential equations.
We will use an integrator that samples its independent variable
at uniform intervals, each of which is called a *step*. Consider this
equation:

$$D^2 x(t) = F(t, x(t)) \tag{3.1}$$

The essential idea is that a discrete approximation to the second
derivative of the unknown function is a linear combination of second derivatives of some previous steps. The particular coefficients
are chosen by numerical analysis and are not of interest here.

$$\frac{x(t+h) - 2x(t) + x(t-h)}{h^2} = \sum_{j=0}^{k} A(j) F(t - jh, x(t - jh)) \tag{3.2}$$

where h is the step size and A is the array of magic coefficients.

For example, Stormer's integrator of order 2 is

$$x(t+h) - 2x(t) + x(t-h) \tag{3.3}$$

$$= \frac{h^2}{12} (13 F(t, x(t)) - 2 F(t - h, x(t - h)) + F(t - 2h, x(t - 2h)))$$

---

[1]ODE means "ordinary differential equation," meaning a differential equation
with a single independent variable.

To use this to compute the future of x we write a program. The procedure returned by `stormer-2` is an integrator for a given function and step size, that given a history of values of x, produces an estimate of the value of x at the next time, $x(t + h)$. The procedures `t` and `x` extract previous times and values of x from the history: (`x 0 history`) returns $x(t)$, (`x 1 history`) returns $x(t - h)$, and (`x 2 history`) returns $x(t - 2h)$. We access the time of a step from a history similarly: (`t 1 history`) returns $t - h$.

```
(define (stormer-2 F h)
  (lambda (history)
    (+ (* 2 (x 0 history))
       (* -1 (x 1 history))
       (* (/ (expt h 2) 12)
          (+ (* 13 (F (t 0 history) (x 0 history)))
             (* -2 (F (t 1 history) (x 1 history)))
             (F (t 2 history) (x 2 history)))))))
```

The procedure returned by `stepper` takes a history and returns a new history advanced by h for the given integrator.

```
(define (stepper h integrator)
  (lambda (history)
    (extend-history (+ (t 0 history) h)
                    (integrator history)
                    history)))
```

The procedure `stepper` is used in the procedure `evolver` to produce a procedure `step` that will advance a history by one step. The `step` procedure is used in the procedure `evolve` that advances the history by a given number of steps of size h. We explicitly use specialized integer arithmetic here (the procedures named `n:>` and `n:-`) for counting steps. This will allow us to use different types of arithmetic for everything else without affecting simple counting.[2]

---

[2]Because we anticipated varying the meanings of many operators in the MIT/GNU Scheme system, we made a special set of operators that name primitive procedures we might need later. We named the copies with the prefix `n:`. In MIT/GNU Scheme the original primitive procedures are always available, with their original names, in the `system-global-environment`, so we could have chosen to get them from there.

```
(define (evolver F h make-integrator)
  (let ((integrator (make-integrator F h)))
    (let ((step (stepper h integrator)))
      (define (evolve history n-steps)
        (if (n:> n-steps 0)
            (evolve (step history) (n:- n-steps 1))
            history))
      evolve)))
```

A second-order differential equation like equation 3.1 generally needs two initial conditions to determine a unique trajectory: $x(t_0)$ and $x'(t_0)$ are sufficient to get $x(t)$ for all t. But the Störmer multistep integrator we are using requires three history values, $x(t_0)$, $x(t_0 - h)$, and $x(t_0 - 2h)$, to compute the next value $x(t_0 + h)$. So to evolve the trajectory with this integrator we must start with an initial history that has three past values of x.

Consider the very simple differential equation:

$$D^2 x(t) + x(t) = 0$$

In the form shown in equation 3.1 the right-hand side is:

```
(define (F t x) (- x))
```

Because all the solutions of this equation are linear combinations of sinusoids, we can get the simple sine function by initializing the history with three values of the sine function:

```
(define numeric-s0
  (make-initial-history 0 .01 (sin 0) (sin -.01) (sin -.02)))
```

where the procedure `make-initial-history` takes the following arguments:

```
(make-initial-history t h x(t) x(t − h) x(t − 2h))
```

Using Scheme's built-in arithmetic, after 100 steps of size $h = .01$ we get a good approximation to $\sin(1)$:

```
(x 0 ((evolver F .01 stormer-2) numeric-s0 100))
.8414709493275624
(sin 1)
.8414709848078965
```

3.1.2   Modulating arithmetic operators

Let's consider the possibility of modulating what is meant by addition, multiplication, etc., for new data types unimagined by our example's programmer. Suppose we change our arithmetic operators to operate on and produce symbolic expressions rather than numerical values. This can be useful in debugging purely numerical calculations, because if we supply symbolic arguments we can examine the resulting symbolic expressions to make sure that the program is calculating what we intend it to. This can also be the basis of a partial evaluator for optimization of numerical programs.

Here is one way to accomplish this goal. We introduce the idea of an *arithmetic package*. An arithmetic package, or just *arithmetic*, is a map from operator names to their operations (implementations). We can install an arithmetic in the user's read-eval-print environment to replace the default bindings of the operators named in the arithmetic with the arithmetic's implementations.

The procedure `make-arithmetic-1` generates a new arithmetic package. It takes a name for the new arithmetic, and an operation-generator procedure that given an operator name constructs an *operation*, here a handler procedure, for that operator. The procedure `make-arithmetic-1` calls the operation-generator procedure with each arithmetic operator, accumulating the results into a new arithmetic package. For symbolic arithmetic, the operation is implemented as a procedure that creates a symbolic expression by consing the operator name onto the list of its arguments.

```
(define symbolic-arithmetic-1
  (make-arithmetic-1 'symbolic
    (lambda (operator)
      (lambda args (cons operator args)))))
```

To use this newly defined arithmetic, we install it. This redefines the arithmetic operators to use this arithmetic:[3]

```
(install-arithmetic! symbolic-arithmetic-1)
```

---

[3]A recent Scheme standard [109] introduced "libraries," which provide a way to specify bindings of the free references in a program. We could use libraries to connect an arithmetic with the code that uses it. But here we demonstrate the ideas by modifying the read-eval-print environment.

`install-arithmetic!` changes the values of the user's global variables that are the names of the arithmetic operators defined in the arithmetic to their values in that arithmetic. For example, after this install:

```
(+ 'a 'b)
(+ a b)

(+ 1 2)
(+ 1 2)
```

Now we can observe the result of taking one step of the Stormer evolution:[4][5]

```
(pp (x 0
        ((evolver F 'h stormer-2)
         (make-initial-history 't 'h 'xt 'xt-h 'xt-2h)
         1)))
(+ (+ (* 2 xt) (* -1 xt-h))
   (* (/ (expt h 2) 12)
      (+ (+ (* 13 (negate xt)) (* -2 (negate xt-h)))
         (negate xt-2h))))
```

We could easily produce simplified expressions by replacing the `cons` in `symbolic-arithmetic-1` with an algebraic simplifier, and then we would have a symbolic manipulator. (We will explore algebraic simplification in section 4.2.)

This transformation was ridiculously easy, and yet our original design didn't make any provisions for symbolic computation. We could just as easily add support for vector arithmetic, matrix arithmetic, etc.

Problems with redefining operators

The ability to redefine operators *after the fact* gives both extreme flexibility and ways to make whole new classes of bugs! (We anticipated such a problem in the `evolver` procedure and avoided it

---

[4]The procedure `pp` prints a list "prettily" by using line breaks and indentation to reveal the list's structure.

[5]You may have noticed that in these symbolic expressions the additions and multiplications are expressed as binary operations, even though in Scheme they are allowed to take many arguments; the installer implements the n-ary versions as nested binary operations. Similarly, the unary - is converted to **negate**. Subtractions and divisions with multiple arguments are also realized as nested binary operations.

by using the special arithmetic operators `n:>` and `n:-` for counting steps.)

There are more subtle problems. A program that depends on the exactness of operations on integers may not work correctly for inexact floating-point numbers. This is exactly the risk that comes with the evolution of biological or technological systems— some mutations will be fatal! On the other hand, some mutations will be extremely valuable. But that risk must be balanced against the cost of narrow and brittle construction.

Indeed, it is probably impossible to prove very much about a program when the primitive procedures can be redefined, except that it will work when restricted to the types it was defined for. This is an easy but dangerous path for generalization.

3.1.3 Combining arithmetics

The symbolic arithmetic cannot do numerical calculation, so we have broken our integration example by replacing the operator definitions. We really want an operator's action to depend on its arguments: for example, numerical addition for `(+ 1 2)` but building a list for `(+ 'a 'b)`. Thus the arithmetic packages must be able to determine which handler is appropriate for the arguments tendered.

An improved arithmetic abstraction

By annotating each operation with an *applicability specification*, often shortened to just an *applicability*, we can combine different kinds of arithmetic. For example, we can combine symbolic and numeric arithmetic so that a combined operation can determine which implementation is appropriate for its arguments.

An applicability specification is just a list of *cases*, each of which is a list of predicates, such as `number?` or `symbolic?`. A procedure is deemed applicable to a sequence of arguments if the arguments satisfy one of the cases—that is, if each predicate in the case is true of the corresponding argument. For example, for binary arithmetic operators, we would like the numeric operations to be applicable in just the case `(number? number?)` and the symbolic operations to be applicable in these cases: `((number? symbolic?) (symbolic? number?) (symbolic? symbolic?))`.

We use `make-operation` to make an operation that includes an applicability for the handler procedure, like this:

```
(define (make-operation operator applicability procedure)
  (list 'operation operator applicability procedure))
```

It is then possible to get the applicability for an operation:

```
(define (operation-applicability operation)
  (caddr operation))
```

We introduce an abstraction for writing applicability information for an operation. The procedure `all-args` takes two arguments, the first being the number of arguments that the operation
accepts (its *arity*, as on page 26), and the second being a predicate
that must be true of each argument. It returns an applicability
specification that can be used to determine if the operation is applicable to the arguments supplied to it. In a numeric arithmetic,
each operation takes numbers for each of its arguments.

Using `all-args` we can implement an operation constructor for
the simplest operations:

```
(define (simple-operation operator predicate procedure)
  (make-operation operator
                  (all-args (operator-arity operator)
                            predicate)
                  procedure))
```

We will also find it useful to have a *domain predicate* that is
true for the objects (such as functions or matrices) that a given
arithmetic's operations take as arguments—for example, `number?`
for numeric arithmetic. To support this more elaborate idea we
will create a constructor `make-arithmetic` for arithmetic packages.
The procedure `make-arithmetic` is like `make-arithmetic-1` (see
page 71) but has additional arguments.

```
(make-arithmetic name
                 domain-predicate
                 base-arithmetic-packages
                 map-of-constant-name-to-constant
                 map-of-operator-name-to-operation)
```

An arithmetic package produced by `make-arithmetic` has a name
that is useful for debugging. It has the domain predicate noted
above. It has a list of arithmetic packages, called the *bases*, that
the new arithmetic will be built from. In addition, the arithmetic
will contain a set of named constants, and a set of operators along

with their corresponding operations. The final two arguments are used to generate these sets.

An example of the use of a base arithmetic is vectors. A vector is represented as an ordered sequence of coordinates: consequently an arithmetic on vectors is defined in terms of arithmetic on its coordinates. So the base arithmetic for a vector arithmetic is the appropriate arithmetic for the vector's coordinates. A vector arithmetic with numeric coordinates will use a numeric arithmetic as its base, while a vector arithmetic with symbolic coordinates will use a symbolic arithmetic as its base. For brevity, we often use the term "over" to specify the base, as in "vectors over numbers" or "vectors over symbols."

The base arithmetics also determine the constants and operators that the derived arithmetic will define. The defined constants will be the union of the constants defined by the bases, and the defined operators will be the union of their operators. If there are no bases, then standard sets of constant and operator names will be defined.

Using these new capabilities, we can define a numeric arithmetic with applicability information. Since numeric arithmetic is built on the Scheme substrate, the appropriate handler for the operator for Scheme number arguments is just the value of the operator symbol for the Scheme implementation. Also, certain symbols, such as the identity constants for addition and multiplication, are specially mapped.

```
(define numeric-arithmetic
  (make-arithmetic 'numeric number? '()
    (lambda (name)                    ;constant generator
      (case name
        ((additive-identity) 0)
        ((multiplicative-identity) 1)
        (else (default-object))))
    (lambda (operator)                ;operation generator
      (simple-operation operator number?
        (get-implementation-value
          (operator->procedure-name operator))))))
```

The last two lines of this code find the procedure defined by the Scheme implementation that is named by the operator.[6]

---

[6]The procedure `default-object` produces an object that is different from any possible constant. The procedure `default-object?` identifies that value.

We can similarly write the `symbolic-extender` constructor to construct a symbolic arithmetic based on a given arithmetic.

```
(define (symbolic-extender base-arithmetic)
  (make-arithmetic 'symbolic symbolic? (list base-arithmetic)
    (lambda (name base-constant)          ;constant generator
      base-constant)
    (let ((base-predicate
            (arithmetic-domain-predicate base-arithmetic)))
      (lambda (operator base-operation) ;operation generator
        (make-operation operator
                        (any-arg (operator-arity operator)
                                 symbolic?
                                 base-predicate)
                        (lambda args
                          (cons operator args)))))))
```

One difference between this and the numeric arithmetic is that the symbolic arithmetic is applicable whenever *any* argument is a symbolic expression.[7] This is indicated by the use of `any-arg` rather than `all-args`; `any-arg` matches if at least one of the arguments satisfies the predicate passed as the second argument, and all the other arguments satisfy the predicate passed as the third argument.[8] Also notice that this symbolic arithmetic is based on a provided `base-arithmetic`, which will allow us to build a variety of such arithmetics.

Applicability specifications are not used as guards on the handlers: they do not prevent the application of a handler to the wrong arguments. The applicability specifications are used only to distinguish among the possible operations for an operator when arithmetics are combined, as explained below.

A combinator for arithmetics

The symbolic and numeric arithmetics are of the same shape, by construction. The `symbolic-extender` procedure produces an

---

[7]Another difference you may have noticed is that the constant-generator and operation-generator procedures for the numeric arithmetic have only one formal parameter, while the generator procedures for the symbolic extender have two. The symbolic arithmetic is built on a base arithmetic, so the constant or operation for the base arithmetic is given to the generator.

[8]The call (`any-arg 3 p1? p2?`) will produce an applicability specification with seven cases, because there are seven ways that this applicability can be satisfied: ((p2? p2? p1?) (p2? p1? p2?) (p2? p1? p1?) (p1? p2? p2?) (p1? p2? p1?) (p1? p1? p2?) (p1? p1? p1?))

arithmetic with the same operators as the base arithmetic it is given. Making a combinator language for building composite arithmetics from parts might be a good approach.

The procedure `add-arithmetics`, below, is a combinator for arithmetics. It makes a new arithmetic whose domain predicate is the disjunction of the given arithmetics' domain predicates, and each of whose operators is mapped to the union of the operations for the given arithmetics.[9]

```
(define (add-arithmetics . arithmetics)
  (add-arithmetics* arithmetics))

(define (add-arithmetics* arithmetics)
  (if (n:null? (cdr arithmetics))
      (car arithmetics)                ;only one arithmetic
      (make-arithmetic 'add
                       (disjoin*
                        (map arithmetic-domain-predicate
                             arithmetics))
                       arithmetics
                       constant-union
                       operation-union)))
```

The third argument to `make-arithmetic` is a list of the arithmetic packages being combined. The arithmetic packages must be compatible in that they specify operations for the same named operators. The fourth argument is `constant-union`, which combines multiple constants. Here this selects one of the argument constants for use in the combined arithmetic; later we will elaborate on this.[10]

```
(define (constant-union name . constants)
  (let ((unique
         (remove default-object?
                 (delete-duplicates constants eqv?))))
    (if (n:pair? unique)
        (car unique)
        (default-object))))
```

---

[9]`disjoin*` is a predicate combinator. It accepts a list of predicates and produces the predicate that is their disjunction.

[10]Making this arbitrary choice is not really reasonable. For example, a vector's zero is not only distinct from the numerical zero, but also is not the same for vectors of different dimension. We have chosen to ignore this problem here.

The last argument is `operation-union`, which constructs the operation for the named operator in the resulting arithmetic. An operation is applicable if it is applicable in any of the arithmetics that were combined.

```
(define (operation-union operator . operations)
  (operation-union* operator operations))

(define (operation-union* operator operations)
  (make-operation operator
                  (applicability-union*
                   (map operation-applicability operations))
                  (lambda args
                    (operation-union-dispatch operator
                                              operations
                                              args))))
```

The procedure `operation-union-dispatch` must determine the operation to use based on the arguments supplied. It chooses the operation from the given arithmetics that is appropriate to the given arguments and applies it to the arguments. If more than one of the given arithmetics has an applicable operation, the operation from the first arithmetic in the arguments to `add-arithmetics` is chosen.

```
(define (operation-union-dispatch operator operations args)
  (let ((operation
         (find (lambda (operation)
                 (is-operation-applicable? operation args))
               operations)))
    (if (not operation)
        (error "Inapplicable operation:" operator args))
    (apply-operation operation args)))
```

A common pattern is to combine a base arithmetic with an extender on that arithmetic. The combination of numeric arithmetic and a symbolic arithmetic built on numeric arithmetic is such a case. So we provide an abstraction for that pattern:

```
(define (extend-arithmetic extender base-arithmetic)
  (add-arithmetics base-arithmetic
                   (extender base-arithmetic)))
```

We can use `extend-arithmetic` to combine the numeric arithmetic and the symbolic arithmetic. Since the applicability cases are disjoint—all numbers for numeric arithmetic and at least one symbolic expression for symbolic arithmetic—the order of arguments to `add-arithmetics` is irrelevant here, except for possible performance issues.

```
(define combined-arithmetic
  (extend-arithmetic symbolic-extender numeric-arithmetic))

(install-arithmetic! combined-arithmetic)
```

Let's try the composite arithmetic:

```
(+ 1 2)
```
3

```
(+ 1 'a)
```
(+ 1 a)

```
(+ 'a 2)
```
(+ a 2)

```
(+ 'a 'b)
```
(+ a b)

The integrator still works numerically (compare page 70):

```
(define numeric-s0
  (make-initial-history 0 .01 (sin 0) (sin -.01) (sin -.02)))

(x 0 ((evolver F .01 stormer-2) numeric-s0 100))
```
.8414709493275624

It works symbolically (compare page 72):

```
(pp (x 0
       ((evolver F 'h stormer-2)
        (make-initial-history 't 'h 'xt 'xt-h 'xt-2h)
        1)))
```
(+ (+ (2 xt) (* -1 xt-h))*
*   (* (/ (expt h 2) 12)*
*   (+ (+ (* 13 (negate xt)) (* -2 (negate xt-h)))*
*   (negate xt-2h))))*

And it works in combination, with numeric history but symbolic step size h:

```
(pp (x 0 ((evolver F 'h stormer-2) numeric-s0 1)))
```
(+ 9.999833334166664e-3
*   (* (/ (expt h 2) 12)*
*   -9.999750002487318e-7))*

Notice the power here. We have combined code that can do symbolic arithmetic and code that can do numeric arithmetic. We have created a system that can do arithmetic that depends on both abilities. This is not just the union of the two abilities— it is the cooperation of two mechanisms to solve a problem that neither could solve by itself.

3.1.4   Arithmetic on functions

Traditional mathematics extends arithmetic on numerical quantities to many other kinds of objects. Over the centuries "arithmetic" has been extended to complex numbers, vectors, linear transformations and their representations as matrices, etc. One particularly revealing extension is to functions. We can combine functions of the same type using arithmetic operators:

$$(f + g)(x) = f(x) + g(x)$$
$$(f - g)(x) = f(x) - g(x)$$
$$(fg)(x) = f(x)g(x)$$
$$(f/g)(x) = f(x)/g(x)$$
$$\vdots$$

The functions that are combined must have the same domain and codomain, and an arithmetic must be defined on the codomain.

The extension to functions is not hard. Given an arithmetic package for the codomain of the functions that we wish to combine, we can make an arithmetic package that implements the function arithmetic, assuming that functions are implemented as procedures.

```
(define (pure-function-extender codomain-arithmetic)
  (make-arithmetic 'pure-function function?
                   (list codomain-arithmetic)
    (lambda (name codomain-constant)    ; *** see below
      (lambda args codomain-constant))
    (lambda (operator codomain-operation)
      (simple-operation operator function?
        (lambda functions
          (lambda args
            (apply-operation codomain-operation
                             (map (lambda (function)
                                    (apply function args))
                                  functions)))))))))
```

Notice that the constant generator (with comment ✱✱✱) must produce a constant function for each codomain constant. For example, the additive identity for functions must be the function of any number of arguments that returns the codomain additive identity.

Combining a functional arithmetic with the arithmetic that operates on the codomains makes a useful package:

```
(install-arithmetic!
  (extend-arithmetic pure-function-extender
                     numeric-arithmetic))
```

```
((+ cos sin) 3)
```
-.8488724885405782

```
(+ (cos 3) (sin 3))
```
-.8488724885405782

By building on `combined-arithmetic` we can get more interesting results:

```
(install-arithmetic!
  (extend-arithmetic pure-function-extender
                     combined-arithmetic))
```

```
((+ cos sin) 3)
```
-.8488724885405782

```
((+ cos sin) 'a)
```
(+ (cos a) (sin a))

```
(* 'b ((+ cos sin) (+ (+ 1 2) 'a)))
```
(b (+ (cos (+ 3 a)) (sin (+ 3 a))))*

The mathematical tradition also allows one to mix numerical quantities with functions by treating the numerical quantities as constant functions of the same type as the functions they will be combined with.

$$(f + 1)(x) = f(x) + 1 \tag{3.4}$$

We can implement the coercion of numerical quantities to constant functions quite easily, by minor modifications to the procedure `pure-function-extender`:

```
(define (function-extender codomain-arithmetic)
  (let ((codomain-predicate
         (arithmetic-domain-predicate codomain-arithmetic)))
    (make-arithmetic 'function
                     (disjoin codomain-predicate function?)
                     (list codomain-arithmetic)
      (lambda (name codomain-constant)
        codomain-constant)
      (lambda (operator codomain-operation)
        (make-operation operator
                        (any-arg (operator-arity operator)
                                 function?
                                 codomain-predicate)
          (lambda things
            (lambda args
              (apply-operation codomain-operation
                (map (lambda (thing)
                       ;; here is the coercion:
                       (if (function? thing)
                           (apply thing args)
                           thing))
                     things)))))))))
```

To allow the coercion of codomain quantities, such as numbers, to constant functions, the domain of the new function arithmetic must contain both the functions and the elements of the codomain of the functions (the possible values of the functions). The operator implementation is applicable if any of the arguments is a function; and functions are applied to the arguments that are given. Note that the constant generator for the make-arithmetic doesn't need to rewrite the codomain constants as functions, since the constants can now be used directly.

With this version we can

```
(install-arithmetic!
 (extend-arithmetic function-extender combined-arithmetic))

((+ 1 cos) 'a)
(+ 1 (cos a))

(* 'b ((+ 4 cos sin) (+ (+ 1 2) 'a)))
(* b (+ 4 (cos (+ 3 a)) (sin (+ 3 a))))
```

This raises an interesting problem: we have symbols, such as a and b, that represent literal numbers, but nothing to represent literal functions. For example, if we write

```
(* 'b ((+ 'c cos sin) (+ 3 'a)))
```

our arithmetic will treat c as a literal number. But we might wish to have c be a literal function that combines as a function. It's difficult to do this with our current design, because c carries no type information, and the context is insufficient to distinguish usages.

But we can make a literal function that has no properties except for a name. Such a function just attaches its name to the list of its arguments.

```
(define (literal-function name)
  (lambda args
    (cons name args)))
```

With this definition we can have a literal function c correctly combine with other functions:

```
(* 'b ((+ (literal-function 'c) cos sin) (+ (+ 1 2) 'a)))
(* b (+ (+ (c (+ 3 a)) (cos (+ 3 a))) (sin (+ 3 a))))
```

This is a narrow solution that handles a useful case.

3.1.5   Problems with combinators

The arithmetic structures we have been building up to now are an example of the use of combinators to build complex structures by combining simpler ones. But there are some serious drawbacks to building this system using combinators. First, some properties of the structure are determined by the means of combination. For example, we pointed out that add-arithmetics prioritized its arguments, such that their order can matter. Second, the layering implicit in this design, such that the codomain arithmetic must be constructed prior to the function arithmetic, means that it's impossible to augment the codomain arithmetic after the function arithmetic has been constructed. Finally, we might wish to define an arithmetic for functions that return functions. This cannot be done in a general way within this framework, without introducing another mechanism for self reference, and self reference is cumbersome to arrange.

Combinators are powerful and useful, but a system built of combinators is not very flexible. One problem is that the shapes of the parts must be worked out ahead of time: the generality that will be available depends on the detailed plan for the shapes of the parts, and there must be a localized plan for how the parts are combined. This is not a problem for a well-understood domain, such as arithmetic, but it is not appropriate for open-ended construction. In section 3.2 we will see how to add new kinds of arithmetic incrementally, without having to decide where they go in a hierarchy, and without having to change the existing parts that already work.

Other problems with combinators are that the behavior of any part of a combinator system must be independent of its context. A powerful source of flexibility that is available to a designer is to build systems that *do* depend upon their context. By varying the context of a system we can obtain variation of the behavior. This is quite dangerous, because it may be hard to predict how a variation will behave. However, carefully controlled variations can be useful.

Exercise 3.1: Warmup with boolean arithmetic

In digital design the boolean operations *and*, *or*, and *not* are written with the operators *, +, and -, respectively.

There is a Scheme predicate `boolean?` that is true only of `#t` and `#f`. Use this to make a boolean arithmetic package that can be combined with the arithmetics we have. Note that all other arithmetic operators are undefined for booleans, so the appropriate result of applying something like `cos` to a boolean is to report an error.

The following template could help get you started:

```
(define boolean-arithmetic
  (make-arithmetic 'boolean boolean? '()
    (lambda (name)
      (case name
        ((additive-identity) #f)
        ((multiplicative-identity) #t)
        (else (default-object))))
    (lambda (operator)
      (let ((procedure
             (case operator
               ((+) <...>)
               ((-) <...>)
               ((*) <...>)
               ((negate) <...>)
               (else
                (lambda args
                  (error "Operator undefined in Boolean"
                         operator)))))))
        (simple-operation operator boolean? procedure)))))
```

In digital design the operator - is typically used only as a unary operator and is realized as **negate**. When an arithmetic is installed, the binary operators +, *, -, and / are generalized to be *n*-ary operators. The unary application (- *operand*) is transformed by the installer into (**negate** *operand*). Thus to make - work, you will need to define the unary boolean operation for the operator **negate**.

Exercise 3.2: Vector arithmetic

We will make and install an arithmetic package on geometric vectors. This is a big assignment that will bring to the surface many of the difficulties and inadequacies of the system we have developed so far.

a. We will represent a vector as a Scheme **vector** of numerical quantities. The elements of a vector are coordinates relative to some Cartesian axes. There are a few issues here. Addition (and subtraction) is defined only for vectors of the same dimension, so your arithmetic must know about dimensions. First, make an arithmetic that defines only addition, negation, and subtraction of vectors over a base arithmetic of operations applicable to the coordinates of vectors. Applying any other operation to a vector should report an error. Hint: The following procedures will be helpful:

```
(define (vector-element-wise element-procedure)
  (lambda vecs      ; Note: this takes multiple vectors
    (ensure-vector-lengths-match vecs)
    (apply vector-map element-procedure vecs)))

(define (ensure-vector-lengths-match vecs)
  (let ((first-vec-length (vector-length (car vecs))))
    (if (any (lambda (v)
               (not (n:= (vector-length v)
                         first-vec-length)))
             vecs)
        (error "Vector dimension mismatch:" vecs))))
```

The use of **apply** here is subtle. One way to think about it is to imagine that the language supported an ellipsis like this:

```
(define (vector-element-wise element-procedure)
  (lambda (v1 v2 ...)
    (vector-map element-procedure v1 v2 ...)))
```

Build the required arithmetic and show that it works for numerical vectors and for vectors with mixed numerical and symbolic coordinates.

b. Your vector addition required addition of the coordinates. The coordinate addition procedure could be the value of the + operator that will be made available in the user environment by `install-arithmetic!`, or it could be the addition operation from the base arithmetic of your vector extension. Either of these would satisfy many tests, and using the installed addition may actually be more general. Which did you use? Show how to implement the other choice. How does this choice affect your ability to make future extensions to this system? Explain your reasoning.

Hint: A nice way to control the interpretation of operators in a procedure is to provide the procedure to use for each operator as arguments to a "maker procedure" that returns the procedure needed. For example, to control the arithmetic operations used in `vector-magnitude` one might write:

```
(define (vector-magnitude-maker + * sqrt)
  (let ((dot-product (dot-product-maker + *)))
    (define (vector-magnitude v)
      (sqrt (dot-product v v)))
    vector-magnitude))
```

c. What shall we do about multiplication? First, for two vectors it is reasonable to define multiplication to be their dot product. But there is a bit of a problem here. You need to be able to use both the addition and multiplication operations, perhaps from the arithmetic on the coordinates. This is not hard to solve. Modify your vector arithmetic to define multiplication of two vectors as their dot product. Show that your dot product works.

d. Add vector magnitude to your vector arithmetic, extending the numerical operator `magnitude` to give the length of a vector. The code given above is most of the work!

e. Multiplication of a vector by a scalar or multiplication of a scalar by a vector should produce the scalar product (the vector with each coordinate multiplied by the scalar). So multiplication can mean either dot product or scalar product, depending on the types of its arguments. Modify your vector arithmetic to make this work. Show that your vector arithmetic can handle both dot product and scalar product. Hint: The `operation-union` procedure on page 78 enables a very elegant way to solve this problem.

Exercise 3.3: Ordering of extensions

Consider two possible orderings for combining your vector extension (exercise 3.2) with the existing arithmetics:

```
(define vec-before-func
 (extend-arithmetic
  function-extender
  (extend-arithmetic vector-extender combined-arithmetic)))
```

```
(define func-before-vec
 (extend-arithmetic
  vector-extender
  (extend-arithmetic function-extender combined-arithmetic)))
```

How does the ordering of extensions affect the properties of the resulting arithmetic? The following procedure makes points on the unit circle:

```
(define (unit-circle x)
  (vector (sin x) (cos x)))
```

If we execute each of the following expressions in environments resulting from installing `vec-before-func` and `func-before-vec`:

```
((magnitude unit-circle) 'a)
```

```
((magnitude (vector sin cos)) 'a)
```

The result (unsimplified) should be:

```
(sqrt (+ (* (sin a) (sin a)) (* (cos a) (cos a))))
```

However, each of these expressions fails with one of the two orderings of the extensions. Is it possible to make an arithmetic for which both evaluate correctly? Explain.

3.2 Extensible generic procedures

Systems built by combinators, as in section 3.1, result in beautiful diamond-like systems. This is sometimes the right idea, and we will see it arise again, but it is very hard to add to a diamond. If a system is built as a ball of mud, it is easy to add more mud.[11]

One organization for a ball of mud is a system erected on a substrate of extensible generic procedures. Modern dynamically typed programming languages, such as Lisp, Scheme, and Python, usually have built-in arithmetic that is generic over a variety of types of numerical quantities, such as integers, floats, rationals, and complex numbers [115, 64, 105]. But systems built on these languages are usually not easily extensible after the fact.

---

[11] At the APL-79 conference Joel Moses is reported to have said: "APL is like a beautiful diamond—flawless, beautifully symmetrical. But you can't add anything to it. If you try to glue on another diamond, you don't get a bigger diamond. Lisp is like a ball of mud. Add more and it's still a ball of mud—it still looks like Lisp." But Joel denies that he said this.

The problems we indicated in section 3.1.5 are the result of using the combinator `add-arithmetics`. To solve these problems we will abandon that combinator. However, the arithmetic package abstraction is still useful, as is the idea of an extender. We will build an arithmetic package in which the operations use generic procedures that can be dynamically augmented with new behavior. We can then extend the generic arithmetic and add the extensions to the generic arithmetic.[12]

We will start by implementing generic procedures, which are procedures that can be dynamically extended by adding handlers after the generic procedures are defined. A generic procedure is a dispatcher combined with a set of *rules*, each of which describes a handler that is appropriate for a given set of arguments. Such a rule combines a handler with its applicability.

Let's examine how this might work, by defining a generic procedure named `plus` that works like addition with numeric and symbolic quantities:

```
(define plus (simple-generic-procedure 'plus 2 #f))

(define-generic-procedure-handler plus
  (all-args 2 number?)
  (lambda (a b) (+ a b)))

(define-generic-procedure-handler plus
  (any-arg 2 symbolic? number?)
  (lambda (a b) (list '+ a b)))

(plus 1 2)
3
```

---

[12] A mechanism of this sort is implicit in most "object-oriented languages," but it is usually tightly bound to ontological mechanisms such as inheritance. The essential idea of extensible generics appears in SICP [1] and is usefully provided in `tinyCLOS` [66] and `SOS` [52].

A system of extensible generics, based on predicate dispatching, is used to implement the mathematical representation system in SICM [121]. A nice exposition of predicate dispatching is given by Ernst [33].

The idea that generic procedures are a powerful tool has been percolating in the Lisp community for decades. The fullest development of these ideas is in the Common Lisp Object System (`CLOS`) [42]. The underlying structure is beautifully expressed in the Metaobject Protocol [68]. It is further elaborated in the "Aspect-oriented programming" movement [67].

```
(plus 1 'a)
(+ 1 a)

(plus 'a 2)
(+ a 2)

(plus 'a 'b)
(+ a b)
```

The procedure `simple-generic-procedure` takes three arguments:
The first is an arbitrary name to identify the procedure when debugging; the second is the procedure's arity. The third argument
is used to provide a default handler; if none is supplied (indicated
by `#f`), then if no specific handler is applicable an error is signaled. Here `plus` is bound to the new generic procedure returned
by `simple-generic-procedure`. It is a Scheme procedure that can
be called with the specified number of arguments.

The procedure `define-generic-procedure-handler` adds a rule
to an existing generic procedure. Its first argument is the generic
procedure to be extended; the second argument is an applicability specification (as on page 73) for the rule being added; and
the third argument is the handler for arguments that satisfy that
specification.

```
(define-generic-procedure-handler generic-procedure
                                  applicability
                                  handler-procedure)
```

It is often necessary to specify a rule in which different arguments
are of different types. For example, to make a vector arithmetic
package we need to specify the interpretation of the * operator.
If both arguments are vectors, the appropriate handler computes
the dot product. If one argument is a scalar and the other is a
vector, then the appropriate handler scales the vector elements by
the scalar. The applicability argument is the means by which this
is accomplished.

The `simple-generic-procedure` constructor we used above to
make the generic procedure `plus` is created with the procedure
`generic-procedure-constructor`

```
(define simple-generic-procedure
  (generic-procedure-constructor make-simple-dispatch-store))
```

where `make-simple-dispatch-store` is a procedure that encapsulates a strategy for saving, retrieving, and choosing a handler.

The `generic-procedure-constructor` takes a dispatch-store constructor and produces a generic-procedure constructor that itself takes three arguments—a name that is useful in debugging, an arity, and a default handler to be used if there are no applicable handlers. If the default handler argument is `#f`, the default handler signals an error:

```
((generic-procedure-constructor dispatch-store-constructor)
 name
 arity
 default-handler)
```

The reason why generic procedures are made in this way is that we will need families of generic procedures that differ in the choice of dispatch store.

In section 3.2.3, we will see one way to implement this mechanism. But first let's see how to use it.

3.2.1   Generic arithmetic

We can use this new generic-procedure mechanism to build arithmetic packages in which the operators map to operations that are implemented as generic procedures. This will allow us to make self-referential structures. For example, we might want to make a generic arithmetic that includes vector arithmetic where both the vectors and the components of a vector are manipulated by the same generic procedures. We could not build such a structure using just `add-arithmetics` introduced earlier.

```
(define (make-generic-arithmetic dispatch-store-maker)
  (make-arithmetic 'generic any-object? '()
    constant-union
    (let ((make-generic-procedure
            (generic-procedure-constructor
             dispatch-store-maker)))
      (lambda (operator)
        (simple-operation operator
                          any-object?
                          (make-generic-procedure
                           operator
                           (operator-arity operator)
                           #f))))))
```

The `make-generic-arithmetic` procedure creates a new arithmetic. For each arithmetic operator, it constructs an operation that is applicable to any arguments and is implemented by a generic procedure. (The predicate `any-object?` is true of anything.) We can install this arithmetic in the usual way.

But first, let's define some handlers for the generic procedures. It's pretty simple to do now that we have the generic arithmetic object. For example, we can grab the operations and constants from any already-constructed arithmetic.

```
(define (add-to-generic-arithmetic! generic-arithmetic
                                    arithmetic)
  (add-generic-arith-constants! generic-arithmetic
                                arithmetic)
  (add-generic-arith-operations! generic-arithmetic
                                 arithmetic))
```

This takes a generic arithmetic package and an ordinary arithmetic package with the same operators. It merges constants into the generic arithmetic using `constant-union`. And for each operator of the given arithmetic it adds a handler to the corresponding generic procedure.

Adding a handler for a particular operator uses the standard generic procedure mechanism, extracting the necessary applicability and procedure from the arithmetic's operation.

```
(define (add-generic-arith-operations! generic-arithmetic
                                       arithmetic)
  (for-each
   (lambda (operator)
     (let ((generic-procedure
            (simple-operation-procedure
             (arithmetic-operation operator
                                   generic-arithmetic)))
           (operation
            (arithmetic-operation operator arithmetic)))
       (define-generic-procedure-handler
         generic-procedure
         (operation-applicability operation)
         (operation-procedure operation))))
   (arithmetic-operators arithmetic)))
```

The `add-generic-arith-operations!` procedure finds, for each operator in the given arithmetic, the generic procedure that must be augmented. It then defines a handler for that generic procedure that is the handler for that operator in the given arithmetic, using the applicability for that handler in the given arithmetic.

The code for adding the constants from an arithmetic to the generic arithmetic is similar. For each constant name in the generic arithmetic it finds the entry in the association of names to constant values in the generic arithmetic. It then replaces the constant value with the `constant-union` of the existing constant and the constant it got for that same name from the given arithmetic.

```
(define (add-generic-arith-constants! generic-arithmetic
                                      arithmetic)
  (for-each
   (lambda (name)
     (let ((binding
            (arithmetic-constant-binding name
                                         generic-arithmetic))
           (element
            (find-arithmetic-constant name arithmetic)))
       (set-cdr! binding
                 (constant-union name
                                 (cdr binding)
                                 element))))
   (arithmetic-constant-names generic-arithmetic)))
```

Fun with generic arithmetics

We can add many arithmetics to a generic arithmetic to give it interesting behavior:

```
(let ((g
       (make-generic-arithmetic make-simple-dispatch-store)))
  (add-to-generic-arithmetic! g numeric-arithmetic)
  (add-to-generic-arithmetic! g
    (function-extender numeric-arithmetic))
  (add-to-generic-arithmetic! g
    (symbolic-extender numeric-arithmetic))
  (install-arithmetic! g))
```

This produces a generic arithmetic that combines numeric arithmetic with symbolic arithmetic over numeric arithmetic and function arithmetic over numeric arithmetic:

```
(+ 1 3 'a 'b)
(+ (+ 4 a) b)
```

And we can even run some more complex problems, as on page 79:

```
(pp (x 0 ((evolver F 'h stormer-2) numeric-s0 1)))
(+ 9.999833334166664e-3
  (* (/ (expt h 2) 12)
    -9.999750002487318e-7))
```

As before, we can mix symbols and functions:

```
(* 'b ((+ cos sin) 3))
(* b -.8488724885405782)
```

but the following will signal an error, trying to add the symbolic quantities (cos a) and (sin a) as numbers:

```
(* 'b ((+ cos sin) 'a))
```

We get this error because cos and sin are numeric operators, like +. Since we have symbolic arithmetic over numeric arithmetic, these operators are extended so that for symbolic input, here a, they produce symbolic outputs, (cos a) and (sin a). We also added function arithmetic over numeric arithmetic, so if functions are numerically combined (here by +) their outputs may be combined only if the outputs are numbers. But the symbolic results cannot be added numerically. This is a consequence of the way we built the arithmetic g.

But there is magic in generic arithmetic. It can be closed: all extensions to the generic arithmetic can be made over the generic arithmetic!

```
(let ((g
        (make-generic-arithmetic make-simple-dispatch-store)))
  (add-to-generic-arithmetic! g numeric-arithmetic)
  (extend-generic-arithmetic! g symbolic-extender)
  (extend-generic-arithmetic! g function-extender)
  (install-arithmetic! g))
```

Here we use a new procedure extend-generic-arithmetic! that captures a common pattern.

```
(define (extend-generic-arithmetic! generic-arithmetic
                                    extender)
  (add-to-generic-arithmetic! generic-arithmetic
    (extender generic-arithmetic)))
```

Now we can use complex mixed expressions, because the functions
are defined over the generic arithmetic:

```
(* 'b ((+ 'c cos sin) (+ 3 'a)))
(* b (+ (+ c (cos (+ 3 a))) (sin (+ 3 a))))
```

We can even use functions that return functions:

```
(((+ (lambda (x) (lambda (y) (cons x y)))
     (lambda (x) (lambda (y) (cons y x))))
  3)
 4)
(+ (3 . 4) (4 . 3))
```

So perhaps we have achieved nirvana?

3.2.2   Construction depends on order!

Unfortunately, there is a severe dependence on the order in which
rules are added to the generic procedures. This is not surprising,
because the construction of the generic procedure system is by
assignment. We can see this by changing the order of construction:

```
(let ((g
       (make-generic-arithmetic make-simple-dispatch-store)))
  (add-to-generic-arithmetic! g numeric-arithmetic)
  (extend-generic-arithmetic! g function-extender)    ;*
  (extend-generic-arithmetic! g symbolic-extender)    ;*
  (install-arithmetic! g))
```

and then we will find that the example

```
(* 'b ((+ 'c cos sin) (+ 3 'a)))
```

which worked in the previous arithmetic, fails because the symbolic arithmetic captures (+ 'c cos sin) to produce a symbolic
expression, which is not a function that can be applied to (+ 3 a).
The problem is that the applicability of the symbolic operation
for + accepts arguments with at least one symbolic argument and
other arguments from the domain predicate of the base. But the
symbolic arithmetic was created over the generic arithmetic as a
base, and the domain predicate of a generic arithmetic accepts
anything! There is also a function operation for + that is applicable to the same arguments, but it has not been chosen because
of the accidental ordering of the extensions. Unfortunately, the

choice of rule is ambiguous. It would be better to not have more than one applicable operation.

One way to resolve this problem is to restrict the symbolic quantities to represent numbers. We can do this by building our generic arithmetic so that the symbolic arithmetic is over the numeric arithmetic, as we did on page 92, rather than over the entire generic arithmetic:

```
(let ((g
       (make-generic-arithmetic make-simple-dispatch-store)))
  (add-to-generic-arithmetic! g numeric-arithmetic)
  (extend-generic-arithmetic! g function-extender)
  (add-to-generic-arithmetic! g
       (symbolic-extender numeric-arithmetic))
  (install-arithmetic! g))
```

This works, independent of the ordering, because there is no ambiguity in the choice of rules. So now the 'c will be interpreted as a constant to be coerced to a constant function by the function extender.

```
(* 'b ((+ 'c cos sin) (+ 3 'a)))
(* b (+ (+ c (cos (+ 3 a))) (sin (+ 3 a))))
```

Unfortunately, we may want to have symbolic expressions over other quantities besides numbers. We cannot yet implement a general solution to this problem. But if we really want a literal function named c, we can use literal-function as we did earlier:

```
(* 'b ((+ (literal-function 'c) cos sin) (+ 3 'a)))
(* b (+ (+ (c (+ 3 a)) (cos (+ 3 a))) (sin (+ 3 a))))
```

This will work independent of the order of construction of the generic arithmetic.

With this mechanism we are now in a position to evaluate the Stormer integrator with a literal function:

```
(pp (x 0 ((evolver (literal-function 'F) 'h stormer-2)
          (make-initial-history 't 'h 'xt 'xt-h 'xt-2h)
          1)))
(+ (+ (* 2 xt) (* -1 xt-h))
   (* (/ (expt h 2) 12)
      (+ (+ (* 13 (f t xt))
            (* -2 (f (- t h) xt-h)))
         (f (- t (* 2 h)) xt-2h))))
```

This is pretty ugly, and it would be worse if we looked at the output of two integration steps. But it is interesting to look at the result of simplifying a two-step integration. Using a magic symbolic-expression simplifier we get a pretty readable expression. This can be useful for debugging a numerical process.

```
(+ (* 2 (expt h 2) (f t xt))
   (* -1/4 (expt h 2) (f (+ (* -1 h) t) xt-h))
   (* 1/6 (expt h 2) (f (+ (* -2 h) t) xt-2h))
   (* 13/12
      (expt h 2)
      (f (+ h t)
         (+ (* 13/12 (expt h 2) (f t xt))
            (* -1/6 (expt h 2) (f (+ (* -1 h) t) xt-h))
            (* 1/12 (expt h 2) (f (+ (* -2 h) t) xt-2h))
            (* 2 xt)
            (* -1 xt-h))))
   (* 3 xt)
   (* -2 xt-h))
```

For example, notice that there are only four distinct top-level calls to the acceleration function f. The second argument to the fourth top-level call uses three calls to f that have already been computed. If we eliminate common subexpressions we get:

```
(let* ((G84 (expt h 2)) (G85 (f t xt)) (G87 (* -1 h))
       (G88 (+ G87 t)) (G89 (f G88 xt-h)) (G91 (* -2 h))
       (G92 (+ G91 t)) (G93 (f G92 xt-2h)))
  (+ (* 2 G84 G85)
     (* -1/4 G84 G89)
     (* 1/6 G84 G93)
     (* 13/12 G84
        (f (+ h t)
           (+ (* 13/12 G84 G85)
              (* -1/6 G84 G89)
              (* 1/12 G84 G93)
              (* 2 xt)
              (* -1 xt-h))))
     (* 3 xt)
     (* -2 xt-h)))
```

Here we clearly see that there are only four distinct calls to f. Though each integration step in the basic integrator makes three calls to f, the two steps overlap on two intermediate calls. While this is obvious for such a simple example, we see how symbolic evaluation might help in understanding a numerical computation.

3.2.3 Implementing generic procedures

We have used generic procedures to do amazing things. But how do we make such a thing work?

Making constructors for generic procedures

On page 89 we made a simple generic procedure constructor:

```
(define simple-generic-procedure
  (generic-procedure-constructor make-simple-dispatch-store))
```

The procedure `generic-procedure-constructor` is given a "dispatch strategy" procedure; it returns a generic-procedure constructor that takes a name, an arity, and a default-handler specification. When this procedure is called with these three arguments it returns a generic procedure that it associates with a newly constructed metadata store for that procedure, which holds the name, the arity, an instance of the dispatch strategy, and the default handler, if any. The dispatch-strategy instance will maintain the handlers, their applicabilities, and the mechanism for deciding which handler to choose for given arguments to the generic procedure.

The code that implements `generic-procedure-constructor` is:

```
(define (generic-procedure-constructor dispatch-store-maker)
  (lambda (name arity default-handler)
    (let ((metadata
           (make-generic-metadata
             name arity (dispatch-store-maker)
             (or default-handler
                 (error-generic-procedure-handler name)))))
      (define (the-generic-procedure . args)
        (generic-procedure-dispatch metadata args))
      (set-generic-procedure-metadata! the-generic-procedure
                                       metadata)
      the-generic-procedure)))
```

This implementation uses `the-generic-procedure`, an ordinary Scheme procedure, to represent the generic procedure, and a metadata store (for rules, etc.) that determines the procedure's behavior. This store is associated with the generic procedure using a "sticky note" (as on page 28) and can later be obtained by calling `generic-procedure-metadata`. This allows procedures such as `define-generic-procedure-handler` to modify the metadata of a given generic procedure.

The argument to `generic-procedure-constructor` is a procedure that creates a dispatch store for saving and retrieving handlers. The dispatch store encapsulates the strategy for choosing a
handler.

Here is the simple dispatch-store constructor we have used so
far. The dispatch store is implemented as a message-accepting
procedure:

```
(define (make-simple-dispatch-store)
  (let ((rules '()) (default-handler #f))
    (define (get-handler args)
      ;; body will be shown in text below.
      ...)
    (define (add-handler! applicability handler)
      ;; body will be shown in text below.
      ...)
    (define (get-default-handler) default-handler)
    (define (set-default-handler! handler)
      (set! default-handler handler))
    (lambda (message)        ; the simple dispatch store
      (case message
        ((get-handler) get-handler)
        ((add-handler!) add-handler!)
        ((get-default-handler) get-default-handler)
        ((set-default-handler!) set-default-handler!)
        ((get-rules) (lambda () rules))
        (else (error "Unknown message:" message))))))
```

The simple dispatch store just maintains a list of the rules,
each of which pairs an applicability with a handler. When the
`get-handler` internal procedure is called with arguments for the
generic procedure, it scans the list sequentially for a handler whose
applicability is satisfied by the arguments tendered; it returns the
handler, or `#f` if it doesn't find one:

```
(define (get-handler args)
  (let ((rule
         (find (lambda (rule)
                 (predicates-match? (car rule) args))
               rules)))
    (and rule (cdr rule))))
```

There are many possible strategies for choosing handlers to run.
The above code returns the first applicable handler in the list.

Another strategy is to return all applicable handlers. If more than one handler is applicable, perhaps all should be tried (in parallel?) and the results compared! Passing a dispatch-store constructor as an argument to `generic-procedure-constructor` allows the strategy to be chosen when the generic-procedure constructor is created, rather than being hard-coded into the implementation.

Adding handlers to generic procedures

The handler definition procedure (see below) adds new rules by calling the internal procedure `add-handler` of the dispatch store. For `make-simple-dispatch-store` above, `add-handler` adds the new rule to the front of the list of rules. (But if there was already a rule for handling that applicability, it just replaces the handler.)

```
(define (add-handler! applicability handler)
  (for-each (lambda (predicates)
              (let ((p (assoc predicates rules)))
                (if p
                    (set-cdr! p handler)
                    (set! rules
                          (cons (cons predicates handler)
                                rules)))))
            applicability))
```

The `define-generic-procedure-handler` procedure uses the metadata table to get the metadata record for the generic procedure. It asks the dispatch store for the `add-handler!` procedure and uses that procedure to add a rule to the metadata that associates the applicability with the handler. The dispatch-store instance is retrieved from the metadata of the generic procedure by `generic-metadata-dispatch-store`.

```
(define (define-generic-procedure-handler generic-procedure
                                          applicability
                                          handler)
  (((generic-metadata-dispatch-store
     (generic-procedure-metadata generic-procedure))
    'add-handler!)
   applicability
   handler))
```

Finally, the heart of the mechanism is the dispatch, called by a generic procedure (`the-generic-procedure` on page 97), which finds an appropriate handler and applies it. The default handler,

as supplied during construction of the generic procedure, is called
if there is no applicable handler.[13]

```
(define (generic-procedure-dispatch metadata args)
  (let ((handler
         (get-generic-procedure-handler metadata args)))
    (apply handler args)))

(define (get-generic-procedure-handler metadata args)
  (or ((generic-metadata-getter metadata) args)
      ((generic-metadata-default-getter metadata))))
```

The power of extensible generics

Construction of a system on a substrate of extensible generic procedures is a powerful idea. In our example it is possible to define
what is meant by addition, multiplication, etc., for new data types
unimagined by the language designer. For example, if the arithmetic operators of a system are implemented as extensible generics, a user may extend them to support arithmetic on quaternions,
vectors, matrices, integers modulo a prime, functions, tensors, differential forms, ... This is not just making new capabilities possible; it also extends old programs, so a program that was written
to manipulate simple numerical quantities may become useful for
manipulating scalar-valued functions.

We have seen that there are potential problems associated with
this use of extensible generic procedures. On the other hand, some
"mutations" will be extremely valuable. For example, it is possible to extend arithmetic to symbolic quantities. The simplest way
to do this is to make a generic extension to all of the operators to
take symbolic quantities as arguments and return a data structure
representing the indicated operation on the arguments. With the
addition of a simplifier of algebraic expressions we suddenly have
a symbolic manipulator. This is useful in debugging purely numerical calculations, because if we give them symbolic arguments
we can examine the resulting symbolic expressions to make sure

---

[13]`generic-metadata-getter` and `generic-metadata-default-getter` retrieve
the `get-handler` procedure and the `get-default-handler` procedure from the
dispatch-store instance stored in the metadata of the generic procedure.

that the program is calculating what we intend it to. It is also the basis of a partial evaluator for optimization of numerical programs. And functional differentiation can be viewed as a generic extension of arithmetic to a compound data type (see section 3.3). The scmutils system we use to teach classical mechanics [121] implements differentiation in exactly this way.

Exercise 3.4: Functional values

The generic arithmetic structure allows us to close the system so that functions that return functions can work, as in the example

```
(((* 3
     (lambda (x) (lambda (y) (+ x y)))
     (lambda (x) (lambda (y) (vector y x))))
   'a)
 4)
(* (* 3 (+ a 4)) #(4 a))
```

a. How hard is it to arrange for this to work in the purely combinator-based arithmetic introduced in section 3.1? Why?

b. Exercise 3.3 on page 86 asked about the implications of ordering of vector and functional extensions. Is the generic system able to support both expressions discussed there (and copied below)? Explain.

```
((magnitude unit-circle) 'a)
((magnitude (vector sin cos)) 'a)
```

c. Is there any good way to make the following work at all?

```
((vector cos sin) 3)
#(-.9899924966004454 .1411200080598672)
```

Show code that makes this work or explain the difficulties.

Exercise 3.5: A weird bug

Consider the +-like ("plus-like") procedure in arith.scm, shown below, which implements *n*-ary procedures + and * as part of installing an arithmetic. It returns a pair of a name and a procedure; the installer will bind the name to the procedure.

It seems that it is written to execute the get-identity procedure that computes the identity every time the operation is called with no arguments.

```
(define (+-like operator identity-name)
  (lambda (arithmetic)
    (let ((binary-operation
           (find-arithmetic-operation operator arithmetic)))
      (and binary-operation
           (let ((binary
                  (operation-procedure binary-operation))
                 (get-identity
                  (identity-name->getter identity-name
                                         arithmetic)))
             (cons operator
                   (lambda args
                     (case (length args)
                       ((0) (get-identity))
                       ((1) (car args))
                       (else (pairwise binary args)))))))))))
```

Perhaps the identity for an operator should be computed only once, not every time the handler is called. As a consequence, it is proposed that the code should be modified as follows:

```
(define (+-like operator identity-name)
  (lambda (arithmetic)
    (let ((binary-operation
           (find-arithmetic-operation operator arithmetic)))
      (and binary-operation
           (let ((binary
                  (operation-procedure binary-operation))
                 (identity
                  ((identity-name->getter identity-name
                                          arithmetic))))
             (cons operator
                   (lambda args
                     (case (length args)
                       ((0) identity)
                       ((1) (car args))
                       (else (pairwise binary args)))))))))))
```

However, this has a subtle bug! Can you elicit the bug? Can you explain it?

Exercise 3.6: Matrices

Matrices are ubiquitous in scientific and technical computing.

a. Make and install an arithmetic package for matrices of numbers, with operations +, -, negate, and *. This arithmetic needs to be able to know the number of rows and the number of columns in a matrix, since matrix multiplication is defined only if the number of columns in the first matrix is equal to the number of rows in the second one.

Make sure that your multiplier can multiply a matrix with a scalar or with a vector. For matrices to play well with vectors you probably need to distinguish row vectors and column vectors. How does this affect the design of the vector package? (See exercise 3.2 on page 85.)

You may assume that the vectors and matrices are of small dimension, so you do not need to deal with sparse representations. A reasonable representation of a matrix is a Scheme vector in which each element is a Scheme vector representing a row.

b. Vectors and matrices may contain symbolic numerical quantities. Make this work.

c. Matrix inversion is appropriate for your arithmetic. If a symbolic matrix is dense, the inverse may take space that is factorial in the dimension. Why?

Note: We are not asking you to implement matrix inversion.

Exercise 3.7: Literal vectors and matrices

It is also possible to have arithmetic on literal matrices and literal vectors with an algebra of symbolic expressions of vectors and matrices. Can you make symbolic algebra of these compound structures play well with vectors and matrices that have symbolic numerical expressions as elements? Caution: This is quite hard. Perhaps it is appropriate as part of a long-term project.

3.3 Example: Automatic differentiation

One remarkable application of extensible generic procedures is *automatic differentiation*.[14] This is a beautiful way to obtain a program that computes the derivative of the function computed by a given program.[15] Automatic differentiation is now an important component in machine learning applications.

We will see that a simple way to implement automatic differentiation is to extend the generic arithmetic primitives to work

---

[14]The term *automatic differentiation* was introduced by Wengert [129] in 1964.

[15]The derivative here is the derivative of a function, not the derivative of an expression. If f is a function, the derivative Df of f is a new function, which when applied to x gives a value $Df(x)$. Its relation to an expression derivative is:

$$Df(t) = \left. \frac{d}{dx} f(x) \right|_{x=t}$$

with *differential objects*, a new compound data type. This will enable the automatic differentiation of symbolic as well as numerical functions. It will also enable us to make automatic differentiation work with higher-order procedures—procedures that return other procedures as values.

Here is a simple example of automatic differentiation to illustrate what we are talking about:

```
((derivative (lambda (x) (expt x 3))) 2)
12
```

Note that the derivative of the function that computes the cube of its argument is a new function, which when given 2 as its argument returns 12 as its value.

If we extend the arithmetic to handle symbolic expressions, and we do some algebraic simplification on the result, we get:

```
((derivative (lambda (x) (expt x 3))) 'a)
(* 3 (expt a 2))
```

And the full power of the programming language is available, including higher-order procedures. This kind of system is useful in working with the very large expressions that occur in interesting physics problems.[16]

Let's look at a simple application: the computation of the roots of an equation by Newton's method. The idea is that we want to find values of x for which $f(x) = 0$. If f is sufficiently smooth, and we have a sufficiently close guess x_0, we can improve the guess by computing a new guess x_1 by the formula:

$$x_{n+1} = x_n - \frac{f(x_n)}{Df(x_n)}$$

This can be repeated, as necessary, to get a sufficiently accurate result. An elementary program to accomplish this is:

---

[16]The automatic differentiation code we present here is derived from the code that we wrote to support the advanced classical mechanics class that Sussman teaches at MIT with Jack Wisdom [121, 122].

```
(define (root-newton f initial-guess tolerance)
  (let ((Df (derivative f)))
    (define (improve-guess xn)
      (- xn (/ (f xn) (Df xn))))
    (let loop ((xn initial-guess))
      (let ((xn+1 (improve-guess xn)))
        (if (close-enuf? xn xn+1 tolerance)
            xn+1
            (loop xn+1))))))
```

Notice that the local procedure named Df in root-newton is a procedure that computes the derivative of the function computed by the procedure passed in as f.

For example, suppose we want to know the angle θ in the first quadrant for which $\cos(\theta) = \sin(\theta)$. (The answer is $\pi/4 \approx$ .7853981633974484) We can write:

```
(define (cs theta)
  (- (cos theta) (sin theta)))
```

```
(root-newton cs 0.5 1e-8)
.7853981633974484
```

This result is correct to full machine accuracy.

3.3.1 How automatic differentiation works

The program for automatic differentiation is directly derived from the definition of the derivative. Suppose that given a function f and a point x in its domain, we want to know the value of the function at a nearby point $f(x + \Delta x)$, where Δx is a small increment. The derivative of a function f is defined to be the function Df whose value for particular arguments x is something that can be "multiplied" by an increment Δx of the argument to get the best possible linear approximation to the increment in the value of f:

$$f(x + \Delta x) \approx f(x) + Df(x)\,\Delta x$$

We implement this definition using a data type that we call a *differential object*. A differential object $[x, \delta x]$ can be thought of as a number with a small increment, $x + \delta x$. But we treat it as a new numerical quantity similar to a complex number: it has two components, a *finite part* and an *infinitesimal part*.[17] We extend each primitive arithmetic function to work with differential objects: each primitive arithmetic function f must know its derivative function Df, so that:

$$[x, \delta x] \xrightarrow{f} [f(x), Df(x)\delta x] \qquad (3.5)$$

Note that the derivative of f at the point x, $Df(x)$, is the coefficient of δx in the infinitesimal part of the resulting differential object.

Now here is the powerful idea: If we then pass the result of $f([x, \delta x])$ (equation 3.5) through another function g, we obtain the chain-rule answer we would hope for:

$$[f(x), Df(x)\delta x] \xrightarrow{g} [g(f(x)), Dg(f(x))Df(x)\delta x]$$

Thus, if we can compute the results of all primitive functions on differential objects, we can compute the results of all compositions of functions on differential objects. Given such a result, we can extract the derivative of the composition: the derivative is the coefficient of the infinitesimal increment in the resulting differential object.

To extend a generic arithmetic operator to compute with differential objects, we need only supply a procedure that computes the derivative of the primitive arithmetic function that the operator names. Then we can use ordinary Scheme compositions to get the derivative of any composition of primitive functions.[18]

---

[17]Differential objects like these are sometimes referred to as *dual numbers*. Dual numbers, introduced by Clifford in 1873 [20], extend the real numbers by adjoining one new element ϵ with the property $\epsilon^2 = 0$. However, in order to conveniently compute multiple derivatives (and derivatives of functions with multiple arguments) it helps to introduce a new infinitesimal part for each independent variable. So our differential algebra space is much more complicated than the single-ϵ dual number space. Our differential objects are also something like the hyperreal numbers, invented by Edwin Hewitt in 1948 [59].

[18]This idea was "discovered" by Dan Zuras (then of Hewlett Packard Corporation) and Gerald Jay Sussman in an all-night programming binge in 1992. We assumed at the time that this had also been discovered by many others, and indeed it had [129, 12], but we were overjoyed when we first understood the idea ourselves! See [94] for a formal exposition of automatic differentiation.

Given a procedure implementing a unary function f, the procedure `derivative` produces a new procedure `the-derivative` that computes the derivative of the function computed by f.[19] When applied to some argument, x, the derivative creates a new infinitesimal increment `dx` and adds it to the argument to get the new differential object $[x, \delta x]$ that represents $x + \delta x$. The procedure f is then applied to this differential object and the derivative of f is obtained by extracting the coefficient of the infinitesimal increment `dx` from the value:

```
(define (derivative f)
  (define (the-derivative x)
    (let* ((dx (make-new-dx))
           (value (f (d:+ x (make-infinitesimal dx)))))
      (extract-dx-part value dx)))
  the-derivative)
```

The procedure `make-infinitesimal` makes a differential object whose finite part is zero and whose infinitesimal part is dx. The procedure `d:+` adds differential objects. The details will be explained in section 3.3.3.

Extending the primitives

We need to make handler procedures that extend the primitive arithmetic generic procedures to operate on differential objects. For each unary procedure we have to make the finite part of the result and the infinitesimal part of the result, and we have to put the results together, as expressed in equation 3.5. So the handler for a unary primitive arithmetic procedure that computes function f is constructed by `diff:unary-proc` from the procedure f for f and the procedure df for its derivative Df. These are glued together using special addition and multiplication procedures `d:+` and `d:*` for differential objects, to be explained in section 3.3.3.

```
(define (diff:unary-proc f df)
  (define (uop x)        ; x is a differential object
    (let ((xf (finite-part x))
          (dx (infinitesimal-part x)))
      (d:+ (f xf) (d:* (df xf) dx))))
  uop)
```

---

[19]We will get to binary functions soon. This is just to make the idea clear before things get complicated. We will extend to n-ary functions in section 3.3.2

For example, the `sqrt` procedure handler for differential objects
is just:

```
(define diff:sqrt
  (diff:unary-proc sqrt (lambda (x) (/ 1 (* 2 (sqrt x))))))
```

The first argument of `diff:unary-proc` is the `sqrt` procedure and
the second argument is a procedure that computes the derivative
of `sqrt`.

We add the new handler to the generic `sqrt` procedure using

```
(assign-handler! sqrt diff:sqrt differential?)
```

where `differential?` is a predicate that is true only of differential
objects. The procedure `assign-handler!` is just shorthand for a
useful pattern:

```
(define (assign-handler! procedure handler . preds)
  (define-generic-procedure-handler procedure
    (apply match-args preds)
    handler))
```

And the procedure `match-args` makes an applicability specification from a sequence of predicates.

Handlers for other unary primitives are straightforward:[20]

```
(define diff:exp (diff:unary-proc exp exp))
```

```
(define diff:log (diff:unary-proc log (lambda (x) (/ 1 x))))
```

```
(define diff:sin (diff:unary-proc sin cos))
```

```
(define diff:cos
        (diff:unary-proc cos (lambda (x) (* -1 (sin x)))))
```
$\vdots$

Binary arithmetic operations are a bit more complicated.

$$g(x + \Delta x, y + \Delta y) \approx g(x,y) + \partial_0 g(x,y)\, \Delta x + \partial_1 g(x,y)\, \Delta y \quad (3.6)$$

where $\partial_0 f$ and $\partial_1 f$ are the partial derivative functions of f with
respect to the two arguments. Let f be a function of two argu-

---

[20]We are showing the definitions of handlers but we are not showing the assignment of the handlers here.

ments; then $\partial_0 f$ is a new function of two arguments that computes the partial derivative of f with respect to its first argument:

$$\partial_0 f(x,y) = \frac{\partial}{\partial u} f(u,v)\bigg|_{u=x,v=y}$$

So the rule for binary operations is

$$([x,\delta x],[y,\delta y]) \overset{f}{\longmapsto} [f(x,y), \partial_0 f(x,y)\delta x + \partial_1 f(x,y)\delta y]$$

To implement binary operations we might think that we could simply follow the plan for unary operations, where d0f and d1f are the two partial derivative functions:

```
(define (diff:binary-proc f d0f d1f)
  (define (bop x y)
    (let ((dx (infinitesimal-part x))
          (dy (infinitesimal-part y))
          (xf (finite-part x))
          (yf (finite-part y)))
      (d:+ (f xf yf)
           (d:+ (d:* dx (d0f xf yf))
                (d:* (d1f xf yf) dy)))))
  bop)
```

This is a good plan, but it isn't quite right: it doesn't ensure that the finite and infinitesimal parts are consistently chosen for the two arguments. We need to be more careful about how we choose the parts. We will explain this technical detail and fix it in section 3.3.3, but let's go with this approximately correct code for now.

Addition and multiplication are straightforward, because the partial derivatives are simple, but division and exponentiation are more interesting. We show the assignment of handlers only for diff:+ because all the others are similar.

```
(define diff:+
  (diff:binary-proc +
                    (lambda (x y) 1)
                    (lambda (x y) 1)))

(assign-handler! + diff:+ differential? any-object?)
(assign-handler! + diff:+ any-object? differential?)
```

```
(define diff:*
  (diff:binary-proc *
                    (lambda (x y) y)
                    (lambda (x y) x)))

(define diff:/
  (diff:binary-proc /
                    (lambda (x y)
                      (/ 1 y))
                    (lambda (x y)
                      (* -1 (/ x (square y))))))
```

The handler for exponentiation $f(x,y) = x^y$ is a bit more complicated. The partial with respect to the first argument is simple: $\partial_0 f(x,y) = yx^{y-1}$. But the partial with respect to the second argument is usually $\partial_1 f(x,y) = x^y \log x$, except for some special cases:

```
(define diff:expt
  (diff:binary-proc expt
    (lambda (x y)
      (* y (expt x (- y 1))))
    (lambda (x y)
      (if (and (number? x) (zero? x))
          (if (number? y)
              (if (positive? y)
                  0
                  (error "Derivative undefined: EXPT"
                         x y))
              0)
          (* (log x) (expt x y))))))
```

Extracting the derivative's value

To compute the value of the derivative of a function, we apply the function to a differential object and obtain a result. We have to extract the derivative's value from that result. There are several possibilities that must be handled. If the result is a differential object, we have to pull the derivative's value out of the object. If the result is not a differential object, the derivative's value is zero. There are other cases that we have not mentioned. This calls for a generic procedure with a default that produces a zero.

```
(define (extract-dx-default value dx) 0)

(define extract-dx-part
  (simple-generic-procedure 'extract-dx-part 2
                            extract-dx-default))
```

In the case where a differential object is returned, the coefficient of dx is the required derivative. This will turn out to be a bit complicated, but the basic idea can be expressed as follows:

```
(define (extract-dx-differential value dx)
  (extract-dx-coefficient-from (infinitesimal-part value) dx))

(define-generic-procedure-handler extract-dx-part
  (match-args differential? diff-factor?)
  extract-dx-differential)
```

The reason this is not quite right is that for technical reasons the structure of a differential object is more complex than we have already shown. It will be fully explained in section 3.3.3.

Note: We made the extractor generic to enable future extensions to functions that return functions or compound objects, such as vectors, matrices, and tensors. (See exercise 3.12 on page 124.)

Except for the fact that there may be more primitive operators and data structures to be included, this is all that is really needed to implement automatic differentiation! All of the procedures referred to in the handlers are the usual generic procedures on arithmetic; they may include symbolic arithmetic and functional arithmetic.

3.3.2 Derivatives of *n*-ary functions

For a function with multiple arguments we need to be able to compute the partial derivatives with respect to each argument. One way to do this is:[21]

```
(define ((partial i) f)
  (define (the-derivative . args)
    (if (not (< i (length args)))
        (error "Not enough arguments for PARTIAL" i f args))
    (let* ((dx (make-new-dx))
           (value
            (apply f (map (lambda (arg j)
                            (if (= i j)
                                (d:+ arg
                                     (make-infinitesimal dx))
                                arg))
                          args (iota (length args))))))
      (extract-dx-part value dx)))
  the-derivative)
```

---

[21]For an alternative strategy, see exercise 3.8 on page 113.

Here we are extracting the coefficient of the infinitesimal `dx` in the result of applying `f` to the arguments supplied with the ith argument incremented by `dx`.[22]

Now consider a function g of two arguments. Expanding on equation 3.6 we find that the derivative Dg is multiplied by a vector of increments to the arguments:

$$g(x + \Delta x, y + \Delta y) \approx g(x,y) + Dg(x,y) \cdot (\Delta x, \Delta y)$$
$$= g(x,y) + [\partial_0 g(x,y), \partial_1 g(x,y)] \cdot (\Delta x, \Delta y)$$
$$= g(x,y) + \partial_0 g(x,y)\,\Delta x + \partial_1 g(x,y)\,\Delta y$$

The derivative Dg of g at the point x,y is the pair of partial derivatives in square brackets. The inner product of that *covector* of partials with the *vector* of increments is the increment to the function g. The `general-derivative` procedure computes this result:

```
(define (general-derivative g)
  (define ((the-derivative . args) . increments)
    (let ((n (length args)))
      (assert (= n (length increments)))
      (if (= n 1)
          (* ((derivative g) (car args))
             (car increments))
          (reduce (lambda (x y) (+ y x))
                  0
                  (map (lambda (i inc)
                         (* (apply ((partial i) g) args)
                            inc))
                       (iota n)
                       increments)))))
  the-derivative)
```

Unfortunately `general-derivative` does not return the structure of partial derivatives. It is useful in many contexts to have a derivative procedure `gradient` that actually gives the covector of partial derivatives. (See exercise 3.10.)

---

[22]The procedure `iota` returns a list of consecutive integers from 0 through `(length args)`.

Exercise 3.8: Partial derivatives

Another way to think about partial derivatives is in terms of λ-calculus currying. Draw a diagram of how the data must flow. Use currying to fix the arguments that are held constant, producing a one-argument procedure that the ordinary derivative will be applied to. Write that version of the partial derivative procedure.

Exercise 3.9: Adding handlers

There are primitive arithmetic functions for which we did not add handlers for differential objects, for example `tan`.

a. Add handlers for `tan` and `atan1` (`atan1` is a function of one argument).

b. It would be really nice to have `atan` optionally take two arguments, as in the Scheme Report [109], because we usually want to preserve the quadrant we are working in. Fix the generic procedure `atan` to do this correctly—using `atan1` for one argument and `atan2` if given two arguments. Also, install an `atan2` handler for differentials. Remember, it must coexist with the `atan1` handler.

Exercise 3.10: Vectors and covectors

As described above, the idea of derivative can be generalized to functions with multiple arguments. The **gradient** of a function of multiple arguments is the covector of partial derivatives with respect to each of the arguments.

a. Develop data types for vectors and covectors such that the value of $Dg(x, y)$ is the covector of partials. Write a **gradient** procedure that delivers that value. Remember, the product of a vector and a covector should be their inner product—the sum of the componentwise products of their elements.

b. Notice that if the input to a function is a vector, that is similar to multiple inputs, so the output of the gradient should be a covector. Note also that if the input to a function is a covector, then the output of the gradient should be a vector. Make this work.

3.3.3 Some technical details

Although the idea behind automatic differentiation is not complicated, there are a number of subtle technical details that must be addressed for it to work correctly.

Differential algebra

If we want to compute a second derivative we must take a derivative of a derivative function. The evaluation of such a function will have two infinitesimals in play. To enable the computation of multiple derivatives and derivatives of functions of several variables we define an algebra of differential objects in "infinitesimal space." The objects are multivariate power series in which no infinitesimal increment has exponent greater than one.[23]

A differential object is represented by a tagged list of the terms of a power series. Each term has a coefficient and a list of infinitesimal incremental factors. The terms are kept sorted, in descending order. (Order is the number of incrementals. So $\delta x \delta y$ is higher order than δx or δy.) Here is a quick and dirty implementation:[24]

```
(define differential-tag 'differential)

(define (differential? x)
  (and (pair? x) (eq? (car x) differential-tag)))

(define (diff-terms h)
  (if (differential? h)
      (cdr h)
      (list (make-diff-term h '()))))
```

The term list is just the `cdr` of the differential object. However, if we are given an object that is not explicitly a differential object, for example a number, we coerce it to a differential object with a single term and with no incremental factors. When we make a differential object from a (presorted) list of terms, we always try to return a simplified version, which may be just a number, which is not explicitly a differential object:

---

[23]The formal algebraic details were clarified by Hal Abelson around 1994, as part of an effort to fix a bug. The code was painfully reworked in 1997 by Sussman with the help of Hardy Mayer and Jack Wisdom.

[24]A nicer version would use record structures, but that would be harder to debug without having a way to print them nicely.

```
(define (make-differential terms)
  (let ((terms                            ; Nonzero terms
         (filter
          (lambda (term)
            (let ((coeff (diff-coefficient term)))
              (not (and (number? coeff) (= coeff 0)))))
          terms)))
    (cond ((null? terms) 0)
          ((and (null? (cdr terms))
                ;; Finite part only:
                (null? (diff-factors (car terms))))
           (diff-coefficient (car terms)))
          ((every diff-term? terms)
           (cons differential-tag terms))
          (else (error "Bad terms")))))
```

In this implementation the terms are also represented as tagged lists, each containing a coefficient and an ordered list of factors.

```
(define diff-term-tag 'diff-term)

(define (make-diff-term coefficient factors)
  (list diff-term-tag coefficient factors))

(define (diff-term? x)
  (and (pair? x) (eq? (car x) diff-term-tag)))

(define (diff-coefficient x)
  (cadr x))

(define (diff-factors x)
  (caddr x))
```

To compute derivatives we need to be able to add and multiply differential objects:

```
(define (d:+ x y)
  (make-differential
   (+diff-termlists (diff-terms x) (diff-terms y))))

(define (d:* x y)
  (make-differential
   (*diff-termlists (diff-terms x) (diff-terms y))))
```

and we also need this:

```
(define (make-infinitesimal dx)
  (make-differential (list (make-diff-term 1 (list dx)))))
```

Addition of term lists is where we enforce and use the sorting of terms, with higher-order terms coming earlier in the lists. We can add two terms only if they have the same factors. And if the sum of the coefficients is zero we do not include the resulting term.

```
(define (+diff-termlists l1 l2)
  (cond ((null? l1) l2)
        ((null? l2) l1)
        (else
          (let ((t1 (car l1)) (t2 (car l2)))
            (cond ((equal? (diff-factors t1) (diff-factors t2))
                   (let ((newcoeff (+ (diff-coefficient t1)
                                      (diff-coefficient t2))))
                     (if (and (number? newcoeff)
                              (= newcoeff 0))
                         (+diff-termlists (cdr l1) (cdr l2))
                         (cons
                          (make-diff-term newcoeff
                                          (diff-factors t1))
                          (+diff-termlists (cdr l1)
                                           (cdr l2))))))
                  ((diff-term>? t1 t2)
                   (cons t1 (+diff-termlists (cdr l1) l2)))
                  (else
                   (cons t2
                         (+diff-termlists l1 (cdr l2)))))))))
```

Multiplication of term lists is straightforward, if we can multiply individual terms. The product of two term lists l1 and l2 is the term list resulting from adding up the term lists resulting from multiplying every term in l1 by every term in l2.

```
(define (*diff-termlists l1 l2)
  (reduce (lambda (x y)
            (+diff-termlists y x))
          '()
          (map (lambda (t1)
                 (append-map (lambda (t2)
                               (*diff-terms t1 t2))
                             l2))
               l1)))
```

A term has a coefficient and a list of factors (the infinitesimals). In a differential object no term may have an infinitesimal with an exponent greater than one, because $\delta x^2 = 0$. Thus, when we multiply two terms we must check that the lists of factors we are merging have no factors in common. This is the reason that *diff-terms returns a list of the product term or an empty list, to be appended in *diff-termlists. We keep the factors sorted when we merge the two lists of factors; this makes it easier to sort the terms.

```
(define (*diff-terms x y)
  (let ((fx (diff-factors x)) (fy (diff-factors y)))
    (if (null? (ordered-intersect diff-factor>? fx fy))
        (list (make-diff-term
                (* (diff-coefficient x) (diff-coefficient y))
                (ordered-union diff-factor>? fx fy)))
        '())))
```

Finite and infinitesimal parts

A differential object has a finite part and an infinitesimal part. Our diff:binary-proc procedure on page 109 is not correct for differential objects with more than one infinitesimal. To ensure that the parts of the arguments x and y are selected consistently we actually use:

```
(define (diff:binary-proc f d0f d1f)
  (define (bop x y)
    (let ((factor (maximal-factor x y)))
      (let ((dx (infinitesimal-part x factor))
            (dy (infinitesimal-part y factor))
            (xe (finite-part x factor))
            (ye (finite-part y factor)))
        (d:+ (f xe ye)
             (d:+ (d:* dx (d0f xe ye))
                  (d:* (d1f xe ye) dy))))))
  bop)
```

where factor is chosen by maximal-factor so that both x and y contain it in a term with the largest number of factors.

The finite part of a differential object is all terms except for terms containing the maximal factor in a term of highest order, and the infinitesimal part is the remaining terms, all of which contain that factor.

Consider the following computation:

$$f(x + \delta x, y + \delta y) =$$
$$f(x, y) + \partial_0 f(x, y) \cdot \delta x + \partial_1 f(x, y) \cdot \delta y + \partial_0 \partial_1 f(x, y) \cdot \delta x \delta y$$

The highest-order term is $\partial_0 \partial_1 f(x, y) \cdot \delta x \delta y$. It is symmetrical with respect to x and y. The crucial point is that we may break the differential object into parts in any way consistent with any one of the maximal factors (here δx or δy) being primary. It doesn't matter which is chosen, because mixed partials of $\mathbf{R}^n \longrightarrow \mathbf{R}$ commute.[25]

```
(define (finite-part x #!optional factor)
  (if (differential? x)
      (let ((factor (default-maximal-factor x factor)))
        (make-differential
         (remove (lambda (term)
                   (memv factor (diff-factors term)))
                 (diff-terms x))))
      x))
```

```
(define (infinitesimal-part x #!optional factor)
  (if (differential? x)
      (let ((factor (default-maximal-factor x factor)))
        (make-differential
         (filter (lambda (term)
                   (memv factor (diff-factors term)))
                 (diff-terms x))))
      0))
```

```
(define (default-maximal-factor x factor)
  (if (default-object? factor)
      (maximal-factor x)
      factor))
```

How extracting really works

As explained on page 114, to make it possible to take multiple derivatives or to handle functions with more than one argument, a differential object is represented as a multivariate power series in which no infinitesimal increment has exponent greater than one. Each term in this series has a coefficient and a list of infinitesi-

---

[25]The fact that any factor of any highest-order term in the series can be used was a central insight of Hal Abelson in the 1994 revision of this idea.

mal incremental factors. This complicates the extraction of the derivative with respect to any one incremental factor. Here is the real story:

In the case where a differential object is returned we must find those terms of the result that contain the infinitesimal factor dx for the derivative we are evaluating. We collect those terms, removing dx from each. If there are no terms left after taking out the ones with dx, the value of the derivative is zero. If there is exactly one term left, which has no differential factors, then the coefficient of that term is the value of the derivative. But if there are remaining terms with differential factors, we must return the differential object with those residual terms as the value of the derivative.

```
(define (extract-dx-differential value dx)
  (let ((dx-diff-terms
         (filter-map
          (lambda (term)
            (let ((factors (diff-factors term)))
              (and (memv dx factors)
                   (make-diff-term (diff-coefficient term)
                                   (delv dx factors)))))
          (diff-terms value))))
    (cond ((null? dx-diff-terms) 0)
          ((and (null? (cdr dx-diff-terms))
                (null? (diff-factors (car dx-diff-terms))))
           (diff-coefficient (car dx-diff-terms)))
          (else (make-differential dx-diff-terms)))))

(define-generic-procedure-handler extract-dx-part
  (match-args differential? diff-factor?)
  extract-dx-differential)
```

Higher-order functions

For many applications we want our automatic differentiator to work correctly for functions that return functions as values:

```
(((derivative
   (lambda (x)
     (lambda (y z)
       (* x y z))))
  2)
 3
 4)
;Value: 12
```

Including literal functions and partial derivatives makes this even more interesting.

```
((derivative
  (lambda (x)
    (((partial 1) (literal-function 'f))
     x 'v)))
 'u)
((((partial 0) ((partial 1) f)) u v)
```

And things can get even more complicated:

```
(((derivative
   (lambda (x)
     (derivative
       (lambda (y)
         ((literal-function 'f)
          x y)))))
  'u)
 'v)
(((partial 0) ((partial 1) f)) u v)
```

Making this work introduces serious complexity in the procedure `extract-dx-part`.

If the result of applying a function to a differential object is a function—a derivative of a derivative, for example—we need to defer the extraction until that function is called with arguments: In a case where a function is returned, as in

```
(((derivative
   (lambda (x)
     (derivative
       (lambda (y)
         (* x y)))))
  'u)
 'v)
1
```

we cannot extract the derivative until the function is applied to arguments. So we defer the extraction until we get the value resulting from that application. We extend our generic extractor:

```
(define (extract-dx-function fn dx)
  (lambda args
    (extract-dx-part (apply fn args) dx)))

(define-generic-procedure-handler extract-dx-part
  (match-args function? diff-factor?)
  extract-dx-function)
```

Unfortunately, this version of `extract-dx-function` has a subtle bug.[26] Our patch is to wrap the body of the new deferred procedure with code that remaps the factor `dx` to avoid the unpleasant conflict. So, we change the handler for functions to:

```
(define (extract-dx-function fn dx)
  (lambda args
    (let ((eps (make-new-dx)))
      (replace-dx dx eps
        (extract-dx-part
          (apply fn
            (map (lambda (arg)
                   (replace-dx eps dx arg))
                 args))
          dx)))))
```

This creates a brand-new factor `eps` and uses it to stand for `dx` in the arguments, thus preventing collision with any other instances of `dx`.

Replacement of the factors is itself a bit more complicated, because the code has to grovel around in the data structures. We will make the replacement a generic procedure, so we can extend it to new kinds of data. The default is that the replacement is just the identity on the object:

---

[26]A bug of this class was pointed out to us by Alexey Radul in 2011. The general problem was first identified by Siskind and Perlmutter in 2005 [111]: the differential tags created to distinguish the infinitesimals incrementing an argument for a derivative calculation can be confused in the evaluation of a derivative of a function whose value is a function. The deferred derivative procedure may be called more than once, using the tag that was created for the outer derivative calculation. More recently, Jeff Siskind showed us another bug that plagued our patch for the first one: there was a potential collision between a tag occurring in an argument and a tag inherited from the lexical scope of a derivative function. These very subtle bugs are explained, along with a careful analysis of ways to fix them, in a beautiful paper by Manzyuk et al. [87].

```
(define (replace-dx-default new-dx old-dx object) object)

(define replace-dx
  (simple-generic-procedure 'replace-dx 3
                            replace-dx-default))
```

For a differential object we have to actually go in and substitute
the new factor for the old one, and we have to keep the factor lists
and the resulting terms sorted:

```
(define (replace-dx-differential new-dx old-dx object)
  (make-differential
   (combine-like-terms
    (sort (map (lambda (term)
                 (make-diff-term
                  (diff-coefficient term)
                  (sort (substitute new-dx old-dx
                                    (diff-factors term))
                        diff-factor>?)))
               (diff-terms object))
          diff-term>?))))

(define-generic-procedure-handler replace-dx
  (match-args diff-factor? diff-factor? differential?)
  replace-dx-differential)
```

Finally, if the object is itself a function we have to defer it until
arguments are available to compute a value:

```
(define (replace-dx-function new-dx old-dx fn)
  (lambda args
    (let ((eps (make-new-dx)))
      (replace-dx old-dx eps
        (replace-dx new-dx old-dx
          (apply fn
            (map (lambda (arg)
                   (replace-dx eps old-dx arg))
                 args)))))))

(define-generic-procedure-handler replace-dx
  (match-args diff-factor? diff-factor? function?)
  replace-dx-function)
```

This is quite a bit more complicated than we might expect. It
actually does three replacements of the differential factors. This
is to prevent collisions with factors that may be free in the body

of `fn` that are inherited from the lexical environment of definition of the function `fn`.[27]

Exercise 3.11: The bug!

Before we became aware of the bug pointed out in footnote 26 on page 121, the procedure `extract-dx-function` was written:

```
(define (extract-dx-function fn dx)
  (lambda args
    (extract-dx-part (apply fn args) dx)))
```

Demonstrate the reason for the use of the `replace-dx` wrapper by constructing a function whose derivative is wrong with this earlier version of `extract-dx-part` but is correct in the fixed version. This is not easy! You may want to read the references pointed at in footnote 26.

3.3.4   Literal functions of differential arguments

For simple arguments, applying a literal function is just a matter of constructing the expression that is the application of the function expression to the arguments. But literal functions must also be able to accept differential objects as arguments. When that happens, the literal function must construct (partial) derivative expressions for the arguments that are differentials. For the ith argument of an n-argument function the appropriate derivative expression is:

```
(define (deriv-expr i n fexp)
  (if (= n 1)
      '(derivative ,fexp)
      '((partial ,i) ,fexp)))
```

Some arguments may be differential objects, so a literal function must choose, for each argument, a finite part and an infinitesimal part. Just as for binary arithmetic handlers, the maximal factor must be consistently chosen. Our literal functions are able to take many arguments, so this may seem complicated, but we wrote the `maximal-factor` procedure to handle many arguments. This is explained in section 3.3.3.

If there are no differential objects among the arguments we just cons up the required expression. If there are differential objects

---

[27]This is carefully explained in Manzyuk et al. [87].

we need to make a derivative of the literal function. To do this we find a maximal factor from all of the arguments and separate out the finite parts of the arguments—the terms that do not have that factor. (The infinitesimal parts are the terms that have that factor.) The partial derivatives are themselves literal functions with expressions that are constructed to include the argument index. The resulting differential object is the inner product of the partial derivatives at the finite parts of the arguments with the infinitesimal parts of the arguments.

This is all brought together in the following procedure:

```
(define (literal-function fexp)
  (define (the-function . args)
    (if (any differential? args)
        (let ((n (length args))
              (factor (apply maximal-factor args)))
          (let ((realargs
                 (map (lambda (arg)
                        (finite-part arg factor))
                      args))
                (deltargs
                 (map (lambda (arg)
                        (infinitesimal-part arg factor))
                      args)))
            (let ((fxs (apply the-function realargs))
                  (partials
                   (map (lambda (i)
                          (apply (literal-function
                                  (deriv-expr i n fexp))
                                 realargs))
                        (iota n))))
              (fold d:+ fxs
                    (map d:* partials deltargs)))))
        `(,fexp ,@args)))
  the-function)
```

Exercise 3.12: Functions with structured values

We made the **extract-dx-part** procedure generic (page 110) so we could extend it for values other than differential objects and functions. Extend **extract-dx-part** to work with derivatives of functions that return vectors. Note: You also have to extend the **replace-dx** generic procedure (page 122) in the extractor.

3.4   Efficient generic procedures

In section 3.2.3 we dispatched to a handler by finding an applicable rule using the dispatch store provided in the metadata:

```
(define (generic-procedure-dispatch metadata args)
  (let ((handler
          (get-generic-procedure-handler metadata args)))
    (apply handler args)))
```

The implementation of the dispatch store (on page 98) we used (on page 89) to make the `simple-generic-procedure` constructor was rather crude. The simple dispatch store maintains the rule set as a list of rules. Each rule is represented as a pair of an applicability and a handler. The applicability is a list of lists of predicates to apply to tendered arguments. The way a generic procedure constructed by `simple-generic-procedure` finds an appropriate handler is to sequentially scan the list of rules looking for an applicability that is satisfied by the arguments.

This is seriously inefficient, because the applicability of many rules may have the same predicate in a given operand position: For example, for multiplication in a system of numerical and symbolic arithmetic there may be many rules whose first predicate is `number?`. So the `number?` predicate may be applied many times before finding an applicable rule. It would be good to organize the rules so that finding an applicable one does not perform redundant tests. This is usually accomplished by the use of an index.

3.4.1   Tries

One simple index mechanism is based on the *trie*.[28]

A trie is traditionally a tree structure, but more generally it may be a directed graph. Each node in the trie has edges connecting to successor nodes. Each edge has an associated predicate. The data being tested is a linear sequence of features, in this case the arguments to a generic procedure.

Starting at the root of the trie, the first feature is taken from the sequence and is tested by each predicate on an edge emanating

---

[28]The trie data structure was invented by Edward Fredkin in the early 1960s.

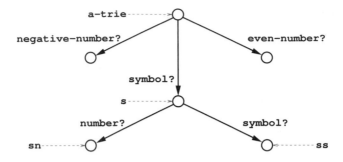

Figure 3.1   A trie can be used to classify sequences of features. A trie is a directed graph in which each edge has a predicate. Starting at the root, the first feature is tested by each predicate on an edge proceeding from the root. If a predicate is satisfied, the process moves to the node at the end of that edge and the next feature is tested. This is repeated with successive features. The classification of the sequence is the set of terminal nodes arrived at.

from the root node. The successful predicate's edge is followed to the next node, and the process repeats with the remainder of the sequence of features. When we run out of features, the current node will contain the associated value, in this case an applicable handler for the arguments.

It is possible that at any node, more than one predicate may succeed. If this happens, then all of the successful branches must be followed. Thus there may be multiple applicable handlers, and there must be a separate means of deciding what to do.

Here is how we can use a trie. Evaluating the following sequence of commands will incrementally construct the trie shown in figure 3.1.

```
(define a-trie (make-trie))
```

We can add an edge to this trie

```
(define s (add-edge-to-trie a-trie symbol?))
```

where `add-edge-to-trie` returns the new node that is at the target end of the new edge. This node is reached by being matched against a symbol.

We can make chains of edges, which are referenced by lists of the corresponding edge predicates

```
(define sn (add-edge-to-trie s number?))
```

The node `sn` is reached from the root via the path (`list symbol?` `number?`). Using a path, there is a simpler way to make a chain of edges than repeatedly calling `add-edge-to-trie`:

```
(define ss (intern-path-trie a-trie (list symbol? symbol?)))
```

We can add a value to any node (here we show symbolic values, but we will later store values that are procedural handlers):

```
(trie-has-value? sn)
```
#f

```
(set-trie-value! sn '(symbol number))
```

```
(trie-has-value? sn)
```
#t

```
(trie-value sn)
```
(symbol number)

We can also use a path-based interface to set values

```
(set-path-value! a-trie (list symbol? symbol?)
                 '(symbol symbol))
```

```
(trie-value ss)
```
(symbol symbol)

Note that both `intern-path-trie` and `set-path-value!` reuse existing nodes and edges when possible, adding edges and nodes where necessary.

Now we can match a feature sequence against the trie we have constructed so far:

```
(equal? (list ss) (get-matching-tries a-trie '(a b)))
```
#t

```
(equal? (list s) (get-matching-tries a-trie '(c)))
```
#t

We can also combine matching with value fetching. The procedure `get-a-value` finds all matching nodes, picks one that has a value, and returns that value.

```
(get-a-value a-trie '(a b))
```
(symbol symbol)

But not all feature sequences have an associated value:

```
(get-a-value a-trie '(-4))
;Unable to match features: (-4)
```

We can incrementally add values to nodes in the trie:

```
(set-path-value! a-trie (list negative-number?)
                 '(negative-number))
(set-path-value! a-trie (list even-number?)
                 '(even-number))

(get-all-values a-trie '(-4))
((even-number) (negative-number))
```

where `get-all-values` finds all the nodes matching a given feature sequence and returns their values.

Given this trie implementation, we can make a dispatch store that uses a trie as its index:

```
(define (make-trie-dispatch-store)
  (let ((delegate (make-simple-dispatch-store))
        (trie (make-trie)))
    (define (get-handler args)
      (get-a-value trie args))
    (define (add-handler! applicability handler)
      ((delegate 'add-handler!) applicability handler)
      (for-each (lambda (path)
                  (set-path-value! trie path handler))
                applicability))
    (lambda (message)
      (case message
        ((get-handler) get-handler)
        ((add-handler!) add-handler!)
        (else (delegate message))))))
```

We make this dispatch store simple by delegating most of the operations to a simple dispatch store. The operations that are not delegated are `add-handler!`, which simultaneously stores the handler in the simple dispatch store and also in the trie, and `get-handler`, which exclusively uses the trie for access. The simple dispatch store manages the default handler and also the set of rules, which is useful for debugging. This is a simple example of the use of delegation to extend an interface, as opposed to the better-known inheritance idea.

Exercise 3.13: Trie rules

To make it easy to experiment with different dispatch stores, we gave
`generic-procedure-constructor` and `make-generic-arithmetic` the
dispatch store maker. For example, we can build a full generic arithmetic as on page 95 but using `make-trie-dispatch-store` as follows:

```
(define trie-full-generic-arithmetic
  (let ((g (make-generic-arithmetic make-trie-dispatch-store)))
    (add-to-generic-arithmetic! g numeric-arithmetic)
    (extend-generic-arithmetic! g function-extender)
    (add-to-generic-arithmetic! g
      (symbolic-extender numeric-arithmetic))
    g))
```

```
(install-arithmetic! trie-full-generic-arithmetic)
```

a. Does this make any change to the dependence on order that we wres-
tled with in section 3.2.2?

b. In general, what characteristics of the predicates could produce situations where there is more than one appropriate handler for a sequence
of arguments?

c. Are there any such situations in our generic arithmetic code?

We have provided a crude tool to measure the effectiveness
of our dispatch strategy. By wrapping any computation with
`with-predicate-counts` we can find out how many times each
dispatch predicate is called in an execution. For example, evaluating `(fib 20)` in a generic arithmetic with a trie-based dispatch
store may yield something like this:[29]

```
(define (fib n)
  (if (< n 2)
      n
      (+ (fib (- n 1)) (fib (- n 2))))))
```

```
(with-predicate-counts (lambda () (fib 20)))
(109453 number)
(109453 function)
(54727 any-object)
(109453 symbolic)
6765
```

---

[29]The names printed for predicates by `with-predicate-counts` do not end in
a question mark; for example the name printed for the predicate `number?` is
simply `number`. The reason for this is obscure, and the curious are welcome to
track it down in the code.

Exercise 3.14: Dispatch efficiency: gotcha!

Given this performance tool it is instructive to look at executions of

```
(define (test-stormer-counts)
  (define (F t x) (- x))
  (define numeric-s0
    (make-initial-history 0 .01 (sin 0) (sin -.01) (sin -.02)))
  (with-predicate-counts
   (lambda ()
     (x 0 ((evolver F 'h stormer-2) numeric-s0 1)))))
```

for the rule-list–based dispatch in `make-simple-dispatch-store`, in the
arithmetic you get by:

```
(define full-generic-arithmetic
  (let ((g (make-generic-arithmetic make-simple-dispatch-store)))
    (add-to-generic-arithmetic! g numeric-arithmetic)
    (extend-generic-arithmetic! g function-extender)
    (add-to-generic-arithmetic! g
          (symbolic-extender numeric-arithmetic))
    g))
```

```
(install-arithmetic! full-generic-arithmetic)
```

and the trie-based version (exercise 3.13), in the arithmetic you get by:

```
(install-arithmetic! trie-full-generic-arithmetic)
```

For some problems the trie should have much better performance than
the simple rule list. We expect that the performance will be better with
the trie if we have a large number of rules with the same initial segment.

Understanding this is important, because the fact that sometimes
the trie does not help with the performance appears counterintuitive.
We explicitly introduced the trie to avoid redundant calls. Explain this
phenomenon in a concise paragraph.

For an additional insight, look at the performance of (`fib 20`) in the
two implementations.

When more than one handler is applicable for a given sequence
of arguments, it is not clear how to use those handlers; addressing
this situation is the job of a *resolution policy*. There are many
considerations when designing a resolution policy. For example,
a policy that chooses the most specific handler is often a good
policy; however, we need more information to implement such a
policy. Sometimes it is appropriate to run all of the applicable
handlers and compare their results. This can be used to catch
errors and provide a kind of redundancy. Or if we have partial
information provided by each handler, such as a numerical interval, the results of different handlers can be combined to provide
better information.

3.4.2 Caching

With the use of tries we have eliminated redundant evaluation of argument predicates. We can do better by using abstraction to eliminate the evaluation of predicates altogether. A predicate identifies a set of objects that are distinguished from all other objects; in other words, the predicate and the set it distinguishes are effectively the same. In our trie implementation, we use the equality of the predicate procedures to avoid redundancy; otherwise we would have redundant edges in the trie and it would be no help at all. This is also why the use of combinations of predicates doesn't mix well with the trie implementation.

The problem here is that we want to build an index that discriminates objects according to predicates, but the opacity of procedures makes them unreliable when used as keys to the index. What we'd really like is to assign a name to the set distinguished by a given predicate. If we had a way to get that name from a given object by superficial examination, we could avoid computing the predicate at all. This name is a "type"; but in order to avoid confusion we will refer to this name as a *tag*.

Given a way to get a tag from an object, we can make a cache that saves the handler resulting from a previous dispatch and reuses it for other dispatches whose arguments have the same tag pattern. But in the absence of explicitly attached tags, there are limitations to this approach, because we can only discriminate objects that share an implementation-specified representation. For example, it's easy to distinguish between a number and a symbol, but it's not easy to distinguish a prime number, because it's unusual for an implementation to represent them specially.

We will return to the problem of explicit tagging in section 3.5, but in the meantime it is still possible to make a useful cache using the representation tags from the Scheme implementation. Given an implementation-specific procedure `implementation-type-name` to obtain the representation tag of an object, we can make a cached dispatch store:

```
(define a-cached-dispatch-store
  (cache-wrapped-dispatch-store (make-trie-dispatch-store)
                                implementation-type-name))
```

This dispatch store wraps a cache around a trie dispatch store, but it could just as well wrap a simple dispatch store.

The heart of the cached dispatch store is a memoizer built on a hash table. The key for the hash table is the list of representation tags extracted by the `implementation-type-name` procedure from the arguments. By passing `implementation-type-name` into this dispatch-store wrapper (as `get-key`) we can use it to make cached dispatch stores for more powerful tag mechanisms that we will develop soon.

```
(define (cache-wrapped-dispatch-store dispatch-store get-key)
  (let ((get-handler
          (simple-list-memoizer
            eqv?
            (lambda (args) (map get-key args))
            (dispatch-store 'get-handler))))
    (lambda (message)
      (case message
        ((get-handler) get-handler)
        (else (dispatch-store message))))))
```

The call to `simple-list-memoizer` wraps a cache around its last argument, producing a memoized version of it. The second argument specifies how to get the cache key from the procedure's arguments. The `eqv?` argument specifies how the tags will be identified in the cache.

Exercise 3.15: Cache performance

Using the same performance tool we introduced for exercise 3.14 on page 130, make measurements for execution of (`test-stormer-counts`) and (`fib 20`) in the cached version of dispatch with the same generic arithmetics explored in exercise 3.14. Record your results. How do they compare?

3.5   Efficient user-defined types

In section 3.4.2 we introduced tags as part of a caching mechanism for dispatch. Each argument is mapped to a tag, and the list of tags is then used as a key in a cache to obtain the handler. If the cache has a handler associated with this list of tags, it is used. If not, the trie of predicates is used to find the appropriate handler and it is entered into the cache associated with the list of tags.

This mechanism is pretty crude: the predicates that can be used for the applicability specifications are restricted to those that always give the same boolean value for any two objects with the same tag. So the discrimination of types cannot be any finer than the available tags. The tags were implementation-specific symbols, such as `pair`, `vector`, or `procedure`. So this severely limits the possible predicates. We could not have rules that distinguish between integers that satisfy `even-integer?` and integers that satisfy `odd-integer?`, for example.

What is needed is a system of tagging that makes it computationally easy to obtain the tag associated with a data item, but where the tags are not restricted to a small set of implementation-specific values. This can be accomplished by attaching a tag to each data item, either with an explicit data structure or via a table of associations.

We have several problems interwoven here: we want to use predicates in applicability specifications; we want an efficient mechanism for dispatch; and we want to be able to specify relationships between predicates that can be used in the dispatch. For example, we want to be able to say that the predicate `integer?` is the disjunction of the predicates `even-integer?` and `odd-integer?`, and also that `integer?` is the disjunction of `positive-integer?`, `negative-integer?`, and `zero?`.

To capture such relationships we need to put metadata on the predicates; but adding an associative lookup to get the metadata of a predicate, as we did with the arity of a function (on page 28), adds too much overhead, because the metadata will contain references to other tags, and chasing these references must be efficient.

One way out is to register the needed predicates. Registration creates a new kind of tag, a data structure that is associated with the predicate. The tag will be easy to attach to objects that are accepted by the predicate. The tag will provide a convenient place to store metadata.

We will construct a system in which each distinct object can have only one tag and where relationships between predicates can be declared. This may appear to be overly simple, but it is adequate for our purposes.

3.5.1   Predicates as types

Let's start with some *simple predicates*. For example, the primitive procedure `exact-integer?` is preregistered in our system as a simple predicate:

```
(predicate? exact-integer?)
#t
```

Now let's define a new predicate that's not a primitive. We will
build it on this particularly slow test for prime numbers.

```
(define (slow-prime? n)
  (and (n:exact-positive-integer? n)
       (n:>= n 2)
       (let loop ((k 2))
         (or (n:> (n:square k) n)
             (and (not (n:= (n:remainder n k) 0))
                  (loop (n:+ k 1)))))))
```

Note that all of the arithmetic operators are prefixed with n: to
ensure that we get the underlying Scheme operations.

We construct the `prime-number?` abstract predicate, with a
name for use in error messages and a criterion, `slow-prime?`, for
an object to be considered a prime number:

```
(define prime-number?
  (simple-abstract-predicate 'prime-number slow-prime?))
```

The procedure `simple-abstract-predicate` creates an *abstract
predicate*, which is a clever trick for memoizing the result of an
expensive predicate (in this case `slow-prime?`). An abstract predicate has an associated constructor that is used to make a *tagged
object*, consisting of the abstract predicate's tag and an object.
The constructor requires that the object to be tagged satisfies
the expensive predicate. The resulting tagged object satisfies the
abstract predicate, as well as carrying its tag. Consequently the
tagged object can be tested for the property defined by the expensive predicate by using the fast abstract predicate (or, equiv-
alently, by dispatching on its tag).

For example, the abstract predicate `prime-number?` is used to
tag objects that are verified prime numbers, for the efficient implementation of generic dispatch. This is important because we
do not want to execute `slow-prime?` during the dispatch to determine whether a number is prime. So we build a new *tagged
object*, which contains both a *tag* (the tag for `prime-number?`) and
a *datum* (the raw prime number). When a generic procedure is
handed a tagged object, it can efficiently retrieve its tag and use
that as a cache key.

In order to make tagged objects, we use `predicate-constructor` to get the constructor associated with the abstract predicate:

```
(define make-prime-number
  (predicate-constructor prime-number?))

(define short-list-of-primes
  (list (make-prime-number 2)
        (make-prime-number 7)
        (make-prime-number 31)))
```

The constructor `make-prime-number` requires that its argument be prime, as determined by `slow-prime?`: the only objects that can be tagged by this constructor are prime numbers.

```
(make-prime-number 4)
;Ill-formed data for prime-number: 4
```

3.5.2   Relationships between predicates

The sets that we can define with abstract predicates can be related to one another. For example, the primes are a subset of the positive integers. The positive integers, the even integers, and the odd integers are subsets of the integers. This is important because any operation that is applicable to an integer is applicable to any element of any subset, but there are operations that can be applied to an element of a subset that cannot be applied to all elements of an enclosing superset. For example, the even integers can be halved without leaving a remainder, but that is not true of the full integers.

When we defined `prime-number?`, we effectively defined a set of objects. But that set has no relation to the set defined by `exact-integer?`:

```
(exact-integer? (make-prime-number 2))
#f
```

We would like these sets to be properly related, which is done by adding some metadata to the predicates themselves:

```
(set-predicate<=! prime-number? exact-integer?)
```

This procedure `set-predicate<=!` modifies the metadata of its argument predicates to indicate that the set defined by the first argument is a (non-strict) subset of the set defined by the second argument. In our case, the set defined by `prime-number?` is declared to be a subset of the set defined by `exact-integer?`. Once this is done, `exact-integer?` will recognize our objects:

```
(exact-integer? (make-prime-number 2))
#t
```

3.5.3   Predicates are dispatch keys

The abstract predicates we have defined are suitable for use in generic dispatch. Even better, they can be used as cache keys to make dispatch efficient. As we described above, when a predicate is registered, a new tag is created and associated with the predicate. All we need is a way to get the tag for a given object: the procedure `get-tag` does this.

If we pass `get-tag` to `cache-wrapped-dispatch-store` as its `get-key` argument, we have a working implementation. However, since the set defined by a predicate can have subsets, we need to consider a situation where there are multiple potential handlers for some given arguments. There are a number of possible ways to resolve this situation, but the most common is to identify the "most specific" handler by some means, and invoke that one. Since the subset relation is a partial order, it may not be clear which handler is most specific, so the implementation must resolve the ambiguity by independent means.

Here is one such implementation. It uses a procedure `rule<` to sort the matching rules into an appropriate order, then chooses a handler from the result.[30]

---

[30]The procedure `is-generic-handler-applicable?` abstracts the handler checking that we previously did using `predicates-match?` in `get-handler` on page 98. This gives us a hook for later elaboration.

```
(define (make-subsetting-dispatch-store-maker choose-handler)
  (lambda ()
    (let ((delegate (make-simple-dispatch-store)))
      (define (get-handler args)
        (let ((matching
                (filter (lambda (rule)
                          (is-generic-handler-applicable?
                           rule args))
                        ((delegate 'get-rules)))))
          (and (n:pair? matching)
               (choose-handler    ; from sorted handlers
                (map cdr (sort matching rule<))
                ((delegate 'get-default-handler))))))
      (lambda (message)
        (case message
          ((get-handler) get-handler)
          (else (delegate message)))))))
```

The procedure `make-most-specific-dispatch-store` chooses
the first of the sorted handlers to be the effective handler:

```
(define make-most-specific-dispatch-store
  (make-subsetting-dispatch-store-maker
   (lambda (handlers default-handler)
     (car handlers))))
```

Another possible choice is to make a "chaining" dispatch store,
in which each handler gets an argument that can be used to invoke
the next handler in the sorted sequence. This is useful for cases
where a subset handler wants to extend the behavior of a superset
handler rather than overriding it. We will see an example of this
in the clock handler of the adventure game in section 3.5.4.

```
(define make-chaining-dispatch-store
  (make-subsetting-dispatch-store-maker
   (lambda (handlers default-handler)
     (let loop ((handlers handlers))
       (if (pair? handlers)
           (let ((handler (car handlers))
                 (next-handler (loop (cdr handlers))))
             (lambda args
               (apply handler (cons next-handler args))))
           default-handler)))))
```

Either one of these dispatch stores can be made into a cached dispatch store by adding a caching wrapper:

```
(define (make-cached-most-specific-dispatch-store)
  (cache-wrapped-dispatch-store
    (make-most-specific-dispatch-store)
    get-tag))

(define (make-cached-chaining-dispatch-store)
  (cache-wrapped-dispatch-store
    (make-chaining-dispatch-store)
    get-tag))
```

Then we create the corresponding generic-procedure constructors:

```
(define most-specific-generic-procedure
  (generic-procedure-constructor
   make-cached-most-specific-dispatch-store))

(define chaining-generic-procedure
  (generic-procedure-constructor
   make-cached-chaining-dispatch-store))
```

3.5.4   Example: An adventure game

One traditional way to model a world is "object-oriented programming." The idea is that the world being modeled is made up of objects, each of which has independent local state, and the coupling between the objects is loose. Each object is assumed to have particular behaviors. An object may receive messages from other objects, change its state, and send messages to other objects. This is very natural for situations where the behavior we wish to model does not depend on the collaboration of multiple sources of information: each message comes from one other object. This is a tight constraint on the organization of a program.

There are other ways to break a problem into pieces. We have looked at "arithmetic" enough to see that the meaning of an operator, such as *, can depend on the properties of multiple arguments. For example, the product of a number and a vector is a different operation from the product of two vectors or of two numbers. This kind of problem is naturally formulated in terms of generic procedures.[31]

---

[31] In languages such as Haskell and Smalltalk, multiple arguments are handled by dispatching on the first argument, producing an object that then dispatches on the second argument, etc.

Consider the problem of modeling a world made of "places," "things," and "people" with generic procedures. How should the state variables that are presumed to be local to the entities be represented and packaged? What operations are appropriately generic over what kinds of entities? Since it is natural to group entities into types (or sets) and to express some of the operations as appropriate for all members of an inclusive set, how is subtyping to be arranged? Any object-oriented view will prescribe specific answers to these design questions; here we have more freedom, and must design the conventions that will be used.

To illustrate this process we will build a world for a simple adventure game. There is a network of rooms connected by passages and inhabited by a variety of creatures, some of which are *autonomous* in that they can wander around. There is an *avatar* that is controlled by the player. There are things, some of which can be picked up and carried by the creatures. There are ways that the creatures can interact: a troll can bite another creature and damage it; any creature can take a thing carried by another creature.

Every entity in our world has a set of named properties. Some of these are fixed and others are changeable. For example, a room has exits to other rooms. These represent the topology of the network and cannot be changed. A room also has contents, such as the creatures who are currently in the room and things that may be acquired. The contents of a room change as creatures move around and as they carry things to and from other rooms. We will computationally model this set of named properties as a table from names to property values.

There is a set of generic procedures that are appropriate for this world. For example, some things, such as books, creatures, and the avatar, are movable. In every case, moving a thing requires deleting it from the contents of the source, adding it to the contents of the destination, and changing its location property. This operation is the same for books, people, and trolls, all of which are members of the "movable things" set.

A book can be read; a person can say something; a troll can bite a creature. To implement these behaviors there are specific properties of books that are different from the properties of people or those of trolls. But these different kinds of movable things have some properties in common, such as location. So when such a thing is instantiated, it must make a table for all of its properties, including those inherited from more inclusive sets. The rules for implementing the behavior of operators such as move must be able to find appropriate handlers for manipulating the properties in each case.

The game

Our game is played on a rough topological map of MIT. There are various autonomous agents (non-player characters), such as students and officials. The registrar, for example, is a troll. There are movable and immovable things, and movable things can be taken by an autonomous agent or the player's avatar. Although this game has little detail, it can be expanded to be very interesting.

We create a session with an avatar named `gjs` who appears in a random place. The game tells the player about the environment of the avatar.

```
(start-adventure 'gjs)
You are in dorm-row
You see here: registrar
You can exit: east
```

Since the registrar is here it is prudent to leave! (He may bite, and after enough bites the avatar will die.)

```
(go 'east)
gjs leaves via the east exit
gjs enters lobby-7
You are in lobby-7
You can see: lobby-10 infinite-corridor
You can exit: up west east
alyssa-hacker enters lobby-7
alyssa-hacker says: Hi gjs
ben-bitdiddle enters lobby-7
ben-bitdiddle says: Hi alyssa-hacker gjs
registrar enters lobby-7
registrar says: Hi ben-bitdiddle alyssa-hacker gjs
```

Notice that several autonomous agents arrive after the avatar, and that they do so one at a time. So we see that the report is for an interval of simulated time rather than a summary of the state at an instant. This is an artifact of our implementation rather than a deliberate design choice.

Unfortunately the registrar has followed, so it's time to leave again.

```
(say "I am out of here!")
```
gjs says: I am out of here!

```
(go 'east)
```
gjs leaves via the east exit
gjs enters lobby-10
You are in lobby-10
You can see: lobby-7 infinite-corridor great-court
You can exit: east south west up

```
(go 'up)
```
gjs leaves via the up exit
gjs enters 10-250
You are in 10-250
You see here: blackboard
You can exit: up down

Room 10-250 is a lecture hall, with a large blackboard. Perhaps we can take it?

```
(take-thing 'blackboard)
```
blackboard is not movable

So sad—gjs loves blackboards. Let's keep looking around.

```
(go 'up)
```
gjs leaves via the up exit
gjs enters barker-library
You are in barker-library
You see here: engineering-book
You can exit: up down
An earth-shattering, soul-piercing scream is heard...

Apparently, a troll (maybe the registrar) has eaten someone. However, here is a book that should be takable, so we take it and return to the lecture hall.

```
(take-thing 'engineering-book)
```
gjs picks up engineering-book

```
(go 'down)
```
gjs leaves via the down exit
gjs enters 10-250
You are in 10-250
Your bag contains: engineering-book
You see here: blackboard
You can exit: up down

From the lecture hall we return to `lobby-10`, where we encounter `lambda-man`, who promptly steals our book.

```
(go 'down)
gjs leaves via the down exit
gjs enters lobby-10
gjs says: Hi lambda-man
You are in lobby-10
Your bag contains: engineering-book
You see here: lambda-man
You can see: lobby-7 infinite-corridor great-court
You can exit: east south west up
alyssa-hacker enters lobby-10
alyssa-hacker says: Hi gjs lambda-man
lambda-man takes engineering-book from gjs
gjs says: Yaaaah! I am upset!
```

The object types

To create an object in our game, we define some properties with `make-property`, define a type predicate with `make-type`, get the predicate's associated instantiator with `type-instantiator`, and call that instantiator with appropriate arguments.

How do we make a troll? The `make-troll` constructor for a troll takes arguments that specify the values for properties that are specific to the particular troll being constructed. The troll will be created in a given place with a `restlessness` (proclivity to move around), an `acquisitiveness` (proclivity to take things), and a `hunger` (proclivity to bite other people).

```
(define (create-troll name place restlessness hunger)
  (make-troll 'name name
              'location place
              'restlessness restlessness
              'acquisitiveness 1/10
              'hunger hunger))
```

We create two trolls: `grendel` and `registrar`. They are initially placed in random places, with some random proclivities.

```
(define (create-trolls places)
  (map (lambda (name)
         (create-troll name
                       (random-choice places)
                       (random-bias 3)
                       (random-bias 3)))
       '(grendel registrar)))
```

The procedure `random-choice` randomly selects one item from the list it is given. The procedure `random-bias` chooses a number (in this case 1, 2, or 3) and returns its reciprocal.

The troll type is defined as a predicate that is true only of trolls. The `make-type` procedure is given a name for the type and a descriptor of the properties that are specific to trolls. (Only trolls have a `hunger` property.)

```
(define troll:hunger
  (make-property 'hunger 'predicate bias?))

(define troll?
  (make-type 'troll (list troll:hunger)))
```

The troll is a specific type of autonomous agent. Thus the set of trolls is a subset of (<=) the set of autonomous agents.

```
(set-predicate<=! troll? autonomous-agent?)
```

The constructor for trolls is directly derived from the predicate that defines the type, as is the accessor for the `hunger` property.

```
(define make-troll
  (type-instantiator troll?))

(define get-hunger
  (property-getter troll:hunger troll?))
```

Autonomous agents are occasionally stimulated by the "clock" to take some action. The distinctive action of the troll is to bite other people.

```
(define-clock-handler troll? eat-people!)
```

A biased coin is flipped to determine whether the troll is hungry at the moment. If it is hungry it looks for other people (trolls are people too!), and if there are some it chooses one to bite, causing the victim to suffer some damage. The narrator describes what happens.

```
(define (eat-people! troll)
  (if (flip-coin (get-hunger troll))
      (let ((people (people-here troll)))
        (if (n:null? people)
            (narrate! (list (possessive troll) "belly rumbles")
                      troll)
            (let ((victim (random-choice people)))
              (narrate! (list troll "takes a bite out of"
                              victim)
                        troll)
              (suffer! (random-number 3) victim))))))
```

The procedure `flip-coin` generates a random fraction between 0 and 1. If that fraction is greater than the argument, it returns true. The procedure `random-number` returns a positive number less than or equal to its argument.

The procedure `narrate!` is used to add narration to the story. The second argument to `narrate!` (`troll` in the above code) may be anything that has a location. The narrator announces its first argument in the location thus determined. One can only hear that announcement if one is in that location.

We said that a troll is a kind of autonomous agent. The autonomous agent type is defined by its predicate, which specifies the properties that are needed for such an agent. We also specify that the set of autonomous agents is a subset of the set of all persons.

```
(define autonomous-agent:restlessness
  (make-property 'restlessness 'predicate bias?))

(define autonomous-agent:acquisitiveness
  (make-property 'acquisitiveness 'predicate bias?))

(define autonomous-agent?
  (make-type 'autonomous-agent
             (list autonomous-agent:restlessness
                   autonomous-agent:acquisitiveness)))

(set-predicate<=! autonomous-agent? person?)
```

The constructor for trolls specified values for the properties `restlessness` and `acquisitiveness`, which are needed to make an autonomous agent, in addition to the `hunger` property specific to trolls. Since trolls are autonomous agents, and autonomous agents are persons, there must also be values for the properties of a person and all its supersets. In this system almost all properties have default values that are automatically filled if not specified. For example, all objects need names; the `name` was specified in the constructor for trolls. But a person also has a `health` property, necessary to accumulate damage, and this property value was not explicitly specified in the constructor for trolls.

The generic procedures

Now that we have seen how objects are built, we will look at how to implement their behavior. Specifically, we will see how generic procedures are an effective tool for describing complex behavior.

We defined `get-hunger`, which is used in `eat-people!`, in terms of `property-getter`. A getter for a property of objects of a given type is implemented as a generic procedure that takes an object as an argument and returns the value of the property.

```
(define (property-getter property type)
  (let ((procedure      ; the getter
          (most-specific-generic-procedure
           (symbol 'get- (property-name property))
           1                ; arity
           #f)))            ; default handler
    (define-generic-procedure-handler procedure
      (match-args type)
      (lambda (object)
        (get-property-value property object)))
    procedure))
```

This shows the construction of a generic procedure with a generated name (for example `get-hunger`) that takes one argument, and the addition of a handler that does the actual access. The last argument to `most-specific-generic-procedure` is the default handler for the procedure; specifying `#f` means that the default is to signal an error.

We also used `define-clock-handler` to describe an action to take when the clock ticks. That procedure just adds a handler to a generic procedure `clock-tick!`, which is already constructed.

```
(define (define-clock-handler type action)
  (define-generic-procedure-handler clock-tick!
    (match-args type)
    (lambda (super object)
      (super object)
      (action object))))
```

This generic procedure supports "chaining," in which each handler gets an extra argument (in this case super) that when called causes any handlers defined on the supersets of the given object to be called. The arguments passed to super have the same meaning as the arguments received here; in this case there's just one argument and it is passed along. This is essentially the same mechanism used in languages such as Java, though in that case it's done with a magic keyword rather than an argument.

The clock-tick! procedure is called to trigger an action, not to compute a value. Notice that the action we specify will be taken after any actions specified by the supersets. We could have chosen to do the given action first and the others later, just by changing the order of the calls.

The real power of the generic procedure organization is illustrated by the mechanisms for moving things around. For example, when we pick up the engineering book, we move it from the room to our bag. This is implemented with the move! procedure:

```
(define (move! thing destination actor)
  (generic-move! thing
                 (get-location thing)
                 destination
                 actor))
```

The move! procedure is implemented in terms of a more general procedure generic-move! that takes four arguments: the thing to be moved, the thing's current location, its destination location, and the actor of the move procedure. This procedure is generic because the movement behavior potentially depends on the types of all of the arguments.

When we create generic-move! we also specify a very general handler to catch cases that are not covered by more specific handlers (for specific argument types).

```
(define generic-move!
  (most-specific-generic-procedure 'generic-move! 4 #f))

(define-generic-procedure-handler generic-move!
  (match-args thing? container? container? person?)
  (lambda (thing from to actor)
    (tell! (list thing "is not movable")
           actor)))
```

The procedure `tell!` sends the message (its first argument) to the `actor` that is trying to move the `thing`. If the `actor` is the avatar, the message is displayed.

In the demo we picked up the book. We did that by calling the procedure `take-thing` with the name `engineering-book`. This procedure resolves the name to the thing and then calls `take-thing!`, which invokes `move!`:

```
(define (take-thing name)
  (let ((thing (find-thing name (here))))
    (if thing
        (take-thing! thing my-avatar)))
  'done)

(define (take-thing! thing person)
  (move! thing (get-bag person) person))
```

There are two procedures here. The first is a user-interface procedure to give the player a convenient way of describing the thing to be taken by giving its name. It calls the second, an internal procedure that is also used in other places.

To make this work we supply a handler for `generic-move!` that is specialized to moving mobile things from places to bags:

```
(define-generic-procedure-handler generic-move!
  (match-args mobile-thing? place? bag? person?)
  (lambda (mobile-thing from to actor)
    (let ((new-holder (get-holder to)))
      (cond ((eqv? actor new-holder)
             (narrate! (list actor
                             "picks up" mobile-thing)
                       actor))
            (else
             (narrate! (list actor
                             "picks up" mobile-thing
                             "and gives it to" new-holder)
                       actor)))
      (if (not (eqv? actor new-holder))
          (say! new-holder (list "Whoa! Thanks, dude!")))
      (move-internal! mobile-thing from to))))
```

If the `actor` is taking the `thing`, the `actor` is the `new-holder`. But it is possible that the `actor` is picking up the `thing` in the `place` and putting it into someone else's bag!

The say! procedure is used to indicate that a person has said
something. Its first argument is the person speaking, and the
second argument is the text being spoken. The move-internal!
procedure actually moves the object from one place to another.

To drop a thing we use the procedure drop-thing to move it
from our bag to our current location:

```
(define (drop-thing name)
  (let ((thing (find-thing name my-avatar)))
    (if thing
        (drop-thing! thing my-avatar)))
  'done)

(define (drop-thing! thing person)
  (move! thing (get-location person) person))
```

The following handler for generic-move! enables dropping a
thing. The actor may be dropping a thing from its own bag or it
might pick up something from another person's bag and drop it.

```
(define-generic-procedure-handler generic-move!
  (match-args mobile-thing? bag? place? person?)
  (lambda (mobile-thing from to actor)
    (let ((former-holder (get-holder from)))
      (cond ((eqv? actor former-holder)
             (narrate! (list actor
                             "drops" mobile-thing)
                       actor))
            (else
             (narrate! (list actor
                             "takes" mobile-thing
                             "from" former-holder
                             "and drops it")
                       actor)))
      (if (not (eqv? actor former-holder))
          (say! former-holder
                (list "What did you do that for?")))
      (move-internal! mobile-thing from to))))
```

Yet another `generic-move!` handler provides for gifting or stealing something, by moving a thing from one bag to another bag. Here the behavior depends on the relationships among the actor, the original holder of the thing, and the final holder of the thing.

```
(define-generic-procedure-handler generic-move!
  (match-args mobile-thing? bag? bag? person?)
  (lambda (mobile-thing from to actor)
    (let ((former-holder (get-holder from))
          (new-holder (get-holder to)))
      (cond ((eqv? from to)
             (tell! (list new-holder "is already carrying"
                          mobile-thing)
                    actor))
            ((eqv? actor former-holder)
             (narrate! (list actor
                             "gives" mobile-thing
                             "to" new-holder)
                       actor))
            ((eqv? actor new-holder)
             (narrate! (list actor
                             "takes" mobile-thing
                             "from" former-holder)
                       actor))
            (else
             (narrate! (list actor
                             "takes" mobile-thing
                             "from" former-holder
                             "and gives it to" new-holder)
                       actor)))
      (if (not (eqv? actor former-holder))
          (say! former-holder (list "Yaaaah! I am upset!")))
      (if (not (eqv? actor new-holder))
          (say! new-holder
                (list "Whoa! Where'd you get this?")))
      (if (not (eqv? from to))
          (move-internal! mobile-thing from to)))))
```

Another interesting case is the motion of a person from one place to another. This is implemented by the following handler:

```
(define-generic-procedure-handler generic-move!
  (match-args person? place? place? person?)
  (lambda (person from to actor)
    (let ((exit (find-exit from to)))
      (cond ((or (eqv? from (get-heaven))
                 (eqv? to (get-heaven)))
             (move-internal! person from to))
            ((not exit)
             (tell! (list "There is no exit from" from
                          "to" to)
                    actor))
            ((eqv? person actor)
             (narrate! (list person "leaves via the"
                             (get-direction exit) "exit")
                       from)
             (move-internal! person from to))
            (else
             (tell! (list "You can't force"
                          person
                          "to move!")
                    actor)))))))
```

There can be many other handlers, but the important thing to
see is that the behavior of the move procedure can depend on the
types of all of the arguments. This provides a clean decomposition
of the behavior into separately understandable chunks. It is rather
difficult to achieve such an elegant decomposition in a traditional
object-oriented design, because in such a design one must choose
one of the arguments to be the principal dispatch center. Should
it be the thing being moved? the source location? the target
location? the actor? Any one choice will make the situation more
complex than necessary.

As Alan Perlis wrote: "It is better to have 100 functions operate
on one data structure than 10 functions on 10 data structures."

Implementing properties

We saw that the objects in our game are created by defining
some properties with `make-property`, defining a type predicate
with `make-type`, getting the predicate's associated instantiator
with `type-instantiator`, and calling that instantiator with appropriate arguments. This simple description hides a complex
implementation that is worth exploring.

The interesting aspect of this code is that it provides a simple
and flexible mechanism for managing the properties that are associated with a type instance, which is robust when subtyping is

used. Properties are represented by abstract objects rather than names, in order to avoid namespace conflicts when subtyping. For example, a type `mammal` might have a property named `forelimb` that refers to a typical front leg. A subtype `bat` of `mammal` might have a property with the same name that refers to a different object, a wing! If the properties were specified by their names, then one of these types would need to change its name. In this implementation, the property objects are specified by themselves, and two properties with the same name are distinct.

The procedure `make-property` creates a data type containing a name, a predicate, and a default-value supplier. Its first argument is the property's name, and the rest of the arguments are a property list with additional metadata about the property. For example, see the definition of `troll:hunger` on page 143. We will ignore how the property list is parsed since it's not interesting.[32]

```
(define (make-property name . plist)
  (guarantee n:symbol? name)
  (guarantee property-list? plist)
  (%make-property name
                  (get-predicate-property plist)
                  (get-default-supplier-property plist)))
```

A property is implemented as a Scheme *record* [65], which is a data structure that consists of a set of named fields. It is defined by elaborate syntax that specifies a constructor, a type predicate, and an accessor for each field:

```
(define-record-type <property>
    (%make-property name predicate default-supplier)
    property?
  (name property-name)
  (predicate property-predicate)
  (default-supplier property-default-supplier))
```

---

[32]The `make-property` procedure uses a helper called `guarantee` to do argument checking. The first argument to `guarantee` is a predicate (preferably a registered predicate) and the second argument is an object to be tested. There may be a third argument, to identify the caller. If the object doesn't satisfy the predicate, `guarantee` signals an error. The procedure `guarantee-list-of` works similarly except that it requires the object to be a list of elements satisfying the predicate.

We have used `assert` earlier in this text. `assert` is more convenient for posing assertions that must be true where they are made. `guarantee` is preferable for the more restricted case of argument type checking.

We chose to give the primitive record constructor %make-property a name with an initial percent sign (%). We often use the initial percent sign to indicate a low-level procedure that will not be used except to support a higher-level abstraction. The %make-property procedure is used only in make-property, which in turn is used by other parts of the system.

Given a set of properties, we can construct a type predicate:

```
(define (make-type name properties)
  (guarantee-list-of property? properties)
  (let ((type
          (simple-abstract-predicate name instance-data?)))
    (%set-type-properties! type properties)
    type))
```

A type predicate is an ordinary abstract predicate (see page 134) along with the specified properties, which are stored in an association using %set-type-properties!. Those specified properties aren't used by themselves; instead they are aggregated with the properties of the supersets of this type. The object being tagged satisfies instance-data?. It is an association from the properties of this type to their values.

```
(define (type-properties type)
  (append-map %type-properties
              (cons type (all-supertypes type))))
```

And type-instantiator builds the instantiator, which accepts a property list using property names as keys, parses that list, and uses the resulting values to create the instance data, which associates each property of this instance with its value. It also calls the set-up! procedure, which gives us the ability to do type-specific initialization.

```
(define (type-instantiator type)
  (let ((constructor (predicate-constructor type))
        (properties (type-properties type)))
    (lambda plist
      (let ((object
              (constructor (parse-plist plist properties))))
        (set-up! object)
        object))))
```

Exercise 3.16: Adventure warmup

Load the adventure game and start the simulation by executing the command (start-adventure *your-name*). Walk your avatar around. Find some takable object and take it. Drop the thing you took in some other place.

Exercise 3.17: Health

Change the representation of the health of a person to have more possible values than are given in the initial game. Scale your representation so that the probability of death from a troll bite is the same as it was before you changed the representation. Also make it possible to recover from a nonfatal troll bite, or other loss of health, by some cycles of rest.

Exercise 3.18: Medical help

Make a new place, the medical center. Make it easily accessible from the Green building and the Gates tower. If a person who suffers a nonfatal injury (perhaps from a troll bite) makes it to the medical center, their health may be restored.

Exercise 3.19: A *palantir*

Make a new kind of thing called a *palantir* (a "seeing stone," as in Tolkien's *Lord of the Rings*). Each instance of a *palantir* can communicate with any other instance; so if there is a *palantir* in lobby-10 and another in dorm-row, you can observe the goings-on in dorm-row by looking into a *palantir* in lobby-10. (Basically, a *palantir* is a magical surveillance camera and display.)

Plant a few immovable *palantiri* in various parts of the campus, and enable your avatar to use one. Can you keep watch on the positions of your friends? Of the trolls?

Can you make an autonomous person other than your avatar use a *palantir* for some interesting purpose? The university's president might be a suitable choice.

Exercise 3.20: Invisibility

Make an "Invisibility Cloak" that any person (including an avatar) can acquire to become invisible, thus invulnerable to attacks by trolls. However, the cloak must be discarded (dropped) after a short time, because possession of the cloak slowly degrades the person's health.

Exercise 3.21: Your turn

Now that you have had an opportunity to play with our "world" of characters, places, and things, extend this world in some substantial way, limited only by your creativity. One idea is to have mobile places, such as elevators, which have entrances and exits that change with time, and are perhaps controllable by persons. But that is just one suggestion—invent something you like!

Exercise 3.22: Multiple players

This is a pretty big project rather than a simple exercise.

a. Extend the adventure game so that there can be multiple players, each controlling a personal avatar.

b. Make it possible for players to be on different terminals.

3.6   Summary

The use of generic procedures introduced in this chapter is both powerful and dangerous—it is not for the faint of heart. Allowing the programmer to dynamically change the meanings of the primitive operators of the language can result in unmanageable code. But if we are careful to extend operators to only new types of arguments, without changing their behavior on the original types, we can get powerful extensions without breaking any old software. Most programming languages do not allow the freedom to modify the existing behavior of primitive operators, for good reason. However, many of the ideas here are portable and can be safely used. For example, in many languages, as diverse as C++ and Haskell, one can overload operators to have new meanings on user-defined types.

Extensions of arithmetic are pretty tame, but we must be aware of the problems that can come up, and the subtle bugs that can be evoked: addition of integers is associative, but addition of floating-point numbers is not associative; multiplication of numbers is commutative, but multiplication of matrices is not. And if we extend addition to be concatenation of strings, that extension is not commutative. On the good side, it is straightforward to extend arithmetic to symbolic expressions containing literal numbers as well as purely numerical quantities. It is not difficult, but lots of work, to continue to expand to functions, vectors, matrices, and tensors. However, we eventually run into real problems with the ordering of extensions—symbolic vectors are not the same as vectors with symbolic coordinates! We also can get into complications with the typing of symbolic functions.

One beautiful example of the power of extensible generics is the almost trivial implementation of forward-mode automatic differentiation by extending each primitive arithmetic procedure to handle differential objects. However, making this work correctly with higher-order functions that return functions as values was difficult. (Of course, most programmers writing applications that need automatic differentiation do not need to worry about this complication.)

In our system the "type" is represented by a predicate that is true of elements of that type. In order to make this efficient we introduced a predicate registration and tagging system that allowed us to add declarations of relationships among the types. For example, we could have prime numbers be a subset of the integers, so numbers that satisfy the user-defined `prime?` predicate automatically satisfy the `integer?` predicate.

Once we have user-defined types with declared subset relationships, we enter a new realm of possibilities. We demonstrated this with a simple but elegantly extensible adventure game. Because our generic procedures dispatch on the types of all of their arguments, the descriptions of the behaviors of the entities in our adventure game are much simpler and more modular than they would be if we dispatched on the first argument to produce a procedure that dispatched on the second argument, and so on. So modeling these behaviors in a typical single-dispatch object-oriented system would be more complicated.

We used tagged data to efficiently implement extensible generic procedures. The data was tagged with the information required to decide which procedures to use to implement the indicated operations. But once we have the ability to tag data, there are other uses tags can be put to. For example, we may tag data with its provenance, or how it was derived, or the assumptions it was based on. Such audit trails may be useful for access control, for tracing the use of sensitive data, or for debugging complex systems [128]. So there is power in the ability to attach arbitrary tags to any data item, in addition to the use of tags to determine the handlers for generic procedures.

4
Pattern Matching

Pattern matching is a technology that supports the creation of domain-specific languages and other systems that should have an additive character.

Pattern matching is a generalization of equality testing. In equality testing we compare two objects to determine that they have the same structure and contents. In pattern matching, we generalize equality testing to allow some parts of the structure and contents to be unspecified. A *pattern* specifies certain parts of the data exactly, but it has "holes" (*pattern variables*) that match the unspecified parts of the data. We may impose constraints on what a pattern variable can match, and we may require that multiple instances of the same pattern variable match the same thing.

A pattern can be matched to a part of a larger datum; the context of the match is unspecified. The ability to work with partial information means that only the specified parts of the pattern are assumptions about the data matched; there are few or no assumptions about the unspecified parts.

This property of pattern matching enables the construction of very flexible rule-based systems. In a rule-based system one can add new rules to add new capabilities, though there are difficulties associated with how rules are defined and how they interact with one another. For example, if more than one rule is applicable, the results may depend on the ordering of application. We already encountered problems with the interaction of rules, in the board-game rule interpreter. (See the critique on page 63.)

Besides the use of patterns to match data that meets a partial specification, patterns can themselves represent partially known information. Merging such patterns (*unification*) can generate more specific information than the individual patterns contribute.

Another use of pattern matching is as a generalization of generic procedures. Generic procedures allow us to do miraculous things by modulating the meanings of the free variables in a program. We may think of the program that employs a generic procedure, such as that bound to +, as advertising for a handler that can do the job of "+ing" the arguments supplied. A handler attached to a generic procedure is applicable if the arguments supplied satisfy the predicates provided when it was attached. But the language for advertising jobs that need to be done is rather limited—all we have is a single symbol, in this case +. If we instead use patterns to advertise jobs to be done and other patterns to advertise procedures that might do those jobs, we have a much richer language: *pattern-directed invocation.*

4.1   Patterns

The elementary laws of algebra can be expressed as equivalence of patterns:

$$a \times (b + c) \Longleftrightarrow a \times b + a \times c$$

This is the distributive law of multiplication over addition. It says that we can replace one side with the other without changing the value of the expression. Each side of the law is a pattern, with pattern variables a, b, and c, and pattern constants $\times$ and $+$. What the law says is that if we find an algebraic expression that is the product of something and a sum of terms, we can replace it with a sum of two products, and vice versa.

Let's see how to organize programs based on pattern matching. A key idea here will be compilation of patterns into combinators that are the pieces of a matcher. In section 4.2 we will demonstrate this in a term-rewriting system for elementary algebra.

A Language of Patterns

The first job is to make up our language of patterns. We will start with something simple. We will make our patterns out of Lisp (Scheme) lists. Unlike the mathematical example above, we will not have reserved symbols, such as $\times$ and $+$, so we will have to distinguish pattern variables from pattern constants. A pattern variable can be represented by a list beginning with the query symbol, ?. This is a traditional choice. So in this language the patterns that make up the distributive law may be represented as follows, assuming that we are manipulating Lisp prefix mathematical expressions:

```
(* (? a) (+ (? b) (? c)))

(+ (* (? a) (? b)) (* (? a) (? c)))
```

You might complain that we could have used distinguished symbols, such as ?a instead of the long-winded (? a). That would be fine, but that choice would make it a bit harder to extend, say if we want a variable that is restricted to match only numbers. Of course, we can add syntax later if it is helpful, but remember Alan Perlis's maxim: "Syntactic sugar causes cancer of the semicolon." With our simple list representation we are able to restrict the pattern variable (? a) to match only numbers by adding the predicate describing the restriction to its list representation: (? a ,number?).

One constraint on our design of the matcher is that the second pattern above should match

```
(+ (* (cos x) (exp y)) (* (cos x) (sin z)))
```

where a=(cos x), b=(exp y), and c=(sin z).

But it should not match

```
(+ (* (cos x) (exp y)) (* (cos (+ x y)) (sin z)))
```

because there is no consistent assignment possible for (? a), unless, somehow, x=(+ x y).[1] We will learn about that sort of situation when we study unification matching in section 4.4; here we will decide that there is no match possible.

Another constraint on the matcher, which will have an important influence on its structure, is the need to match an unknown number of consecutive elements in a list. For example, suppose we want to make a rule to replace a sum of squares of a sine and a cosine with 1, even if they are not consecutive in the sum:

```
(+ ... (expt (sin theta) 2) ... (expt (cos theta) 2) ...)
(+ 1 ... ... ...)
```

The ... here may stand for many terms. We will use a *segment variable*, written with the prefix ??, to match many terms. So the pattern we will write is:

```
(+ (?? t1)
   (expt (sin (? x)) 2)
   (?? t2)
   (expt (cos (? x)) 2)
   (?? t3))
```

---

[1] Of course, a very clever matcher could deduce that y=0, under the assumption that we are dealing with numbers.

We needed three segment variables here. The segment variable
(?? t1) will match the terms before the sine term, (?? t2) will
match the terms between the sine term and the cosine term, and
(?? t3) will match the terms after the cosine term.

Segment variables have a profound effect, because we don't
know how long a segment is until we find the next part that
matches, and we may be able to match the same data item many
ways. For example, there may be squares of both sines and cosines
of two different angles in the same sum. Even simpler, the pattern

```
(a (?? x) (?? y) (?? x) c)
```

can match the datum

```
(a b b b b b c)
```

in four different ways. (Notice that the segment variable x must
eat up the same number of bs in the two places it appears in
the pattern.) So the matcher must do a search over the space of
possible assignments to the segment variables.

4.2   Term rewriting

Term-rewriting systems are powerful tools for creating domain-
specific languages for manipulating expression-like information.
If we have a syntactic system of expressions, where we may need
to replace some subexpressions with "equivalent" subexpressions,
we can often use a rule-based term-rewriting system to describe
those transformations. For example, many compiler optimizations
can be expressed as local rewrites of program fragments in a larger
context. The essential features of a term-rewriting system are the
use of a pattern matcher to identify the information to be transformed, and a template system for instantiating the replacement.

There has been extensive research [72] into the problem of constructing convergent term-rewriting systems from equational theories (systems of "equivalent" expressions), but we won't get into
that here. Also, there is a superficial similarity between the patterns matched against and the templates for instantiation, which
may suggest the possibility of making bidirectional rules; we won't

look at that either. First we develop a simple unidirectional system, in which patterns are used to recognize inputs and templates are used to make outputs.

Here is an approximation to some algebraic simplification rules:

```
(define algebra-1
  (rule-simplifier
   (list
    ;; Associative law of addition
    (rule '(+ (? a) (+ (? b) (? c)))
          '(+ (+ ,a ,b) ,c))
    ;; Commutative law of multiplication
    (rule '(* (? b) (? a))
          (and (expr<? a b)
               '(* ,a ,b)))
    ;; Distributive law of multiplication over addition
    (rule '(* (? a) (+ (? b) (? c)))
          '(+ (* ,a ,b) (* ,a ,c)))))))
```

There are three rules in `algebra-1`. The first rule implements the associative law of addition, the second implements the commutative law of multiplication, and the third implements the distributive law of multiplication over addition.

Each rule is composed of two parts: a pattern to match a subexpression, and a *consequent* expression. If the pattern matches, the consequent is evaluated. If the value of the consequent is #f the rule is not applicable. Otherwise the result of the evaluation replaces the matched subexpression. Notice that we use the backquote mechanism described on page 391 to simplify writing the consequent expression.

The rules are gathered in a list for the `rule-simplifier` procedure. The result is a simplifier procedure that can be applied to an algebraic expression.

```
(algebra-1 '(* (+ y (+ z w)) x))
(+ (+ (* x y) (* x z)) (* w x))
```

Notice the restriction predicate, `expr<?`, in the consequent of the rule for the commutative law:

```
(rule '(* (? b) (? a))
      (and (expr<? a b)
           '(* ,a ,b)))
```

If the consequent expression returns #f, that match is considered
to have failed. The system backtracks into the matcher to look for
an alternative match; if none are forthcoming, the rule is not applicable. In the commutative law the restriction predicate expr<?
imposes an ordering on algebraic expressions. The reason for this
restriction is left as exercise 4.1.

Exercise 4.1: Guard expressions

Why is the (expr<? a b) restriction necessary in the commutative law?
What would go wrong if there were no restriction?

4.2.1   Segment variables in algebra

The algebra-2 rule system is far more interesting. It is built
with the assumption that addition and multiplication are *n*-ary
operations. We need segment variables to make this work. We
also use the number? predicate in variable restrictions to support
rules for numerical simplification.

```
(define algebra-2
  (rule-simplifier
   (list
    ;; Sums
    (rule '(+ (? a))
          a)                        ; unary + is identity
    (rule '(+ (?? a) (+ (?? b)) (?? c))
          '(+ ,@a ,@b ,@c))         ; associative: use n-ary +
    (rule '(+ (?? a) (? y) (? x) (?? b))
          (and (expr<? x y)         ; commutative
               '(+ ,@a ,x ,y ,@b)))

    ;; Products
    (rule '(* (? a))
          a)                        ; unary * is identity
    (rule '(* (?? a) (* (?? b)) (?? c))
          '(* ,@a ,@b ,@c))         ; associative: use n-ary *
    (rule '(* (?? a) (? y) (? x) (?? b))
          (and (expr<? x y)         ; commutative
               '(* ,@a ,x ,y ,@b)))

    ;; Distributive law
    (rule '(* (?? a) (+ (?? b)) (?? c))
          '(+ ,@(map (lambda (x) '(* ,@a ,x ,@c)) b)))
```

```
;; Numerical simplifications
(rule '(+ 0 (?? x))
      '(+ ,@x))
(rule '(+ (? x ,number?) (? y ,number?) (?? z))
      '(+ ,(+ x y) ,@z))
(rule '(* 0 (?? x))
      0)
(rule '(* 1 (?? x))
      '(* ,@x))
(rule '(* (? x ,number?) (? y ,number?) (?? z))
      '(* ,(* x y) ,@z))
)))
```

With `algebra-2` we implement some numerical simplifications, in addition to dealing with multiple arguments to sums and products. Notice that we used the backquote mechanism to build patterns that include the predicate `number?` as restrictions on the variables, in addition to its use for constructing the consequent expressions. For further understanding of the simplifier, see exercise 4.2.

Now we can get these results:

```
(algebra-2 '(* (+ y (+ z w)) x))
(+ (* w x) (* x y) (* x z))

(algebra-2 '(+ (* 3 (+ x 1)) -3))
(* 3 x)
```

At this point we can see how it may be possible to extend such a system to simplify large classes of algebraic expressions.

Exercise 4.2: Term ordering

According to the predicate `expr<?`, an expression that is explicitly a number is less than any expression that is not explicitly a number.

a. In `algebra-2` how does the ordering on expressions imposed by the commutative laws make the numerical simplification rules effective?

b. Suppose that the commutative laws did not force an ordering. How would we have to express the numerical simplification rules? Explain why numerical simplification would become very expensive.

Exercise 4.3: Sorting efficiency

The ordering in the commutative laws evolves an order n^2 bubble sort on the terms of a sum and the factors of a product. This can get pretty bad if there are many terms, as in a serious algebra problem. Is there some way in this system to make a more efficient sort? If not, why not? If so, how would you arrange it?

Exercise 4.4: Collecting terms

The system we have described does not collect like terms. For example:

```
(algebra-2 '(+ (* 4 x) (* 3 x)))
(+ (* 3 x) (* 4 x))
```

Make a new system `algebra-3` that includes rules that cause the collection of like terms, leaving the result as a sum of terms. Demonstrate your solution. Your solution must be able to handle problems like

```
(algebra-3
  '(+ y (* x -2 w) (* x 4 y) (* w x) z (* 5 z) (* x w) (* x y 3)))
(+ y (* 6 z) (* 7 x y))
```

4.2.2 Implementation of rule systems

Now that we have some experience with the use of a pattern-based rule system, let's dive in to see how it works.

We implement a rule as a procedure that matches the rule's pattern against a given expression. If the match succeeds, the rule evaluates its consequent in an environment in which the pattern variables are bound to their matched data. Rule procedures take success and failure continuations that can be used to backtrack into the consequent or pattern-match part of a rule.[2]

The `rule-simplifier` procedure used above is a constructor for a simple recursive simplifier. It produces `simplify-expression`, a procedure that takes an expression and uses the rules to simplify the expression. It recursively simplifies all the subexpressions of an expression and then applies the rules to simplify the resulting expression. It does this repeatedly until the process converges. Thus the expression returned is a fixed point of the simplification process.

---

[2]See section 5.4.2 on page 273 for more examples and explanation of this success/failure pattern.

```
(define (rule-simplifier the-rules)
  (define (simplify-expression expression)
    (let ((subexpressions-simplified
             (if (list? expression)
                 (map simplify-expression expression)
                 expression)))
      (try-rules subexpressions-simplified the-rules
        (lambda (result fail)    ; A: success continuation
          (simplify-expression result))
        (lambda ()               ; B: failure continuation
          subexpressions-simplified))))
  simplify-expression)
```

The procedure `try-rules` just scans the list of rules, sequencing the scan by means of the `succeed` and `fail` continuations.

```
(define (try-rules data rules succeed fail)
  (let per-rule ((rules rules))
    (if (null? rules)
        (fail)                  ; out of rules: go to B above
        (try-rule data
                  (car rules)
                  succeed       ; if rule succeeds go to A above
                  (lambda () ; if rule fails try other rules
                    (per-rule (cdr rules)))))))

(define (try-rule data rule succeed fail)
  (rule data succeed fail))
```

Rule construction is implemented by the procedure `make-rule`, which takes a rule pattern and a handler that implements the consequent expression. For example, the commutative law rule on page 161 can be made directly with make-rule:

```
(make-rule '(* (? b) (? a))
  (lambda (b a)
    (and (expr<? a b)
         '(* ,a ,b))))
```

The handler (lambda (b a) ...) needs to get arguments that are the values of the pattern variables named a and b from the dictionary produced by the matcher procedure. The rule applies the handler to a list of these values in the order in which they appear in the pattern. Thus the handler must be written with its parameters in that order.

The rule constructor `make-rule` compiles the pattern into a match procedure. The rule it returns is a procedure that uses that match procedure to match the data. If the match succeeds, the rule applies the handler to values of the pattern variables resulting from the match.

We will learn how a pattern is compiled into a match procedure in section 4.3; all we need to know here is that the match procedure can be run using `run-matcher` and that if the match succeeds, the third argument to `run-matcher` is called with a *dictionary*. The dictionary `dict` is a mapping of pattern variables to the subexpressions that they were matched against. If the match fails, `run-matcher` returns #f, and the rule fails.

```
(define (make-rule pattern handler)
  (let ((match-procedure (match:compile-pattern pattern)))
    (define (the-rule data succeed fail)
      (or (run-matcher match-procedure data
            (lambda (dict)
              (let ((result
                      (apply handler
                             (match:all-values dict))))
                (and result
                     (succeed result
                              (lambda () #f)))))))
          (fail)))
    the-rule))
```

The procedure `match:all-values` returns the values of the pattern variables in the order in which they appear in the pattern.

4.2.3   Aside: Magic macrology

Compare the rule definition given on page 161:

```
(rule '(* (? b) (? a))
      (and (expr<? a b)
           '(* ,a ,b)))
```

with what `make-rule` needs for its arguments:

```
(make-rule '(* (? b) (? a))
  (lambda (b a)
    (and (expr<? a b)
         '(* ,a ,b))))
```

The names a and b are repeated: they occur both in the pattern and in the parameter list of the handler, in the same order.

This is both obnoxious to write and error-prone, because we must remember to repeat the names, and we can make a mistake if we repeat them incorrectly or in the wrong order.

This is a case for syntactic abstraction, otherwise known as a *macro*. The following rather magical code fragment transforms the rule definition into the desired call to make-rule:

```
(define-syntax rule
  (er-macro-transformer
   (lambda (form rename compare)
     (let ((pattern (cadr form))
           (handler-body (caddr form))
           (r-make-rule (rename 'make-rule))
           (r-lambda (rename 'lambda)))
       `(,r-make-rule ,pattern
                      (,r-lambda
                       ,(match:pattern-names pattern)
                       ,handler-body)))))))
```

We can at least partially check this macro with the following magic incantation that expands the macros that appear in an expression:

```
(pp (syntax '(rule '(* (? b) (? a))
                   (and (expr<? a b)
                        `(* ,a ,b)))
            (the-environment)))
(make-rule '(* (? b) (? a))
           (lambda (b a)
             (and (expr<? a b)
                  (list '* a b))))
```

We see that the rule expands into a call to make-rule with the pattern and its handler procedure. This is the expression that is evaluated to make the rule. In more conventional languages, a macro, such as rule, expands directly into code that is substituted for the macro call. However, this process is not referentially transparent, because the macro expansion may use symbols that conflict with the user's symbols. In Scheme we try to avoid this problem, allowing a user to write *hygienic macros* that cannot cause conflicts. But this is more complicated than just substituting one expression for another. We will not try to explain the problems or the solutions here, but we will just use the solutions described in the MIT/GNU Scheme reference manual [51].

4.2.4   Pattern-directed invocation

The rule executive, `try-rules`, can also be used to implement procedures that use patterns for dispatching on input properties. The arguments to a pattern operator are matched against the pattern operator's rule pattern. The consequent of the matching rule computes the value to be returned.

For example, we could write the traditional factorial procedure, distributing the conditional as follows:

```
(define factorial
  (make-pattern-operator
   (rule '(0) 1)
   (rule '((? n ,positive?))
         (* n (factorial (- n 1))))))

(factorial 10)
3628800
```

We could also use this mechanism to build procedures whose behavior depends on the number of arguments supplied. For example, the Lisp – operator is negation when applied to one argument and subtraction when applied to multiple arguments:

```
(define -
  (make-pattern-operator
   (rule '((? x)) (n:- 0 x))
   (rule '((? x) (?? y)) (n:- x (apply n:+ y)))))
```

We can allow a pattern operator to be extended with additional rules dynamically. Such pattern operators are analogous to generic procedures, allowing the programmer to distribute the rule definitions nonlocally. For example, in a peephole optimizer we may want to group various optimizations with different parts of the code generator of a compiler.

```
(define peephole (make-pattern-operator))

(attach-rule! peephole
  (rule '((push (? reg1))
          (pop (? reg2)))
        (if (eqv? reg1 reg2)
            '()
            '((move ,reg1 ,reg2)))))
```

```
(attach-rule! peephole
  (rule '((or (? reg) (? const1 ,unsigned-integer?))
          (or (? reg) (? const2 ,unsigned-integer?)))
        '((or ,reg
              ,(bitwise-or const1 const2)))))
```

The first rule could be in the control-structure part of the optimizer, and the second rule could be located with the logical arithmetic part of the optimizer.

Here is one way to implement pattern operators. The last rule passed to `make-pattern-operator` is the *default* rule. It is always tried last, no matter what other rules may be added later.

```
(define (make-pattern-operator . rules)
  (let ((rules
          (cons 'rules
                (if (pair? rules)
                    (except-last-pair rules)
                    '())))
        (default-rule
          (and (pair? rules)
               (last rules))))
    (define (the-operator . data)
      (define (succeed value fail) value)
      (define (fail)
        (error "No applicable operations:" data))
      (try-rules data
                 (cdr rules)
                 succeed
                 (if default-rule
                     (lambda ()
                       (try-rule data
                                 default-rule
                                 succeed
                                 fail))
                     fail)))
    (set-pattern-metadata! the-operator rules)
    the-operator))
```

We use `set-pattern-metadata!` to attach the rule list as a "sticky note" to an operator, and we use `pattern-metadata` to retrieve it in the code below. We have procedures to add a rule to the front (`override-rule!`) or to the end (`attach-rule!`) of an operator's rule list:

```
(define (attach-rule! operator rule)
  (let ((metadata (pattern-metadata operator)))
    (set-cdr! metadata
              (append (cdr metadata)
                      (list rule)))))

(define (override-rule! operator rule)
  (let ((metadata (pattern-metadata operator)))
    (set-cdr! metadata
              (cons rule (cdr metadata)))))
```

4.3   Design of the matcher

Now that we have seen some of the power of pattern matching, we
will explore how it works. Our matcher is constructed from a family of match procedures (or *matchers*), and some combinators that
combine them to produce compound matchers.[3] Each primitive
element of the pattern is represented by a primitive matcher, and
the only combination, list, is represented by a combinator that
combines matchers for the list elements to make a compound one.

All match procedures take three arguments: a list containing
data to be matched, a dictionary of bindings of pattern variables,
and a continuation procedure (succeed) to be called if the match
is successful. The arguments to succeed must be the new dictionary resulting from the match and the number of items that
were consumed from the input list. This number will be used for
determining where to proceed after a segment match returns. A
match procedure returns #f if the match is unsuccessful.

There are three primitive match procedures and one combinator. Let's go through them. We will also need a small procedure
that we can pass to a match procedure as its succeed argument
to report the result:

```
(define (result-receiver dict n-eaten)
  `(success ,(match:bindings dict) ,n-eaten))
```

Pattern constants
The procedure match:eqv takes a pattern constant, such as x,
and produces a match procedure, eqv-match, that succeeds if and
only if the first data item is equal (using eqv?) to the pattern
constant. It does not add to the dictionary. The second argument

---

[3]This strategy for building pattern matchers was first described by Carl Hewitt
in his PhD thesis [56].

to `succeed` is the number of items matched, which is 1 for this match procedure.

```
(define (match:eqv pattern-constant)
  (define (eqv-match data dictionary succeed)
    (and (pair? data)
         (eqv? (car data) pattern-constant)
         (succeed dictionary 1)))
  eqv-match)
```

For example:

```
(define x-matcher (match:eqv 'x))

(x-matcher '(x) (match:new-dict) result-receiver)
(success () 1)

(x-matcher '(y) (match:new-dict) result-receiver)
#f
```

Element variables

The procedure `match:element` is used to make a match procedure, `element-match`, for a pattern variable, such as `(? x)`, that is intended to match a single item.

When matching an *element variable* there are two possibilities: either the element variable already has a value or it does not yet have a value. If the variable has a value, it is bound in the dictionary. In that case the match succeeds if and only if the binding's value is equal (using `equal?`) to the first data item. If the variable does not have a value, it is not bound. In that case the match succeeds, extending the dictionary by adding a binding of the variable to the first data item. In either case of success, we indicate that the number of items consumed is 1.

```
(define (match:element variable)
  (define (element-match data dictionary succeed)
    (and (pair? data)
         (let ((binding (match:lookup variable dictionary)))
           (if binding
               (and (equal? (match:binding-value binding)
                            (car data))
                    (succeed dictionary 1))
               (succeed (match:extend-dict variable
                                           (car data)
                                           dictionary)
                        1)))))
  element-match)
```

Here are some examples. A match binding is a list: the first element is the variable name; the second element is the value; and the third element is the variable's type (here all are ? element variables).

```
((match:element '(? x))
 '(a) (match:new-dict) result-receiver)
(success ((x a ?)) 1)

((match:element '(? x))
 '(a b) (match:new-dict) result-receiver)
(success ((x a ?)) 1)

((match:element '(? x))
 '((a b) c) (match:new-dict) result-receiver)
(success ((x (a b) ?)) 1)
```

Segment variables

The procedure `match:segment` is used to make a match procedure, `segment-match`, for a pattern variable, such as `(?? x)`, that is intended to match a sequence of items. A segment-variable matcher is more complicated than an element-variable matcher because it can consume an unknown number of data items. Thus a segment matcher must inform its caller not only of the new dictionary, but also of how many items from the data were eaten.

When matching a segment variable there are two possibilities: either the segment variable already has a value or it does not yet have a value. If the segment variable has a value, the value must match the data; this is checked by `match:segment-equal?` on page 174. If the segment variable does not yet have a value, it must be given one.

The matcher, `segment-match`, returned by `match:segment`, succeeds with some initial sublist of the data, `(list-head data i)`, as a possible assignment to the segment variable. (It starts with i=0, assuming that the segment will eat no items from the data.) However, if that success leads to a later failure in the match, the segment matcher tries to eat one more element than it had already tried (by executing `(lp (+ i 1))`). If the segment matcher runs out of data items, it fails to match. This is the key to the backtracking search that is needed when there are segment variables.

```
(define (match:segment variable)
  (define (segment-match data dictionary succeed)
    (and (list? data)
         (let ((binding (match:lookup variable dictionary)))
           (if binding
               (match:segment-equal?
                data
                (match:binding-value binding)
                (lambda (n) (succeed dictionary n)))
               (let ((n (length data)))
                 (let lp ((i 0))
                   (and (<= i n)
                        (or (succeed (match:extend-dict
                                      variable
                                      (list-head data i)
                                      dictionary)
                                     i)
                            (lp (+ i 1)))))))))))
  segment-match)
```

For example:

```
((match:segment '(?? a))
 '(z z z) (match:new-dict) result-receiver)
(success ((a () ??)) 0)
```

Of course, a zero-length segment is okay.

If we want to see all of the possible matches, we change the result receiver to return #f after printing the successful result. This causes the matcher procedure to come up with an alternative value, if possible.

```
(define (print-all-results dict n-eaten)
  (pp '(success ,(match:bindings dict) ,n-eaten))
  ;; by returning #f we force backtracking.
  #f)
```

```
((match:segment '(?? a))
 '(z z z) (match:new-dict) print-all-results)
(success ((a () ??)) 0)
(success ((a (z) ??)) 1)
(success ((a (z z) ??)) 2)
(success ((a (z z z) ??)) 3)
#f
```

Now, returning to the case of a segment variable that already has a value, we need to make sure that the value matches an initial segment of the data. This is handled by `match:segment-equal?`. It compares the elements of the value against the data. If that works, it returns by calling `ok` (the procedure passed as its third argument) with the number of elements consumed from the data (which must be the length of the value); otherwise it returns `#f`.

```
(define (match:segment-equal? data value ok)
  (let lp ((data data) (value value) (n 0))
    (cond ((pair? value)
           (if (and (pair? data)
                    (equal? (car data) (car value)))
               (lp (cdr data) (cdr value) (+ n 1))
               #f))
          ((null? value) (ok n))
          (else #f))))
```

Matching lists

Finally, there is the `match:list` combinator, which takes a list of match procedures and makes a match procedure that matches a data list if and only if the given matchers eat up all of the elements in the data list. It applies the matchers in succession. Each matcher tells the list combinator how many items to jump over before passing the remaining data to the next matcher.

```
(define (match:list matchers)
  (define (list-match data dictionary succeed)
    (and (pair? data)
         (let lp ((data-list (car data))
                  (matchers matchers)
                  (dictionary dictionary))
           (cond ((pair? matchers)
                  ((car matchers)
                   data-list
                   dictionary
                   (lambda (new-dictionary n)
                     ;; The essence of list matching:
                     (lp (list-tail data-list n)
                         (cdr matchers)
                         new-dictionary))))
                 ((pair? data-list) #f)   ;unmatched data
                 ((null? data-list) (succeed dictionary 1))
                 (else #f)))))
  list-match)
```

Notice that the matcher, `list-match`, returned by the `match:list` combinator has exactly the same interface as the other matchers, allowing it to be incorporated into a combination. The fact that all of the basic match procedures have exactly the same interface makes this a system of combinators.

Now we can make a matcher that matches a list of any number of elements, starting with the symbol a, ending with the symbol b, and with a segment variable (?? x) between them, by the combination:

```
((match:list (list (match:eqv 'a)
                   (match:segment '(?? x))
                   (match:eqv 'b)))
 '((a 1 2 b))
 (match:new-dict)
 result-receiver)
(success ((x (1 2) ??)) 1)
```

This was a successful match. The dictionary returned has exactly one entry: x=(1 2), and the match ate precisely one element (the list (a 1 2 b)) from the list supplied.

```
((match:list (list (match:eqv 'a)
                   (match:segment '(?? x))
                   (match:eqv 'b)))
 '((a 1 2 b 3))
 (match:new-dict)
 result-receiver)
#f
```

This was a failure, because there was nothing to match the 3 after the b in the input data.

The dictionary

The dictionary we will use is just a headed list of bindings. Each binding is a list of the variable's name, its value, and its type.

```
(define (match:new-dict)
  (list 'dict))

(define (match:bindings dict)
  (cdr dict))

(define (match:new-bindings dict bindings)
  (cons 'dict bindings))
```

```
(define (match:extend-dict var value dict)
  (match:new-bindings dict
                      (cons (match:make-binding var value)
                            (match:bindings dict))))

(define (match:lookup var dict)
  (let ((name
         (if (symbol? var)
             var
             (match:var-name var))))
    (find (lambda (binding)
            (eq? name (match:binding-name binding)))
          (match:bindings dict))))

(define (match:make-binding var value)
  (list (match:var-name var)
        value
        (match:var-type var)))

(define match:binding-name car)
(define match:binding-type caddr)

(define match:binding-value
  (simple-generic-procedure 'match:binding-value 1 cadr))
```

The accessor `match:binding-value` is just `cadr`, but is made generic to allow future extensions. This will be needed in the code supporting section 4.5.

4.3.1   Compiling patterns

We can automate the construction of pattern matchers from patterns with an elementary compiler. The compiler produces as its value a match procedure appropriate for the pattern it is given, which has exactly the same interface as the elementary matchers given above.

The match-procedure interface is convenient for composing matchers, but not very friendly to humans. For playing with the matcher it is more convenient to use:

```
(define (run-matcher match-procedure datum succeed)
  (match-procedure (list datum)
                   (match:new-dict)
                   (lambda (dict n)
                     (and (= n 1)
                          (succeed dict)))))
```

With this interface we are hiding several details about match procedures: we wrap the incoming datum in a list; we check that exactly one element of that list (the datum) has been matched; and we provide the initial dictionary.

Some simple examples are:

```
(run-matcher
 (match:compile-pattern '(a ((? b) 2 3) (? b) c))
 '(a (1 2 3) 2 c)
 match:bindings)
#f
```

```
(run-matcher
 (match:compile-pattern '(a ((? b) 2 3) (? b) c))
 '(a (1 2 3) 1 c)
 match:bindings)
((b 1 ?))
```

As we saw before, some patterns involving segment variables may match in many ways, and we can elicit all of the matches by failing back into the matcher to select the next one, until they are all exhausted:

```
(run-matcher
 (match:compile-pattern '(a (?? x) (?? y) (?? x) c))
 '(a b b b b b b c)
 print-all-matches)
((y (b b b b b)) ??) (x () ??))
((y (b b b b)) ??) (x (b) ??))
((y (b b)) ??) (x (b b) ??))
((y () ??) (x (b b b) ??))
#f
```

The possible matches require both instances of (?? x) to match the same data.

The procedure `print-all-matches` prints the bindings and forces a failure.

```
(define (print-all-matches dict)
  (pp (match:bindings dict))
  #f)
```

To make this compiler we need to define the syntax of pattern variables. For now we have a very simple syntax: a pattern variable is a list of the type (? or ??) and the name.

```
(define (match:var-type var)
  (car var))

(define (match:var-type? object)
  (memq object match:var-types))

(define match:var-types '(? ??))

(define (match:named-var? object)
  (and (pair? object)
       (match:var-type? (car object))
       (n:>= (length object) 2)
       (symbol? (cadr object))))

(define (match:element-var? object)
  (and (match:var? object)
       (eq? '? (match:var-type object))))

(define (match:segment-var? object)
  (and (match:var? object)
       (eq? '?? (match:var-type object))))
```

This code is more complex than one might expect, because we
will extend the variable syntax in section 4.5 and some of the
exercises.

```
(define match:var-name
  (simple-generic-procedure 'match:var-name 1
    (constant-generic-procedure-handler #f)))

(define-generic-procedure-handler match:var-name
  (match-args match:named-var?)
  cadr)
```

The default handler is a procedure that always returns false, and
at this time there is only one substantive handler, which retrieves
the name of a named variable.

We also make the predicate that determines if its argument is
a match variable generic, although at this time the only objects
that satisfy match:var? are named variables.

```
(define match:var?
  (simple-generic-procedure 'match:var? 1
    (constant-generic-procedure-handler #f)))

(define-generic-procedure-handler match:var?
  (match-args match:named-var?)
  (constant-generic-procedure-handler #t))
```

The compiler maps a pattern to the corresponding matcher:

```
(define (match:compile-pattern pattern)
  (cond ((match:var? pattern)
         (case (match:var-type pattern)
           ((?) (match:element pattern))
           ((??) (match:segment pattern))
           (else (error "Unknown var type:" pattern))))
        ((list? pattern)
         (match:list (map match:compile-pattern pattern)))
        (else   ; constant
         (match:eqv pattern)))))
```

By varying this compiler, we can change the syntax of patterns
any way we like.

```
(run-matcher
 (match:compile-pattern '(a ((? b) 2 3) (? b) c))
 '(a (1 2 3) 1 c)
 match:bindings)
((b 1 ?))
```

Exercise 4.5: Backtracking

In the example on page 177 we got multiple matches, by returning #f
from the success procedure print-all-matches. This is probably pretty
mysterious. How does it work? Explain, in a short but clear paragraph,
how the sequence of matches is generated.

4.3.2   Match-variable restrictions

Often we want to restrict the kind of object that can be matched
by a pattern variable. For example, we may want to make a
pattern in which a variable can match only a positive integer.
One way to do this, which we used in our term-rewriting system in
section 4.2.1, is to allow a variable to carry a predicate for testing
the datum for acceptability. For example, we may be interested in
finding positive integer powers of sine functions. We could write
the pattern we want as follows:

```
'(expt (sin (? x)) (? n ,exact-positive-integer?))
```

We cannot use simple quotation for such a pattern, because the
predicate expression (here exact-positive-integer?) must be
evaluated before being included in the pattern. As in term rewriting (section 4.2), we use the backquote mechanism to do this.

To make a matcher that can check that data satisfies such a predicate, we add a single line to `match:element`:

```
(define (match:element variable)
  (define (element-match data dictionary succeed)
    (and (pair? data)
         (match:satisfies-restriction? variable (car data))
         (let ((binding (match:lookup variable dictionary)))
           (if binding
               (and (equal? (match:binding-value binding)
                            (car data))
                    (succeed dictionary 1))
               (succeed (match:extend-dict variable
                                           (car data)
                                           dictionary)
                        1)))))
  element-match)

(define (match:satisfies-restriction? var value)
  (or (not (match:var-has-restriction? var))
      ((match:var-restriction var) value)))
```

Exercise 4.6: Pattern alternatives: choice is good

An interesting way to extend our pattern language is to introduce a choice operator:

```
(?:choice pattern ...)
```

This should compile into a matcher that tries to match each of the given *pattern*s in order from left to right, returning the first successful match, or `#f` if none match. (This should remind you of regular expression "alternation" (see page 40), but the name "choice" is more traditional in pattern matching.)

For example:

```
(run-matcher
 (match:compile-pattern '(?:choice a b (? x) c))
 'z
 match:bindings)
((x z ?))

(run-matcher
 (match:compile-pattern
  '((? y) (?:choice a b (? x ,string?) (? y ,symbol?) c)))
 '(z z)
 match:bindings)
((y z ?))
```

```
(run-matcher
 (match:compile-pattern '(?:choice b (? x ,symbol?)))
  'b
  print-all-matches)
()
((x b ?))
 #f
```

To do: Implement a new matcher procedure, `match:choice`, for this new pattern schema. Augment the pattern compiler appropriately.

Exercise 4.7: Naming in patterns

Another extension is to provide named patterns, analogous to Scheme's `letrec`.

Naming allows shorter, more modular patterns while also supporting recursive subpatterns, including mutually recursive subpatterns.

For instance, the pattern:

```
(?:pletrec ((odd-even-etc (?:choice () (1 (?:ref even-odd-etc))))
            (even-odd-etc (?:choice () (2 (?:ref odd-even-etc)))))
   (?:ref odd-even-etc))
```

should match all lists of the following form (including the empty list):

```
(1 (2 (1 (2 (1 ...))))))
```

Here, `?:pletrec` introduces a block of mutually recursive pattern definitions while `?:ref` substitutes a defined pattern in place (in order to distinguish such references from literal symbols like a and from pattern variables like (? x)).

To do: Implement these new `?:pletrec` and `?:ref` pattern schemas. One approach is to implement new matcher procedures, `match:pletrec` and `match:ref`, then augment the pattern compiler appropriately. Other approaches may also work. Explain your approach briefly if it is subtle or non-obvious.

To think (before you do!): In a proper environment-based `letrec`-like implementation, nested `?:pletrec` instances would introduce distinct contour lines for scoping. But the control structure of our pattern matcher does not make this easy.

The matcher procedures traverse the pattern and data in left-to-right depth-first order, binding the first textual appearance of each distinct pattern variable (like (? x)) to its corresponding datum and then treating each subsequent textual appearance in the pattern as a constraining instance. This is achieved by threading the dictionary through the depth-first control path. Pay particular attention to the appearance of `new-dictionary` in the body of `match:list`. This control structure, in essence, decrees that the leftmost, deepest instance of each unique pattern variable is a defining instance in an implicit flat global name-space, with all subsequent downstream appearances being constraining instances.

So let's not worry about that scoping complexity in this exercise. Specifically, just as pattern variables all share a common global name-space, so too can your pattern definitions.

Of course, if you are really ambitious, you can implement lexical scop-ing by rewriting all the existing matcher interfaces to accept an extra **pattern-environment** parameter. But that is a job for another time and place (in exercise 4.9).

Exercise 4.8: Hoist by our own petard

On the surface it may appear that it would be easy to extend this matcher system to allow vector patterns and vector data. But we made a strong assumption in the design of this matcher—that it is a matcher of list patterns on list data.

a. What would it take to liberate this code from that assumption so that you could make a matcher that encompassed both kinds of compound data? Or arbitrary sequences? What sorts of changes are required? Do you need to change the interface to a match procedure?

b. Make it so! (This is lots of work.)

Exercise 4.9: General pattern language

Even with the addition of **?:pletrec** and **?:ref** in exercise 4.7, the pattern matcher we have is not a complete language, in that it does not support namespace scoping and parametric patterns. For example, we cannot write the following pattern, which is intended to match only lists of symbols that are palindromes.

```
(?:pletrec ((palindrome
             (?:pnew (x)
               (?:choice ()
                         ((? x ,symbol?)
                          (?:ref palindrome)
                          (? x))))))
  (?:ref palindrome))
```

For this to work in any reasonable way, **?:pnew** creates fresh lexically scoped pattern variables that can be referred to only in the body of the **?:pnew**.

A fully worked-out pattern language is a wonderful subsystem to have, but it is not easy to build.

To do: Flesh out this idea to produce a full pattern language. Not for the faint of heart!

4.4   Unification match

Pattern matching is, as we have said, a kind of equality testing between structured data items. It is a generalization of equality testing because we allow some parts of the data to be unspecified, by allowing pattern variables that match the unspecified parts of the data. But we require that every occurrence of the same pattern variable must match equivalent data.

So far our matchers have been one-sided: we match a pattern with variables against data that contains no variables, producing a dictionary—a map from each variable in the pattern to a matching piece of the data. If we substitute the matching value for each variable into the original pattern we make a *substitution instance* of the pattern. The resulting instance is always equivalent to the original data.

We are about to remove the limitation that the data has no variables: we will allow variables on both sides of the match. This powerful kind of match is called *unification*. The result of a successful unification is also a dictionary, but the values for variables may contain variables, and the dictionary may not give values for every variable in the patterns. If we substitute the values associated with variables in the dictionary for variables that appear in either of the two given patterns, we obtain a substitution instance of both initial patterns. This substitution instance, which may contain variables, is called the *unifier* of the patterns. The unifier is the most general common substitution instance of the two patterns: any other common substitution instance of the two patterns is a substitution instance of the unifier. The unifier is unique, up to renaming of the variables, so unification is well defined.[4]

Unification was first described by J. A. Robinson in his famous invention of the resolution procedure for theorem proving [104].[5]

For a simple example, suppose we have several sources of partial information about Ben Franklin's dates of birth and death:

---

[4]The unifier is unique for patterns with only element variables. This is a theorem; we will not prove it here. In section 4.4.4 we will extend our unifier to include segment variables. However, when the patterns have segment variables, unification will generally yield multiple matches.

[5]For an extensive survey of unification see [6].

```
(define a
  '(((? gn) franklin) (? bdate) ((? dmo) (? dday) 1790)))

(define b
  '((ben franklin) ((? bmo) 6 1705) (apr 17 (? dyear))))

(define c
  '((ben (? fn)) (jan (? bday) 1705) (apr 17 (? dyear))))
```

The unification of two expressions will give us a dictionary of the values of the variables that are derived from the match. We can use that dictionary to construct the unifier of the two patterns:

```
(unifier a b)
```
((ben franklin) ((? bmo) 6 1705) (apr 17 1790))

```
(unifier a c)
```
((ben franklin) (jan (? bday) 1705) (apr 17 1790))

```
(unifier b c)
```
((ben franklin) (jan 6 1705) (apr 17 (? dyear)))

Each of these results is more fully specified than the partial information provided by any source. We can further combine all three sources to get a full picture:

```
(unifier a (unifier b c))
```
((ben franklin) (jan 6 1705) (apr 17 1790))

```
(unifier b (unifier a c))
```
((ben franklin) (jan 6 1705) (apr 17 1790))

```
(unifier c (unifier a b))
```
((ben franklin) (jan 6 1705) (apr 17 1790))

Often there are constraints among the variables in an expression. For example, there may be multiple instances of the same variable, which must remain consistent, as in the following derivation:

```
(define addition-commutativity
  '(= (+ (? u) (? v)) (+ (? v) (? u))))

(unifier '(= (+ (cos (? a)) (exp (? b))) (? c))
         addition-commutativity)
```
(= (+ (cos (? a)) (exp (? b))) (+ (exp (? b)) (cos (? a))))

4.4.1 How unification works

We can think of unification as a kind of equation solving. If we think of the patterns as structured partial information, unifying them is testing the proposition that the two patterns are partial information about the same thing. For the patterns to unify, the corresponding parts must unify. So unification is setting up equations among the corresponding parts and solving for the unknowns (the pieces of information left unspecified in each pattern).

The process is analogous to the way we solve numerical equations. The goal is to eliminate as many variables in the equations as we can. The result is a list of substitutions of expressions for the eliminated variables. No substitution expression may refer to any eliminated variable. We scan the equations for one that can be solved for one of the variables in it. Solving for a variable isolates it, finding an equivalent expression that does not contain the variable. We eliminate the variable by replacing all occurrences of it with the newly discovered value (the equivalent expression), both in the remaining equations and in the values associated with previously eliminated variables in the substitution list. We then add the new substitution to the substitution list. We repeat until there are no more equations to be solved or we encounter a contradiction. The result is either a successful substitution list or a report of the contradiction.

In unification the "equations" are the matches of the corresponding parts of the two input patterns, and the "substitution list" is the dictionary. One way to implement unification is to walk the common structure of the input patterns. As in one-sided matching, the patterns are represented by list structure. If a variable is encountered on either side of the match, it is bound, in the dictionary, to the data on the other side.

If there are multiple occurrences of a variable in the original patterns, each subsequent occurrence must match the value bound by the first occurrence. This is ensured by the fact that every time a variable is encountered, it is looked up in the dictionary, and if there is a binding for the variable, its value is used instead of the variable. Also, every time a new binding is made and entered into the dictionary, the new binding is used to replace all instances of the newly eliminated variable in the values for other variables in the dictionary.

To obtain the `unifier` of two patterns we `unify` them to get the dictionary of substitutions, if they can be unified. If not, `unify` returns `#f`, indicating a failure. The dictionary is then used to instantiate one of the patterns; it doesn't matter which is chosen. The procedure `match:dict-substitution` replaces every instance of a variable in the pattern expression `pattern1` that has a binding in the dictionary `dict` with its value in the dictionary.

```
(define (unifier pattern1 pattern2)
  (let ((dict (unify pattern1 pattern2)))
    (and dict
         ((match:dict-substitution dict) pattern1))))
```

The main interface to the unifier is `unify`, which returns the dictionary result of a successful match, or `#f` if the match was unsuccessful.

```
(define (unify pattern1 pattern2)
  (unify:internal pattern1 pattern2
                  (match:new-dict)
                  (lambda (dict) dict)))
```

The `unify:internal` entry point gives more control of the matching process. It takes the two patterns to be unified, a dictionary that may have some bindings specified, and a success continuation (`succeed`) that will be called if the match succeeds. The success continuation provided by `unify`, above, just returns the dictionary. In section 4.4.4, when we add code to experiment with segment variables in the patterns, we will be able to extract multiple matches by returning `#f` from `succeed`, indicating that the result was not the one wanted. The ability to backtrack into the matcher also simplifies other interesting semantic extensions, such as incorporating algebraic expressions and equation solving into the match process.[6]

---

[6] In the guts of this unifier it is convenient for a failure to make an explicit call to a failure continuation. But in `unify:internal` we transition to a different convention for indicating a failure: returning `#f` from a success continuation. This is to make the convention for use of the unifier the same as the convention for use of the matcher of section 4.3.

This is an interesting transition. In the rule system in section 4.2.2 we used explicit success and failure continuations, so to use the matcher in the rule system we had to make the reverse transition: the matcher used the `#f` convention, so `make-rule` (on page 166) had to implement the transition.

In `unify:internal` the patterns to be unified, `pattern1` and `pattern2`, are wrapped in lists. The unifier program will compare these lists term by term, building a dictionary that makes corresponding terms equal. The match succeeds if both lists of terms are simultaneously exhausted. At the top level, in `unify:internal`, the term lists just contain the two given patterns, but the central unification procedure, `unify:dispatch`, will recursively descend into the pattern, comparing subpatterns of the patterns as lists of terms.[7]

```
(define (unify:internal pattern1 pattern2 dict succeed)
  ((unify:dispatch (list pattern1) (list pattern2))
   dict
   (lambda (dict fail rest1 rest2)
     (or (and (null? rest1) (null? rest2)
              (succeed dict))
         (fail)))
   (lambda () #f)))
```

The procedure `unify:dispatch`, which takes two input lists of terms, is the core of the recursive descent matcher. The match process depends on the contents of the term lists. For example, if both term lists begin with a constant, as in `(ben franklin)` and `(ben (? fn))`, the constants must be compared, and the match can proceed only if the constants are equal. If one term list begins with a variable, the other can begin with any term, and the variable must be bound to the term it matches. (If both are variables, one of the variables will be eliminated in favor of the other.) So, if one term list is `((? bmo) 6 1705)` and the other is `(jan (? bday) 1705)`, then the variable `(? bmo)` must be bound to the value `jan` for the match to proceed. If both term lists start with a list that is not a variable, the match must recursively match the corresponding sublists before proceeding to match the rest of the given term lists. For example, in unifying b and c in the Ben Franklin example, after the first terms are matched the dictionary contains

---

The choice of convention for implementing failure in a backtracking system is usually a matter of style, but the use of an explicit failure continuation is often easier to extend. Luckily, it is easy to interface these disparate ways of implementing backtracking.

[7]As in the pattern matching system described in section 4.3, the unification matcher is organized around lists of terms to allow later extension to segment variables.

a binding of fn to franklin and the remaining termlists are (((?
bmo) 6 1705) (apr 17 (? dyear))) and ((jan (? bday) 1705)
(apr 17 (? dyear))). Both of these term lists begin with a list,
so the matching must recurse to compare the sublists ((? bmo) 6
1705) and (jan (? bday) 1705).

The procedure unify-dispatcher returned by unify:dispatch
takes three arguments: a dictionary, a success continuation, and a
failure continuation. If both term lists are exhausted, the match
succeeds. If there are more terms to be matched, the generic
procedure unify:gdispatch calls an appropriate match procedure
that depends on the contents of the two term lists. If the match
succeeds, it means that the initial terms of the two term lists
could be unified relative to the given dictionary. So the success
continuation is called with the new dictionary dict*, a new failure
continuation fail*, and the unmatched tails, rest1 and rest2, of
the input lists. These tails are then matched by a recursive call
to unify:dispatch.

```
(define (unify:dispatch terms1 terms2)
  (define (unify-dispatcher dict succeed fail)
    (if (and (null? terms1) (null? terms2))
        (succeed dict fail terms1 terms2)
        ((unify:gdispatch terms1 terms2)
         dict
         (lambda (dict* fail* rest1 rest2)
           ((unify:dispatch rest1 rest2)
            dict* succeed fail*))
         fail)))
  unify-dispatcher)
```

The generic procedure unify:gdispatch has handlers for the
cases described above: matching two constants, matching two
term lists, and matching a variable to something. (Because it
is generic, it can be extended for new kinds of matching.) The
default handler, for cases such as matching a constant to a term
list, is unify:fail:

```
(define (unify:fail terms1 terms2)
  (define (unify-fail dict succeed fail)
    (fail))
  unify-fail)

(define unify:gdispatch
  (simple-generic-procedure 'unify 2 unify:fail))
```

In this unifier the term lists are matched term by term, so the job of a handler is to match the first terms of the two term lists. Thus the applicability of a handler depends only on the first term of each term list. To simplify the applicability specification we introduce `car-satisfies`, which takes a predicate and produces a new predicate ensuring that there is a first term in the list and that term satisfies the argument predicate.

```
(define (car-satisfies pred)
  (lambda (terms)
    (and (pair? terms)
         (pred (car terms)))))
```

Any term that is not a match variable or a list is a constant. Constants match only when they are equal:

```
(define (unify:constant-terms terms1 terms2)
  (let ((first1 (car terms1)) (rest1 (cdr terms1))
        (first2 (car terms2)) (rest2 (cdr terms2)))
    (define (unify-constants dict succeed fail)
      (if (eqv? first1 first2)
          (succeed dict fail rest1 rest2)
          (fail)))
    unify-constants))

(define (constant-term? term)
  (and (not (match:var? term))
       (not (list? term))))

(define-generic-procedure-handler unify:gdispatch
  (match-args (car-satisfies constant-term?)
              (car-satisfies constant-term?))
  unify:constant-terms)
```

The handler `unify:list-terms` is where the recursive descent actually happens. Because the first term of each term list is itself a list, the matcher must recurse to match those sublists. If the match of the sublists succeeds, the match must continue with the rest of the input termlists. (Note that the recursive match will succeed only if all of the terms of the two sublists match; so the unmatched sublist tails passed to the success continuation will be empty and are ignored.)

```
(define (unify:list-terms terms1 terms2)
  (let ((first1 (car terms1)) (rest1 (cdr terms1))
        (first2 (car terms2)) (rest2 (cdr terms2)))
    (define (unify-lists dict succeed fail)
      ((unify:dispatch first1 first2)
       dict
       (lambda (dict* fail* null1 null2)
         (succeed dict* fail* rest1 rest2))
       fail))
    unify-lists))

(define (list-term? term)
  (and (not (match:var? term))
       (list? term)))

(define-generic-procedure-handler unify:gdispatch
  (match-args (car-satisfies list-term?)
              (car-satisfies list-term?))
  unify:list-terms)
```

So far our code implements recursive descent and the matching
of constants. Obvious contradictions like matching two different
symbols or a symbol to a list produce a failure. In order to solve
interesting equations we must be able to match terms with variables. When we find variables, we may add new bindings to the
dictionary. The part of the equation solver that deals with variables is the procedure `maybe-substitute`.

The procedure `maybe-substitute` gets one term list `var-first`
that starts with a variable. It matches that variable with the first
term of the second term list, `terms`.

If a variable is matched against itself we have a tautology, and
the match succeeds with an unchanged dictionary. If the variable already has a value, we replace the variable with its value
and match the resulting list against the term list `terms`. Finally,
if the variable does not have a value, we can eliminate it using
`do-substitute`, which is responsible for adding a binding from
`var` to `term` when possible.

```
(define (maybe-substitute var-first terms)
  (define (unify-substitute dict succeed fail)
    (let ((var (car var-first)) (rest1 (cdr var-first))
          (term (car terms)) (rest2 (cdr terms)))
      (cond ((and (match:element-var? term)
                  (match:vars-equal? var term))
             (succeed dict fail rest1 rest2))
            ((match:has-binding? var dict)
             ((unify:dispatch
               (cons (match:get-value var dict) rest1)
               terms)
              dict succeed fail))
            (else
             (let ((dict* (do-substitute var term dict)))
               (if dict*
                   (succeed dict* fail rest1 rest2)
                   (fail))))))))
  unify-substitute)
```

In do-substitute we first use the old dictionary to clean the incoming term by replacing any previously eliminated variables with their values. Then we check if there are any restrictions on what objects var may match. Finally we check for any occurrences of var in the cleaned term (term*). If the cleaned term contains a reference to var, the match cannot proceed.[8] If our match passes all these tests, we make a new dictionary that includes the new binding of var to the cleaned term. The binding values in the new dictionary must also be cleaned of references to var.

---

[8] In the unification literature this is called the "occurs check." The occurs check is used to prevent trying to obtain a solution to an equation like $x = f(x)$. Such a fixed-point equation may be solvable, in some cases, if we know more about the function f, but this unifier is a *syntactic* matcher. One could put in a hook at this point to ask for a more powerful equation solver to help, but we are not doing that. Most Prolog systems avoid implementing the occurs check for efficiency reasons.

```
(define (do-substitute var term dict)
  (let ((term* ((match:dict-substitution dict) term)))
    (and (match:satisfies-restriction? var term*)
         (or (and (match:var? term*)
                  (match:vars-equal? var term*))
             (not (match:occurs-in? var term*)))
         (match:extend-dict var term*
           (match:map-dict-values
            (match:single-substitution var term*)
            dict)))))
```

Now that we know how to handle variables we just have to install this handler in our generic dispatcher procedure. The only subtlety here is that the variable to be eliminated may appear in either term list. We must guarantee that the term list containing the variable is the first argument to `maybe-substitute`.

```
(define (element? term)
  (any-object? term))

(define-generic-procedure-handler unify:gdispatch
  (match-args (car-satisfies match:element-var?)
              (car-satisfies element?))
  (lambda (var-first terms)
    (maybe-substitute var-first terms)))

(define-generic-procedure-handler unify:gdispatch
  (match-args (car-satisfies element?)
              (car-satisfies match:element-var?))
  (lambda (terms var-first)
    (maybe-substitute var-first terms)))
```

At this point we have a complete, correct, and competent traditional unifier.[9] It is written with generic procedures, so it can easily be extended to work with other kinds of data. And with only a small amount of work we can add semantic attachments, such as the commutativity of lists beginning with the symbols + and *. As we shall see, we can also add support for new kinds of syntactic variables, such as segment variables. But before we do that we will look at a real application: type inference.

---

[9]Because unification is so important, there has been a great deal of work developing efficient algorithms. Memoization can be used to make large improvements. For an extensive exposition of unification algorithms see [6].

Exercise 4.10: Unifying vectors

This unifier can be extended to handle data and patterns that are made of other data types, such as vectors. Make handlers for vectors without transforming the vectors to lists (the easy way out!).

Exercise 4.11: Unifying strings

Extend the unifier to allow unification of strings. This could be fun, but you need to invent a syntactic mechanism for representing string variables inside a string. This is pretty delicate, because you may have to represent a string variable with a string expression. This gets into quotation problems—please try not to invent a baroque mechanism. Also, make sure that you don't make assumptions that will prevent you from introducing string segment variables later. (See exercise 4.21 on page 209.)

Exercise 4.12: Variable restrictions

We added support for restrictions on variables as we did in the one-sided matcher: we just put a clause for that into the main conditional in the procedure `do-substitute`. But there are subtle problems.

- What should happen if a restricted variable is matched against another restricted variable?

- When the variable is first bound to its target, after passing the restriction, it is uniformly eliminated. But the restriction is then lost, preventing it from killing an unsuitable later part of the match.

Your task is to understand these problems and determine how to ameliorate them. How important could this be for any applications you might consider? Is there a solution that fits nicely into our implementation strategy?

Exercise 4.13: Unifying with pattern combinators?

Unlike our earlier one-sided pattern matcher, our unification matcher does not compile the patterns into match procedures that combine to build a match procedure for the pattern. But a system of match procedures is potentially more efficient, because it avoids the syntactic analysis of the patterns while matching. Can the unification matcher be broken up in a similar way? If not, why not? Is it a good idea to do so? If not, why not? If so, do it! (This is hard!)

4.4.2 Application: Type inference

One classic application of unification matching is type inference: given a program and some type information about parts of the program, deduce type information about other parts of the program. For example, if we know that < is a procedure that takes two numerical arguments and produces a boolean value, then if we analyze the expression (g (< x (f y))), we can deduce that f and g are unary procedures; g accepts a boolean argument; f returns a numerical value; and x has a numerical value. If this information is used to deduce properties of the program that the expression is embedded in, we can learn a great deal about the program. Here is an analysis of the expression:

```
(pp (infer-program-types '(g (< x (f y)))))
(t (? type:17)
   ((t (type:procedure ((boolean-type)) (? type:17)) g)
    (t (boolean-type)
       ((t (type:procedure ((numeric-type) (numeric-type))
                           (boolean-type))
          <)
        (t (numeric-type) x)
        (t (numeric-type)
           ((t (type:procedure ((? y:12)) (numeric-type)) f)
            (t (? y:12) y)))))))
```

This is the abstract tree of the given expression, annotated with types. Each subexpression *x* has been expanded into a *typed expression* of the form (t *type x*). For example, the reference to g has the type:

```
(type:procedure ((boolean-type)) (? type:17))
```

As expected, g is a procedure that accepts a boolean argument, but we have no information about its value. The unknown value type is represented by the pattern variable (? type:17).

Let's consider a more substantial example:

```
(define foo
  (infer-program-types
   '(define fact
      (lambda (n)
        (begin
          (define iter
            (lambda (product counter)
              (if (> counter n)
                  product
                  (iter (* product counter)
                        (+ counter 1)))))
          (iter 1 1))))))
```

The result in foo is rather verbose. So we look at it with a simplifier that puts it into "human readable" form.

```
(pp (simplify-annotated-program foo))
(begin
 (define fact
   (lambda (n)
     (declare-type n (numeric-type))
     (define iter
       (lambda (product counter)
         (declare-type product (numeric-type))
         (declare-type counter (numeric-type))
         (if (> counter n)
             product
             (iter (* product counter)
                   (+ counter 1)))))
     (declare-type iter
       (type:procedure ((numeric-type) (numeric-type))
                       (numeric-type)))
     (iter 1 1)))
 (declare-type fact
   (type:procedure ((numeric-type)) (numeric-type))))
```

Here we see that the type inference program was able to determine the complete type of the factorial program—that it is a procedure that takes one numerical input and produces a numerical output. This is reported in a declaration:

```
(declare-type fact
  (type:procedure ((numeric-type)) (numeric-type)))
```

The type of the internal definition iter has also been determined: it takes two numerical arguments and produces a numerical result.

```
(declare-type iter
  (type:procedure ((numeric-type) (numeric-type))
                  (numeric-type)))
```

Also, the type of each internal variable has been determined, and an appropriate declaration has been posted:

```
(declare-type n (numeric-type))
(declare-type product (numeric-type))
(declare-type counter (numeric-type))
```

4.4.3 How type inference works

The process of type inference has four phases.

1. The given program is annotated with type variables for all subexpressions of the program.
2. Constraints on the type variables are formulated based on the semantic structure of the program.
3. The constraints are unified to eliminate as many of the variables as possible.
4. The annotated program is specialized using the dictionary produced by unification of the constraints to make a new annotated program whose type annotations incorporate the constraints.

The plan is implemented in this procedure:

```
(define (infer-program-types expr)
  (let ((texpr (annotate-program expr)))
    (let ((constraints (program-constraints texpr)))
      (let ((dict (unify-constraints constraints)))
        (if dict
            ((match:dict-substitution dict) texpr)
            '***type-error***)))))
```

This procedure complains if the program expression cannot be consistently typed. However, it gives no explanation about why it failed; this could be accomplished by passing information back in the failure continuations.

Annotation

The `annotate-program` procedure is implemented in terms of a generic procedure, `annotate-expr`, to allow easy extension for new language features.

```
(define (annotate-program expr)
  (annotate-expr expr (top-level-env)))

(define annotate-expr
  (simple-generic-procedure 'annotate-expr 2 #f))
```

The `annotate-expr` procedure takes an environment for bindings of the type variables. It is initialized with the top-level environment created below.

There are simple handlers for annotating simple kinds of expressions. If an explicit number appears as a subexpression it is given a constant type, constructed by (numeric-type):

```
(define-generic-procedure-handler annotate-expr
  (match-args number? any-object?)
  (lambda (expr env)
    (make-texpr (numeric-type) expr)))
```

The procedure make-texpr constructs a typed expression from a type and an expression. Its parts can be selected with texpr-type and texpr-expr.

However, we may not a priori know a type for an identifier, which is represented by a symbol. The procedure get-var-type tries to find the identifier's type in the environment, and failing that, creates a unique type variable for the type annotation of all occurrences of the identifier in that lexical context:

```
(define-generic-procedure-handler annotate-expr
  (match-args symbol? any-object?)
  (lambda (expr env)
    (make-texpr (get-var-type expr env) expr)))
```

We may know types for some identifiers, such as primitive procedures of the language. These are provided in the top-level environment. The primitive procedures shown here have procedure types with type constants (e.g., (numeric-type)) for their arguments and values:

```
(define (top-level-env)
  (list (make-top-level-env-frame)))

(define (make-top-level-env-frame)
  (let ((binary-numerical
         (let ((v (numeric-type)))
           (procedure-type (list v v) v)))
        (binary-comparator
         (let ((v (numeric-type)))
           (procedure-type (list v v) (boolean-type)))))
    (list (cons '+ binary-numerical)
          ...
          (cons '= binary-comparator)
          (cons '< binary-comparator)
          ...)))
```

For a conditional expression, a type variable is created for the value of the conditional expression, and each subexpression is recursively annotated:

```
(define-generic-procedure-handler annotate-expr
  (match-args if-expr? any-object?)
  (lambda (expr env)
    (make-texpr (type-variable)
        (make-if-expr
         (annotate-expr (if-predicate expr) env)
         (annotate-expr (if-consequent expr) env)
         (annotate-expr (if-alternative expr) env)))))
```

There are annotation handlers for every kind of expression. We will not show all of them, but the annotation of a lambda expression is interesting:

```
(define-generic-procedure-handler annotate-expr
  (match-args lambda-expr? any-object?)
  (lambda (expr env)
    (let ((env* (new-frame (lambda-bvl expr) env)))
      (make-texpr
       (procedure-type (map (lambda (name)
                               (get-var-type name env*))
                            (lambda-bvl expr))
                       (type-variable))
       (make-lambda-expr (lambda-bvl expr)
                         (annotate-expr (lambda-body expr)
                                        env*))))))
```

Just as in an interpreter or compiler, the annotation of a lambda expression makes a new environment frame to hold information about the bound variables; in this case we create one type variable for each bound variable. We create a procedure type for the value of the lambda expression, with the type variables we just created for the bound variables and a type variable for the value, and we recursively annotate the body.

Constraints

The program-constraints procedure formulates constraints on the type variables based on the semantic structure of the program. It is also implemented using a generic procedure with handlers for each expression type.

```
(define (program-constraints texpr)
  (program-constraints-1 (texpr-type texpr)
                         (texpr-expr texpr)))

(define program-constraints-1
  (simple-generic-procedure 'program-constraints-1 2 #f))
```

This generic procedure takes two arguments: the type of an expression and the expression itself. It returns a list of constraints on the types that it discovers in its study of the expression. It walks the expression tree, discovering and formulating type constraints where they may be found.

Here is the handler for conditionals:

```
(define-generic-procedure-handler program-constraints-1
  (match-args type-expression? if-expr?)
  (lambda (type expr)
    (append
     (list (constrain (boolean-type)
                      (texpr-type (if-predicate expr)))
           (constrain type
                      (texpr-type (if-consequent expr)))
           (constrain type
                      (texpr-type (if-alternative expr))))
     (program-constraints (if-predicate expr))
     (program-constraints (if-consequent expr))
     (program-constraints (if-alternative expr)))))
```

This handler formulates three type constraints that it adds to the constraints it recursively formulates in the three subexpressions of the conditional. The first constraint is that the value of the predicate expression is a boolean. The second and third constraints are that the type of the value of the conditional is the same as the types of the value of the consequent expression and the value of the alternative expression.

The constraints are represented as equations:

```
(define (constrain lhs rhs)
  `(= ,lhs ,rhs))
```

(The identifiers `lhs` and `rhs` are mnemonic for "left-hand side" and "right-hand side" respectively.)

The type constraint for a `lambda` expression is that the type of the value returned by the `lambda` expression's procedure is the

same as the type of the value of its body. This is combined with
the constraints formulated for the body.

```
(define-generic-procedure-handler program-constraints-1
  (match-args type-expression? lambda-expr?)
  (lambda (type expr)
    (cons (constrain (procedure-type-codomain type)
                     (texpr-type (lambda-body expr)))
          (program-constraints (lambda-body expr)))))
```

The constraints for a procedure call are that the operator's type
is a procedure type, the types of the operand expressions match
the argument types of the procedure, and the type of the value
returned by the procedure is the type of the call.

```
(define-generic-procedure-handler program-constraints-1
  (match-args type-expression? combination-expr?)
  (lambda (type expr)
    (cons (constrain (texpr-type (combination-operator expr))
                     (procedure-type
                      (map texpr-type
                           (combination-operands expr))
                      type))
          (append
            (program-constraints (combination-operator expr))
            (append-map program-constraints
                        (combination-operands expr))))))
```

Unification

Each constraint discovered is an equation of two type expressions.
So we now have a set of equations to solve. This is accomplished
by unifying the left-hand side (lhs) and right-hand side (rhs) of
each equation. All these unifications must be done in the same
variable-binding context so as to solve them simultaneously. Since
unification of two lists unifies corresponding elements of the lists,
we can just combine the constraints into one giant unification:

```
(define (unify-constraints constraints)
  (unify (map constraint-lhs constraints)
         (map constraint-rhs constraints)))
```

The dictionary returned by `unify-constraints` is then used by
`infer-program-types` (on page 196) to instantiate the typed program.

Critique

Although this small type-inference system is a nice demonstration of unification, it is not very good at type inference: it doesn't really handle procedures very well. For example, consider the simple case:

```
(pp (infer-program-types
      '(begin (define id (lambda (x) x))
              (id 2))))
```

This apparently works correctly, returning

```
(t (numeric-type)
   (begin
     (t (type:procedure ((numeric-type)) (numeric-type))
        (define id
          (t (type:procedure ((numeric-type)) (numeric-type))
             (lambda (x) (t (numeric-type) x)))))
     (t (numeric-type)
        ((t (type:procedure ((numeric-type)) (numeric-type))
            id)
         (t (numeric-type) 2)))))
```

But notice that the identity procedure has been typed as having a numeric argument and a numeric value, because the procedure was used with a numeric argument. However, the correct type for the identity procedure should not require any specific kind of argument. More generally, the type of a procedure should not depend on its use in an example. This confusion causes a failure to type a perfectly reasonable piece of code:

```
(infer-program-types
  '(begin (define id (lambda (x) x))
          (id 2)
          (id #t)))
***type-error***
```

Exercise 4.14: Procedures

The specific problem shown in the critique above is not very hard to fix, but the general case is complicated. How can we handle procedures passed as arguments and returned as values? Remember that there may be free variables in a procedure that are lexically bound where the procedure was defined.

Work out a fix for this problem, and make it as general as you can.

Exercise 4.15: Parametric types

This exercise examines what it takes to extend this type-inference system to work with parametric types. For example, the Scheme `map` procedure operates on lists of objects of any type.

a. What must be done to extend the system to support parametric types? Does this extension require us to modify the unifier? If so, explain why it is necessary. If not, explain why it is not necessary.

b. Implement the changes required to allow parametric types to be used.

Exercise 4.16: Union types

The type-inference system we have outlined here does not have any support for union types. For example, the addition operator + is defined for numeric arithmetic. But what if we want + to be both addition of numbers and concatenation of strings?

a. What must be done to extend the system to support union types? Does this extension require us to modify the unifier? If so, explain why it is necessary. If not, explain why it is not necessary.

b. Implement the changes required to allow union types to be used. Note: This is not easy.

Exercise 4.17: Side effects

The type-inference system we have outlined here is adequate for pure functional programs. Can it be elegantly extended to work for programs with assignment? If you think so, explain and demonstrate your design. If you think not, explain your reasons.

This is not easy. It may be a nice term project to understand this and make it work.

Exercise 4.18: Is this practical?

Is our implementation of type inference practical?

a. Estimate the orders of growth of time and space of the annotation and constraints phases with the size of the program being analyzed.

b. Estimate the order of growth of time and space of the giant unification phase, using the algorithm shown. What about the best known algorithms for unification? (This will take some library research.)

c. Is there a way to break up the giant unification phase into parts so that the whole has better asymptotic behavior?

4.4.4 Adding segment variables—an experiment!

Adding segment variables to the unifier is exciting: we are not sure exactly what we will get.[10] But our careful use of generic procedures will ensure that no program that depends on the behavior of the unifier without the addition of segment variables (such as the type inference example) will produce wrong answers as a consequence of this experiment. Indeed, the organization of the unifier in terms of generic procedures makes such experiments relatively unproblematic.[11]

The use of predicates for the dispatch controls the interaction between element variables and segment variables. For example, a segment variable may incorporate an element variable into a segment it accumulates, but an element variable may not have a segment variable as its value. Thus, we must change our definition of the predicate `element?` (on page 192) to exclude segment variables:

```
(define (element? term)
  (not (match:segment-var? term)))
```

We need generic handlers for the segment variable cases. The `unify:gdispatch` handler for term lists that start with a segment variable is `maybe-grab-segment`, which is installed as follows. The list known to contain the segment variable is always passed as the first argument to `maybe-grab-segment` (as we did with `maybe-substitute`).[12]

---

[10]Others have added segment variables to pattern matchers or unifiers [5], with some success. Apparently there are versions of Prolog that have segment variables [34]. A detailed theoretical treatment of an algorithm that includes sequence variables (another name for segment variables) in a unifier can be found in Kutsia's PhD thesis [79]. However, here we are not trying to build a complete and correct segment unifier. We are just trying to show how easy it is to add some useful new behavior to the elementary unification procedure already built.

[11]The extension to segments is very subtle. We thank Kenny Chen, Will Byrd, and Michael Ballantyne for helping us think about this experiment.

[12]The procedure `complement` is a combinator for predicates: `complement` makes a new predicate that is the negation of its argument.

```
(define-generic-procedure-handler unify:gdispatch
  (match-args (car-satisfies match:segment-var?)
              (complement (car-satisfies match:segment-var?)))
  (lambda (var-first terms)
    (maybe-grab-segment var-first terms)))

(define-generic-procedure-handler unify:gdispatch
  (match-args (complement (car-satisfies match:segment-var?))
              (car-satisfies match:segment-var?))
  (lambda (terms var-first)
    (maybe-grab-segment var-first terms)))
```

In matching two termlists that each start with a segment variable, there is a special case to be handled: if both lists start with the same segment variable, we can dismiss the tautology without further work. Otherwise it is possible that we will get a match starting with either variable. But there are cases where a good match is obtained with one variable but not the other, depending on the further occurrences of the variables in the patterns. To make sure we don't miss a match starting with one of the variables, we make the match symmetrical by trying the other order if the first one fails.

```
(define (unify:segment-var-var var-first1 var-first2)
  (define (unify-seg-var-var dict succeed fail)
    (if (match:vars-equal? (car var-first1) (car var-first2))
        (succeed dict fail (cdr var-first1) (cdr var-first2))
        ((maybe-grab-segment var-first1 var-first2)
         dict
         succeed
         (lambda ()
           ((maybe-grab-segment var-first2 var-first1)
            dict
            succeed
            fail)))))
  unify-seg-var-var)

(define-generic-procedure-handler unify:gdispatch
  (match-args (car-satisfies match:segment-var?)
              (car-satisfies match:segment-var?))
  unify:segment-var-var)
```

The procedure `maybe-grab-segment` is analogous to the procedure `maybe-substitute` (on page 191) used for element variables. The case of matching a segment variable against itself was handled by `unify:segment-var-var`; so `maybe-grab-segment` starts by checking if the segment variable at the start of `var-first` has a value. If so, we replace the variable with its value and match the resulting list against the term list `terms`. Because the binding of a segment variable is the list of elements that it gobbles, we use `append` to replace the segment variable with its value. The more complex job of matching an unbound segment variable is passed on to `grab-segment`.

```
(define (maybe-grab-segment var-first terms)
  (define (maybe-grab dict succeed fail)
    (let ((var (car var-first)))
      (if (match:has-binding? var dict)
          ((unify:dispatch
            (append (match:get-value var dict)
                    (cdr var-first))
            terms)
           dict succeed fail)
          ((grab-segment var-first terms)
           dict succeed fail))))
  maybe-grab)
```

The procedure `grab-segment` is where the segment matching and backtracking actually happen. The term list is broken into two parts: an initial segment and the rest of the terms (`terms*`). The initial segment (`initial`) starts out empty and `terms*` is the whole term list. The match tries to proceed with the segment variable bound to `initial`. If that fails, the failure continuation tries to match with an element moved from `terms*` to `initial`. This is repeated until either a match succeeds or the match of the entire term list fails:

```
(define (grab-segment var-first terms)
  (define (grab dict succeed fail)
    (let ((var (car var-first)))
      (let slp ((initial '()) (terms* terms))
        (define (continue)
          (if (null? terms*)
              (fail)
              (slp (append initial (list (car terms*)))
                   (cdr terms*))))
        (let ((dict* (do-substitute var initial dict)))
          (if dict*
              (succeed dict* continue (cdr var-first) terms*)
              (continue))))))
  grab)
```

This appears to be all that is required to make a unifier with an experimental extension for segment variables. With segment variables we must expect to get multiple matches. We can reject a match, forcing the program to backtrack, to get an alternative. Note that each dictionary entry is a list containing the name of the variable, the value, and the type of the variable.

We can use the unifier as a one-sided matcher. For example, there are exactly two ways to match the distributive law pattern to the given algebraic expression, as we see:[13]

```
(let ((pattern '(* (?? a) (+ (?? b)) (?? c)))
      (expression '(* x y (+ z w) m (+ n o) p)))
  (unify:internal pattern expression (match:new-dict)
    (lambda (dict)
      (pp (match:bindings dict))
      #f)))
((c (m (+ n o) p) ??) (b (z w) ??) (a (x y) ??))
((c (p) ??) (b (n o) ??) (a (x y (+ z w) m) ??))
#f
```

Both of these dictionaries produce the same substitution instance:

```
(* x y (+ z w) m (+ n o) p)
```

But in an algebraic manipulator we really want both dictionaries, because each of them represents a different application of the distributive law.

Things get more complicated and much less clear when segment variables match against lists containing segment variables:

```
(let ((p1 '(a (?? x) (?? y) (?? x) c))
      (p2 '(a b b b (?? w) b b b c)))
  (unify:internal p1 p2 (match:new-dict)
    (lambda (dict)
      (pp (match:bindings dict))
      #f)))

((y (b b b (?? w) b b b) ??) (x () ??))
((y (b b (?? w) b b) ??) (x (b) ??))
((y (b (?? w) b) ??) (x (b b) ??))
```

---

[13] This is a one-sided match that could also be done with the earlier matcher, but this ability to match expressions with variables on both sides of the match is useful.

```
((w () ??) (y () ??) (x (b b b) ??))
((w () ??) (y () ??) (x (b b b) ??))
((y ((?? w)) ??) (x (b b b) ??))
((y () ??) (w () ??) (x (b b b) ??))
((w ((?? y)) ??) (x (b b b) ??))
((w () ??) (y () ??) (x (b b b) ??))
#f
```

Apparently, there are many ways to make this match. But many of the dictionaries are really different ways of constructing the same substitution instance. To see this clearly, we construct the substitution instance in each case:

```
(let ((p1 '(a (?? x) (?? y) (?? x) c))
      (p2 '(a b b b (?? w) b b b c)))
  (unify:internal p1 p2 (match:new-dict)
    (lambda (dict)
      (and dict
           (let ((subst (match:dict-substitution dict)))
             (let ((p1* (subst p1)) (p2* (subst p2)))
               (if (not (equal? p1* p2*))
                   (error "Bad dictionary"))
               (pp p1*))))
      #f)))
```

```
(a b b b (?? w) b b b c)
(a b b b (?? w) b b b c)
(a b b b (?? w) b b b c)
(a b b b b b b c)
(a b b b b b b c)
(a b b b (?? w) b b b c)
(a b b b b b b c)
(a b b b (?? y) b b b c)
(a b b b b b b c)
#f
```

So we see that each "solution" is a valid solution to the problem of finding values for the variables that when substituted back into the given patterns make the patterns the same. In this case five of the solutions are equivalent. These five are the most general unifiers, and they are unique up to renaming of the variables. The other four are not as general as possible. But unification is supposed to produce the unique most general common substitution instance of the two input patterns, up to renaming of variables. So with segments, this very useful pattern matcher is not really a unifier.

Actually, the problem is a bit worse. There are perfectly good matches that are not found by this program. Here is an example:

```
;;; A missing match!
(unify:internal '(((?? x) 3) ((?? x)))
                '((4 (?? y)) (4 5))
                (match:new-dict)
                (lambda (dict)
                  (pp (match:bindings dict))
                  #f))
#f
```

But these expressions do match, with the following bindings:

```
((x (4 5) ??) (y (5 3) ??))
```

How sad! But there is a moral to this story. Using generic procedures, we can make possibly problematic extensions to a correct algorithm without undermining its correctness for uses of the unextended algorithm. The extensions may be useful for some purposes, even without satisfying the correctness requirements of the unextended algorithm.

Exercise 4.19: Can we fix these problems?

We have a problem with unifying patterns containing segment variables. We may miss some matches; we may generate multiple copies of the same solution; and some of the solutions, although valid solutions of the problem to make the input patterns equal, are not maximally general. Let's think about fixing this.

a. Write a wrapper for `unify:internal` that collects all of the solutions. This is not hard if you use assignments, but it might be more fun to look for a functional solution—but don't try too hard!

b. Now that you have all of the solutions, it is easy to eliminate duplicates. Create the result of substituting from each solution into the inputs. You can check that the results of the two substitutions are equal—this is a check that the algorithm for solving is correct. Now save the pair of one substitution and one result for each distinct result. Be careful: The name of a variable doesn't matter, so two resulting dictionaries represent the same solution if you can get one by uniformly renaming variables in the other.

c. If any result in the collection is a substitution instance of another result, it is not a most general common specialization of the two inputs.

Write the predicate `substitution-instance?` to filter those out. You are now left with the collection of the most general common specializations that this algorithm will generate. Return these.

d. Figure out a way to avoid missing matches like the "A missing match!" shown above. Is there a simple extension of the code shown that can handle this kind of match? Note: This is an extremely difficult problem.

Exercise 4.20: More general matches

Beyond the nasty problems shown above, there is an interesting subtlety that is not addressed by the unifier. Consider the following problem:

```
(unifier '((?? x) 3) '(4 (?? y)))
(4 3)
```

Here we see a perfectly good match, but it is not the most general one possible. The problem is that there can be any number of things between the 4 and the 3. A better answer would be:

```
(4 (?? z) 3)
```

Figure out how to get this answer. This requires a significant extension to the unifier.

Exercise 4.21: Strings with segments

If you did not do exercise 4.11 (page 193), do it now. But here we want you to add string segment variables. This can be useful in matching segments of DNA!

4.5   Pattern matching on graphs

The pattern matching we have developed so far is for matching list structures. Such structures are excellent for representing expressions, such as algebraic expressions or the abstract syntax trees of computer-language expressions. However, pattern matching can be used to make systems that operate on a much wider range of data. If the structure of interest can be characterized by an accessibility relation, it may be appropriate to describe the structure as a graph of *nodes* representing "places" and *edges* representing "path elements" describing how the places are interconnected. An electrical circuit is an example of such a structure, where the circuit parts and circuit nodes are places and the accessibility relation is just the description of the interconnect. A board game like chess or checkers is another, where the board squares may be represented by nodes in a graph and the adjacency of squares may be represented by edges in the graph.

We will implement a graph as a collection of nodes and edges. Our graphs are immutable in the sense that once a node or an edge is added, it cannot be modified; the graph can be changed only by adding more nodes and edges. This will have consequences that we will see in section 4.5.4.

A node contains a collection of edges, and an edge is a combination of a *label* and a *value*. The label of an edge is an object that is unique under `eqv?`, usually a symbol or a number. The value of an edge is a Scheme object, often another node.

This implementation will work with concrete graphs (where all of the nodes and edges are available at the time we build the graph) and lazy graphs (where the graph is extended, as necessary, at the time of access). In the simpler world of linear sequences, a list is a concrete graph and a stream is a lazy graph that is generated when referenced.

We will first look at a simple example to see how graphs work. We will then use an extended example, a chess referee, to explore more complex uses of graphs and pattern matching on graphs.

4.5.1   Lists as graphs

We start with the simple but familiar world of lists. The `cons` cells are the nodes, which will be made with `g:cons` and whose `car` and `cdr` will be implemented as edges labeled with `car` and `cdr` and accessed by `g:car` and `g:cdr`:

```
(define (g:cons car cdr)
  (let ((pair (make-graph-node 'pair)))
    (pair 'connect! 'car car)
    (pair 'connect! 'cdr cdr)
    pair))

(define (g:car pair) (pair 'edge-value 'car))
(define (g:cdr pair) (pair 'edge-value 'cdr))
```

To represent lists as graphs we need a special end marker for lists:

```
(define nil (make-graph-node 'nil))

(define (g:null) nil)

(define (g:null? object) (eqv? object nil))
```

The conversion of a list to a list graph is:

```
(define (list->graph list)
  (if (pair? list)
      (g:cons (car list) (list->graph (cdr list)))
      (g:null)))
```

and a simple example works as expected:

```
(define g (list->graph '(a b c)))

(and (eqv? 'a (g:car g))
     (eqv? 'b (g:car (g:cdr g)))
     (eqv? 'c (g:car (g:cdr (g:cdr g))))
     (g:null? (g:cdr (g:cdr (g:cdr g)))))
#t
```

We can modify the list-graph constructor to allow lazy graphs, with nodes that are created as edges are traversed:

```
(define (list->lazy-graph list)
  (if (pair? list)
      (g:cons (delay (car list))
              (delay (list->lazy-graph (cdr list))))
      (g:null)))
```

Here we used the Scheme [109] `delay` to construct a *promise* that will evaluate the delayed (postponed) expression when the promise is `forced`. Streams [13] (lazy lists) are usually constructed using `delay` and `force`.

4.5.2 Implementing graphs

We have to be able to make *graph nodes* and connect them to other nodes by *edges*. We will represent a graph node as a *bundle procedure*: a collection of delegate procedures that can be called by name.[14]

---

[14]For an example of how a graph node is used, see `g:cons` on page 210. For a more complete description of bundle procedures see page 395.

```
(define (make-graph-node name)
  (let ((edges '()))
    (define (get-name) name)
    (define (all-edges) (list-copy edges))
    (define (%find-edge label)
      (find (lambda (edge)
              (eqv? label (edge 'get-label)))
            edges))
    (define (has-edge? label)
      (and (%find-edge label) #t)) ; boolean value
    (define (get-edge label)
      (let ((edge (%find-edge label)))
        (if (not edge)
            (error "No edge with this label:" label))
        edge))
    (define (edge-value label)
      ((get-edge label) 'get-value))
    (define (connect! label value)
      (if (has-edge? label)
          (error "Two edges with same label:" label))
      (set! edges
            (cons (make-graph-edge label value) edges)))
    (define (maybe-connect! label value)
      (if (not (default-object? value))
          (connect! label value)))
    (bundle graph-node? get-name all-edges has-edge?
            get-edge edge-value connect! maybe-connect!)))
```

The argument to `make-graph-node` is the name of the new node; this is shown when printing a node object. The first argument to the `bundle` macro is a predicate that the generated bundle will satisfy. In this case, it is defined as

```
(define graph-node? (make-bundle-predicate 'graph-node))
```

We will not show the definitions of other bundle predicates since they are similar.

Edges are also represented as bundle procedures. An edge may have a concrete value or the value may be a promise (constructed by `delay`) to produce the value when asked. The latter provides for lazy graph structures.

```
(define (make-graph-edge label value)
  (define (get-label) label)
  (define (get-value)
    (if (promise? value)
        (force value)
        value))
  (bundle graph-edge? get-label get-value))
```

Exercise 4.22: More lazy graphs

We have shown how to make concrete lists and lazy lists. How about some more interesting structures?

Perhaps it would be nice to have a dynamically extensible tree. For example, a game tree could be usefully built this way: we may want to elaborate the tree both in breadth and depth as resources become available. Make an example of such a tree that can be extended as more plausible moves are considered at each level, and as more levels are added for consideration.

4.5.3 Matching on graphs

We might want to search a graph for interesting features. One way to do this is to try to match patterns to the graph. A pattern for a graph could specify an alternating sequence of nodes and edges: a *path*. Such a pattern can be matched by starting at a node and trying to follow the path specified by the pattern.

Imagine, for example, that we have a chessboard and chess pieces. The board squares are nodes of a graph. The nodes representing adjacent squares are connected to a given node by edges. We can label the edges, as seen by the player playing White, by compass directions: `north, south, east, west, northeast, southeast, northwest, southwest`. Going `north` is toward the Black side of the board, and going `south` is toward the White side of the board.

Given such an arrangement, we can specify a move where a knight may move north-north-east as:

```
(define basic-knight-move
  '((? source-node ,(occupied-by 'knight))
    north (?)
    north (?)
    east (? target-node ,maybe-opponent)))
```

This pattern shares several characteristics with those we've looked at in previous sections: element variables are introduced by the ? character; they can have names (e.g., `source-node`); and they can have restrictions (e.g., `(occupied-by 'knight)`). We introduce the syntax `(?)` to indicate an anonymous element variable.

The pattern match starts with `source-node`, traverses two edges labeled `north`—with nodes that we don't care about—and finally travels `east` to reach `target-node`. We call this kind of pattern a *path pattern*, or in the context of chess, a *move pattern*.

Of course, this is only one possible knight move. But we can generate all possible knight moves by symmetries: we can reflect the knight move east-west, we can rotate it clockwise by 90 degrees, and we can rotate it by 180 degrees:

```
(define all-knight-moves
  (symmetrize-move basic-knight-move
                   reflect-ew rotate-90 rotate-180))
```

The `symmetrize-move` procedure applies all possible combinations of these three symmetries to produce eight moves. The order in which the symmetry transformations are applied doesn't matter for the transformations we use.

```
(define (symmetrize-move move . transformations)
  (let loop ((xforms transformations) (moves (list move)))
    (if (null? xforms)
        moves
        (loop (cdr xforms)
              (append moves
                      (map (rewrite-path-edges (car xforms))
                           moves))))))
```

where `rewrite-path-edges` applies its argument to each edge label in a move, producing a new move with substituted edge labels.

One example of such a symmetry transformation is

```
(define (reflect-ew label)
  (case label
    ((east) 'west)
    ((northeast) 'northwest)
    ((northwest) 'northeast)
    ((southeast) 'southwest)
    ((southwest) 'southeast)
    ((west) 'east)
    (else label)))
```

and the others are similar remappings of the compass directions.

The resulting list of all knight moves is

```
((source north (?) north (?) east target)
 (source north (?) north (?) west target)
 (source east (?) east (?) south target)
 (source east (?) east (?) north target)
 (source south (?) south (?) west target)
 (source south (?) south (?) east target)
 (source west (?) west (?) north target)
 (source west (?) west (?) south target))
```

where we have simplified the printing by replacing the restricted source and target node variables with *source* and *target*.

Knight moves are special in chess, in that a knight can move over squares occupied by either a friend or an opponent to get to the target square. Rooks, bishops, and queens may not pass through an occupied square, but they may pass through many unoccupied squares on their way to a target square. We need a way to specify such a repeated traversal. We use (* ...) to specify a repeated traversal:

```
(define basic-queen-move
  '((? source-node ,(occupied-by 'queen))
    (* north (?* ,unoccupied))
    north (? target-node ,maybe-opponent)))
```

The queen may move north through any number of unoccupied squares to the target square. The notation (?* ...) is a new kind of pattern variable that can be used only inside a (* ...) pattern. Like a simple pattern variable, it matches one element, but instead of saving just a single matched value, it collects a list of all elements matched in the repeat. All of the queen's possible moves are then:

```
(define all-queen-moves
  (symmetrize-move basic-queen-move
               rotate-45 rotate-90 rotate-180))
```

Pawns have more complicated rules. A pawn is (almost) the only piece whose possible moves depend on its position or the position of a neighboring opponent.[15] A pawn may go north one or two steps from its initial position, but it may go only one step north if not in its initial position. A pawn may take one step northeast or northwest if and only if that move takes an opponent piece. Finally, a pawn in the penultimate row may move into the last row and be promoted into any piece, usually a queen.[16]

---

[15] Castling is another special case. Castling is allowed under restricted circumstances: when the king and the rook are in their initial positions, the squares between the king and rook are unoccupied, and the king is not in check and will not have to traverse or land in a square where it would be in check.

[16] There is also a pawn move, en passant capture, that depends on the opponent's previous move.

Exercise 4.23: Filling out chess moves

We have shown how to make patterns for knight moves and queen moves, but we have not made patterns for moves for all chess pieces.

a. Rook moves and bishop moves are similar to queen moves, but more restricted: a rook cannot move diagonally, and a bishop can move *only* diagonally. Make patterns for all bishop moves and all simple rook moves.

b. Pawn moves are much more complicated. Make a set of patterns for all possible pawn moves (except en passant captures).

c. Make a set of patterns for the king's very limited ways to move. Don't worry about castling or the rule that a king cannot be moved into check.

d. Castling is the final special case. It involves both the king and a rook. Make a set of castling patterns. (See footnote 15.)

4.5.4 Chessboards and alternate graph views

The chessboard, as a graph, incorporates an exciting idea. We want the same patterns to work for both players. But the edges describing directions are different: `north` for White is `south` for Black and `east` for White is `west` for Black! This makes little difference for the major pieces (the rooks, knights, bishops, kings, queens) with symmetrical move patterns, but White pawns can move only `north` and Black pawns can move only `south`. In any case, it would be pleasant to make the move descriptions the same for both players.

We want the two players to have different views of the board graph: we want the meanings of the edge labels to be relative to the player. If the player playing White sees a `north` edge from (the node representing) square A to square B we want the player playing Black to see a `north` edge from square B to square A.

To make this work we introduce *graph views*. A graph view is a reversible mapping from one edge label to another. When a graph view is applied to a node, it returns a copy of that node in which the edges are renamed.

In the case of chess the relevant view is with the board rotated 180 degrees:

```
(define rotate-180-view
  (make-graph-view 'inverse rotate-180 rotate-180))
```

where `make-graph-view` makes a graph view. The procedure `graph-node-view` applies a view to a node:

```
(graph-node-view node view)
```

White will see a node directly and Black will see the same node projected through the `rotate-180-view`. Given this map, all operations look the same to both White and Black.

Using a graph view takes care of *relative* addressing, where we are looking at neighbors of a given node. But we also need to do *absolute* addressing, where the node to find is specified by a row and column. Each color wants to see similar addressing, where the home row is 0, and the opponent's home row is 7; likewise each color sees the leftmost column as 0 and the rightmost as 7.[17] White's addresses are the default, and Black's are inverted with the procedure `invert-address`.

Let's make a board. The following code is specific to chess, since we're not focusing on making an abstract domain. We make an 8×8 array of nodes representing squares, each with an address. We iterate through all possible square addresses, connecting each node to each of its neighbors by an edge with the appropriate label. Then we populate the sides with pieces.

```
(define chess-board-size 8)
(define chess-board-indices (iota chess-board-size))
(define chess-board-last-index (last chess-board-indices))

(define (make-chess-board)
  (let ((board (make-chess-board-internal)))
    (for-each (lambda (address)
                (connect-up-square address board))
              board-addresses)
    (populate-sides board)
    board))
```

The possible addresses for chess-board squares are all pairs of integers from 0 to 7:

```
(define board-addresses
  (append-map (lambda (y)
                (map (lambda (x)
                       (make-address x y))
                     chess-board-indices))
              chess-board-indices))
```

---

[17]We use zero-based indexing, unlike the traditional chess conventions, but this is not important except for input and output to players.

The procedure `make-chess-board-internal` makes the array of nodes for squares as a list of rows, each of which is a list of columns for that row. It returns a bundle procedure with a handful of delegates to manipulate the board.

```
(define (make-chess-board-internal)
  (let ((nodes
          (map (lambda (x)
                 (map (lambda (y)
                        (make-graph-node (string x "," y)))
                      chess-board-indices))
               chess-board-indices)))
    (let loop ((turn 0))
      See below for the delegate definitions.
      (bundle #f node-at piece-at piece-in address-of
              set-piece-at color next-turn)))))
```

The `turn` variable is the current turn, starting with zero. Even turns are White, and odd turns are Black, as shown by the delegate procedure `color`:

```
(define (color) (if (white-move?) 'white 'black))
(define (white-move?) (even? turn))
```

The delegate procedure `node-at` gets the node at a given address. If this is a Black turn, it translates the address and applies the node view.

```
(define (node-at address)
  (define (get-node address)
    (list-ref (list-ref nodes (address-x address))
              (address-y address)))
  (if (white-move?)
      (get-node address)
      (graph-node-view (get-node (invert-address address))
                       rotate-180-view)))
```

The inverse of `node-at` is the delegate procedure `address-of`. Each node has an edge, labeled with `address`, with its address as the value. As with `node-at`, if this is a Black move the returned address must be translated.

```
(define (address-of node)
  (let ((address (node 'edge-value 'address)))
    (if (white-move?)
        address
        (invert-address address))))
```

The delegate procedure `next-turn` advances the board after a move is made:

```
(define (next-turn) (loop (+ turn 1)))
```

Connecting the squares to their neighbors does address arithmetic to handle (literal) edge cases, creating a labeled edge between each square and each of its neighbors. It also creates the `address` edge for each node.

```
(define (connect-up-square address board)
  (let ((node (board 'node-at address)))
    (node 'connect! 'address address)
    (for-each-direction
     (lambda (label x-delta y-delta)
       (let ((x+ (+ (address-x address) x-delta))
             (y+ (+ (address-y address) y-delta)))
         (if (and (<= 0 x+ chess-board-last-index)
                  (<= 0 y+ chess-board-last-index))
             (node 'connect! label
                   (board 'node-at
                          (make-address x+ y+)))))))))
```

```
(define (for-each-direction procedure)
  (procedure 'north 0 1)
  (procedure 'northeast 1 1)
  (procedure 'east 1 0)
  (procedure 'southeast 1 -1)
  (procedure 'south 0 -1)
  (procedure 'southwest -1 -1)
  (procedure 'west -1 0)
  (procedure 'northwest -1 1))
```

An address is represented as a list of column and row number:

```
(define (make-address x y) (list x y))
(define (address-x address) (car address))
(define (address-y address) (cadr address))
```

```
(define (address= a b)
  (and (= (address-x a) (address-x b))
       (= (address-y a) (address-y b))))
```

```
(define (invert-address address)
  (make-address (- chess-board-last-index
                   (address-x address))
                (- chess-board-last-index
                   (address-y address))))
```

A piece is represented by data incorporating its piece type and its color. Our convention is that at the nth turn, each piece on the board will be connected to the node representing the square it occupies by an edge from that node with the label n. This is a consequence of graph immutability; otherwise we could just use a side effect to modify the edge. To populate the board, we connect each piece to the node for its initial square with an edge labeled 0.

```
(define (populate-sides board)

  (define (populate-side color home-row pawn-row)

    (define (do-column col type)
      (add-piece col home-row type)
      (add-piece col pawn-row 'pawn))

    (define (add-piece col row type)
      ((board 'node-at (make-address col row))
       'connect! 0 (make-piece type color)))

    (do-column 0 'rook)
    (do-column 1 'knight)
    (do-column 2 'bishop)
    (do-column 3 'queen)
    (do-column 4 'king)
    (do-column 5 'bishop)
    (do-column 6 'knight)
    (do-column 7 'rook))

  (populate-side 'white 0 1)
  (populate-side 'black 7 6))
```

We can now start a game:

```
(define the-board)

(define (start-chess-game)
  (set! the-board (make-chess-board))
  (print-chess-board the-board))
```

And we get this nice chessboard image:

```
;;;     0    1    2    3    4    5    6    7
;;;   +----+----+----+----+----+----+----+----+
;;; 7 | Rb | Nb | Bb | Qb | Kb | Bb | Nb | Rb |
;;;   +----+----+----+----+----+----+----+----+
;;; 6 | Pb | Pb | Pb | Pb | Pb | Pb | Pb | Pb |
;;;   +----+----+----+----+----+----+----+----+
;;; 5 |    |    |    |    |    |    |    |    |
;;;   +----+----+----+----+----+----+----+----+
;;; 4 |    |    |    |    |    |    |    |    |
;;;   +----+----+----+----+----+----+----+----+
;;; 3 |    |    |    |    |    |    |    |    |
;;;   +----+----+----+----+----+----+----+----+
;;; 2 |    |    |    |    |    |    |    |    |
;;;   +----+----+----+----+----+----+----+----+
;;; 1 | Pw | Pw | Pw | Pw | Pw | Pw | Pw | Pw |
;;;   +----+----+----+----+----+----+----+----+
;;; 0 | Rw | Nw | Bw | Qw | Kw | Bw | Nw | Rw |
;;;   +----+----+----+----+----+----+----+----+
;;; white to move
```

4.5.5 Chess moves

Now that we have a chessboard, populated with pieces, we need
a way to move those pieces around. If a piece is in a particular
square at a particular turn, the node representing that square has
an edge, with the turn as its label, whose value is the piece. The
following delegate procedures in `make-chess-board-internal` on
page 218 are relevant here:

```
(define (piece-at address)
  (piece-in (node-at address)))

(define (piece-in node)
  (and (node 'has-edge? turn)
       (node 'edge-value turn)))

(define (set-piece-at address piece)
  ((node-at address) 'connect! (+ turn 1) piece))
```

We use `piece-at` to obtain a piece that we expect to move, given its address. Of course, it is always a good idea to check for obvious errors.

```
(define (get-piece-to-move board from)
  (let ((my-piece (board 'piece-at from)))
    (if (not my-piece)
        (error "No piece in this square:" from))
    (if (not (eq? (board 'color) (piece-color my-piece)))
        (error "Can move only one's own pieces:"
               my-piece from))
    my-piece))
```

To actually make a move we pick the piece up and set it down in the target square. However, this move is allowed only if the target square is empty or if it is occupied by an opponent piece to be captured.

```
(define (simple-move board from to)
  (let ((my-piece (get-piece-to-move board from)))
    (let ((captured (board 'piece-at to)))
      (if (not (no-piece-or-opponent? captured my-piece))
          (error "Can't capture piece of same color:"
                 captured)))
    ;; The move looks good; make it so:
    (board 'set-piece-at to my-piece)
    ;; Now update all the unaffected pieces to
    ;; the next state of the board:
    (for-each (lambda (address)
                (if (not (or (address= from address)
                             (address= to address)))
                    (let ((p (board 'piece-at address)))
                      (if p
                          (board 'set-piece-at address p)))))
              board-addresses)
    (board 'next-turn)))
```

Notice that we didn't put in a check that the piece we want to move is able to make that move. Our only descriptions of the legal moves available to each kind of piece are in the graph patterns that we built in section 4.5.3. In exercise 4.24 on page 225 we will fix this problem.

But first, let's use the matcher to determine whether a move described by such a path pattern is a capture:

```
(define (capture? board from path)
  (let* ((my-piece (get-piece-to-move board from))
         (dict
          (graph-match path
                       (match:extend-dict chess-board:var  ;**
                                          board
                                          (match:new-dict))
                       (board 'node-at from))))
    (and dict
         (let* ((target (match:get-value 'target-node dict))
                (captured (board 'piece-in target)))
           (and captured
                `(capture ,my-piece
                          ,captured
                          ,(board 'address-of target)))))))
```

The line marked by ;** adds a special binding in the initial dictionary, which is used by some pattern restrictions that need to interrogate the board.

For convenience, chess-move updates the board with a move, then prints the board for the player who will move next.

```
(define (chess-move from to)
  (set! the-board (simple-move the-board from to))
  (print-chess-board the-board))
```

To demonstrate this code we can make an interesting position:

```
(define (giuoco-piano-opening)
  (start-chess-game)
  (chess-move '(4 1) '(4 3))          ;W: P-K4
  (chess-move '(3 1) '(3 3))          ;B: P-K4
  (chess-move '(6 0) '(5 2))          ;W: N-KB3
  (chess-move '(6 0) '(5 2))          ;B: N-QB3
  (chess-move '(5 0) '(2 3))          ;W: B-QB4
  (chess-move '(2 0) '(5 3)))         ;B: B-QB4

(giuoco-piano-opening)
```

After lots of printout, we obtain the following board position:

```
;;;      0    1    2    3    4    5    6    7
;;;    +----+----+----+----+----+----+----+----+
;;; 7  | Rb |    | Bb | Qb | Kb |    | Nb | Rb |
;;;    +----+----+----+----+----+----+----+----+
;;; 6  | Pb | Pb | Pb | Pb |    | Pb | Pb | Pb |
;;;    +----+----+----+----+----+----+----+----+
;;; 5  |    |    | Nb |    |    |    |    |    |
;;;    +----+----+----+----+----+----+----+----+
;;; 4  |    |    | Bb |    | Pb |    |    |    |
;;;    +----+----+----+----+----+----+----+----+
;;; 3  |    |    | Bw |    | Pw |    |    |    |
;;;    +----+----+----+----+----+----+----+----+
;;; 2  |    |    |    |    |    | Nw |    |    |
;;;    +----+----+----+----+----+----+----+----+
;;; 1  | Pw | Pw | Pw | Pw |    | Pw | Pw | Pw |
;;;    +----+----+----+----+----+----+----+----+
;;; 0  | Rw | Nw | Bw | Qw | Kw |    |    | Rw |
;;;    +----+----+----+----+----+----+----+----+
;;; white to move
```

At this point the White Knight at King Bishop 3 is attacking
the Black Pawn at King 5. It is not a good idea to take that piece
because it is defended by the Black Knight at Queen-Bishop 6,
and one should not exchange a knight for a pawn. However, we
can use a graph pattern from the knight moves to check that this
is a possible capture:

```
(capture? the-board
          (make-address 5 2)
          '((? source-node ,(occupied-by 'knight))
            north (?) north (?)
            west (? target-node ,maybe-opponent)))
(capture (knight white) (pawn black) (4 4))
```

Indeed, it is the only possible capture for this knight:

```
(filter-map (lambda (path)
              (capture? the-board
                        (make-address 5 2)
                        path))
            all-knight-moves)
((capture (knight white) (pawn black) (4 4)))
```

Exercise 4.24: Legal chess moves

In exercise 4.23 on page 216 we made a library of patterns for all legal chess moves. Modify the `simple-move` program (page 222) to check that the piece being moved is allowed to move in the way requested.

4.5.6 Implementing graph matching

The entry point for using a graph pattern is:

```
(define (graph-match path dict object)
  ((gmatch:compile-path path) object dict
    (lambda (object* dict*)
      dict*)))
```

We compile the path pattern into a match procedure that takes the graph object (a node) to start from, an initial dictionary, and a success continuation. If the pattern successfully matches a sequence of edges starting with that node, it calls the success continuation, which takes the node (`object*`) at the end of the matched path and a dictionary of bindings accumulated in the match, as described in section 4.3.[18] If the pattern fails to match the given object the match procedure returns `#f`.

The patterns that we are using for matching against graphs are *expressions* of a small language that we want to compile into match procedures. The syntax of graph-pattern expressions can be described in BNF. Here a postfix * indicates 0 or more occurrences, postfix + indicates 1 or more, and postfix ? indicates 0 or 1 occurrence. An infix | indicates alternatives. Items surrounded in " are literal strings. For example, a pattern variable to match a single element starts with (?, has an optional name and optional predicate, and ends with).

---

[18]But notice that the success continuation of the graph-matcher procedure is different from the success continuation of the expression-matcher procedure. The expression-matcher success continuation takes a dictionary and a number of elements eaten by the matcher (to make segments work), whereas the graph-matcher success continuation takes the final node and the dictionary resulting from matching the matched part of the graph.

```
<edge> = <edge-label> <target>
<edge-label> = <symbol>
<target> = <node-var> | <object-var> | <constant>
<node-var> = <single-var>
<object-var> = <single-var> | <sequence-var>
<single-var> = "(?" <var-name>? <unary-predicate>? ")"
<sequence-var> = "(?*" <var-name>? <unary-predicate>? ")"
<var-name> = <symbol>

<path> = <node-var> <path-elements>
<path-elements> = <path-element>*

<path-element> =
    <edge>
  | "(*" <path-elements> ")"      ; repeat any number of times
  | "(+" <path-elements> ")"      ; repeat at least once
  | "(opt" <path-elements> ")"    ; one or zero instances
  | "(or" <ppath-elements>+ ")"
  | "(and" <ppath-elements>+ ")"
<ppath-elements> = "(" <path-elements> ")"
```

In our graph-matching language every path in a graph starts with a node variable. A node variable is a single-element variable, which satisfies the predicate `match:element-var?`. We compile a path as follows:

```
(define (gmatch:compile-path path)
  (if (and (pair? path) (match:element-var? (car path)))
      (gmatch:finish-compile-path (cdr path)
        (gmatch:compile-var (car path)))
      (error "Ill-formed path:" path)))
```

Here we check that the first element of `path` is an element variable; if so, we compile it into a variable matcher. The remainder of the path, if any, is compiled by `finish-compile-path`:[19]

```
(define (gmatch:finish-compile-path rest-elts matcher)
  (if (null? rest-elts)
      matcher
      (gmatch:seq2 matcher
                   (gmatch:compile-path-elts rest-elts))))
```

---

[19] Although the actual name of the procedure is `gmatch:finish-compile-path`, we abbreviate such names to elide the `gmatch:` prefix in text explanations.

where seq2 produces a match procedure that sequentially matches
its match-procedure arguments:

```
(define (gmatch:seq2 match-first match-rest)
  (define (match-seq object dict succeed)
    (match-first object dict
                 (lambda (object* dict*)
                   (match-rest object* dict* succeed)))))
  match-seq)
```

The variable matcher match-first, produced by compile-var,
will match the initial node of the path, and the resulting dictionary dict* is then used by the result of compile-path-elts
(match-rest) to match the remainder of the path, starting with
the edge object*.

There are only a few cases for compiling path-element patterns.
Either the path starts with an edge label and a target node, or it
starts with a special match form (*, +, opt, or, and):

```
(define (gmatch:compile-path-elts elts)
  (let ((elt (car elts))
        (rest (cdr elts)))
    (cond ((and (symbol? elt) (pair? rest))
           (gmatch:finish-compile-path (cdr rest)
             (gmatch:compile-edge elt (car rest))))
          ((pair? elt)
           (gmatch:finish-compile-path rest
             (gmatch:compile-path-elt elt)))
          (else
           (error "Ill-formed path elements:" elts)))))
```

An edge may be labeled by any symbol that is not one of the special symbols (*, +, opt, or, and) used by graph-matcher patterns.
The matcher for a simple labeled edge is then compiled by:

```
(define (gmatch:compile-edge label target)
  (let ((match-target (gmatch:compile-target target)))
    (define (match-edge object dict succeed)
      (and (graph-node? object)
           (object 'has-edge? label)
           (match-target (object 'edge-value label)
                         dict succeed)))
    match-edge))
```

The edge matcher, match-edge, checks that the object is a graph
node, that there is an edge with the given label emanating from

that object, and that the target of the edge (the `edge-value`) will match (using `match-target`) the pattern for the target in the graph-match pattern. The match procedure `match-target` used in `match-edge` is made by the compiler `compile-target`.

There are only two possibilities when compiling a target: a variable or a constant.

```
(define (gmatch:compile-target elt)
  (if (match:var? elt)
      (gmatch:compile-var elt)
      (let ()
        (define (match-constant object dict succeed)
          (and (eqv? elt object)
               (succeed object dict)))
        match-constant)))
```

The special match forms are handled by `compile-path-elt`:

```
(define (gmatch:compile-path-elt elt)
  (let ((keyword (car elt))
        (args (cdr elt)))
    (case keyword
      ((*) (gmatch:compile-* args))
      ((+) (gmatch:compile-+ args))
      ((opt) (gmatch:compile-opt args))
      ((or) (gmatch:compile-or args))
      ((and) (gmatch:compile-and args))
      (else (error "Ill-formed path element:" elt)))))
```

Compiling a pattern with optional path elements works as follows: There is a recursive call to `compile-path-elts` with the path element patterns for the optional sequence of path elements, to obtain `matcher`, the matcher for the elements that are optionally present in the path. When `match-opt` is applied to a graph node object, the matcher for those path elements is applied; but if it fails, returning `#f`, the match succeeds with the original object and the original dictionary.

```
(define (gmatch:compile-opt elts)
  (let ((matcher (gmatch:compile-path-elts elts)))
    (define (match-opt object dict succeed)
      (or (matcher object dict succeed)
          (succeed object dict)))
    match-opt))
```

A pattern with repeated path elements, for example the pattern
(* north (?* ,unoccupied)) in basic-queen-moves on page 215,
is compiled like this:

```
(define (gmatch:compile-* elts)
  (gmatch:* (gmatch:compile-path-elts elts)))
```

As for a pattern requiring an optional sequence of path elements,
the compiler is called recursively to obtain a matcher for the potentially repeated sequence, which is then passed to gmatch:*:

```
(define (gmatch:* matcher)
  (define (match-* object dict succeed)
    (or (matcher object dict
                 (lambda (object* dict*)
                   (match-* object* dict* succeed)))
        (succeed object dict)))
  match-*)
```

The graph-pattern matcher match-* tries to use the matcher
passed to it on the graph node object supplied. If it succeeds,
match-* calls itself recursively to try the part of the graph where
the last match left off. Eventually it will fail to progress, succeed-
ing with the graph object that matcher failed on.

Compiling patterns requiring at least one, but possibly many,
repetitions of a sequence of path elements, indicated with +, is
similar to *. It uses gmatch:* as above, but requires at least one
matching element first:

```
(define (gmatch:compile-+ elts)
  (let ((matcher (gmatch:compile-path-elts elts)))
    (gmatch:seq2 matcher (gmatch:* matcher))))
```

The remaining special path patterns are and and or, each of
which contains a number of subpath patterns. An and element
must match all of the subpath patterns starting at the current
node. An or element must match at least one of the subpath
patterns starting at the current node.

```
(define (gmatch:compile-and elt-lists)
  (gmatch:and (map gmatch:compile-path-elts elt-lists)))
```

```
(define (gmatch:compile-or elt-lists)
  (gmatch:or (map gmatch:compile-path-elts elt-lists)))
```

The procedures and and or are where the real work happens:

```
(define (gmatch:and matchers)
  (lambda (object dict succeed)
    (if (null? matchers)
        (succeed object dict)
        (let loop ((matchers matchers) (dict dict))
          ((car matchers) object dict
           (if (null? (cdr matchers))
               succeed
               (lambda (object* dict*)
                 (loop (cdr matchers) dict*)))))))))

(define (gmatch:or matchers)
  (lambda (object dict succeed)
    (let loop ((matchers matchers))
      (if (pair? matchers)
          (or ((car matchers) object dict succeed)
              (loop (cdr matchers)))
          #f))))
```

The procedure compile-var compiles a pattern variable. It is called from compile-path and compile-target, and has four mutually exclusive cases to handle variables with or without the optional name and predicate:

```
(define (gmatch:compile-var var)
  (cond ((match-list? var gmatch:var-type?)
         (gmatch:var-matcher (car var) #f #f))
        ((match-list? var gmatch:var-type? symbol?)
         (gmatch:var-matcher (car var) (cadr var) #f))
        ((match-list? var gmatch:var-type? symbol? procedure?)
         (gmatch:var-matcher (car var) (cadr var) (caddr var)))
        ((match-list? var gmatch:var-type? procedure?)
         (gmatch:var-matcher (car var) #f (cadr var)))
        (else
         (error "Ill-formed variable:" var))))
```

The procedure var-type? matches the type symbol of a pattern variable: ? or ?*. To recognize the four cases of variables, compile-var uses a utility procedure match-list?, which is true if its first argument is a list and each element of the list satisfies the corresponding predicate argument.

```
(define (match-list? datum . preds)
  (let loop ((preds preds) (datum datum))
    (if (pair? preds)
        (and (pair? datum)
             ((car preds) (car datum))
             (loop (cdr preds) (cdr datum)))
        (null? datum))))
```

The procedure `var-matcher` is the matcher for variables, now that we have decoded their syntax.

```
(define (gmatch:var-matcher var-type var-name restriction)
  (define (match-var object dict succeed)
    (and (or (not restriction)
             (restriction object dict))
         (if var-name
             (let ((dict*
                    (gmatch:bind var-type var-name object
                                 dict)))
               (and dict*
                    (succeed object dict*)))
             (succeed object dict))))
  match-var)
```

Here `bind` adds a binding for `var-name` with value `object`, returning a new dictionary. If the dictionary already has such a binding, and its value is different from `object`, `bind` returns `#f` to indicate a match failure.

And with this we have finished the graph matcher.

Exercise 4.25: Graph matching

The graph matcher described here is very useful, but there are problems for which it isn't well suited. What is an interesting problem that requires extension(s) to the matcher? Find such a problem, define and implement the extension(s), and demonstrate its use on some examples.

4.6 Summary

Patterns are fun, but they are also a very useful way to organize parts of a system for additivity. In this chapter we have seen how to build a term-rewriting system. A rule-based term-rewriting system makes it easy to write programs that do successive replacements of parts of an expression with "equivalent" parts, terminating when no more rules are applicable. Such systems are important components of larger systems that do symbolic manipulation. Algebraic expression simplification is one application, but compilers do huge amounts of this kind of manipulation, to compute optimizations and sometimes to generate code.

We also saw a flexible way to construct a pattern matcher, by "compiling" a pattern into a combination of simple matchers that all have the same interface structure. This makes it easy to add new features and to make such a system very efficient. When we add segment variables, which match an unspecified number of elements, to such a matcher we find that we have to implement a backtracking system, because there may be multiple possible matches to any particular data if the pattern has more than one segment variable. This complicates matters significantly. Besides the intrinsic complexity of backtracking, the backtracking in the pattern matcher must be interfaced to the backtracking system in the rule executive that uses the patterns. We will examine more general ways of dealing with backtracking in section 5.4. We will investigate even more powerful backtracking strategies in section 7.5.2.

If we model partially specified data as patterns with holes (represented by pattern variables), then we find that we need to match patterns against each other to collect the constraints on the data so that we can sharpen the specification. We explored *unification*: the process of merging partial information structures of this kind. This is essentially a way of setting up and solving symbolic equations for the missing parts of the data. Unification is very powerful, and we showed how to make a simple type-inference engine using unification in this way.

We found that the ideas of pattern matching can be extended to operate on general graphs rather than just hierarchical expressions. This made it easy to work with such complex graphs as chess boards, where we used patterns to specify legal chess moves.

Patterns and pattern matching can be a way to express computational thought, and on some problems can be more revealing than other programming methods. But be careful: pattern matching is not the answer to all of the world's problems, so let's not become addicted to it.

5
Evaluation

One of the best ways to attack a problem is to make up a domain-specific language in which the solution is easily expressed. If the language you make up is powerful enough, many problems that are similar to the one you are attacking will have easy-to-express solutions in your language. This strategy is especially effective if you start with a flexible mechanism. We explored this idea in limited contexts in chapters 2, 3, and 4. Here we will pursue this idea in full generality.

When we make up a language we must give it meaning. If we want the expressions of the language to describe computational processes, we must build a mechanism that, when given expressions in the language, evolves the desired process. An *interpreter* is just such a mechanism. We will explore this creative realm starting with an extensible version of the applicative order Scheme `eval/apply` interpreter similar to the ones described in SICP [1], Chapter 4.

Scheme procedures are strict, requiring each argument to be evaluated before the body of the procedure is entered. We next generalize our interpreter, adding declarations to the formal parameter list of a procedure. These declarations will allow a procedure to defer evaluation of the corresponding argument to when its value is actually needed, providing for lazy evaluation, with or without memoization of the value. This declaration mechanism can also be used for other information, such as types and units.

An interpreter is rather inefficient, because it must analyze the expression to be interpreted in order to know what to do at each step. This effort is repeated each time the interpreter encounters the same expression. So we next separate the interpretation into two phases, analysis and execution. The analysis phase examines the expression and compiles an execution procedure, which when called will perform the intent of the expression. The execution procedure runs without access to the expression it was compiled from. The execution procedures all have the same form, and constitute a system of combinators.

We next add McCarthy's `amb` operator to allow us to do non-deterministic evaluation and search. Remarkably, this requires no change to the analysis part of the evaluator. The only change required is in the format of the execution procedures, which are re-expressed in continuation-passing style. The use of continuation-passing style suggests exposing the underlying continuation to the programmer.

The procedure `call/cc` that exposes the underlying continuation is a standard procedure in Scheme, and it turns out that all we need is `call/cc` to implement `amb` directly in Scheme, so we conclude by showing how to do this.

5.1   Generic `eval`/`apply` interpreter

Our first interpreter is constructed to be extensible. All significant parts are generic procedures, and we are careful to avoid unnecessary commitments. Let's start.

The essence of the interpreter is in two procedures: `eval` and `apply`. The procedure `eval` takes an expression and an environment as inputs. The expression is a combination of subexpressions that are syntactically glued together. The environment gives meanings to some of the symbols that appear in the expression. There are other symbols that have meanings that are fixed in the definition of `eval`.[1] But most expressions are interpreted as combinations of an *operator* and *operands*. Evaluation of the operator should yield a procedure and evaluation of the operands should yield arguments. The procedure and arguments are then passed to `apply`. The procedure usually names the arguments with *formal parameters*. The procedure `apply` evaluates the *body* of the procedure (using `eval`) in an environment in which the formal parameters of the procedure are *bound* to the arguments. This is the central computational loop of the interpreter.

What we just described is the traditional applicative-order interpreter plan. In our interpreter we will pass the unevaluated operands and the environment for their evaluation to `apply` to make it possible to implement a variety of evaluation strategies, such as normal order as well as applicative order.

---

[1]But because our `eval` is a generic procedure, the set of symbols that are defined by eval may be changed easily and even dynamically.

The language we will be implementing is a Lisp variant.[2] This implies that the code is expressed as list structures. In Lisp all compound expressions are lists, some of which start with distinguished keywords. Compound expressions that have distinguished keywords are called *special forms*. The compound expressions that are not special forms are interpreted as applications of procedures to arguments. The implementation will be organized as a set of rules for each expression type, with the exception of applications, which are distinguished by not being special forms. With each rule we give the syntactic definition of the expression type. This strategy can be used to implement almost any language, though a new parser would be needed. With Lisp the reader converts the character-string input into list structures, which are natural representations of the abstract syntax tree (AST) of the language. With other languages the AST is more elaborate and the parser is much more complicated.

5.1.1 eval

We define g:eval as a generic procedure with two arguments.

```
(define g:eval
  (simple-generic-procedure 'eval 2 default-eval))
```

The default case for eval is an *application* (sometimes described as a *combination*).

```
(define (default-eval expression environment)
  (cond ((application? expression)
         (g:apply (g:advance
                    (g:eval (operator expression)
                            environment))
                  (operands expression)
                  environment))
        (else
         (error "Unknown expression type" expression))))
```

---

[2]Our interpreter's implementation is made simpler by the use of Scheme as the implementation language. We inherit the Scheme reader, so our syntax is very simple; we inherit tail recursion, so we don't need to pay special care when implementing procedure calls; and we use Scheme procedures as primitives. If we were to choose a different implementation language, for example C, we would have many more issues to contend with. Nevertheless, it is possible to build this kind of interpreter in any language.

In Lisp-based languages the operator of a list representing an application is the first element of the list and the operands are the rest of the elements of the list.

```
(define (application? exp) (pair? exp))
(define (operator app) (car app))
(define (operands app) (cdr app))
```

Note how the code above follows the pattern we described on page 235. We are presenting both the interpretation of a particular syntactic construct (application), and the definition of its syntax. Also as we explained there, it is necessary to handle applications as the default case of the generic procedure, because there is no special keyword identifying an application in Lisp—instead it is identified by being a list *not* starting with one of the distinguished keywords.

An application first evaluates the operator part of the expression and then passes that value to `g:apply` along with the operands of the expression and the current environment. However, after evaluating the operator, we pass the value to the generic procedure `g:advance`. The purpose of `g:advance` is to continue evaluations that have been postponed. We will not need to postpone evaluations until section 5.2, so until then `g:advance` is just an identity function:[3]

```
(define g:advance
  (simple-generic-procedure 'g:advance 1 (lambda (x) x)))
```

This is not the traditional way that `apply` is defined. By passing along the unevaluated operands and the environment of the application we leave open the option to introduce normal-order evaluation as well as applicative-order evaluation; we also enable the implementation of declarations on the formal parameters, and perhaps some other options.

For each non-application expression type we provide a handler. Self-evaluating expressions return themselves:

---

[3] The use of the `g:` prefix in `g:apply` and other names serves to identify those names as specific to this "generic" interpreter. In later sections we introduce different versions of the interpreter, each of which has its own prefix.

```
(define-generic-procedure-handler g:eval
  (match-args self-evaluating? environment?)
  (lambda (expression environment) expression))
```

In Lisp languages the self-evaluating expressions include the numbers, the boolean values, and strings. In Scheme, number? is a rather complicated predicate. The objects that satisfy number? include integers of arbitrary size, rational fractions, reals, and complex numbers.[4]

```
(define (self-evaluating? exp)
  (or (number? exp)
      (boolean? exp)
      (string? exp)))
```

There may be other self-evaluating expressions, so to make that option really flexible we could have defined self-evaluating? as a generic procedure. But here this is not necessary, because we could just make another handler for g:eval to define any other self-evaluating expression type that we might want to add.

Quotations are required in languages that allow manipulation of the symbolic expressions of the language.[5] A quotation is an expression that protects a subexpression from evaluation.

```
(define-generic-procedure-handler g:eval
  (match-args quoted? environment?)
  (lambda (expression environment)
    (text-of-quotation expression)))
```

In Lisp-based languages the list-structure representation of a quoted expression is a list beginning with the keyword quote. The reader (parser) for Lisp expands any expression beginning with an apostrophe character (e.g., '(a b c)) into a quoted expression (here (quote (a b c))).

```
(define (quoted? exp) (tagged-list? exp 'quote))
(define (text-of-quotation quot) (cadr quot))
```

---

[4]Reals are usually represented in the computer as floating-point numbers. The parts of a Scheme complex number may be integers or rational fractions, as well as reals.

[5]The understanding of quotation and its relationship to evaluation has deep consequences in analytic philosophy. One good exposition of this is in the 1982 PhD thesis of Brian Cantwell Smith [112].

A *tagged list* is just a list beginning with a given unique symbol:

```
(define (tagged-list? e t) (and (pair? e) (eq? (car e) t)))
```

Scheme variables are just looked up in the environment. In other languages there are more complex rules about variables. For example, in C there are *lvalues* and *rvalues*, and they are handled differently.

```
(define-generic-procedure-handler g:eval
  (match-args variable? environment?)
  lookup-variable-value)
```

In Lisp-based languages the variables are represented by symbols.[6]

```
(define (variable? exp) (symbol? exp))
```

The procedure `lookup-variable-value` looks up its argument in the given environment. If no value is found for that variable, it looks for a value in the underlying Scheme.[7] If no value is found, an `Unbound variable` error is signaled.

Binary conditional expressions (*if-then-else*) have a simple handler. If the predicate part of the expression evaluates to a true value, evaluate the consequent part of the expression, otherwise evaluate the alternative part of the expression.

```
(define-generic-procedure-handler g:eval
  (match-args if? environment?)
  (lambda (expression environment)
    (if (g:advance
         (g:eval (if-predicate expression) environment))
        (g:eval (if-consequent expression) environment)
        (g:eval (if-alternative expression) environment))))
```

We must call `g:advance` on the evaluated predicate because we need to know the value to make the decision. Notice that the

---

[6]A symbol is an atomic object that is named by a string of characters. What makes a symbol interesting is that it is unique: any two instances of a symbol with the same character-string name may be presumed to be identical (they are `eq?`).

[7]Many of the Scheme primitives found this way will work, such as `car` or `+`. However, primitives that take procedures as arguments, such as `map` or `filter`, will not accept nonprimitive procedures (i.e., those created by this interpreter from `lambda` expressions). This is addressed in exercise 5.5 on page 249.

evaluator for `if` uses the `if` construct of the embedding language to do the work!

The Lisp syntax for the `if` expression is simple. If no alternative is specified, the value of the `if` expression with a false predicate is the value of the global variable `the-unspecified-value`.

```
(define (if? exp) (tagged-list? exp 'if))
(define (if-predicate exp) (cadr exp))
(define (if-consequent exp) (caddr exp))

(define (if-alternative exp)
  (if (not (null? (cdddr exp)))
      (cadddr exp)
      'the-unspecified-value))

(define (make-if pred conseq alternative)
  (list 'if pred conseq alternative))
```

The first really interesting special form is the specification of an anonymous procedure, represented by a `lambda` expression. A `lambda` expression is a special form, the constructor for procedures. Evaluation of a `lambda` expression constructs a procedure from the formal parameters, the body, and the current environment. The environment must be carried by the procedure if the variables in the language are lexically scoped. In a lexically scoped language the free variables in the body of the `lambda` expression (those that are not formal parameters) are given meanings from the lexical context (where the `lambda` expression appears textually).

```
(define-generic-procedure-handler g:eval
  (match-args lambda? environment?)
  (lambda (expression environment)
    (make-compound-procedure
     (lambda-parameters expression)
     (lambda-body expression)
     environment)))
```

The syntax for `lambda` expressions is:

```
(define (lambda? exp) (tagged-list? exp 'lambda))

(define (lambda-parameters lambda-exp) (cadr lambda-exp))

(define (lambda-body lambda-exp)
  (let ((full-body (cddr lambda-exp)))
    (sequence->begin full-body)))
```

```
(define (make-lambda parameters body)
  (cons 'lambda
        (cons parameters
              (if (begin? body)
                  (begin-actions body)
                  (list body)))))
```

Note that the body of a `lambda` expression may contain several expressions. These are intended to be evaluated in sequence, to allow for side-effecting actions, such as assignment, or I/O control actions, such as printing. This is handled by `sequence->begin`, which creates a `begin` special form.

```
(define (sequence->begin seq)
  (cond ((null? seq) seq)
        ((null? (cdr seq)) (car seq))
        (else
         (make-begin
          (append-map (lambda (exp)
                        (if (begin? exp)
                            (begin-actions exp)
                            (list exp)))
                      seq)))))
```

Notice that the procedure `sequence->begin` flattens nested `begin` forms, preserving the order of execution. The syntax and evaluation of `begin` forms is defined and described on page 242.

Derived expression types

The expression types already introduced are sufficient to conveniently write most programs, but it is often nice to have some syntactic sugar. These can be implemented by transformations of expressions into combinations of simpler ones. Macros are a way to generalize such transformations; but we choose not to build a macro expander as part of our interpreter.[8] Here we explicitly

---

[8] The real problem with macros is that they can introduce bindings that can inadvertently conflict with existing bindings, making them referentially opaque. There are several attacks on the referential-opacity problem, leading to the development of Scheme *hygienic* macro systems. See [73, 74, 8, 31]. Also, drastically modifying a language by introducing special forms makes it harder for a reader to understand a program—the reader must learn the new special forms before reading the program that uses them.

show how the Lisp multi-armed conditional can be turned into a
nest of if expressions:

```
(define-generic-procedure-handler g:eval
  (match-args cond? environment?)
  (lambda (expression environment)
    (g:eval (cond->if expression)
            environment)))
```

The procedure cond->if is a rather simple data manipulation:

```
(define (cond->if cond-exp)
  (define (expand clauses)
    (cond ((null? clauses)
           (error "COND: no values matched"))
          ((else-clause? (car clauses))
           (if (null? (cdr clauses))
               (cond-clause-consequent (car clauses))
               (error "COND: ELSE not last"
                      cond-exp)))
          (else
           (make-if (cond-clause-predicate (car clauses))
                    (cond-clause-consequent (car clauses))
                    (expand (cdr clauses)))))))
  (expand (cond-clauses cond-exp)))
```

And here is the syntax for the cond special form:

```
(define (cond? exp) (tagged-list? exp 'cond))

(define (cond-clauses exp) (cdr exp))

(define (cond-clause-predicate clause) (car clause))

(define (cond-clause-consequent clause)
  (sequence->begin (cdr clause)))

(define (else-clause? clause)
  (eq? (cond-clause-predicate clause) 'else))
```

Because cond allows a sequence of actions for the consequent of a
clause, this definition also depends on sequence->begin.

Local variables can be introduced with let expressions. These
are implemented by translation into a combination with an explicit
lambda expression:

```
(define-generic-procedure-handler g:eval
  (match-args let? environment?)
  (lambda (expression environment)
    (g:eval (let->combination expression)
            environment)))
```

The syntax for let is:

```
(define (let? exp) (tagged-list? exp 'let))
```

```
(define (let-bound-variables let-exp)
  (map car (cadr let-exp)))
```

```
(define (let-bound-values let-exp)
  (map cadr (cadr let-exp)))
```

```
(define (let-body let-exp)
  (sequence->begin (cddr let-exp)))
```

```
(define (let->combination let-exp)
  (let ((names (let-bound-variables let-exp))
        (values (let-bound-values let-exp))
        (body (let-body let-exp)))
    (cons (make-lambda names body)
          values)))
```

Effects

If there are operations in the language that have effects, like assignment or printing, they must be sequenced, because the order is essential. In Scheme we syntactically represent such sequences of operations with begin:

```
(define-generic-procedure-handler g:eval
  (match-args begin? environment?)
  (lambda (expression environment)
    (evaluate-sequence (begin-actions expression)
                       environment)))
```

```
(define (begin? exp) (tagged-list? exp 'begin))
(define (begin-actions begin-exp) (cdr begin-exp))
(define (make-begin actions) (cons 'begin actions))
```

The real work is actually in the sequence evaluation:

```
(define (evaluate-sequence actions environment)
  (cond ((null? actions)
         (error "Empty sequence"))
        ((null? (cdr actions))
         (g:eval (car actions) environment))
        (else
         (g:eval (car actions) environment)
         (evaluate-sequence (cdr actions)
                            environment))))
```

The value returned by evaluating a nonempty sequence of expressions is the value of the last expression in the sequence. But effects caused by executing expressions in the sequence happen in the order of the sequence.

Most effects are implemented by assignment of variables. (Indeed, input/output operations are usually implemented in hardware by assignment to particular sensitive locations in the address space.) In Scheme we allow a program to assign to a variable in the lexical environment of the assignment statement:

```
(define-generic-procedure-handler g:eval
  (match-args assignment? environment?)
  (lambda (expression environment)
    (set-variable-value! (assignment-variable expression)
                        (g:eval (assignment-value expression)
                                environment)
                        environment)))
```

The syntax for assignment is:

```
(define (assignment? exp) (tagged-list? exp 'set!))
(define (assignment-variable assn) (cadr assn))
(define (assignment-value assn) (caddr assn))
```

We also allow definition, the creation of a new variable with a given value. A definition creates a new variable in the most local lexical environment frame of the definition statement.

```
(define-generic-procedure-handler g:eval
  (match-args definition? environment?)
  (lambda (expression environment)
    (define-variable! (definition-variable expression)
                      (g:eval (definition-value expression)
                              environment)
                      environment)
    (definition-variable expression)))
```

The syntax for definitions is more complicated than the syntax for assignment, because we allow multiple ways to define a procedure:[9]

```
(define (definition? exp) (tagged-list? exp 'define))

(define (definition-variable defn)
  (if (variable? (cadr defn))        ; (DEFINE  foo        ...)
      (cadr  defn)
      (caadr defn)))                 ; (DEFINE (foo ...) ...)

(define (definition-value defn)
  (if (variable? (cadr defn))        ; (DEFINE  foo        ...)
      (caddr defn)
      (cons 'lambda                  ; (DEFINE (foo p...) b...)
            (cons (cdadr defn)       ; =(DEFINE  foo
                  (cddr  defn)))))) ;    (LAMBDA (p...) b...))
```

This completes the usual list of special forms that define the syntax of the language. Of course, the generic procedure implementation enables creation of new special forms easily, allowing the language to grow to make it more convenient to express computational ideas that were not well supported in the base language. But a language with many different syntactic constructs may be difficult to learn, document, and use; this is a classic engineering tradeoff (remember Alan Perlis's maxim on page 159).

5.1.2 apply

The traditional Scheme apply takes two arguments, the procedure to be applied and the evaluated arguments to be passed to the procedure. This is sufficient for Scheme, because Scheme is a strict

---

[9]MIT/GNU Scheme allows a more general syntax for definitions, with recursive expansion of the cadr of the define form (see page 383). We do not do this here.

applicative-order language with only lexically scoped variables. By generalizing the interface to `apply` to take three arguments—the procedure to be applied, the *un*evaluated operands, and the calling environment—we make it possible to include procedures that require normal-order evaluation for some parameters (e.g., call by need) or procedures that make declarations on parameters, such as types and units. We will make some extensions like these in section 5.2. The environment argument also makes it possible to accommodate non-lexically scoped variables, but we will not do so; it is generally a bad idea. We will start out with Scheme applicative order, with generic hooks for extension.

Our `apply` is a generic procedure with three arguments:

```
(define g:apply
  (simple-generic-procedure 'apply 3 default-apply))

(define (default-apply procedure operands calling-environment)
  (error "Unknown procedure type" procedure))
```

We will need handlers for the various kinds of procedures. Some procedures, like arithmetic addition (usually named by the + operator), are *strict*: they need all of their arguments evaluated before they can compute a value. In Scheme all procedures are strict, including primitive procedures (implemented in the system or hardware below the level of the language). So we need a generic handler for strict primitives:

```
(define-generic-procedure-handler g:apply
  (match-args strict-primitive-procedure?
              operands?
              environment?)
  (lambda (procedure operands calling-environment)
    (apply-primitive-procedure procedure
      (eval-operands operands calling-environment))))
```

The application of a primitive procedure is "magic" at this level of detail. The operands evaluator, like `if` on page 238, must call `g:advance` on the result of evaluation to ensure a value.

```
(define (eval-operands operands calling-environment)
  (map (lambda (operand)
         (g:advance (g:eval operand calling-environment)))
       operands))
```

Note that the order of evaluation of the operands is determined by the behavior of `map`.

Procedures constructed by evaluating `lambda` expressions are not primitive. Here we can take apart the procedure. We can grab the formal parameter specifications, which are the names of the formal parameters. We also can extract the body of the procedure, which we will pass to `eval` with an environment that includes the formal parameter bindings. For lexical scoping, that extended environment is built on the environment packaged with the procedure by the evaluation of the `lambda` expression that constructed the procedure.

```
(define-generic-procedure-handler g:apply
  (match-args strict-compound-procedure?
              operands?
              environment?)
  (lambda (procedure operands calling-environment)
    (if (not (n:= (length (procedure-parameters procedure))
                  (length operands)))
        (error "Wrong number of operands supplied"))
    (g:eval (procedure-body procedure)
            (extend-environment
             (procedure-parameters procedure)
             (eval-operands operands calling-environment)
             (procedure-environment procedure)))))
```

Here `strict-compound-procedure?` is true of all compound procedures that have no declarations on any of their parameters.[10]

Driver loop

To interact with this evaluator we need a read-eval-print loop:

```
(define (repl)
  (check-repl-initialized)
  (let ((input (g:read)))
    (write-line (g:eval input the-global-environment))
    (repl)))
```

---

[10]We have made a decision here that limits future extension. The fact that we require the procedure parameters to be a list of the same length as the list of operands means that we cannot extend this `g:apply` handler to allow procedures with optional or rest parameters. So we could not define the traditional Lisp + that takes an unspecified number of arguments and adds them up! But see exercise 5.2.

Here `g:read` issues a prompt, `eval>`, on the terminal. It accepts characters and parses them, converting what it gets into an s-expression. That s-expression is then evaluated with `g:eval` with respect to `the-global-environment` and the result is written back to the terminal. The procedure `repl` calls itself tail recursively. For this to work, the global environment must be initialized:

```
(define the-global-environment
  'not-initialized)

(define (initialize-repl!)
  (set! the-global-environment (make-global-environment))
  'done)

(define (check-repl-initialized)
  (if (eq? the-global-environment 'not-initialized)
      (error
       "Interpreter not initialized. Run (init) first.")))
```

This completes the elementary evaluator.

Exercise 5.1: Unbound-variable handling

In Lisps, including Scheme, attempting to evaluate an unbound symbol is an unbound-variable error. However, in some algebraic processes it is often sensible to allow an unbound symbol to be a self-evaluating object. For example, if we generically extend arithmetic to build algebraic expressions with symbolic values, as we did in chapter 3, it is sometimes useful to allow the following:

```
(+ (* 2 3) (* 4 5))
26

(+ (* a 3) (* 4 5))
(+ (* a 3) 20)
```

Our generic arithmetic supported symbolic extensions: the operators `*` and `+` were extended to build expressions when their arguments were not reducible to numbers. But it did not allow the use of unbound variables as literal numbers. Here the symbol `a` is unbound. We may want it to be self-evaluating.

a. Make a generic extension to `eval` to allow this kind of behavior. To make this work with the numerical primitives (`+`, `*`, `-`, `/`) it is necessary to extend their behavior as well. Note that these operators should be changed in the underlying Scheme environment. As in chapter 3, the generic operator mechanism may be given handlers that work in the underlying Scheme system.

b. Also augment `apply` to allow unbound symbols in the operator position to be interpreted as literal functions, known only by their names: `(+ (f 3) (* 4 5)) ==> (+ (f 3) 20)`

These extensions to `eval` and `apply` are generally dangerous, because they hide real unbound-variable errors. Make them contingent on the value of a user-settable variable: `allow-self-evaluating-symbols`.

Exercise 5.2: *n*-ary procedures

Footnote 10 on page 246 points out a nasty assumption that we put into the `g:apply` handler that implies a restriction on the future expansion of this evaluator. In Scheme, if the `procedure-parameters` of a procedure is not a list but rather a symbol, then that symbol is taken as a single parameter that will be bound to the list of arguments.[11]

In this exercise we change the interpreter to accept a single symbol as the formal parameter list, so that a procedure can be defined to take an indefinite number of arguments. In our interpreter the procedure `lambda-parameters` (page 239) is happy to return a single symbol, and everywhere it is called the result is passed to `make-compound-procedure`. That value is retrieved by `procedure-parameters`, which is used in `g:apply`. So it appears that the only part of the interpreter that needs to be changed is `g:apply`.

Change `g:apply` to work with the new compound procedures. This can be done by rewriting the existing `strict-compound-procedure?` handler of `g:apply` (page 246), but it is both easier and clearer to specialize that handler for the case where the `procedure-parameters` is a list, and to add a new handler for the case where the `procedure-parameters` is a symbol.

Exercise 5.3: Vectors of procedures

In mathematical text a common abuse of notation is to identify a tuple of functions with a function that returns a tuple of values. For example, if `(cos 0.6)` produces `0.8253356149096783` and if `(sin 0.6)` produces

---

[11] In Scheme, a parameter that takes all the arguments after the explicitly declared ones is called a *rest parameter*. If there are explicitly declared parameters we can use an improper list (a chain of pairs in which the last `cdr` is not the empty list) as our parameter list. For example `(lambda (a b . c) ...)` is a procedure that takes at least two arguments, which will be bound to `a` and `b`; any additional arguments supplied (after the first two) are made into a list that is the value of `c`. If there are no explicitly declared parameters and just a rest parameter we use a single symbol to be the name of the rest parameter. For example, in Scheme we can write `(lambda xs ...)` to define a procedure that takes any number of arguments and binds the parameter `xs` to be the list of arguments.

0.5646424733950354 then we expect ((`vector cos sin`) 0.6) to produce #(0.8253356149096783 0.5646424733950354).

Although we had an exercise 3.2 to extend the arithmetic to vectors, those extensions did not modify the underlying language evaluator. This behavior needs an extension to `g:apply` so it can handle vectors of functions as a kind of function. Make this extension, demonstrate it, and show that it interoperates with more conventional code.

Exercise 5.4: Your turn

Invent a fun, interesting construct that can easily be implemented using generic `eval/apply` but would be rather painful without that kind of generic support.

Exercise 5.5: Interoperation with the underlying system

As pointed out on page 238, evaluating the expression

```
eval> (map (lambda (x) (* x x)) '(1 2 3))
```

in our interpreter does not work if the `map` in this expression refers to the `map` procedure from the underlying Scheme system.

However, if we redefine `map` for our interpreter it does work:

```
eval> (define (map f l)
         (if (null? l)
             '()
             (cons (f (car l)) (map f (cdr l)))))
map

eval> (map (lambda (x) (* x x)) '(1 2 3))
(1 4 9)
```

Why does it not work to use the underlying procedures that take procedural arguments, such as `map`? Explain. Outline a strategy to fix the problem and implement your solution. Note: This is subtle to get right, so don't spend infinite time trying to make it work perfectly.

Exercise 5.6: Different quotation

There have been interesting languages with very different evaluation and quotation rules. For example, in MDL (see Wikipedia [91]) a symbol is assumed to be self evaluating, and variables to be looked up are distinguished with a prefix character. Also, in MDL a combination is a special form, but with an implied keyword. Our evaluator can easily be modified to interpret a MDL-like syntax, just by changing the syntax definitions. Try it!

Exercise 5.7: Infix notation

Unlike Lisp, most computer languages use infix notations. If we wanted to include infix expressions in Scheme we might write:

```
(infix
  "fact := lambda n:
            if n == 0
               then 1
               else n*fact(n-1)")

(fact 6)                ; The Lisp procedure is now defined
720

(infix "fact(5)")    ; And it can be used in infix notation.
120
```

This is entirely a small matter of syntax (ha!). However, it is an interesting project to make it work. You do not need to change the interpreter. The work is parsing the character string to compile it into the corresponding Lisp expressions, in the same way that `cond->if` works. Lisp programmers have done this many times, but people who program in Lisp seem to like the native Lisp Polish prefix notation![12] Oh, well...

5.2   Procedures with non-strict arguments

In this section we will investigate adding declarations to the formal parameters of a procedure to allow deferred evaluation of the corresponding operands.

In Scheme, procedures are *strict*. Strict procedures require evaluating all the operands of the calling expression and binding the resulting arguments to the formal parameters before the body of the procedure is evaluated. But for an `if` expression, the predicate part must be evaluated to determine whether to evaluate the consequent part or the alternative part; they won't both be evaluated. This is why `if` must be a special form, not a procedure.

A *non-strict* procedure is one that defers the evaluation of some operands. How can we make it possible for a programmer to define non-strict procedures as needed, rather than just using a few special forms, such as `if`, that are specified in the language definition?

---

[12]Such an infix parser can be found on the website for this book.

For example, suppose we want to make a procedure `unless` that works like the special form `if` in that it does not evaluate the alternatives that are not needed.[13] Using `unless` we could write:

```
(define (fib n)
  (unless (< n 2)
          (+ (fib (- n 1)) (fib (- n 2)))
          n))
```

For this definition of the Fibonacci function to work correctly, the second operand of the `unless` expression should not be evaluated if $n < 2$, and the third operand should not be evaluated if $n \geq 2$. But the first operand of the `unless` expression must always be evaluated to determine the choice.

We need a way to determine which operands of `unless` to evaluate, and which to defer. To do this we introduce a kind of declaration and write:

```
(define (unless condition (usual lazy) (exception lazy))
  (if condition exception usual))
```

Here we define the procedure `unless` in terms of the special form `if`, but we declare that the second and third arguments are lazy.[14] The first argument is, by default, strict.

We could have many kinds of declarations on formal parameters, describing how to handle operands and arguments. A parameter could be declared lazy and memoized, to implement call by need, as are arguments to all procedures in languages like Haskell; a parameter could be declared to require that its argument satisfy given predicates, which could be types and units; etc.

Implementing generalized formal parameters

To implement generalized formal parameters, we need a special applicator that handles the new cases. This is accomplished by adding a single handler to `g:apply`, similar to the earlier one for strict compound procedures (see page 246):

---

[13]You may notice that this definition of `unless` differs from that used in many Lisp languages, including standard Scheme [109] and Emacs Lisp.

[14]Common practice uses the term "lazy evaluation" to mean that the argument's evaluation is postponed and that the result is memoized. Here we separate those ideas and use lazy to mean just postponed.

```
(define-generic-procedure-handler g:apply
  (match-args general-compound-procedure?
              operands?
              environment?)
  (lambda (procedure operands calling-environment)
    (if (not (n:= (length (procedure-parameters procedure))
                  (length operands)))
        (error "Wrong number of operands supplied"))
    (let ((params (procedure-parameters procedure))
          (body (procedure-body procedure)))
      (let ((names (map procedure-parameter-name params))
            (arguments
             (map (lambda (param operand)
                    (g:handle-operand param
                                      operand
                                      calling-environment))
                  params
                  operands)))
        (g:eval body
                (extend-environment names arguments
                (procedure-environment procedure)))))))
```

This differs from the strict applicator in two ways: first, we must extract the names of the parameters, since they could be wrapped in declarations; second, we must handle the operands specially, depending on the declarations. This is done by the generic procedures `procedure-parameter-name` and `g:handle-operand`.

The procedure `procedure-parameter-name` allows us to add declarations to a formal parameter and still be able to retrieve its name. The default handler is the identity function, so the name of an undecorated formal parameter is just itself.

```
(define procedure-parameter-name
  (simple-generic-procedure 'parameter-name 1 (lambda (x) x)))
```

The procedure `g:handle-operand` allows us to choose how to process an operand based on the declarations of the corresponding formal parameter:

```
(define g:handle-operand
  (simple-generic-procedure 'g:handle-operand 3
    (lambda (parameter operand environment)
      (g:advance (g:eval operand environment)))))
```

The default way to handle an operand without declarations is to evaluate the operand, as was previously done by `eval-operands` on page 245.

We need a syntax to allow us to decorate a formal parameter with declarations. Here we choose to use a list beginning with the name of the formal parameter:

```
(define-generic-procedure-handler procedure-parameter-name
  (match-args pair?)
  car)
```

We will start by implementing two kinds of declarations. The first is `lazy`, which means the operand is evaluated only when its value is needed, for example as the predicate of an `if` expression. The second is `lazy memo`, which is like `lazy` except that the first time the operand is evaluated, the value is remembered so that subsequent uses do not require reevaluation.

If a parameter is specified to be lazy (or lazy memoized) the evaluation of the operand must be postponed. The postponed expression must be packaged with the environment that will be used to give values to the free variables in that expression when its value is required.[15]

```
(define-generic-procedure-handler g:handle-operand
  (match-args lazy? operand? environment?)
  (lambda (parameter operand environment)
    (postpone operand environment)))
```

```
(define-generic-procedure-handler g:handle-operand
  (match-args lazy-memo? operand? environment?)
  (lambda (parameter operand environment)
    (postpone-memo operand environment)))
```

Of course, we must extend `g:advance`, which so far has only a default handler (see page 236), to do the postponed evaluation. Notice that the result of `g:advance` may itself be a postponement, so we may have to advance that.

```
(define-generic-procedure-handler g:advance
  (match-args postponed?)
  (lambda (object)
    (g:advance (g:eval (postponed-expression object)
                       (postponed-environment object)))))
```

---

[15]In the original implementations of by-name parameters in Algol-60 these combinations of expression and environment were called *thunks*. Because Scheme programs commonly use procedures with no formal parameters to package an expression to be evaluated later in some other environment, we also call such nullary procedures used in this way *thunks*.

If the expression is postponed with the intent of memoizing the result, the result is saved by `advance-memo!`:

```
(define-generic-procedure-handler g:advance
  (match-args postponed-memo?)
  (lambda (object)
    (let ((value
            (g:advance
              (g:eval (postponed-expression object)
                      (postponed-environment object)))))
      (advance-memo! object value)
      value)))
```

The memoized value never needs to be evaluated again. The `advance-memo!` procedure changes the type of the postponed object to satisfy the predicate `advanced-memo?` and saves the value, making it accessible by `advanced-value`:[16]

```
(define-generic-procedure-handler g:advance
  (match-args advanced-memo?)
  advanced-value)
```

Example: Lazy pairs and lists

Procedures with lazy parameters give us new power. For example, we can define a constructor `kons`, and selectors `kar` and `kdr`, so that we can make pairs without evaluating their contents.[17] Here we have implemented `kons` as a procedure that takes its arguments call by need (memoized lazy). It produces a message acceptor, `the-pair`, for `kar` and `kdr`. It also puts a "sticky note" on `the-pair` for identifying it as the result of `kons`.

```
(define (kons (x lazy memo) (y lazy memo))
  (define (the-pair m)
    (cond ((eq? m 'kar) x)
          ((eq? m 'kdr) y)
          (else (error "Unknown message -- kons" m x y))))
  (hash-table-set! kons-registrations the-pair #t)
  the-pair)
```

---

[16]The procedure `advance-memo!` also drops the pointer from the postponed object to the environment for its evaluation, allowing that environment to be garbage-collected if there are no other pointers to it.

[17]An ancient but important paper by Dan Friedman and David Wise, entitled "Cons should not evaluate its arguments"[40], showed how lazy functional programming can be powerful, but is easily obtained using `kons` rather than `cons`.

```
(define (kar x)
  (x 'kar))

(define (kdr x)
  (x 'kdr))
```

The reason why we need the sticky note is to be able to recognize a kons pair:

```
(define (kons? object)
  (hash-table-exists? kons-registrations object))
```

Using this lazy pair mechanism we can easily implement stream-type processing. Streams are like lists, but they are built as needed by the processes that consume them.[18] Thus a stream that is infinitely long may be processed incrementally, with only a finite portion actual at any time.

Some streams are finite, so it is useful to choose a representation for the empty stream. Let's make it the same as the empty list:

```
(define the-empty-stream '())

(define (empty-stream? thing)
  (null? thing))
```

We can add streams:

```
(define (add-streams s1 s2)
  (cond ((empty-stream? s1) s2)
        ((empty-stream? s2) s1)
        (else
         (kons (+ (kar s1) (kar s2))
               (add-streams (kdr s1) (kdr s2)))))))
```

We can find the *n*th element of a stream:

```
(define (ref-stream stream n)
  (if (= n 0)
      (kar stream)
      (ref-stream (kdr stream) (- n 1))))
```

Given these, we can create a (potentially infinite) stream of Fibonacci numbers with two initial entries and the rest of the stream formed by adding the stream to its kdr:

---

[18]Scheme [109] provides delay and force for implementing streams. For more information about streams see SICP [1] and SRFI-41 [13].

```
(define fibs
  (kons 0 (kons 1 (add-streams (kdr fibs) fibs))))
```

Then we can look at a few Fibonacci numbers

```
(ref-stream fibs 10)
55
```

```
(ref-stream fibs 100)
354224848179261915075
```

The usual doubly recursive Fibonacci program is exponential, so
one could not expect to get the 100th entry in this sequence by that
method; but the fact that the kons pairs are memoized reduces
this to a linear problem. Notice that by this point in the sequence
the ratio of two successive Fibonacci numbers has converged to
the golden ratio in full precision:

```
(inexact
  (/ (ref-stream fibs 100)
     (ref-stream fibs 99)))
1.618033988749895
```

Exercise 5.8: Integrating differential equations

Unfortunately, the use of kons does not, in itself, solve all stream problems. For example, the difficulty alluded to in SICP [1] section 4.2.3
(p. 411) does not automatically dissipate. Suppose we want to integrate a differential equation given some initial conditions. We make the
following definitions:

```
(define (map-stream proc (items lazy memo))
  (if (empty-stream? items)
      items
      (kons (proc (kar items))
            (map-stream proc (kdr items)))))

(define (scale-stream items factor)
  (map-stream (lambda (x) (* x factor))
              items))

(define (integral integrand initial-value dt)
  (define int
    (kons initial-value
          (add-streams (scale-stream integrand dt)
                       int)))
  int)
```

```
(define (solve f y0 dt)
  (define y (integral dy y0 dt))
  (define dy (map-stream f y))
  y)
```

We try to find an approximation to e by integrating $x'(t) = x(t)$ with initial condition $x(0) = 1$. We know that $e = x(1)$ so we write:

```
(ref-stream (solve (lambda (x) x) 1 0.001) 1000)
;Unbound variable: dy
```

We get an error—ugh!

However, now we have the tools to fix this problem. What has to be changed to make this work as expected? Fix this program to get the following behavior:

```
(ref-stream (solve (lambda (x) x) 1 0.001) 1000)
2.716923932235896
```

(Yes, we know this is a terrible approximation to e, but it illustrates a programming point, not a numerical analysis point!)

Exercise 5.9: Why not `kons`?

The `kons` special form is equivalent to a `cons` with both arguments lazy and memoized. If the arguments were not memoized, the computation (`ref-stream fibs 100`) above would take a very long time.

a. Is there ever an advantage to not memoizing? When might it matter?

b. Why could we not have defined `kons` simply as

```
(define (kons (a lazy memo) (d lazy memo))
  (cons a d))
```

using the primitive procedure `cons` imported from Scheme?

c. More generally, the Lisp community has avoided changing `cons` to be `kons`, as recommended by Friedman and Wise (see footnote 17 on page 254). What potentially serious problems are avoided by using `cons` rather than `kons`? Assume that we do not care about small constant factors in performance.

Exercise 5.10: Restricted parameters

One nice idea is to build restrictions into the declaration of a formal parameter. We might want to require that an arbitrary predicate be true of a parameter, similar to our use of restrictions in pattern variables in section 4.3.2. For example, we might want a procedure to take three arguments: the first is any integer, but the second is prime, and the third is unrestricted. This might be notated:

```
(define (my-proc (n integer?) (p prime?) g)
  ...)
```

Unfortunately, this kind of ad hoc design does not play well with other
declarations, like `lazy` and `memo`, unless we legislate the order of the
declarations or make them reserved identifiers. Suppose, for convenience,
we declare `lazy` and `memo` to be special keywords, and require other
declarations to be announced with a keyword, such as `restrict-to` for
a predicate:

```
(define (my-proc (n restrict-to integer?)
                 (p restrict-to prime? lazy)
                 g)
  ...)
```

a. Design an appropriate syntax. Make sure it is extensible in that new
declaration types can be added as needed. Express your syntax in BNF
and change the syntax procedures of your interpreter to implement it.

b. Implement predicate restrictions. If a restriction is violated at run
time, the program should report an error. You may find `guarantee`
useful here.

Exercise 5.11: *n*-ary procedures, again!

a. In exercise 5.2 on page 248 we modified the `g:apply` handler to allow the formal parameters of a procedure to be a single symbol that is
bound to a list of the arguments. Unfortunately, this way of specifying
a rest argument is not natural for a system where the formal parameters
may be decorated with declarations. However, we can invent a decoration syntax that allows us to define procedures with optional and rest
arguments.

For example, if we allow the last formal parameter in the formal
parameter list be decorated with the word `rest`, it should be bound to
the unmatched arguments. This `rest` declaration should be usable with
other declarations on that argument. So we should be able to create
procedures like:

```
(lambda (x
         (y restrict-to integer? lazy)
         (z rest restrict-to list-of-integers?))
  ...)
```

where `list-of-integers?` is a predicate that is true of lists of integers.
The `rest` declaration should be able to be used with other declarations,
such as `lazy` and `restrict-to`.

Make `rest` declarations work!

b. It may also be useful to allow a procedure to have optional arguments, possibly with specified default values. For example, a numerical
procedure could allow the user to specify a tolerance for approximation,
but specify a default value if the user does not supply the tolerance:

```
(lambda (x (epsilon optional flo:ulp-of-one))
  ...)
```

Here `flo:ulp-of-one` is a globally defined symbol that specifies the smallest power of two that when added to 1.0 produces a value that is not equal to 1.0. In the C library it is called `DBL_EPSILON`. (For those few of you who care, in IEEE double-precision floating point the value of `flo:ulp-of-one` is 2.220446049250313e-16.)

Make `optional` declarations work too! Be sure that your extension can mix and match with all other declarations that make sense.

5.3 Compiling to execution procedures

The evaluator that we have been working with is extremely flexible and extensible, but it is dumb: our programs run rather slowly. One culprit is that the evaluator is repeatedly looking at the syntax (however simple) of the program. We avoided this problem in chapter 4 by transforming each matcher pattern into a composition of matcher procedures that all have the same form—a combinator language—in section 4.3. In interpreting a language we can avoid reexamining the syntactic structure by similarly compiling into a composition of execution procedures. So before getting deeper into evaluation, let's make this transition.

The critical idea is to separate the problem of evaluation of an expression relative to an environment into two phases. In the first phase the expression is analyzed and converted into an execution procedure. In the second phase that execution procedure is applied to an environment, producing the expected evaluation result. We implement this idea directly, as the composition of the two phases.

```
(define (x:eval expression environment)
  ((analyze expression) environment))
```

The analysis and conversion of the expression is called *compilation,* and the work that it does is said to be done at *compile time.* The compiler extracts that part of the behavior that does not depend on the values of the free variables in the expression. This is mostly syntactic analysis, but it is also a venue for some optimizations that are implementable by syntactic rules. The resulting execution procedure depends on the mapping of symbols to values specified in the environment; the work it does is said to be done at *run time.*

Analysis of expressions

Since we want to be able to extend the language syntax as needed, we implement the analysis as a generic procedure, with the default being an application of an operator to operands. This has to be a default for Lisp/Scheme because there is no syntactic keyword that distinguishes an application.[19]

```
(define x:analyze
  (simple-generic-procedure 'x:analyze 1 default-analyze))
```

The convention for x:analyze is that it takes an expression as an argument and returns an execution procedure, which takes one argument, an environment.

The procedure analyze captures a common usage pattern:

```
(define (analyze expression)
  (make-executor (x:analyze expression)))
```

The purpose of wrapping the execution procedure with the procedure make-executor is to aid in debugging. The resulting *executor* is also a procedure, with the same arguments and returned value as the execution procedure that it wraps. One useful aspect of this wrapper is that it maintains an "execution trace" that can be helpful while determining how a program got to a point of failure.

As we said, the default analysis is of an application.

```
(define (default-analyze expression)
  (cond ((application? expression)
         (analyze-application expression))
        (else (error "Unknown expression type" expression))))

(define (analyze-application expression)
  (let ((operator-exec (analyze (operator expression)))
        (operand-execs (map analyze (operands expression))))
    (lambda (environment)
      (x:apply (x:advance (operator-exec environment))
               operand-execs
               environment))))
```

Notice the division of labor here: the operator and the operands are extracted from the expression and analyzed to make up the ex-

---

[19] This evaluator differs significantly from the previous ones, so as mentioned in footnote 3 on page 236, we use a new prefix (x:, for "eXecution procedure") to identify analogous procedures.

ecution procedures `operator-exec` and `operand-execs`. This may require significant analysis. The execution procedure for the application is then a procedure (created by the `lambda` expression) that takes an environment and does the application. The procedure `x:apply` (on page 265) is analogous to `g:apply` in the interpreter; but `x:apply` takes execution procedures for the operands, rather than the operand expressions that were used by `g:apply`. The procedure `x:advance`, analogous to `g:advance`, is introduced for the same reason. Every part of the evaluator can be transformed in this way.

The transformation of self-evaluating expressions (such as numbers, boolean values, or strings) is trivial. The only hard part of this is the actual syntax of the expressions, which is handled by the Scheme parser. The text of the programs is parsed into tokens and s-expressions before it ever gets to the evaluator, so we need not concern ourselves with those complexities here.

```
(define (analyze-self-evaluating expression)
  (lambda (environment) expression))

(define-generic-procedure-handler x:analyze
  (match-args self-evaluating?)
  analyze-self-evaluating)
```

Quotation is easy, again because the hard part is in the parser.[20]

```
(define (analyze-quoted expression)
  (let ((qval (text-of-quotation expression)))
    (lambda (environment) qval)))

(define-generic-procedure-handler x:analyze
  (match-args quoted?)
  analyze-quoted)
```

Variables are also easy. Once we identify the variable, all of the work is in the execution procedure.

```
(define (analyze-variable expression)
  (lambda (environment)
    (lookup-variable-value expression environment)))
```

---

[20]In Lisp (and so in Scheme) the extraction of the text of the quotation is simple—it is just a `cadr`—but our intent is to be general enough to accommodate any language syntax. In most languages the extraction of the text of the quotation is much harder.

```
(define-generic-procedure-handler x:analyze
  (match-args variable?)
  analyze-variable)
```

Procedure definitions, expressed in Lisp/Scheme by `lambda` expressions, are an example of a powerful division of labor. Before building the execution procedure, the analyzer (compiler) parses the `lambda` expression, extracting the formal parameter specifications, and compiles the body of the expression. Thus the execution procedure for the `lambda` expression, and the code that eventually executes the body, need not do that work.

```
(define (analyze-lambda expression)
  (let ((vars (lambda-parameters expression))
        (body-exec (analyze (lambda-body expression))))
    (lambda (environment)
      (make-compound-procedure vars body-exec environment))))
```

```
(define-generic-procedure-handler x:analyze
  (match-args lambda?)
  analyze-lambda)
```

The special form `if` is another very clear example of the advantage of separating analysis from execution. The three parts of the `if` expression are analyzed at compile time, allowing the execution procedure to do no more work than extract the boolean value from the predicate to decide whether to do the consequent or the alternative. The analysis of the subexpressions is not necessary to do at run time (when the execution procedure is used).

```
(define (analyze-if expression)
  (let ((predicate-exec
         (analyze (if-predicate expression)))
        (consequent-exec
         (analyze (if-consequent expression)))
        (alternative-exec
         (analyze (if-alternative expression))))
    (lambda (environment)
      (if (x:advance (predicate-exec environment))
          (consequent-exec environment)
          (alternative-exec environment)))))
```

```
(define-generic-procedure-handler x:analyze
  (match-args if?)
  analyze-if)
```

Sequences of expressions to be evaluated are an especially good example of separation of analysis and execution. There is no good reason to recompile a sequence of expressions every time we enter the body of a procedure; this work can be done once and for all at compile time.

The `analyze-begin` procedure first analyzes each subexpression of the `begin` expression, producing a list of execution procedures (preserving the order of the expressions in the `begin` expression). These execution procedures are then glued together using `reduce-right` and a pairwise combinator that takes two execution procedures and produces an execution procedure that executes the two given execution procedures in sequence.[21]

```
(define (analyze-begin expression)
  (reduce-right (lambda (exec1 exec2)
                  (lambda (environment)
                    (exec1 environment)
                    (exec2 environment)))
                #f
                (map analyze
                     (let ((exps
                             (begin-actions expression)))
                       (if (null? exps)
                           (error "Empty sequence"))
                       exps)))))

(define-generic-procedure-handler x:analyze
  (match-args begin?)
  analyze-begin)
```

The treatment of assignments is not problematical in the absence of compiler optimizations.

```
(define (analyze-assignment expression)
  (let ((var
          (assignment-variable expression))
        (value-exec
          (analyze (assignment-value expression))))
    (lambda (environment)
      (set-variable-value! var
                           (value-exec environment)
                           environment)
      'ok)))
```

---

[21] In `analyze-begin` the `reduce-right` procedure will never use the `#f` argument because the `#f` is accessed only if the list of expressions is empty. But that would signal the error `Empty sequence` before the reduction started.

```
(define-generic-procedure-handler x:analyze
  (match-args assignment?)
  analyze-assignment)
```

However, if there are compiler optimizations to be done, assignments pose serious problems. Indeed, assignments introduce time into a program: some things happen before the assignment and some happen after the assignment, and the assignment can change the events that reference the variable that was changed. Thus, for example, common subexpressions may not really have the same value if they reference a variable that can be assigned!

Definitions are not a problem, unless we think of them (and incorrectly use them) as assignments, potentially interfering with compiler optimizations.

```
(define (analyze-definition expression)
  (let ((var
          (definition-variable expression))
        (value-exec
          (analyze (definition-value expression))))
    (lambda (environment)
      (define-variable! var
                        (value-exec environment)
                        environment)
      var)))
```

```
(define-generic-procedure-handler x:analyze
  (match-args definition?)
  analyze-definition)
```

Special forms that are implemented by transformations of expressions, such as cond and let, are really easy in this system; we simply compile the transformed expression. Indeed, this is the place where a very general macro facility could be hooked in.

```
(define-generic-procedure-handler x:analyze
  (match-args cond?)
  (compose analyze cond->if))
```

```
(define-generic-procedure-handler x:analyze
  (match-args let?)
  (compose analyze let->combination))
```

Application of procedures

The execution procedure for an application calls the execution procedure for the operator to obtain the compound procedure to be applied. (See `analyze-application` on page 260.) The operands have also been converted to execution procedures.

The procedure `x:apply` is analogous to `g:apply` in the elementary evaluator (on page 245):

```
(define x:apply
  (simple-generic-procedure 'x:apply 3 default-apply))

(define (default-apply procedure operand-execs environment)
  (error "Unknown procedure type" procedure))
```

Note that the `default-apply` here is the same as the one used by `g:apply` except for the names of the two unused parameters.

As before, we need handlers for application of the various kinds of procedures, with particular kinds of parameters. The application handler for strict primitive procedures has to force the arguments and then execute the primitive procedure.

```
(define-generic-procedure-handler x:apply
  (match-args strict-primitive-procedure?
              executors?
              environment?)
  (lambda (procedure operand-execs environment)
    (apply-primitive-procedure procedure
      (map (lambda (operand-exec)
             (x:advance (operand-exec environment)))
           operand-execs))))
```

The application handler for general procedures is only slightly different than in the elementary evaluator shown earlier. The difference is that we have execution procedures rather than operand expressions to work with.

```
(define-generic-procedure-handler x:apply
  (match-args compound-procedure? executors? environment?)
  (lambda (procedure operand-execs calling-environment)
    (if (not (n:= (length (procedure-parameters procedure))
                  (length operand-execs)))
        (error "Wrong number of operands supplied"))
    (let ((params (procedure-parameters procedure))
          (body-exec (procedure-body procedure)))
      (let ((names (map procedure-parameter-name params))
            (arguments
             (map (lambda (param operand-exec)
                    (x:handle-operand param
                                      operand-exec
                                      calling-environment))
                  params
                  operand-execs)))
        (body-exec (extend-environment names arguments
                                       (procedure-environment procedure)))))))
```

This application handler for compound procedures needs to be
able to deal with the various kinds of formal parameters that may
be present in the compound procedure. This is accomplished, in
our usual way, by making x:handle-operand a generic procedure.
The default, for an operand to be evaluated before entering the
body of the compound procedure, is to immediately execute the
operand execution procedure to obtain a value. However, lazy parameters and memoized lazy parameters need to be able to postpone the execution appropriately.

```
(define x:handle-operand
  (simple-generic-procedure 'x:handle-operand 3
    (lambda (parameter operand-exec environment)
      (operand-exec environment))))

(define-generic-procedure-handler x:handle-operand
  (match-args lazy? executor? environment?)
  (lambda (parameter operand-exec environment)
    (postpone operand-exec environment)))

(define-generic-procedure-handler x:handle-operand
  (match-args lazy-memo? executor? environment?)
  (lambda (parameter operand-exec environment)
    (postpone-memo operand-exec environment)))
```

The postponement of an execution procedure for an operand is
the same as the postponement of an operand expression. But

the handlers for the generic procedure `x:advance` to deal with a postponed operand execution procedure are different from those for `g:advance`: the postponed execution procedure must be called on the postponed environment rather than evaluated relative to that environment (compare with `g:advance` on page 253).

```
(define-generic-procedure-handler x:advance
  (match-args postponed?)
  (lambda (object)
    (x:advance ((postponed-expression object)
                (postponed-environment object)))))

(define-generic-procedure-handler x:advance
  (match-args postponed-memo?)
  (lambda (object)
    (let ((value
           (x:advance ((postponed-expression object)
                       (postponed-environment object)))))
      (advance-memo! object value)
      value)))
```

The handling of operands in this `x:apply` is not very clever. In fact, it does lots of "parsing" of the formal parameter list in the execution procedure, so we really did not fully compile the compound procedure. One step to improve this compilation would be to separate out the handler for strict compound procedures, as we did earlier. Fixing this nastiness is your job in exercise 5.16.

Exercise 5.12: Implementing n-ary procedures

In exercises 5.2 and 5.11 we noted that it is often valuable to have procedures that can take an indefinite number of arguments. The addition and multiplication procedures in Scheme are examples of such procedures.

To define such a procedure in Scheme, we specify the formal parameters of a **lambda** expression as a single symbol rather than a list. That symbol is bound to a list of the arguments supplied. For example, to make a procedure that takes several arguments and returns a list of the squares of the arguments, we can write:

```
(lambda x (map square x))
```

or

```
(define (ss . x) (map square x))
```

and then we can say

```
(ss 1 2 3 4) ==> (1 4 9 16)
```

Modify the analyzing interpreter to allow this construct.

Hint: You do not need to change the code involving `define` or `lambda` in the syntax definitions! This is entirely a change in the analyzer.

Demonstrate that your modification allows this kind of procedure and that it does not cause other troubles.

Exercise 5.13: Simplifying debugging

One problem with this compiler is that the execution procedures are all anonymous `lambda` expressions. So there is little information for a backtrace to report. However, it is easy to improve matters. If we rewrite the procedure that makes execution procedures for applications

```
(define (analyze-application exp)
  (let ((operator-exec (analyze (operator exp)))
        (operand-execs (map analyze (operands exp))))
    (lambda (env)
      (x:apply (x:advance (operator-exec env))
               operand-execs
               env))))
```

like this:

```
(define (analyze-application exp)
  (let ((operator-exec (analyze (operator exp)))
        (operand-execs (map analyze (operands exp))))
    (define (execute-application env)
      (x:apply (x:advance (operator-exec env))
               operand-execs
               env))
    execute-application))
```

then (in MIT/GNU Scheme) the execution procedure will have a name that tells us what kind of execution procedure it is. Implement this idea in all the execution procedures.

Think of, and perhaps implement, other ways we could improve the debuggability of the runtime code without impairing the execution speed. One thing you might do is add the expression `exp` as a "sticky note" on the execution procedure.

Exercise 5.14: Constant folding

Assume we have a declaration to tell the analyzer that certain symbols have a given meaning (for example a declaration that the conventional arithmetic operators {`+`, `-`, `*`, `/`, `sqrt`} refer to known constant procedures). Then any combination of constants with these operators, such as `(/ (+ 1 (sqrt 5)) 2)`, may be evaluated by the analyzer at compile time and the result used instead of executing the computation at run time. This compile-time optimization is called *constant folding*.

Implement constant folding in the analyzer. To do constant folding, the analyzer needs to know which symbols in the program text it can count on to be bound to known values. For example, it needs to know if `car` is actually bound to the primitive selector of pairs. Assume that the analyzer can call a procedure that finds the bindings of known symbols. This procedure should take a symbol and return the value that the analyzer may depend on, or `#f` if the symbol is not under control of the analyzer.

Exercise 5.15: Other optimizations

There are many simple transformations that can improve the execution of a program. For example, we can use our pattern-matching technology to make a term-rewriting system that implements peephole optimization and loop-invariant code motion. Perhaps it would be nice to add common subexpression elimination; but be careful about side effects due to assignments. Add a phase of optimization to the analysis, implement some classic compiler optimizations, and show their effects.

Exercise 5.16: Compiling formal-parameter declarations

Although the transformation to compositions of execution procedures is quite effective, and produces much faster code than straight interpretation, the version we presented is not very clever: the compound-procedure execution procedure for `x:apply` parses the formal parameter list to determine how to handle the operands. This should really be done at compile time rather than run time: the analysis of the `lambda` expression that made the compound procedure should produce an execution procedure that knows what to do with the operands and calling environment.

Figure this out and do it. Make sure that you do not carry the calling environment any further than is absolutely needed.

Note: This is a big project.

5.4   Exploratory behavior

We have already encountered explicit backtracking search for matching segment variables in pattern matching. But even in the absence of segment variables, the implementation of the term-rewriting system required some backtracking search. When a rule's consequent expression determined that the match was not selective enough for the consequent to replace the matched part of the data, even though the antecedent pattern of the rule matched a piece of data, the consequent expression returned `#f`, failing back into the match and perhaps trying a different rule.

Also, the trie mechanism for optimizing the access to a generic procedure handler requires backtracking. The trie chases a sequence of predicates that the sequence of arguments must satisfy. But there may be multiple ways that an initial segment of predicates matches the initial segment of arguments, so there is an implicit search built into the trie mechanism.

We normally think of backtracking, and its extreme use in search, as an AI technique. However, backtracking can be viewed as a way of making systems that are modular and independently evolvable, as in the exploratory behavior of biological systems. Consider a simple but practical example: solving a quadratic equation. There are two roots to a quadratic. We could return both, and assume that the user of the solution knows how to deal with that, or we could return one and hope for the best. (The canonical square-root procedure `sqrt` returns the positive square root, even though there are two square roots!) The disadvantage of returning both solutions is that the receiver of that result must know to try the computation with both and either reject one, or return both results of the computation, which may itself have made some choices. The disadvantage of returning only one solution is that it may not be the right one for the receiver's purpose. This can be a real problem in simulations of physical systems.

Linguistically implicit search

The searches we have explicitly built are okay, but perhaps we can do better by building a backtracking mechanism into the linguistic infrastructure. The square-root procedure should return one of the roots, with the option to change its mind and return the other one if the first choice is determined to be inappropriate by the receiver. It is, and should be, the receiver's responsibility to determine if the ingredients to its computation are appropriate and acceptable. This may itself require a complex computation, involving choices whose consequences may not be apparent without further computation; so the process is recursive. Of course, this gets us into potentially deadly exponential searches through all possible assignments to all the choices that have been made in the program.

It is important to consider the extent to which a search strategy can be separated from the other parts of a program, so that one can interchange search strategies without greatly modifying the program. Here we take the further step of pushing search and search control into the infrastructure that is supported by the language, and not explicitly building search into our program at all. Making search implicit may encourage excessive use of search. As usual, modular flexibility can be dangerous.

This idea has considerable history. In 1961 John McCarthy [90] had the idea of a nondeterministic operator, amb, which could be useful for representing nondeterministic automata. In 1967 Bob Floyd [35] had the idea of building backtracking search into a computer language as part of the linguistic infrastructure. In 1969 Carl Hewitt [56] proposed a language, PLANNER, that embodied these ideas. In the early 1970s Colmerauer, Kowalski, Roussel, and Warren developed Prolog [78], a language based on a limited form of first-order predicate calculus, which made backtracking search implicit.[22]

5.4.1 amb

McCarthy's amb takes any number of arguments. The value of the amb expression is the value of one of the arguments, but we don't know in advance which one is appropriate. For example,

```
(amb 1 2 3)
```

produces the value 1 or 2 or 3, depending on the future of the computation. The expression (amb), with no arguments, has no possible values: it is a computational failure, rejecting the choices previously made.

An expression using amb may have many possible values. To see all the possible values we print one and then cause a failure, forcing the production of the next value, until there are no more to be had.

```
(begin
  (newline)
  (write-line (list (amb 1 2 3) (amb 'a 'b)))
  (amb))
;;; Starting a new problem
(1 a)
(2 a)
(3 a)
(1 b)
(2 b)
(3 b)
;;; There are no more values
```

---

[22]Erik Sandewall's survey [107] of systems that support tools for "nonmonotonic" reasoning gives more context than we can provide here.

Using amb we can generate Pythagorean triples rather easily. We use amb to generate triples of integers and reject the ones that are not Pythagorean.

To facilitate programming with amb, we introduce a helper. We use require as a filter that will force a failure and backtrack if its argument predicate expression is not true.

```
(define (require p)
  (if (not p) (amb) 'ok))
```

To obtain some integer in an interval, we write:

```
(define (an-integer-between low high)
  (require (<= low high))
  (amb low (an-integer-between (+ low 1) high)))
```

With these helpers we can write the search for Pythagorean triples in a very intuitive form:

```
(define (a-pythagorean-triple-between low high)
  (let ((i (an-integer-between low high)))
    (let ((j (an-integer-between i high)))
      (let ((k (an-integer-between j high)))
        (require (= (+ (* i i) (* j j))
                    (* k k)))
        (list i j k)))))
```

```
(begin
  (newline)
  (write-line (a-pythagorean-triple-between 1 20))
  (amb))
;;; Starting a new problem
(3 4 5)
(5 12 13)
(6 8 10)
(8 15 17)
(9 12 15)
(12 16 20)
;;; There are no more values
```

This seems like a generally useful facility. Let's see how we can make it part of our language.

5.4.2 Implementing amb

It is nice that we separated the analysis of the expressions of the language from the execution, because that allows us to change the execution without changing any of the syntactic analysis. So building nondeterministic search into the language is a matter of changing only the execution procedures. The critical step is to transform the execution procedures into continuation-passing style, where in addition to the environment argument, each execution procedure takes two continuation arguments: one, typically named `succeed`, that is called when the computation is successful, and the other, typically named `fail`, that is called when the computation is unsuccessful.

The execution procedure returns a proposed value by calling the success continuation with the value and a failure continuation. The failure continuation is the "complaint department": if some future of the computation does not like the tendered value, it may call the failure continuation with no arguments to demand a different result. (In section 4.3 we used a returned value of #f as a failure indication. In section 4.2.2 we used success and failure continuations. The use of success and failure continuations is more flexible and can be expanded to include information about why the value was rejected.)

So the general pattern of an execution procedure will be:

```
(lambda (environment succeed fail)
  ;; succeed = (lambda (value fail)
                 ;; Try this value.
                 ;; if don't like it (fail).
                 ;; ...)
  ;; fail = (lambda () ...)
  ...
  ;; Try to make a result.  If cannot, (fail).
  ...)
```

The transformation to continuation-passing style is a bit unpleasant, as it expands the code considerably, but it is basically mechanical. For example, the `analyze-application` procedure on page 260 is:

```
(define (analyze-application expression)
  (let ((operator-exec (analyze (operator expression)))
        (operand-execs (map analyze (operands expression))))
    (lambda (environment)
      (x:apply (x:advance (operator-exec environment))
               operand-execs
               environment))))
```

If we transform this code to continuation-passing style we get:[23]

```
(define (analyze-application exp)
  (let ((operator-exec (analyze (operator exp)))
        (operand-execs (map analyze (operands exp))))
    (lambda (env succeed fail)
      (operator-exec env
                     (lambda (operator-value fail-1)
                       (a:advance operator-value
                                  (lambda (procedure fail-2)
                                    (a:apply procedure
                                             operand-execs
                                             env
                                             succeed
                                             fail-2))
                                  fail-1))
                     fail))))
```

This execution procedure is more complicated than the one it was
derived from. In the body of the original execution procedure,
the expression (operator-exec environment) returns a value to
the expression (x:advance ...), which in turn returns a value
to the expression (x:apply ... ...). In the new execution
procedure, these nested expressions are gone. Each procedure
"returns" by calling a procedure that accepts the results of its
computation.

Since we will often have to force a value, it is appropriate to
make an abstraction that captures the forcing. The procedure
execute-strict hides the uninteresting details associated with
the process of forcing the evaluation of a postponed expression in
order to ensure an unpostponed value. In analyze-application
above, it is used to force the value of the operator in order to get
an applicable procedure.

---

[23] In this evaluator we use the a: prefix (for amb) to distinguish analogous
procedures, as explained in footnote 19 on page 260.

```
(define (execute-strict executor env succeed fail)
  (executor env
            (lambda (value fail-1)
              (a:advance value succeed fail-1))
            fail))
```

The procedure `execute-strict` calls the given execution procedure (`executor`). The result of that is then passed to `a:advance` to be forced. The forced value is then passed to the success continuation (`succeed`) of `execute-strict`, effectively returning the result of the forcing to the caller of `execute-strict`.

Using `execute-strict` we can rewrite `analyze-application`:

```
(define (analyze-application exp)
  (let ((operator-exec (analyze (operator exp)))
        (operand-execs (map analyze (operands exp))))
    (lambda (env succeed fail)
      (execute-strict operator-exec
                      env
                      (lambda (procedure fail-2)
                        (a:apply procedure
                                 operand-execs
                                 env
                                 succeed
                                 fail-2))
                      fail))))
```

Each of the execution procedures has to be transformed in this way. We use `execute-strict` in `analyze-if` to force the value of the predicate of the conditional, without which we cannot proceed:

```
(define (analyze-if exp)
  (let ((predicate-exec (analyze (if-predicate exp)))
        (consequent-exec (analyze (if-consequent exp)))
        (alternative-exec (analyze (if-alternative exp))))
    (lambda (env succeed fail)
      (execute-strict predicate-exec
                      env
                      (lambda (pred-value pred-fail)
                        ((if pred-value
                             consequent-exec
                             alternative-exec)
                         env succeed pred-fail))
                      fail))))
```

Most of the transformations are straightforward, and we will not burden you with the details in this text. But there is an

interesting case: assignments. Often in backtracking systems we
need two different kinds of assignment. The usual permanent
assignment, set!, is useful for accumulating information during
a search process, such as how many times a particular branch is
investigated. There is also an undoable assignment maybe-set!
that must be undone if the branch it is on is retracted. The usual
permanent assignment is implemented as:

```
(define (analyze-assignment exp)
  (let ((var (assignment-variable exp))
        (value-exec (analyze (assignment-value exp))))
    (lambda (env succeed fail)
      (value-exec env
                  (lambda (new-val val-fail)
                    (set-variable-value! var new-val env)
                    (succeed 'ok val-fail))
                  fail))))
```

The undoable assignment is more complex. The failure continuation passed with the successful assignment reverts the value of
the assigned variable to its previous value.

```
(define (analyze-undoable-assignment exp)
  (let ((var (assignment-variable exp))
        (value-exec (analyze (assignment-value exp))))
    (lambda (env succeed fail)
      (value-exec env
                  (lambda (new-val val-fail)
                    (let ((old-val
                           (lookup-variable-value var env)))
                      (set-variable-value! var new-val env)
                      (succeed 'ok
                               (lambda ()
                                 (set-variable-value! var
                                                      old-val
                                                      env)
                                 (val-fail)))))
                  fail))))
```

The only other interesting case is the implementation of amb itself. Here is where we have to select the next alternative if the last
one tendered is rejected. This is done by the failure continuation
for the current alternative:

```
(define (analyze-amb exp)
  (let ((alternative-execs
          (map analyze (amb-alternatives exp))))
    (lambda (env succeed fail)
      (let loop ((alts alternative-execs))
        (if (pair? alts)
            ((car alts) env
                        succeed
                        (lambda ()
                          (loop (cdr alts))))
            (fail))))))
```

If there are no alternatives left, the execution procedure for amb calls the failure continuation it was called with. This makes the program execute a depth-first search of the tree of alternatives. The alternatives are examined by cdring down the list of alternatives; thus the search proceeds in left-to-right order.[24]

Except for adjustments to the read-eval-print loop (page 246) to make it work with the continuation-passing structure, that is all there is to it!

Exercise 5.17: A puzzle

Formalize and solve the following puzzle using amb:

Two women (Alyssa and Eva) and four men (Ben, Louis, Cy, and Lem) are seated at a round table, playing cards. Each has a hand; no two of the hands are equally strong.

- Ben is seated opposite Eva.
- The man at Alyssa's right has a stronger hand than Lem has.
- The man at Eva's right has a stronger hand than Ben has.
- The man at Ben's right has a stronger hand than Cy has.
- The man at Ben's right has a stronger hand than Eva has.
- The woman at Lem's right has a stronger hand than Cy has.
- The woman at Cy's right has a stronger hand than Louis has.

What is the arrangement at the table? Is it unique up to rotation of the table? (continued)

---

[24]Our implementation of amb is not quite the idea envisioned by McCarthy. His amb is "prescient" in that it will converge to a value even if one of the alternatives diverges. Since our evaluator does a left-to-right, depth-first search of the alternatives, if *e* is an expression that diverges (computes infinitely or signals an error), our (amb *e* 5) diverges; but McCarthy's amb would return 5. This is explained beautifully by William Clinger [21].

Use `amb` to specify the alternatives that are possible for each choice.
Also determine how many solutions there are if we are not told that
"The man at Ben's right has a stronger hand than Cy has," but rather
that "The man on Ben's right is not Cy." Explain this result.

Note: The most straightforward solution is slow; it takes a few hours
on a laptop (2017). However, there is a clever solution that converges
in only about 2 minutes.[25]

Exercise 5.18: Failure detection

Implement a new construct called `if-fail` that permits a program to
catch the failure of an expression. `if-fail` takes two expressions. It
evaluates the first expression as usual, and returns its value as usual if
the evaluation succeeds. If the evaluation fails, however, the value of the
second expression is returned, as in the following example:

```
(if-fail (let ((x (amb 1 3 5)))
           (require (even? x))
           x)
         'all-odd)
all-odd

(if-fail (let ((x (amb 1 3 4 5)))
           (require (even? x))
           x)
         'all-odd)
4
```

Hint: This is trivial!

Exercise 5.19: Assignment

What are the results of the following evaluations, where `if-fail` is as
specified in exercise 5.18?

```
(let ((pairs '()))
  (if-fail (let ((p (prime-sum-pair '(1 3 5 8) '(20 35 110))))
             (set! pairs (cons p pairs))
             (amb))
           pairs))

(let ((pairs '()))
  (if-fail (let ((p (prime-sum-pair '(1 3 5 8) '(20 35 110))))
             (maybe-set! pairs (cons p pairs))
             (amb))
           pairs))
```

---

[25]These timings are with the embedded exploratory-behavior interpreter itself
interpreted by the underlying Scheme system. If we use the Scheme compiler
to compile the embedded interpreter we get a factor of about 30 speed im-
provement.

You may use the following definitions:

```
(define (prime-sum-pair list1 list2)
  (let ((a (an-element-of list1))
        (b (an-element-of list2)))
    (require (prime? (+ a b)))
    (list a b)))

(define (an-element-of lst)
  (if (null? lst)
      (amb)
      (amb (car lst)
           (an-element-of (cdr lst)))))

(define (prime? n)
  (= n (smallest-divisor n)))

(define (smallest-divisor n)
  (define (find-divisor test-divisor)
    (cond ((> (square test-divisor) n) n)
          ((divides? test-divisor n) test-divisor)
          (else (find-divisor (+ test-divisor 1)))))
  (define (divides? a b)
    (= (remainder b a) 0))
  (find-divisor 2))
```

Exercise 5.20: Choice ordering

The amb mechanism, as written, always tries the choices in the order given in the amb expression. But sometimes we can use contextual information to make a better ordering. For example, in a board game the choice of a move from the possible legal moves should depend on the state of the game board. Let's invent a version of amb that can give us this kind of flexibility. Let's assume that each choice expression is paired with a numerical weight expression:

```
(choose (<weight-1> <choice-1>) ... (<weight-n> <choice-n>))
```

We can evaluate all the weight expressions and use them to choose the next choice expression to be evaluated and returned. Of course, after a choice is made, it is exhausted, and if a failure gets back to this choose form, the remaining weight expressions must be reevaluated before making the next choice.

a. Implement choose so that a choice with the largest weight is chosen.

b. In real situations the weights are usually not strong enough to make a unique choice. Sometimes a good strategy is to make a random choice with probability that is proportional to the computed weights. Implement an alternative chooser pchoose, with the same syntax as choose, that works in this way.

5.5 Exposing the underlying continuations

Now we are in a position to deal with real magic!

Most languages, including Scheme, are organized around the notion of an expression. An expression has a value that it "returns." An expression is made up of subexpressions, each of which has a value that it returns to the bigger expression it is a part of. What is the essential idea of an expression?

Consider the compound expression

```
(+ 1 (* 2 3) (/ 8 2))
```

Of course, this has the value 11. It is computed by evaluating the operator and the operands, then applying the value of the operator (the procedure) to the values of the operands (the arguments).

This process can be clarified by reformulating the computation in *continuation-passing style*. Here we invent new operators **, //, and ++ to name the continuation-passing style multiplication, division, and addition procedures:

```
(define (** m1 m2 continue)
  (continue (* m1 m2)))

(define (// n d continue)
  (continue (/ n d)))

(define (++ a1 a2 continue)
  (continue (+ a1 a2)))
```

These procedures differ from the usual *, /, and + in that they do not return to their caller; rather they are defined to call their last argument with the value computed. The argument that receives the value is called the *continuation* procedure. We used continuation-passing style in sections 4.2.2 and 5.4.2 and also in the unifier on page 188.

The computation of (+ 1 (* 2 3) (/ 8 2)) in continuation-passing style looks like:

```
(** 2 3
    (lambda (the-product)          ; A
      (// 8 2
          (lambda (the-quotient)   ; B
            (++ 1 the-product
                (lambda (the-sum)
                  (++ the-sum the-quotient k)))))))
```

where k is the final continuation procedure, which takes one argument, which is the value 11 of the computation.[26]

In this example the procedure ** computes the product of 2 and 3 and calls its continuation procedure (the lambda expression labeled by comment A) with 6. Thus, in the body of A, the-product is bound to 6. In the body of A the procedure // computes the quotient of 8 and 2 and passes the resulting 4 to the procedure labeled B, where the-quotient is bound to 4. In the body of B the procedure ++ computes the sum of 1, 6, and 4, and passes the resulting 11 to the continuation procedure k.

In continuation-passing style there are no nested expressions that return values. All results are passed to continuation procedures. Thus, there is no need for a stack, because there is nobody waiting for the value returned! Instead, we have linearized our expression tree in the same way that a compiler must in order to compute the value of the expression in a sequential machine.

Underlying continuations
The idea is that the slot in the expression that contains the subexpression is just syntactic sugar for a procedure that accepts the value of the subexpression for later use in continuing the evaluation of the expression. This idea is very powerful, because the continuation represents the entire future of the computation. This deeper understanding of the meaning of an expression allows us to escape from the single-valued expression style of programming, at the considerable cost of complexity and syntactic nesting.

Whenever an expression is evaluated, a continuation exists that expects the result of the expression. If the expression is evaluated at top level, for example, the continuation will take the result, print it on the screen, prompt for the next input, evaluate it, and so on, forever. Most of the time the continuation includes actions specified by user code, as in a continuation that will take the result, multiply it by the value stored in a local variable, add seven, and give the answer to the top-level continuation to be printed. Normally these ubiquitous continuations are hidden behind the scenes, and programmers don't think much about them. Scheme provides the ability for a programmer to get the underlying contin-

---

[26]The idea of continuation-passing style was introduced by computer language theorists to clarify the semantics of computer languages. For a complete history of this idea see [103]. In Scheme the continuations underlying subexpressions are exposed as first-class procedures [120, 61, 109].

uation of an expression. An underlying continuation is a first-class object that can be passed as an argument, returned as a value, and incorporated into a data structure. Most other languages do not support the use of first-class continuations. (Languages that do have them include SML, Ruby, and Smalltalk.)

Explicit underlying continuations are one of the most powerful (and most dangerous) tools of a programmer. Continuations give the programmer explicit control over time. A computation can be captured and suspended at one moment and restored and continued at any future time. This makes it possible to write coroutines (cooperative multitasking), and with the addition of a timer interrupt mechanism we get timesharing (preemptive multitasking). On the occasions that you may need to deal explicitly with continuations, Scheme lets you do so by creating an explicit procedure that is the current continuation. But before we can take charge of this power we need a deeper understanding of continuations.

A continuation is a captured control state of a computation.[27] If a continuation is invoked, the computation continues at the place represented by the continuation. A continuation may represent the act of returning a value of a subexpression to the evaluation of the enclosing expression. The continuation is then a procedure that when invoked returns its argument to the evaluation of the enclosing expression as the value of the subexpression. A continuation can be invoked multiple times, allowing a computation to be resumed at a particular point with different values returned by the continuation. We will see an example shortly.

Scheme provides `call-with-current-continuation` (abbreviated `call/cc`), which gives access to the continuations that underly expression structure. The argument to `call/cc` is a procedure that gets the continuation of the `call/cc` expression as its argument. Again: a continuation is a first-class procedure that takes one argument—the value to be returned when the continuation is called.[28] Here is a simple example:

---

[27]This control state is not to be confused with the full state of a system. The full state is all the information required, along with the program, to determine the future of a computation. It includes all of the current values of mutable variables and data. The continuation does not capture the current values of mutable variables and data.

[28]But note that the Scheme report [109] allows continuations to take any number of arguments.

```
(define foo)

(set! foo
  (+ 1
    (call/cc
      (lambda (k)
        ;; k is the continuation
        ;; of the call/cc expression.
        ;; so if we call k with 6
        ;; then foo will get the value 11
        (k (* 2 3))))
    (/ 8 2)))
```

```
foo
11
```

So `call/cc` calls its argument with the continuation of the `call/cc`. Not very exciting yet! So far this is no different from the straight-forward evaluation of `(+ 1 (* 2 3) (/ 8 2))` .

But procedures in Scheme have indefinite extent. This is a game changer. Let's save the continuation for reuse.

```
(define bar)
(define foo)

(set! foo
  (+ 1
    (call/cc
      (lambda (k)
        (set! bar k)
        (k (* 2 3))))
    (/ 8 2)))
```

```
foo
11
```

```
(bar -2)
```

```
foo
3
```

Wow, look what happened! We saved in `bar` the future of the computation that ultimately gives a value to `foo`. When we called that continuation with another value, the assignment of `foo` was redone, resulting in a different value of `foo`.

5.5.1   Continuations as nonlocal exits

Consider the following simple example of a nonlocal exit continuation (adapted from the Scheme report [109]):

```
(call/cc
 (lambda (exit)
   (for-each (lambda (x)
               (if (negative? x) (exit x)))
             '(54 0 37 -3 245 -19))      ; **
   (exit #t)))
-3
```

Because Scheme's `for-each` procedure walks the list in left-to-right order, the first negative element encountered is -3, which is immediately returned. Had the list contained no negative numbers, the result would have been #t (since the body of the outer `lambda` expression is a sequence of two expressions, the `for-each` expression followed by returning #t).

The use of `call/cc` might appear within some other expression, as in the following definition. (Traditionally, a symbol bound to an underlying continuation starts with the letter k.)

```
(define (first-negative list-of-numbers)
  (call/cc
   (lambda (k_exit)
     (or (call/cc (lambda (k_shortcut)
                    (for-each (lambda (n)
                                (cond ((not (number? n))
                                       (pp '(not-a-number: ,n))
                                       (k_exit #f))
                                      ((negative? n)
                                       (k_shortcut n))
                                      (else
                                       'keep-looking)))
                              list-of-numbers)
                    #f))
         'no-negatives-found))))
```

This behaves as follows:

```
(first-negative '(54 0 37 -3 245 -19))
-3

(first-negative '(54 0 37  3 245  19))
no-negatives-found
```

```
(first-negative '(54 0 37 no 245 -19))
(not-a-number: no)
#f
```

This demonstrates nested continuations, where the outermost
k_exit continuation exits the entire call to `first-negative` while
the inner k_shortcut continuation exits only to the enclosing disjunction, then continues from there.

  In short, if a continuation captured by `call/cc` is ever invoked
with some value, then the computation will continue by returning
that value as the value of the call to `call/cc` that captured it and
resuming execution normally from there.

Exercise 5.21: Nonlocal exits

This exercise is to be done in the native Scheme, where it will be easier
to debug and instrument than in our embedded interpreter. There is a
good implementation of `call/cc` in the native Scheme.

a. Define a simple procedure, `snark-hunt`,[29] that takes a tree as its
argument and recursively descends the tree looking for the symbol `snark`
at any leaf. It should immediately stop searching and return `#t` if one
is found; `#f` otherwise. Use `call/cc`. For example:

```
(snark-hunt '(((a b c) d (e f)) g (((snark . "oops") h) (i . j))))
  #t
```

Note that the input to `snark-hunt` may not be composed solely of proper
lists.

b. How might you verify that `snark-hunt` exits immediately rather than
silently returning through multiple return levels? Define a new procedure, `snark-hunt/instrumented`, to demonstrate this.

  Hint: Setting an exit status flag, then signaling an error on wayward
return paths might work if placed carefully, but simply tracing via `pp`
may be easier. Any quick and dirty hack that works will do. The goal
here is to build your intuition about continuations, not to ship product-
quality code. Briefly explain your strategy.

5.5.2   Nonlocal transfer of control

The preceding was somewhat simplistic, because the continuations
captured were used only for nonlocal exits. But continuations are
more powerful than that: they can be reentered once invoked. The
following example illustrates the idea:[30]

---

[29]See "The Hunting of the Snark," by Lewis Carroll, 1876.

[30]This example is adapted from Wikipedia [25].

```
(define the-continuation #f)

(define (test)
  (let ((i 0))
    ;; The argument to call/cc assigns the
    ;; continuation produced by call/cc to the
    ;; global variable the-continuation.
    (call/cc (lambda (k) (set! the-continuation k)))
    ;; When the-continuation is called, execution
    ;; resumes here.
    (set! i (+ i 1))
    i))
```

The behavior is perhaps surprising. The procedure test creates a local variable i initialized to 0. It also creates a continuation representing the control state of returning from the call/cc expression in the body of the let expression and stores that state in the global variable the-continuation. It then increments i and returns i's new value: 1.

```
(test)
1
```

When the-continuation is called, the call/cc returns to the body of the let expression. Execution proceeds to increment i and return its new value. The continuation can be reused to increment i again and return its new value.

```
(the-continuation 'OK)
2
```

```
(the-continuation 'OK)
3
```

(The argument OK is the value of the call/cc; it is ignored by the let body.)

We save the continuation in another-continuation, so we can make a new one to be stored in the-continuation by executing test again. The call to test creates another instance of i, which is initialized to 0.

```
(define another-continuation the-continuation)
```

```
(test)
1
```

This new continuation is independent of the one we saved in
another-continuation.

```
(the-continuation 'OK)
```
2

```
(another-continuation 'OK) ; uses the saved continuation
```
4

Now consider the following slightly more interesting scenario:

```
(define the-continuation #f)
(define sum #f)

(begin
  (set! sum
        (+ 2 (call/cc
              (lambda (k)
                (set! the-continuation k)
                (k 3)))))
  'ok)
```
ok

```
sum
```
5

```
(the-continuation 4)
```
ok

```
sum
```
6

```
(the-continuation 5)
```
ok

```
sum
```
7

Note carefully how reentering this captured continuation, by calling the-continuation, returns control to the point before the addition and, therefore, before assigning variable sum and returning
the symbol ok. This is why invoking it always returns the symbol
ok. However, sum is assigned the sum of 2 and the argument we
supplied to the-continuation. So when we ask for the value of
sum we get that new sum. This demonstrates how to use a captured continuation to proceed from intermediate return points.
We will see how this mechanism can be used for backtracking in
section 5.5.3.

5.5.3   From continuations to `amb`

It turns out that almost anything we want to do, including implementing `amb`, can be done with just the Scheme native `call/cc`; let's see how to do that.

Indeed, continuations are a natural mechanism for supporting backtracking. A choice can be made, and if that choice turns out to be inappropriate, an alternative choice can be made and its consequences worked out. (Wouldn't we like real life to have this feature!) In our square-root example, the square-root program should return the `amb` of both square roots, where `amb` is the operator that chooses and returns one of them, with the option to provide the other if the first is rejected. The receiver can then just proceed to use the given solution; but if at some point the receiver finds that its computation does not meet some constraint, it can `fail`, causing the `amb` operator to revise its choice and return with the new choice through its continuation. In essence, the continuation allows the generator of choices to be written as a coroutine that interacts with the receiver/tester of the choices.

The heart of the backtracker is `amb-list`, which takes a sequence of sibling thunks, each representing an alternative value for the `amb` expression. The thunks are produced by an `amb` macro, which syntactically transforms `amb` expressions into `amb-list` expressions, as follows:

```
(amb e1 ... en) ==>
  (amb-list (list (lambda () e1) ... (lambda () en)))
```

The `amb` macro (written in portable `syntax-rules` form) is:

```
(define-syntax amb
  (syntax-rules ()
    ((amb exp ...)
     (amb-list (list (lambda () exp) ...)))))
```

For example:

```
(pp (syntax '(amb a b c) user-initial-environment))
(amb-list (list (lambda () a) (lambda () b) (lambda () c)))
```

The search maintains a search schedule, an agenda of thunks that can be called when it is necessary for an `amb` expression to return with a new alternative value. The procedure `amb-list` first adds the thunks for its alternative values to the search schedule and then yields control to the first pending thunk on the schedule. If there are no alternatives (the expression was just (amb)) then the amb-list yields control without adding anything to the search schedule and increments a global counter for auditing the search.

```
(define (amb-list alternatives)
  (if (null? alternatives)
      (set! *number-of-calls-to-fail*
            (+ *number-of-calls-to-fail* 1)))
  (call/cc
   (lambda (k)
     ((add-to-search-schedule)
      (map (lambda (alternative)
             (lambda ()
               (within-continuation k alternative)))
           alternatives))
     (yield))))
```

For a particular amb expression the thunks for the alternatives are constructed so as to return from that amb expression, using the continuation, k, captured at the entrance to their enclosing amb-list.[31]

The way to yield control is to retrieve a thunk specifying an alternative, if any, from the search schedule and execute it. The search schedule is both a stack and a queue; we will see why shortly.

```
(define (yield)
  (if (deque-empty? (*search-schedule*))
      ((*top-level*) 'no-more-alternatives)
      ((pop! (*search-schedule*)))))
```

You may be puzzled by the fact that we call *top-level* and add-to-search-schedule to get the procedures that do the work. We also call *search-schedule* to get the search schedule object. The reason for this indirection is that these are Scheme *parameter* objects (see page 394). We have defined them this way because we will be dynamically binding them to different values, as will be shown shortly. We initialize the *search-schedule* to be empty:

---

[31]The use of the MIT/GNU Scheme extension within-continuation procedure, which here is approximately equivalent to the call (k (alternative)), prevents the capture of pieces of the control stack that are unnecessary for continuing the computation correctly.

```
(define *search-schedule*
  (make-parameter (empty-search-schedule)))
```

The magic is the call/cc in amb-list. The amb-list (and thus the amb) executes the yield. The continuation of this call/cc, and thus of this amb, is put onto the search schedule for each alternative of this amb. When an alternative popped from the search schedule is executed, its value is returned by whatever amb expression put that alternative into the search schedule.

By making the search schedule both a stack and a queue, we can implement both depth-first and breadth-first search, because they differ only in the order of the schedule. This is done by dynamically binding the add-to-search-schedule parameter to the ordering desired, as shown below.

The default is depth first:

```
(define add-to-search-schedule
  (make-parameter add-to-depth-first-search-schedule))
```

The following two procedures can be used to control the search order in the execution of a thunk that encapsulates a problem to be solved, by dynamically binding add-to-search-schedule. For an example of their use, see exercise 5.22 on page 293.

```
(define (with-depth-first-schedule problem-thunk)
  (call/cc
   (lambda (k)
     (parameterize ((add-to-search-schedule
                      add-to-depth-first-search-schedule)
                     (*search-schedule*
                      (empty-search-schedule))
                     (*top-level* k))
       (problem-thunk)))))

(define (with-breadth-first-schedule problem-thunk)
  (call/cc
   (lambda (k)
     (parameterize ((add-to-search-schedule
                      add-to-breadth-first-search-schedule)
                     (*search-schedule*
                      (empty-search-schedule))
                     (*top-level* k))
       (problem-thunk)))))
```

These procedures also locally reinitialize the *search-schedule* and the *top-level* by dynamically binding them, providing control in extent rather than scope. If yield finds no more alternatives it can cause this search to terminate and return the value no-more-alternatives to the caller of with-...-first-schedule. For example:

```
(define search-order-demo
  (lambda ()
    (let ((x (amb 1 2)))
      (pp (list x))
      (let ((y (amb 'a 'b)))
        (pp (list x y))))
    (amb)))
```

```
(with-depth-first-schedule search-order-demo)
(1)
(1 a)
(1 b)
(2)
(2 a)
(2 b)
no-more-alternatives
```

```
(with-breadth-first-schedule search-order-demo)
(1)
(2)
(1 a)
(1 b)
(2 a)
(2 b)
no-more-alternatives
```

The orderings are implemented in terms of the low-level stack and queue mutators. For depth first the alternatives are put onto the front of the schedule, and for breadth first they are put onto the end of the schedule. In both cases they appear on the schedule in the order in which they were supplied to amb.

```
(define (add-to-depth-first-search-schedule alternatives)
  (for-each (lambda (alternative)
              (push! (*search-schedule*) alternative))
            (reverse alternatives)))
```

```
(define (add-to-breadth-first-search-schedule alternatives)
  (for-each (lambda (alternative)
              (add-to-end! (*search-schedule*) alternative))
            alternatives))
```

The parameter `*top-level*` is initialized so that when no alternatives are found, the system continues in the read-eval-print
loop with the given `result`. (In the code above, `yield` passes
the symbol `no-more-alternatives` to the top level.) Note that
`with-...-first-schedule` rebinds `*top-level*`.

```
(define *top-level*
  (make-parameter
   (lambda (result)
     (abort->nearest
      (cmdl-message/active
       (lambda (port)
         (fresh-line port)
         (display "; " port)
         (write result port)))))))
```

To start everything up we also need:

```
(define (init-amb)
  (reset-deque! (*search-schedule*))
  (set! *number-of-calls-to-fail* 0)
  'done)
```

And finally, almost every program using `amb` will need `require`:

```
(define (require p)
  (if (not p) (amb) 'ok))
```

That is all there is to it! It is amazing what one can do with
`call/cc`. So we do not need to make an embedded system to
implement `amb` (as we did in section 5.4.2), if we have `call/cc` in
our native environment.

Other ways to try alternatives

If there are multiple possible ways to solve a subproblem, and
only some of them are appropriate for solving the larger problem,
sequentially trying them as in generate-and-test is only one way
to proceed. For example, if some of the choices lead to very long
(perhaps infinite) computations in the tester while others may
succeed or fail quickly, it is appropriate to allocate each choice to a
thread that may run concurrently. This requires a way for threads
to communicate and perhaps for a successful thread to kill its
siblings. All of this can be arranged with continuations, with the
thread-to-thread communications organized around transactions.

Exercise 5.22: Breadth versus depth

Recall the dumb way to find Pythagorean triples (on page 272). We instrument the searcher with a counter of the number of triples tried:

```
(define (a-pythagorean-triple-between low high)
  (let ((i (an-integer-between low high)))
    (let ((j (an-integer-between i high)))
      (let ((k (an-integer-between j high)))
        (set! triples-tested (+ triples-tested 1))
        (require (= (+ (* i i) (* j j))
                    (* k k)))
        (list i j k)))))

(define triples-tested 0)
```

Consider the following experiment. First we try breadth-first search:

```
(begin (init-amb)          ; to reset failure counter
       (set! triples-tested 0)
       (with-breadth-first-schedule
        (lambda ()
          (pp (a-pythagorean-triple-between 10 20)))))
(12 16 20)

triples-tested
246

*number-of-calls-to-fail*
282
```

And then we try depth-first search:

```
(begin (init-amb)
       (set! triples-tested 0)
       (with-depth-first-schedule
        (lambda ()
          (pp (a-pythagorean-triple-between 10 20)))))
(12 16 20)

triples-tested
156

*number-of-calls-to-fail*
182
```

a. Explain the difference in `triples-tested` between depth-first and breadth-first search (in rough terms, not the exact counts).

b. Explain the difference between the number of triples tested and the `*number-of-calls-to-fail*`. Where are the extra failures coming from?   (continued)

c. Considering that the breadth-first search does more work, why is the following `a-pythagorean-triple-from` search not usable under the depth-first search strategy, although it works fine under the breadth-first strategy?

```
(define (a-pythagorean-triple-from low)
  (let ((i (an-integer-from low)))
    (let ((j (an-integer-from i)))
      (let ((k (an-integer-from j)))
        (require (= (+ (* i i) (* j j)) (* k k)))
        (list i j k)))))

(define (an-integer-from low)
  (amb low (an-integer-from (+ low 1))))

(with-depth-first-schedule
  (lambda ()
    (pp (a-pythagorean-triple-from 10))))
```

Exercise 5.23: Less deterministic nondeterminism

Eva Lu Ator points out that our `amb` implementation is not as non-deterministic as one might sometimes like. Specifically, given a list of alternatives in an `amb` form, we always choose the leftmost alternative first, then the second leftmost, and so on, in left-to-right order.

She suggests that one might wish to override this choice, say, by going from right to left, or even in random order. Specifically, she would like something like:

```
(with-left-to-right-ordering problem-thunk)
(with-right-to-left-ordering problem-thunk)
(with-random-ordering problem-thunk)
```

She's quick to point out that this choice of ordering is independent of the search order (depth-first, breadth-first, or other).

a. Under what circumstances might you want an unordered (random) `amb`? Craft a specific short example to use as a test case in part **b**.

b. Implement these three choice orders and give an example use of each. For simplicity and uniformity, model your code after that for `with-depth-first-schedule`, `add-to-depth-first-search-schedule`, etc. Hint: Feel free to use Scheme's built-in `random` procedure.

Exercise 5.24: Nesting strategies

We intended that the breadth-first and depth-first search strategies could be arbitrarily nested within searches. Does the nesting of depth-first and breadth-first scheduling work correctly as currently implemented? Specifically, design an experiment that exposes the bug (if there is one) or that demonstrates anecdotally that it does work correctly (if it does). Explain your rationale.

This involves crafting experiments that distinguish between depth-first and breadth-first search strategies, then composing them in interesting ways to demonstrate local control over nested searches.

Identify a natural class of problems for which this flexibility is useful— not just hacked together to prove a point.

Exercise 5.25: Undoable assignment

In the embedded interpreter version of amb in section 5.4.2 we showed how to use two kinds of assignment: the usual permanent assignment, indicated by set!, and the undoable assignment, indicated by maybe-set!, which gets undone by backtracking. We can implement a general wrapper for undoable effects in the native-code implementation of this section:

```
(define (effect-wrapper doer undoer)
  (force-next
   (lambda () (undoer) (yield)))
  (doer))

(define (force-next thunk)
  (push! (*search-schedule*) thunk))
```

And we can then implement maybe-set! as a macro:

```
(define-syntax maybe-set!
  (syntax-rules ()
    ((maybe-set! var val)
     (let ((old-val var))
       (effect-wrapper
        (lambda ()
          (set! var val))
        (lambda ()
          (set! var old-val)))))))
```

Unfortunately, this makes sense only for depth-first search; it makes no sense for breadth-first search. Explain why. Is this fixable?

Exercise 5.26: Search control in the embedded system

How could we change the embedded system of section 5.4.2, with analysis to combinators that have success and failure continuations, to enable both depth-first search (as it is now) and breadth-first search? Explain your strategy. Make a new implementation that incorporates this ability to control the search order. Note: This is a rather large transformation.

5.6   Power and responsibility

In this chapter we have seen that we have great power from the
Church-Turing universality of computation. We can never complain: "I cannot express this in the language I must use." If
we know the tricks of interpretation and compilation we can always escape from the confines of any language because it is always
possible to build an appropriate domain-specific language for the
problem at hand. The exposition here uses Scheme as the underlying language and builds powerful Lisp-based languages on
top of Scheme. The reason we use Lisp syntax here is because it
greatly simplifies the exposition of these ideas. (See exercise 5.7
on infix notations. If we had to do this in a language with a complicated syntax the exposition would be many times longer and
more tedious.) But the power of interpretation is available in any
Turing-universal language.

It is important for future flexibility that the languages we build
be simple and general. They must have very few mechanisms:
primitives, means of combination, and means of abstraction. We
want to be able to extend them as needed and to be able to mix
and match the parts of programs. And, most important, when
we have multiple languages, each of which is appropriate for some
part of a problem, there must be good ways for those languages
to interoperate.

With great power comes even greater responsibility. Every time
we create a language we must also document it so that it can
be taught to others. The programs we write today will be read
and modified by others in the future. (Indeed, even when we
read next year what we wrote last year, we will be very different
and we will not remember the details of what we did.) So it is
important that we use this power very sparingly, and that when
we do so we document the result very carefully. Otherwise we will
be leaving an incomprehensible mess for the next programmer (or
for ourselves!) to clean up and rewrite. Don't participate in the
creation of a "Tower of Babel."

The systems that derive from UNIX show both the good and
the bad sides of this issue. The commands all have their own languages. If you know about `awk` and `sed` and `grep` you know that
each has its own language, including the really ugly and badly defined regular-expression language we discussed in section 2.2. Certainly each of those languages helped make the immediate prob-

lems easier to solve. But they do not have a consistent underlying idea that makes them easy to learn and understand. Just think about how the quotation conventions of the shell interact with the quotation conventions of **grep** and you will appreciate this point. To become a UNIX guru you have to learn lots of nasty special-case stuff. On the other hand, UNIX itself has a wonderfully simple and elegant way to glue stuff together: *streams*. Each of the basic UNIX utilities takes input from streams and puts out streams. They can be connected by piping output streams to input streams. This lesson is very worth contemplating.

6
Layering

In section 1.1 we alluded to the idea that programming could learn from the practice of architecture. A programmer might start with an executable skeleton plan (a *parti*) to help try out an idea. When the *parti* looks good the programmer could elaborate it with more information.

For example, declared implementation types may enable the compilation of efficient code and inhibit the occurrence of type errors. Declared dimensions and units may be added to prevent some bugs and support documentation. Assertions of predicates can help with the localization of errors that occur at run time and they could support the automatic or manual construction of proofs of "correctness." Declarations of how much precision is needed for some numerical quantities and operations can give clarity to numerical analysis problems. Suggestions of alternative implementations can enable useful degeneracy in an implementation. We can track the provenance of a result by carrying dependencies.

But the usual way of adding these important and powerful features to the text of a program turns the program text into a tangled mess. To continue with the architecture analogy, it does not separate the served spaces from the servant spaces. The separation of the "essential" features of a program (the code that defines its behavior) from the "accidental" ones (e.g., type information for a compiler or code for logging) has been an important issue. Aspect-oriented programming [67] was an attempt to address part of this problem, by explicitly identifying "cross-cutting concerns" such as logging. Layering is another way to effect the separation.

The ability to annotate any piece of data or code with other data or code is a crucial mechanism in building flexible systems. The decoration of a value is a generalization of the tagging used to support extensible generic operations. Here we introduce the idea of *layered programming*. Both the data and the procedures that process it will be made up of multiple layers that enable additive annotation without introducing clutter.

6.1   Using layers

Layers give us the ability to sketch out a computation and then
elaborate that computation with metadata that is processed along
with the computation. Let's consider some annotations that we
think may be valuable in many situations. For example, suppose
we are interested in using Newton's force law for gravity:

```
(define (F m1 m2 r)
  (/ (* G m1 m2) (square r)))
```

This is a simple numerical calculation, but we can elaborate it to
carry support information and units.

We find Newton's constant G by looking up a recent measurement published by NIST:

```
(define G
  (layered-datum 6.67408e-11
    unit-layer (unit 'meter 3 'kilogram -1 'second -2)
    support-layer (support-set 'CODATA-2018)))
```

Here we show the numerical value of the measurement, the units
of that measurement $(\mathrm{m}^3/(\mathrm{kg}\ \mathrm{s}^2))$, and the source of the data (its
support). We could extend this to also carry the uncertainty in
the measurement as a range in another layer, but we won't do
that here.

We can also find the mass of the Earth, the mass of the Moon,
and the distance to the Moon (semimajor axis) from other sources:

```
(define M-Earth
  (layered-datum 5.9722e24
                 unit-layer (unit 'kilogram 1)
                 support-layer
                 (support-set 'Astronomical-Almanac-2016)))

(define M-Moon
  (layered-datum 7.342e22
                 unit-layer (unit 'kilogram 1)
                 support-layer
                 (support-set 'NASA-2006)))

(define a-Moon
  (layered-datum 384399e3
                 unit-layer (unit 'meter 1)
                 support-layer
                 (support-set 'Wieczorek-2006)))
```

Now we can ask the question, "What is the gravitational force of attraction between the Earth and the Moon at that distance?" and we will get the answer:

```
(pp (F M-earth M-Moon a-moon))
#[layered-datum 1.9805035857209e20]
(base-layer 1.9805035857209e20)
(unit-layer (unit kilogram 1 meter 1 second -2))
(support-layer
 (support-set Wieczorek-2006
              NASA-2006
              Astronomical-Almanac-2016
              CODATA-2018))
```

The result gives the numerical value, the units of that result, and the sources that the result depended upon.

6.2   Implementation of layering

There are two parts to layering. The first is that it must be possible to create a datum that contains multiple layers of information. In our example, we used `layered-datum` to do this. The second part is that we need to be able to enhance a procedure so that it can process each layer (somewhat) independently. A procedure enhanced in this way is called a *layered procedure*.

We also need a way to assign names to layers. Every layer must have a name, so that the layer in a datum can be specified. The name is also used by a layered procedure to connect the processing for that layer to the corresponding layers in the incoming data. We have written our example to use variables to refer to layer names, as in `unit-layer`, which is bound to the name for the unit layer. This makes the user interface independent of the details of how a layer name is specified; this will turn out to be useful.

Another aspect of layer naming is that there must be a distinguished *base layer*, which represents the underlying computation being performed. In our example using `layered-datum`, the base layer's value is distinguished by being the first argument and by not having an associated name.

Layered data can be built from simple data structures. We can use any convenient data structure that can associate a layer name with a value and that permits many such associations. A special name can be used to identify the base layer, making the data structure simple and uniform.

Building layered procedures is more complicated, because the processing for most layers will need some information from the computation in the base layer. For example, suppose we are multiplying two numbers that carry support information. Normally, the support of the result is the union of the supports of the arguments. But suppose one argument has a base-layer value of zero; then the support of the result is the support of the zero, and the support of the other argument is irrelevant.

The base layer must not depend on any non-base layer because that violates the idea of the base layer: that it is an independent computation that the other layers enhance. And a non-base layer should not depend on another non-base layer. A non-base layer generally shouldn't share information with another non-base layer since its behavior would be different depending on the presence or absence of the other layer. This would be inconsistent with our general approach of building additive programs.

So building a layered procedure involves a balance between sharing information from the base layer to the non-base layers and isolating layers in most other cases. We will address this in the next sections as we explore the details of implementing layering.

6.2.1   Layered data

A layered data item is a base value annotated with extra information about that value. The annotation is an association of layer names with their values. For example, the number 2 may be the base value in many data items: if we are dealing in potatoes there may be a 2-dollar price tag on a 2-pound bag of potatoes. Each of these instances of the number 2 must be a distinct data item, with different values (dollars or pounds) for the units layer. There may be other layers as well: the 2-dollar price may have information saying how it was derived from the price paid to the farmer and the cost of transportation and processing.

To address this issue we introduce the *layered datum*. A layered datum is represented as a bundle that contains an association of layers and their values. So a 2-pound quantity of potatoes and a 2-dollar price for potatoes will be separate layered data items:

```
(define (make-layered-datum base-value alist)
  (if (null? alist)
      base-value
      (let ((alist
              (cons (cons base-layer base-value)
                    alist)))
        (define (has-layer? layer)
          (and (assv layer alist) #t))
        (define (get-layer-value layer)
          (cdr (assv layer alist)))
        (define (annotation-layers)
          (map car (cdr alist)))
        (bundle layered-datum?
                has-layer? get-layer-value
                annotation-layers))))
```

The associations between layers and their values are represented as an *association list*, or *alist*—a list of key–value pairs.

For convenience, we provide `layered-datum`, which takes its layer arguments in *property-list* form (alternating layer and value, as in the examples on page 300) and calls `make-layered-datum` with the corresponding alist.

```
(define (layered-datum base-value . plist)
  (make-layered-datum base-value (plist->alist plist)))
```

This design provides great flexibility. There may be many different kinds of layered data, and for each there is no a priori commitment to any particular layer or number of layers. The only common feature is that each layered datum has a distinguished layer, the `base-layer`, which contains the object that all the other layer values are annotations on.

Each layer is represented by a bundle that embodies the specifics of that layer. The simplest is the base layer:

```
(define base-layer
  (let ()
    (define (get-name) 'base)
    (define (has-value? object) #t)
    (define (get-value object)
      (if (layered-datum? object)
          (object 'get-layer-value base-layer)
          object))
    (bundle layer? get-name has-value? get-value)))
```

This shows the primary operation of a layer: the `get-value` operation that fetches the layer value, if present, or returns a default. In the case of the base layer, the default is the object itself.

The *annotation layers* have a little more complexity. In addition to the above, they also manage a set of named procedures that will be explored when we look at layered procedures. The `make-annotation-layer` procedure provides the common infrastructure used by all annotation layers; it calls its `constructor` argument to supply the layer-specific parts.

```
(define (make-annotation-layer name constructor)
  (define (get-name) name)
  (define (has-value? object)
    (and (layered-datum? object)
         (object 'has-layer? layer)))
  (define (get-value object)
    (if (has-value? object)
        (object 'get-layer-value layer)
        (layer 'get-default-value)))
  (define layer
    (constructor get-name has-value? get-value))
  layer)
```

We use `make-annotation-layer` to construct the units layer:

```
(define unit-layer
  (make-annotation-layer 'unit
    (lambda (get-name has-value? get-value)
      (define (get-default-value)
        unit:none)
      (define (get-procedure name arity)
        See definition on page 308.)
      (bundle layer?
              get-name has-value? get-value
              get-default-value get-procedure))))
```

This implementation shows the rest of the layer structure: a provider for the default value, and the procedure `get-procedure` that implements this layer's support for layered procedures, which we will examine in the next section (page 308).

As a convenience for a common use case, `layer-accessor` creates an accessor procedure that is equivalent to calling a layer's `get-value` delegate:

```
(define (layer-accessor layer)
  (lambda (object)
    (layer 'get-value object)))

(define base-layer-value
  (layer-accessor base-layer))
```

6.2.2   Layered procedures

Procedures are also data that can be layered. A layered procedure is similar to a generic procedure, in which there are handlers for different argument types. A layered procedure instead provides implementations for separate layers in the incoming data, and processes all of them to produce a layered result.[1] For example, when combining a numeric layer with a units layer, the procedure can process the numeric parts of the arguments using its numeric layer, and also process the units parts of the arguments using its units layer.

In the numerical example shown in section 6.1, the code F for Newton's force represents the *parti*, the essential plan for the computation to be performed. It operates on numbers; the units annotate the numbers. The layered generic procedures that implement the arithmetic operators, such as multiplication, have a base component that operates on the numbers in the base layer and they have other components, one for each layer that might annotate the numerical base layer. The units layer is an annotation layer that gives more information about the data and the computation, but is not essential to the computation.

In a layered system the base layer must be able to compute without reference to the other layers. But the annotation layers may need access to the values that are in the base layer. If an annotation layer of an argument is missing, the procedure's annotation layer may use a default value or simply not run. In any case, the base layer always runs.

To construct a layered procedure, we need a unique **name** and **arity** for the procedure, and a **base-procedure** to implement the base computation:

---

[1] Note that a layer's implementation for a layered procedure may itself be a generic procedure. Likewise, a handler for a generic procedure may be a layered procedure.

```
(define (make-layered-procedure name arity base-procedure)
  (let* ((metadata
          (make-layered-metadata name arity base-procedure))
         (procedure
          (layered-procedure-dispatcher metadata)))
    (set-layered-procedure-metadata! procedure metadata)
    procedure))
```

Information about the layered procedure is kept in metadata for that procedure. The metadata also manages the handlers for the base layer and the annotation layers.

The metadata for a layered procedure is implemented as a bundle. It is created with the name of the layered procedure, its arity, and the base-procedure (the handler for the base layer). The metadata provides access to each of these. It also provides set-handler! for assigning a handler for an annotation layer and get-handler for retrieving the handler for an annotation layer.

Each annotation layer, for example the unit-layer, provides get-procedure that when given a procedure name and arity returns the appropriate handler for that procedure name and arity for that layer. The get-handler provided by the layered metadata first checks if it has a handler for that layer. If so it returns that handler; otherwise it returns the result of the layer's get-procedure.

```
(define (make-layered-metadata name arity base-procedure)
  (let ((handlers (make-weak-alist-store eqv?)))
    (define (get-name) name)
    (define (get-arity) arity)
    (define (get-base-procedure) base-procedure)
    (define has? (handlers 'has?))
    (define get (handlers 'get))
    (define set-handler! (handlers 'put!))
    (define (get-handler layer)
      (if (has? layer)
          (get layer)
          (layer 'get-procedure name arity)))
    (bundle layered-metadata?
            get-name get-arity get-base-procedure
            get-handler set-handler!)))
```

The actual work of applying a layered procedure is done by layered-procedure-dispatcher. The dispatcher must be able to access and apply the base procedure and the annotation layer procedures that are associated with the layered procedure. All of this information is provided by the metadata.

```
(define (layered-procedure-dispatcher metadata)
  (let ((base-procedure (metadata 'get-base-procedure)))
    (define (the-layered-procedure . args)
      (let ((base-value
             (apply base-procedure
                    (map base-layer-value args)))
            (annotation-layers
             (apply lset-union eqv?
                    (map (lambda (arg)
                           (if (layered-datum? arg)
                               (arg 'annotation-layers)
                               '()))
                         args))))
        (make-layered-datum base-value
          (filter-map          ; drops #f values
           (lambda (layer)
             (let ((handler (metadata 'get-handler layer)))
               (and handler
                    (cons layer
                          (apply handler base-value args)))))
           annotation-layers))))
    the-layered-procedure))
```

When called, a layered procedure first calls `base-procedure` on the base-layer values of the arguments to get the base value. It also determines which annotation layers are applicable by examining each of the arguments; if there are no annotation layers that have handlers, then the result is just the base-layer value, because `make-layered-datum` (on page 303), will return the unannotated base value. Otherwise, each applicable layer's handler is called to produce a value for that layer. The layer-specific handler is given access to the computed `base-value` and the arguments to the layered procedure; it does not need any layer values other than its own and those of the base layer. Generally, the result is a layered datum containing the base value and the values of the applicable annotation layer handlers.

To see how this works in practice, let's look at the implementation for the units layer (on page 304). The `get-procedure` handler of the units layer (below) looks up the layer-specific procedure by name if the layered procedure's name is an arithmetic operator, and then calls the layer-specific procedure with the units from each argument. (There is a special exception for `expt`, whose second argument is not decorated with units—it is a number.) For other procedures, the units handling is undefined, so `get-procedure` returns #f to indicate that.

```
(define (get-procedure name arity)
  (if (operator? name)
      (let ((procedure (unit-procedure name)))
        (case name
          ((expt)
           (lambda (base-value base power)
             (procedure (get-value base)
                        (base-layer-value power))))
          (else
           (lambda (base-value . args)
             (apply procedure (map get-value args))))))
      #f))
```

Notice that because `get-procedure` is an internal procedure of `unit-layer`, it has access to the units layer `get-value` inherited from `make-annotation-layer` (on page 304). We will see `unit-procedure` when we talk about the units implementation in section 6.3.1.

Let's look at an example. Consider the simple procedure `square` that squares its argument.

```
(define (square x) (* x x))
```

We make a layered version of our square procedure, giving the numerical version to the base layer.

```
(define layered-square
  (make-layered-procedure 'square 1 square))
```

This layered squaring procedure behaves the same as the base version:

```
(layered-square 4)
```
16

```
(layered-square 'm)
```
(m m)*

However, if we provide an argument with a units layer, both the base layer and units layer will be processed separately and combined in the output:

```
(pp (layered-square
      (layered-datum 'm
                     unit-layer (unit 'kilogram 1))))
#[layered-datum (* m m)]
(base-layer (* m m))
(unit-layer (unit kilogram 2))
```

6.3   Layered arithmetic

Now that we know how to make layered procedures, we can add layers to an arithmetic. All that is required is to build an arithmetic with a layered procedure for each operation supplied in the base arithmetic. We start with a pleasant arithmetic

```
(define (generic-symbolic)
  (let ((g (make-generic-arithmetic
            make-simple-dispatch-store)))
    (add-to-generic-arithmetic! g numeric-arithmetic)
    (extend-generic-arithmetic! g function-extender)
    (extend-generic-arithmetic! g symbolic-extender)
    g))
```

and build an extender to handle the layers on that substrate:

```
(define generic-with-layers
  (let ((g (generic-symbolic)))
    (extend-generic-arithmetic! g layered-extender)
    g))
```

The layered extender has to do a bit of work. It makes a layered extension arithmetic that operates on layered data. The domain predicate of the layered extension arithmetic is `layered-datum?`. The base predicate for the layered operations is just the domain predicate of the underlying arithmetic, with the extra provision that it must reject layered data items.[2] The constants are the base constants, and for each arithmetic operator the operation is a layered procedure applicable if any argument is layered, with the base procedure inherited from the underlying arithmetic.

---

[2]The procedures `conjoin` and `complement` are combinators for predicates: `conjoin` makes a new predicate that is the boolean **and** of its arguments, and `complement` makes a new predicate that is the negation of its argument.

```
(define (layered-extender base-arith)
  (let ((base-pred
          (conjoin (arithmetic-domain-predicate base-arith)
                   (complement layered-datum?))))
    (make-arithmetic (list 'layered
                           (arithmetic-name base-arith))
                     layered-datum?
                     (list base-arith)
      (lambda (name base-value)
        base-value)
      (lambda (operator base-operation)
        (make-operation operator
          (any-arg (operator-arity operator)
                   layered-datum?
                   base-pred)
          (make-layered-procedure operator
            (operator-arity operator)
            (operation-procedure base-operation)))))))
```

Nearly all of this is boilerplate, including leaving the constant objects alone and requiring that at least one argument to an operation be layered. The only interesting part is the final three lines, in which the base arithmetic's operation procedure is wrapped in a layered procedure. The operator is used as the name of the layered procedure, so that each layer can provide special handling should that operation need it.

6.3.1   Unit arithmetic

We need an arithmetic of units for the units annotation layer on an arithmetic. A unit specification has named base units, and an exponent for each base unit.[3] In the units arithmetic, the product of unit specifications is a new unit specification where the exponent of each base unit is the sum of the exponents of the corresponding base units in the arguments.

```
(unit:* (unit 'kilogram 1 'meter 1 'second -1)
        (unit 'second -1))
(unit kilogram 1 meter 1 second -2)
```

---

[3]Watch out! The "base units" are not to be confused with the base-layer in our layered-data system. A system of units is built on a set of base units, such as kilograms, meters, and seconds. There are derived units, such as the newton, which is a combination of the base units: $1\,\text{N} = 1\,\text{kg} \cdot \text{m} \cdot \text{s}^{-2}$

Here we assume that the base units are just named by symbols, such as `kilogram`.

Representation of unit specifications

To make it easy to create a unit specification, we represent it externally as a property list (with alternating keys and values) of base unit names and exponents.

But internally, it is convenient to represent a unit specification as a tagged alist; so we must convert a raw property list to the alist representation, using `plist->alist`. We keep the alists sorted by the base unit name. In this conversion we do some error checking. The argument list to `unit` must be in the form of a property list. The exponent associated with each base unit name must be an exact rational number (usually an integer). It is an error if a named base unit is duplicated. The sort by base unit names will signal an error if the base unit name is not a symbol.

```
(define (unit . plist)
  (guarantee plist? plist 'unit)
  (let ((alist
         (sort (plist->alist plist)
               (lambda (p1 p2)
                 (symbol<? (car p1) (car p2))))))
    (if (sorted-alist-repeated-key? alist)
        (error "Base unit repeated" plist))
    (for-each (lambda (p)
                (guarantee exact-rational? (cdr p)))
              alist)
    (alist->unit alist)))

(define (sorted-alist-repeated-key? alist)
  (and (pair? alist)
       (pair? (cdr alist))
       (or (eq? (caar alist) (caadr alist))
           (sorted-alist-repeated-key? (cdr alist)))))
```

The procedure `alist->unit` just attaches a unique tag to an alist; and `unit->alist` extracts the alist from a unit specification:

```
(define (alist->unit alist)
  (cons %unit-tag alist))

(define (unit->alist unit)
  (guarantee unit? unit 'unit->alist)
  (cdr unit))
```

Here, the value of %unit-tag is just a unique symbol that we use
to head a unit specification alist. To make the printed output
of unit specifications look like the property lists that we give to
unit to make a unit specification, we arrange that the Scheme
printer prints unit specifications in property list form. This magic
arrangement (not shown here) is triggered by the unit-tag symbol
at the head of the list.

The predicate unit? is true if its argument is a legitimate unit
specification:

```
(define (unit? object)
  (and (pair? object)
       (eq? (car object) %unit-tag)
       (list? (cdr object))
       (every (lambda (elt)
                (and (pair? elt)
                     (symbol? (car elt))
                     (exact-rational? (cdr elt))))
              (cdr object))))
```

Unit arithmetic operations

We construct the unit arithmetic as a mapping between the operator name and the operation that implements the required behavior. Pure numbers, like π, are unitless. When a quantity with
units is multiplied by a unitless number, the result is the units
of the quantity with units. So the unit arithmetic needs a multiplicative identity for unitless numbers—this is unit:none. The
procedure simple-operation combines the operator, the test for
applicability, and the procedure that implements the operation:

```
(define (unit-arithmetic)
  (make-arithmetic 'unit unit? '()
    (lambda (name)
      (if (eq? name 'multiplicative-identity)
          unit:none
          (default-object)))
    (lambda (operator)
      (simple-operation operator
                        unit?
                        (unit-procedure operator)))))
```

We call unit-procedure to get the appropriate procedure for each
operator:

```
(define (unit-procedure operator)
  (case operator
    ((*) unit:*)
    ((/) unit:/)
    ((remainder) unit:remainder)
    ((expt) unit:expt)
    ((invert) unit:invert)
    ((square) unit:square)
    ((sqrt) unit:sqrt)
    ((atan) unit:atan)
    ((abs ceiling floor negate round truncate)
     unit:simple-unary-operation)
    ((+ - max min)
     unit:simple-binary-operation)
    ((acos asin cos exp log sin tan)
     unit:unitless-operation)
    ((angle imag-part magnitude make-polar make-rectangular
            real-part)
     ;; first approximation:
     unit:unitless-operation)
    (else
     (if (eq? 'boolean (operator-codomain operator))
         (if (n:= 1 (operator-arity operator))
             unit:unary-comparison
             unit:binary-comparison)
         unit:unitless-operation)))))
```

For each case above we must provide the appropriate operation. For example, to multiply two unit quantities we must add corresponding exponents and elide any base unit that has zero exponent:

```
(define (unit:* u1 u2)
  (alist->unit
   (let loop ((u1 (unit->alist u1)) (u2 (unit->alist u2)))
     (if (and (pair? u1) (pair? u2))
         (let ((factor1 (car u1)) (factor2 (car u2)))
           (if (eq? (car factor1) (car factor2)) ; same unit
               (let ((n (n:+ (cdr factor1) (cdr factor2))))
                 (if (n:= 0 n)
                     (loop (cdr u1) (cdr u2))
                     (cons (cons (car factor1) n)
                           (loop (cdr u1) (cdr u2)))))
               (if (symbol<? (car factor1) (car factor2))
                   (cons factor1 (loop (cdr u1) u2))
                   (cons factor2 (loop u1 (cdr u2))))))
         (if (pair? u1) u1 u2)))))
```

Some operators, such as `remainder`, `expt`, `invert`, `square`, `sqrt`, and `atan`, require special treatment. The rest of the operators fit into a few simple classes. Simple unary operations, like `negate`, just propagate the units of their argument to their result:

```
(define (unit:simple-unary-operation u)
  u)
```

But some, like the implementation of addition, check that they are not "combining apples and oranges:"

```
(define (unit:simple-binary-operation u1 u2)
  (if (not (unit=? u1 u2))
      (error "incompatible units:" u1 u2))
  u1)
```

Exercise 6.1: Derived units

Although the unit computation given above is correct and reasonably complete, it is not very nice to use. For example, the unit specification for kinetic energy (as shown on page 316) is:

```
(unit kilogram 1 meter 2 second -2)
```

This is correct in terms of the International System of Units (SI) base units {kilogram, meter, second}, but it would be much nicer if expressed in terms of joules, the SI derived unit of energy:

```
(unit joule 1)
```

The full system of SI base units is {kilogram, meter, second, ampere, kelvin, mole, candela}, and there is an approved set of derived units. For example:

- newton = kilogram·meter·second^{-2}
- joule = newton·meter
- coulomb = ampere·second
- watt = joule·second^{-1}
- volt = watt·ampere^{-1}
- ohm = volt·ampere^{-1}
- siemens = ohm^{-1}
- farad = coulomb·volt^{-1}
- weber = volt·second
- henry = weber·ampere^{-1}
- hertz = second^{-1}
- tesla = weber·meter^{-2}
- pascal = newton·meter^{-2}

a. Make a procedure that takes a unit description in terms of SI base units and, if possible, makes a simpler description using derived units.

b. The expression of a unit description in terms of the derived units is not unique—there may be many such equivalent descriptions. This is similar to a problem of algebraic simplification, but the criterion of "simpler" is not obvious. Make a nice version that you like and explain why you like it.

c. It is nice to be able to use the standard abbreviations and multipliers for the units. For example, 1 mA is the nice way to write 0.001 A or 1/1000 ampere. Design and implement a simple extensible system that allows the use of these notational conveniences for both input and output. But remember that "syntactic sugar causes cancer of the semicolon."

6.4 Annotating values with dependencies

One kind of annotation that a programmer may want to deploy in some parts of a program is the tracking of dependencies. Every piece of data (or procedure) came from somewhere. Either it entered the computation as a premise that can be labeled with its external provenance, or it was created by combining other data. We can provide primitive operations of the system with annotation layers that, when processing data with justifications, can annotate the results with appropriate justifications.

Justifications can be at differing levels of detail. The simplest kind of justification is just a set of those premises that contributed to the new data. A procedure such as addition can form a sum with a justification that is just the union of the premises of the justifications of the addends that were supplied. Multiplication is similar, but a zero multiplicand is sufficient to force the product to be zero, so the justifications of the other factors do not need to be included in the justification of the zero product.

Such simple justifications can be computed and carried without much more than a constant overhead, but they can be invaluable in debugging complex processes and in the attribution of credit or blame for outcomes of computations. Just this much is sufficient to support dependency-directed backtracking. (See section 7.5.)

Externally supplied data can be annotated with a *premise* that identifies its origin. More generally, any data value can be annotated with a set of premises, which is called its *support set*. The support set annotating a datum is usually referred to as its *support*. When a support-aware procedure is applied to multiple arguments, it must combine the support sets of the arguments to represent the support of the result.

Managing support sets is a straightforward application of our layered data mechanism. We add a support layer to our generic arithmetic to handle support sets. It coexists with other layers, such as the units layer. So this is an additive feature.

On page 309 we built an arithmetic that supports layered data and procedures:

```
(define generic-with-layers
  (let ((g (generic-symbolic)))
    (extend-generic-arithmetic! g layered-extender)
    g))

(install-arithmetic! generic-with-layers)
```

We don't need to specify what layers are to be supported by `layered-extender`, since it automatically uses the layers in each layered procedure's arguments. So if, say, + is called with arguments that have units, then the result will also have units. But if none of the arguments have units, then neither does the result, and the unit addition procedure is not invoked. Similarly, if the arguments have support, then the result will have support. But if the arguments do not have support, the result will not have support, and the support addition procedure is not invoked.

For example, we can define the kinetic energy of a particle with mass m and velocity v:

```
(define (KE m v)
  (* 1/2 m (square v)))
```

Now we can see the result of evaluating the kinetic energy on some arguments:

```
(pp (KE (layered-datum 'm
                       unit-layer (unit 'kilogram 1)
                       support-layer (support-set 'cph))
        (layered-datum 'v
                       unit-layer (unit 'meter 1 'second -1)
                       support-layer (support-set 'gjs))))
#[layered-datum (* (* 1/2 m) (square v))]
(base-layer (* (* 1/2 m) (square v)))
(unit-layer (unit kilogram 1 meter 2 second -2))
(support-layer (support-set gjs cph))
```

We supply each argument with annotations for the units layer and the support layer. For the support layer we give a set of premises (the support set). Here, each argument is supported by a single premise, `cph` and `gjs` respectively. The value is a layered object with three layers: the base generic arithmetic layer value is the appropriate algebraic expression; the units are correct; and the support set is the set of named premises that contributed to the value.

Here we accepted the definition of `KE` without supplying explicit support for that procedure. More generally, we might want to add such support. For example, we may want to say that `KE` is supported by a premise `KineticEnergy-classical`. Then if we find a result of some complex computation that seems wrong, we can find out which procedures contributed to the wrong answer, as well as the numerical or symbolic input values that were used. We will attack this problem in exercise 6.2.

Not all premises that appear in the arguments to a computation need to appear in a result. For example, if a factor contributing to a product is zero, that is sufficient reason for the product to be zero, independent of any other finite factors. This is illustrated by supplying a zero mass:

```
(pp (KE (layered-datum 0
                       unit-layer (unit 'kilogram 1)
                       support-layer (support-set 'jems))
        (layered-datum 'v
                       unit-layer (unit 'meter 1 'second -1)
                       support-layer (support-set 'gjs))))
#[layered-datum 0]
(base-layer 0)
(unit-layer (unit kilogram 1 meter 2 second -2))
(support-layer (support-set jems))
```

Here the support for the numeric value of the result being zero is just the support supplied for the zero value for the mass.

6.4.1   The support layer

Now we will see how the support layer is implemented. It is somewhat different from the units layer, because units can be combined without any reference to the base layer, whereas the support layer needs to look at the base layer for some operations.

The support layer is somewhat simpler than the units layer, because all but three of the arithmetic operators use the default: the support set of the result is the union of the support sets of the arguments.

```
(define support-layer
  (make-annotation-layer 'support
    (lambda (get-name has-value? get-value)
      (define (get-default-value)
        (support-set))
      (define (get-procedure name arity)
        (case name
          ((*) support:*)
          ((/) support:/)
          ((atan2) support:atan2)
          (else support:default-procedure)))
      (bundle layer?
              get-name has-value? get-value
              get-default-value get-procedure)))))

(define support-layer-value
  (layer-accessor support-layer))

(define (support:default-procedure base-value . args)
  (apply support-set-union (map support-layer-value args)))
```

Multiplication is the first interesting case. The support layer needs to look at the values of the base arithmetic arguments to determine the computation of support. If either argument is zero, then the support for the result is only the support for the zero argument.

```
(define (support:* base-value arg1 arg2)
  (let ((v1 (base-layer-value arg1))
        (v2 (base-layer-value arg2))
        (s1 (support-layer-value arg1))
        (s2 (support-layer-value arg2)))
    (if (exact-zero? v1)
        (if (exact-zero? v2)
            (if (< (length (support-set-elements s1))
                   (length (support-set-elements s2)))
                s1
                s2)    ;arbitrary
            s1)
        (if (exact-zero? v2)
            s2
            (support-set-union s1 s2)))))
```

Division (and arctangent, not shown) also has to examine the base layer to deal with zero arguments. If the dividend is zero, that is sufficient to support the result that the quotient is zero. The divisor won't ever be zero because the base-layer computation will have signaled an error and this code won't be run.

```
(define (support:/ base-value arg1 arg2)
  (let ((v1 (base-layer-value arg1))
        (s1 (support-layer-value arg1))
        (s2 (support-layer-value arg2)))
    (if (exact-zero? v1)
        s1
        (support-set-union s1 s2))))
```

These optimizations for * and / make sense only when we can prove that an argument is really zero, not an unsimplified symbolic expression. (But if an expression simplifies to exact zero we can use that fact!)

```
(define (exact-zero? x)
  (and (n:number? x) (exact? x) (n:zero? x)))
```

The support-set abstraction is implemented as a list starting with the symbol support-set

```
(define (%make-support-set elements)
  (cons 'support-set elements))

(define (support-set? object)
  (and (pair? object)
       (eq? 'support-set (car object))
       (list? (cdr object))))

(define (support-set-elements support-set)
  (cdr support-set))
```

along with a few extra utilities to complete the abstraction.

```
(define (make-support-set elements)
  (if (null? elements)
      %empty-support-set
      (%make-support-set (delete-duplicates elements))))

(define (support-set . elements)
  (if (null? elements)
      %empty-support-set
      (%make-support-set (delete-duplicates elements))))
```

```
(define %empty-support-set
  (%make-support-set '()))

(define (support-set-empty? s)
  (null? (support-set-elements s)))
```

We need to be able to compute the union of support sets and adjoin new elements to them. Since we chose to keep our elements in a list, we can use the lset library from Scheme.[4]

```
(define (support-set-union . sets)
  (make-support-set
   (apply lset-union eqv?
          (map support-set-elements sets))))

(define (support-set-adjoin set . elts)
  (make-support-set
   (apply lset-adjoin eqv? (support-set-elements set) elts)))
```

Exercise 6.2: Procedural responsibility

The support layer based on arithmetic is extremely low level. Every primitive arithmetic operation is support-aware, and there is no way to bypass that work for common conditions. There needs to be a means of abstraction. For example, suppose we have a procedure that computes the numerical definite integral of a function. The units of the numerical value of the integral is the product of the units of the numerical value of the integrand and the units of the numerical value of the limits of integration. (The units of the upper and lower limit must be the same!) However, it is not a good idea to carry the units computation through all of the detailed arithmetic going on in the integration process. It should be possible to annotate the integrator so that the result has the correct units without requiring every internal addition and multiplication to be a layered procedure operating on layered data.

a. Make it possible to allow compound procedures that may be built out of the primitive arithmetic procedures (or possibly not) to modify the support of their results by adding a premise (such as "made by George").

b. Allow compound procedures to be executed in a way that hides their bodies from the support layer. Thus, for example, a trusted library procedure may annotate its result with appropriate support, but the operations in its body will not incur the overhead of computing the support of intermediate results.

c. The support layer is organized around the operators of an arithmetic system. But sometimes it is useful to distinguish the specific occurrences

---

[4]If the support sets get large we can try to represent them much more efficiently, but here we are dealing with only small sets.

of an operator. For example, when dealing with numerical precision it is not very helpful to say that a loss of significance is due to subtraction of almost equal quantities. It would be more helpful to show the particular instance of subtraction that is the culprit. Is there some way to add the ability to identify instances of an operator to the support layer?

Exercise 6.3: Paranoid programming

Sometimes we are not confident that a library procedure does what we expect. In that case it is prudent to "wrap" the library procedure with a test that checks its result. For example, we may be using a program `solve` that takes as inputs a set of equations and a set of unknowns, that may occur in the equations, producing a set of substitutions for the unknowns that satisfy the equations. We might want to wrap the `solve` program with a wrapper that checks that the result of substituting the outputs into the input equations indeed makes them tautologies. But we don't want such a paranoia wrapper to appear as part of our *parti*. How can this sort of thing be implemented as a layer? Explain your design and implement it.

Exercise 6.4: IDE for layered programs

This exercise is a major design project: the invention of and development of an IDE (Integrated Development Environment) for layered systems.

The idea of layered programs, using layered data and layered procedures, is a very nice idea. The goal is to be able to annotate programs with useful and executable metadata—such as type declarations, assertions, units, and support—without cluttering the text of the base program. However, the text of the program must be linked with the text of the annotations, so that as any part of the program is edited, the related layers are also edited. For example, suppose it is necessary to edit the base procedure of some layered procedure. The layers may be information like type declarations or how it handles units and support sets. It would be nice for the editor to show us these layers and how they are connected to the text of the base program, when necessary. Perhaps edits to the text of the base program entail edits to the annotation layers. Sometimes this can be done automatically, but often the programmer must edit the layers.

a. Imagine what you would like to see in an IDE to support the development of layered systems. What would you like to see on a screen? How would you keep the parts that are edited synchronized?

b. Emacs is a powerful infrastructure for building such an IDE. It supports multiple windows and per-window editing modes. It has syntactic support for many computer languages, including Scheme. There are Emacs subsystems, like `org-mode`, that have the flavor of a layered structure for documents. Can this be extended to help with layered programming? Sketch out a way to build your IDE using Emacs.

(continued)

c. Build a small but extensible prototype on the Emacs base, and try it out. What problems do you encounter? Did Emacs really provide a good place to start? If not, why not? Report on your experiment.

d. If your prototype was promising, develop a solid system and make it into a loadable Emacs library, so we can all use your great system.

6.4.2   Carrying justifications

More complex justifications may also record the particular operations that were used to make the data. This kind of annotation can be used to provide explanations (proofs), but it is intrinsically expensive in space—potentially linear in the number of operations performed. However, sometimes it is appropriate to attach a detailed audit history describing the derivation of a data item, to allow some later process to use the derivation for some purpose or to evaluate the validity of the derivation for debugging.[5]

For many purposes, such as legal arguments, it is necessary to know the provenance of data: where it was collected, how it was collected, who collected it, how the collection was authorized, etc. The detailed derivation of a piece of evidence, giving the provenance of each contribution, may be essential to determining if it is admissable in a trial.

The symbolic arithmetic that we built in section 3.1 is one way this can be done. In fact, if symbolic arithmetic is used as a layer on numeric arithmetic, then every numerical value is annotated with its derivation. The symbolic arithmetic annotation could be very expensive, because the symbolic expression for an application of a numerical operator includes the symbolic expressions of its inputs. However, because we need only include a pointer to each input, the space and time cost of annotating each operation is often acceptable.[6] So one may overlay this kind of justification

---

[5] In Patrick Suppes's beautiful *Introduction to Logic* [118] the proofs are written in four columns. The columns are an identifier for the line, the statement for that line, the rule that was used for deriving that line from previous lines, and the set of premises that support the line. This proof structure is actually the inspiration for the way we carry justifications and support sets.

[6] This is not really true. The problem is that the composition of numerical operations may incur no significant memory access cost, but the construction of a symbolic expression, however small, requires access to memory. And memory access time is huge compared with the time to do arithmetic in CPU registers. Sigh...

when it is necessary to provide an explanation, or even temporarily, to track a difficult-to-catch bug.

Exercise 6.5: Justifications

Sketch out the issues involved in carrying justifications for data. Notice that the reason for a value depends on the values that it was derived from and the way those values were combined. What do we do if the reason for a value is some numerically weighted combination of many factors, as in a deep neural network? This is a research question that we need to address to make the systems that affect us accountable.

6.5   The promise of layering

We have only scratched the surface of what can be done with an easy and convenient mechanism for layering of data and programs. It is an open area of research. The development of systems to support such layering can have huge consequence for the future.

Sensitivity analysis is an important feature that can be built using annotated data and layered procedures. For example, in mechanics, if we have a system that evolves the solution of a system of differential equations from some initial conditions, it is often valuable to understand the way a tube of trajectories that surround a reference trajectory deforms. This is usually accomplished by integrating a variational system along with the reference trajectory. Similarly, it may be possible to carry a probability distribution of values around a nominal value along with the nominal value computed in some analyses. This may be accomplished by annotating the values with distributions and providing the operations with overlaying procedures to combine the distributions, guided by the nominals, perhaps implementing Bayesian analysis. Of course, to do this well is not easy.

An even more exciting but related idea is that of perturbational programming. By analogy with the differential equations example, can we program symbolic systems to carry a "tube" of variations around a reference trajectory, thus allowing us to consider small variations of a query? Consider, for example, the problem of doing a search. Given a set of keywords, the system does some magic that comes up with a list of documents that match the keywords. Suppose we incrementally change a single keyword. How sensitive is the search to that keyword? More important, is it possible to reuse some of the work that was done getting the previous result in the incrementally different search? We don't know the answers to these questions, but if it is possible, we want to be able to capture the methods by a kind of perturbational program, built as an overlay on the base program.

Dependencies mitigate inconsistency

Dependency annotations on data give us a powerful tool for organizing human-like computations. For example, all humans harbor mutually inconsistent beliefs: an intelligent person may be committed to the scientific method yet have a strong attachment to some superstitious or ritual practices; a person may have a strong belief in the sanctity of all human life, yet also believe that capital punishment is sometimes justified. If we were really logicians this kind of inconsistency would be fatal: if we really were to simultaneously believe both propositions P and NOT P, then we would have to believe all propositions! But somehow we manage to keep inconsistent beliefs from inhibiting all useful thought. Our personal belief systems appear to be locally consistent, in that there are no contradictions apparent. If we observe inconsistencies we do not crash; we may feel conflicted or we may chuckle.

We can attach to each proposition a set of supporting assumptions, allowing deductions to be conditional on the assumption set. Then, if a contradiction occurs, a process can determine the particular "nogood set" of inconsistent assumptions. The system can then "chuckle," realizing that no deductions based on any superset of those assumptions can be believed. This chuckling process, dependency-directed backtracking, can be used to optimize a complex search process, allowing a search to make the best use of its mistakes. But enabling a process to simultaneously hold beliefs based on mutually inconsistent sets of assumptions without logical disaster is revolutionary.

Restrictions on the use of data

Data is often encumbered by restrictions on the ways it may be used. These encumberances may be determined by statute, by contract, by custom, or by common decency. Some of these restrictions are intended to control the diffusion of the data, while others are intended to delimit the consequences of actions predicated on that data.

The allowable uses of data may be further restricted by the sender: "I am telling you this information in confidence. You may not use it to compete with me, and you may not give it to any of my competitors." Data may also be restricted by the receiver: "I don't want to know anything about this that I may not tell my spouse."

Although the details may be quite involved, as data is passed from one individual or organization to another, the restrictions on the uses to which it may be put are changed in ways that can often be formulated as algebraic expressions. These expressions describe how the restrictions on the use of a particular data item may be computed from the history of its transmission: the encumberances that are added or deleted at each step. When parts of one data set are combined with parts of another data set, the restrictions on the ways that the extracts may be used and the restrictions on the ways that they may be combined must determine the restrictions on the combination. A formalization of this process is a *data-purpose algebra* [53] description.

Data-purpose algebra layers can be helpful in building systems that track the distribution and use of sensitive data to enable auditing and to inhibit the misuse of that data. But this kind of application is much larger than just a simple matter of layering. To make it effective requires ways of ensuring the security of the process, to prevent leakage through uncontrolled channels or compromise of the tracking layers. There is a great deal of research to be done here.

7
Propagation

Decades of programming experience have taken a toll on our collective imagination. We come from a culture of scarcity, where computation and memory were expensive, and concurrency was difficult to arrange and control. This is no longer true. But our languages, our algorithms, and our architectural ideas are based on those assumptions. Our languages are basically sequential and directional—even functional languages assume that computation is organized around values percolating up through expression trees. Multidirectional constraints are hard to express in functional languages.

Escaping the Von Neumann straitjacket

The propagator model of computation [99] provides one avenue of escape. The propagator model is built on the idea that the basic computational elements are propagators, autonomous independent machines interconnected by shared cells through which they communicate. Each propagator machine continuously examines the cells it is connected to, and adds information to some cells based on computations it can make from information it can get from others. Cells accumulate information and propagators produce information.

Since the propagator infrastructure is based on propagation of data through interconnected independent machines, propagator structures are better expressed as wiring diagrams than as expression trees. In such a system partial results are useful, even though they are not complete. For example, the usual way to compute a square root is by successive refinement using Heron's method. In traditional programming, the result of a square root computation is not available to subsequent computations until the required error tolerance is achieved. By contrast, in an analog electrical circuit that performed the same function, the partial results could be used by the next stages as first approximations to their computations. This is not an analog/digital problem—it is organizational. In a propagator mechanism the partial results of a digital process can be made available without waiting for the final result.

Figure 7.1   Kanizsa's triangle is a classic example of a completion illusion. The white triangle is not there!

Filling in details

This makes a natural computational structure for building powerful systems that fill in details. The structure is additive: new ways to contribute information can be included just by adding new parts to a network, whether simple propagators or entire subnetworks. For example, if an uncertain quantity is represented as a range, a new way of computing an upper bound can be included without disturbing any other part of the network.

Filling in details plays an important role in all ways we use information. Consider Kanizsa's triangle (figure 7.1), for example. Given a few fragmentary pieces of evidence we see a white triangle (on a white background!) that isn't there (and that is typically described as brighter than the background). We have filled in the missing details of an implied figure. When we hear speech we fill in the details from the observed context, using the regularities of phonology, morphology, syntax, and semantics. An expert electrical circuit designer who sees a partial schematic diagram fills in details that make a sensible mechanism. This filling in of details is not sequential; it happens opportunistically wherever local deductions can be made from surrounding clues. Deductions may compound, so that if a piece is filled in it forms a new clue for the continuing completion process.

Dependencies and backtracking

Using layering, we incorporate dependencies into the propagator infrastructure in a natural and efficient way. This allows the system to track and preserve information about the provenance of each value. Provenance can be used to provide a coherent explanation of how a value was derived, citing the sources and the rules by which the source material was combined. This is especially important when we have multiple sources, each providing partial information about a value. Dependency tracking also provides a substrate for debugging (and possibly for introspective self-debugging).

Besides foundation beliefs, hypotheticals may be introduced by amb machines, which provide alternative values supported by premises that may be discarded without pain. Unlike systems modeled on expression-based languages such as Lisp, there is no spurious control flow arising from the expression structure to pollute our dependencies and force expensive recomputation of already-computed values when backtracking.

Degeneracy, redundancy, and parallelism

The propagator model incorporates mechanisms to support the integration of redundant (actually degenerate) subsystems so that a problem can be addressed in multiple disparate ways. Multiply redundant designs can be effective in combating attacks: if there is no single thread of execution that can be subverted, an attack that disables or delays one of the paths will not impede the computation, because an alternate path can substitute. Redundant and degenerate parallel computations contribute to integrity and resiliency: computations that proceed along variant paths can be checked to assure integrity. The work of subverting parallel computations increases because of the cross-thread invariants.

The propagator model is essentially concurrent, distributed, and scalable, with strong isolation and a built-in assumption of parallel computation. Multiple independent propagators are computing and contributing to the information in the shared cells, where the information is merged and contradictions are noted and acted upon.

7.1 An example: Distances to stars

Consider a problem of astronomy, the estimation of the distance to stars. This is very hard, because the distances are enormous. Even for the closest stars, for which we can use parallax measurements, with the radius of the Earth's orbit as a baseline, the angular variation of the position of a star is a small part of an

Figure 7.2 The angle θ of the triangle to the distant star erected on the semimajor axis of the Earth's orbit around the Sun is called the parallax of the star. Note that $A/d = \tan(\theta)$. If $\theta = 1$ arcsecond then the distance d is defined to be 1 parsec. The length of the semimajor axis A is 1 Astronomical Unit (AU) = 149597870700 meters.

arcsecond. Indeed, the unit of distance for stellar distances is the *parsec*, which is the altitude of a triangle based on the diameter of the Earth's orbit, where the vertex angle is 2 arcseconds. The parallax is measured by observing the variation of position of the star against the background as the Earth revolves annually around the Sun. (See figure 7.2.)

We define a propagator that relates the parallax of a star, in radians, to the distance to the star, in parsecs:

```
(define-c:prop (c:parallax<->distance parallax distance)
  (let-cells (t (AU AU-in-parsecs))
    (c:tan parallax t)
    (c:* t distance AU)))
```

Here, the special form `define-c:prop` defines a special kind of procedure, a constructor named `c:parallax<->distance`. When `c:parallax<->distance` is given two cells, locally named `parallax` and `distance`, as its arguments, it constructs a constraint propagator that relates those cells. Using the special form `let-cells` it creates two new cells, one locally named `t`, and the other locally named `AU`. The cell named `t` is not initialized; the cell named `AU` is initialized to the numerical value of the Astronomical Unit, the semimajor axis of the Earth's orbit, in parsecs. The cell named `parallax` and the cell named `t` are connected by a primitive constraint propagator constructed by `c:tan`, imposing the constraint

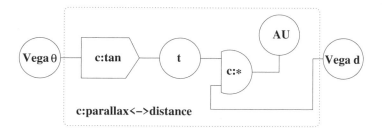

Figure 7.3   Here we see a "wiring diagram" of the propagator system constructed by calling `c:parallax<->distance` on the cells named `Vega-parallax-distance` (Vega d in the diagram) and `Vega-parallax` (Vega θ in the diagram). Circles indicate cells, and other shapes indicate propagators interconnecting the cells. These propagators are not directional—they enforce algebraic constraints. By convention we name constraint-propagator constructors with the prefix `c:`. For example, the propagator constructed by `c:*` enforces the constraint that the product of the contents of the cell `t` and the contents of the cell `Vega-parallax-distance` is the contents of the cell `AU`.

that any value held by `t` must be the tangent of the value held by `parallax`. Similarly, the cells named `t`, `distance`, and `AU` are connected by a primitive constraint propagator constructed by `c:*`, imposing the constraint that the product of the value in cell `t` and the value in cell `distance` is the value in `AU`.

Let's think about the distance to the star Vega, as measured by parallax. We make two cells, `Vega-parallax-distance` for the distance, and `Vega-parallax` for the parallax angle:

```
(define-cell Vega-parallax-distance)
(define-cell Vega-parallax)
```

Now we can interconnect our cells with the propagator constructor that we just defined:

```
(c:parallax<->distance Vega-parallax Vega-parallax-distance)
```

The system of cells and propagators so constructed is illustrated in figure 7.3.

The constraint propagators are themselves made up of directional propagators, as shown in figure 7.4. A directional propaga-

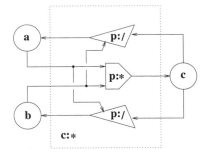

Figure 7.4   The constraint propagator constructed by c:* is made up of three directional propagators. By convention we name the directional-propagator constructors with the prefix p:. The directional multiplier propagator, constructed by p:*, forces the value in c to be the product of the values in cells a and b. The divider propagators, constructed by p:/, force the value in their quotient cells (a and b) to be the result of dividing the value in the dividend cell (c) by the value in the divisor cells (b and a).

tor, such as the multiplier constructed by p:*, adjusts the value in the product cell to be consistent with the values in the multiplier and multiplicand cells. It is entirely appropriate to mix directional propagators and constraint propagators in a propagator system.[1]

Now let's use this small system to compute. Friedrich G. W. von Struve in 1837 published an estimate of the parallax of Vega: 0.125" ± 0.05".[2] This was the first plausible published measurement of the parallax of a star, but because his data was sparse and he later contradicted that data, the credit for the first real measurement goes to Friedrich Wilhelm Bessel, who did a careful measurement of the parallax of the star 61 Cygni in 1838. However, Struve's estimate is quite close to the current best estimate of the parallax of Vega. We tell our propagator system Struve's estimate of 125 milliarcseconds plus or minus 50 milliarcseconds:

---

[1]Constraint propagation was introduced by David Waltz in his doctoral thesis on the interpretation of line drawings [125]. Gerald Jay Sussman and Richard Stallman developed electrical circuit analysis tools based on constraint propagation [119, 114]. Eugene Freuder [39] transformed the constraint-programming ideas into a major intellectual endeavor, with its own journal [24]. Guy Steele's PhD thesis [116] showed how one could construct a programming language based on constraints.

[2]See [127], page 71.

```
(tell! Vega-parallax
       (+->interval (mas->radians 125) (mas->radians 50))
       'FGWvonStruve1837)
```

The procedure `tell!` takes three arguments: a propagator cell, a value for that cell, and a premise symbol describing the provenance of the data. The procedure `mas->radians` converts milliarcseconds to radians. The procedure `+->interval` makes an interval centered on its first argument:

```
(define (+->interval value delta)
  (make-interval (n:- value delta) (n:+ value delta)))
```

So the `Vega-parallax` cell is given the interval

```
(+->interval (mas->radians 125) (mas->radians 50))
(interval 3.6361026083215196e-7 8.48423941941688e-7)
```

Struve's estimate of the error in his result was a pretty big fraction of the estimated parallax. So his estimate for the distance to Vega is pretty wide (roughly 5.7 to 13.3 or 9.5 ± 3.8 parsecs):

```
(get-value-in Vega-parallax-distance)
(interval 5.7142857143291135 13.33333333343721)
```

```
(interval>+- (get-value-in Vega-parallax-distance))
(+- 9.523809523883163 3.8095238095540473)
```

This interval value is supported by the premise `FGWvonStruve1837`.

```
(get-premises Vega-parallax-distance)
(support-set fgwvonstruve1837)
```

We will use a procedure `inquire` that nicely shows the value of the cell and the support for that value:[3]

---

[3]There is also a "reason" for the value, indicated by the list beginning with `because`. In this case the value in the `Vega-parallax-distance` cell was derived by division of the contents of the `AU` cell by the contents of the `t` cell in the propagator made by `c:parallax<->distance`. The directional division propagator `p:/` was part of the constraint propagator `c:*`, which was itself part of the `c:parallax<->distance` constraint propagator. These reasons can get very verbose. We will omit the "because" part of the results of `inquire` when they are not helpful.

By chasing these reasons recursively one can get a very verbose explanation of the derivation of a value. These reasons are the justifications we discussed in section 6.4.2.

```
(inquire Vega-parallax-distance)
((vega-parallax-distance)
 (has-value (interval 5.7143e0 1.3333e1))
 (depends-on fgwvonstruve1837)
 (because
  ((p:/ c:* c:parallax<->distance)
   (au 4.8481e-6)
   (t (interval 3.6361e-7 8.4842e-7))))))
```

A tighter bound, reported by Russell et al. in 1982 [106], is

```
(tell! Vega-parallax
       (+->interval (mas->radians 124.3) (mas->radians 4.9))
       'JRussell-etal1982)
```

which seems pretty close to the center of Struve's estimate. With that measurement, the distance estimate is narrowed to

```
(inquire Vega-parallax-distance)
((vega-parallax-distance)
 (has-value (interval 7.7399 8.3752))
 (depends-on jrussell-etal1982))
```

Notice that our estimate of the distance to Vega now depends only on the Russell measurement. Because the interval of the Russell measurement is entirely contained in the interval of the Struve measurement, the Struve measurement provides no further information. But the cell remembers the Struve measurement and its provenance so it can be recovered, if needed.

By 1995 there were some better measurements:[4]

```
(tell! Vega-parallax
       (+->interval (mas->radians 131) (mas->radians 0.77))
       'Gatewood-deJonge1995)
((vega-parallax)
 (has-value (the-contradiction))
 (depends-on jrussell-etal1982 gatewood-dejonge1995)
 (because
  ((has-value (interval 5.7887e-7 6.2638e-7))
   (depends-on jrussell-etal1982))
  ((has-value (interval 6.3137e-7 6.3884e-7))
   (depends-on gatewood-dejonge1995)))))
```

---

[4]We are lying here! Actually the measurement of Gatewood and de Jonge [43] is a bit different. The center of their measurement was 130 milliarcseconds rather than the 131 that we quote here. We fudged this to make it possible to illustrate a computational point a bit later.

We see that the contradiction depends on the two sources of information. Each source provides an interval, and the intervals do not overlap. Suppose we think that the measurement by Gatewood and de Jonge looks suspicious. Let's retract that premise:

```
(retract! 'Gatewood-deJonge1995)
```

All values that depend on the retracted premise are now retracted, and thus the value that we see for the distance has reverted to

```
(inquire Vega-parallax-distance)
((vega-parallax-distance)
 (has-value (interval 7.7399 8.3752))
 (depends-on jrussell-etal1982))
```

This is what we got from Russell et al.; and indeed that premise supports the value.

But the plot thickens, because the Hipparcos satellite (as reported by Van Leeuwen [83]) made some very impressive measurements of the parallax of Vega:

```
(tell! Vega-parallax
       (+->interval (mas->radians 130.23) (mas->radians 0.36))
       'FvanLeeuwen2007Nov)
((vega-parallax)
 (has-value (the-contradiction))
 (depends-on jrussell-etal1982 fvanleeuwen2007nov)
 (because
  ((has-value (interval 5.7887e-7 6.2638e-7))
   (depends-on jrussell-etal1982))
  ((has-value (interval 6.2963e-7 6.3312e-7))
   (depends-on fvanleeuwen2007nov)))))
```

Which do we believe?[5] Let's reject the Russell result:

```
(retract! 'JRussell-etal1982)
```

```
(inquire Vega-parallax-distance)
((vega-parallax-distance)
 (has-value (interval 7.6576 7.7))
 (depends-on fvanleeuwen2007nov))
```

Here we have the satellite's result isolated.

---

[5]Actually there are some problems with the Hipparcos data. Specifically, the distances measured by Hipparcos to some very bright clusters, such as the Pleiades, are apparently not consistent with better measurements made by very long baseline radio interferometry. But this discrepancy does not damage other Hipparcos measurements.

Now let's add back Gatewood and see what happens:

```
(assert! 'Gatewood-deJonge1995)

(inquire Vega-parallax-distance)
((vega-parallax-distance)
 (has-value (interval 7.6576 7.6787))
 (depends-on gatewood-dejonge1995 fvanleeuwen2007nov))
```

We get a stronger result because the intersection of the intervals of Van Leeuwen and Gatewood is smaller than either separately.[6] (The Gatewood result, (interval 7.589 7.6787), is not shown.)

Magnitudes

There are other ways to estimate the distance to a star. We know that the apparent brightness of a star decreases with the square of the distance from us, so if we knew the intrinsic brightness of the star we could get the distance by measuring its apparent brightness.

By now we have a pretty good theoretical understanding that can give reliable and accurate estimates of the intrinsic brightness of some kinds of stars. For those stars, spectroscopic analysis of the light we receive from the star gives us information about, for example, its state, its chemical composition, and its mass; and from these we can estimate the intrinsic brightness. Vega is a very good example of a star we know a lot about.

Astronomers describe the brightness of a star in *magnitudes*. A difference of 5 magnitudes is defined to be a factor of 100 in brightness.[7] The intrinsic brightness of a star is given as the magnitude it would appear to have if it were situated 10 parsecs away from the observer. This is called the *absolute magnitude* of the star. We can summarize the connection between brightness and

---

[6]This is why we fudged Gatewood and de Jonge's measurement. Their result would not overlap with the Hipparcos result if we quoted it correctly. In fact, the Hipparcos measurement would be entirely contained in the Gatewood and de Jonge error bars.

[7]This admittedly weird system descends from the work of the ancient Greek astronomer Hipparchus (c. 190 BCE – c. 120 BCE). He assigned a numerical brightness to each star in his catalog. He called the brightest stars *first magnitude*, less bright ones *second magnitude*, and the dimmest *sixth magnitude*. The ESA's Hipparcos Space Astrometry Mission (see page 335) was named in honor of Hipparchus.

distance in a neat formula that combines the inverse square law with the definition of magnitudes. If M is the absolute magnitude of a star, m is its apparent magnitude, and d is the distance to the star in parsecs, then $m - M = 5(\log_{10}(d) - 1)$. This formula can be represented by a constraint-propagator constructor:[8]

```
(define-c:prop
  (c:magnitudes<->distance apparent-magnitude
                           absolute-magnitude
                           magnitude-distance)
  (let-cells (dmod dmod/5 ld10 ld
              (ln10 (log 10)) (one 1) (five 5))
    (c:+ absolute-magnitude dmod apparent-magnitude)
    (c:* five dmod/5 dmod)
    (c:+ one dmod/5 ld10)
    (c:* ln10 ld10 ld)
    (c:exp ld magnitude-distance)))
```

Now let's wire up some knowledge of Vega. We define some cells and interconnect them with the propagators:

```
(define-cell Vega-apparent-magnitude)
(define-cell Vega-absolute-magnitude)
(define-cell Vega-magnitude-distance)

(c:magnitudes<->distance Vega-apparent-magnitude
                         Vega-absolute-magnitude
                         Vega-magnitude-distance)
```

We now provide some measurements. Vega is very bright: its apparent magnitude is very close to zero. (The Hubble space telescope was used to make this very precise measurement. See Bohlin and Gilliland [14].)

```
(tell! Vega-apparent-magnitude
       (+->interval 0.026 0.008)
       'Bohlin-Gilliland2004)
```

---

[8]This is a pretty ugly language, because we need to name and create cells for all of the intermediate parts of an expression. There are many ways to make this pretty, but the concepts are clearer if we start out with this crude but very concrete language of wiring diagrams. It is easy to write a small compiler that converts constraints written as algebraic expressions to propagator diagram fragments. (See exercise 7.1 on page 340 and exercise 7.6 on page 367.)

And the absolute magnitude of Vega is also known to rather high precision [44]:

```
(tell! Vega-absolute-magnitude
       (+->interval 0.582 0.014)
       'Gatewood2008)
```

As a consequence we get a pretty nice estimate of the distance to Vega, which depends only on these measurements:

```
(inquire Vega-magnitude-distance)
((vega-magnitude-distance)
 (has-value (interval 7.663 7.8199))
 (depends-on gatewood2008 bohlingilliland2004))
```

Unfortunately, we have the distance in two different cells, so let's connect them with a propagator:

```
(c:same Vega-magnitude-distance Vega-parallax-distance)
```

At this point we have an even better value for the distance to Vega—an interval whose high end is the same as before (on page 336), but whose low end is a bit higher:

```
(inquire Vega-parallax-distance)
((vega-parallax-distance)
 (has-value (interval 7.663 7.6787))
 (depends-on fvanleeuwen2007nov gatewood-dejonge1995
             gatewood2008 bohlingilliland2004))
```

Does the 1995 measurement of Gatewood and de Jonge really matter here? Let's find out:

```
(retract! 'Gatewood-deJonge1995)

(inquire Vega-parallax-distance)
((vega-parallax-distance)
 (has-value (interval 7.663 7.7))
 (depends-on fvanleeuwen2007nov
             gatewood2008
             bohlingilliland2004))
```

Indeed it does. The 1995 measurement pulled in the high end of the interval.

Measurements Improved!

We have two ways of computing the distance to Vega—from parallax and from magnitude. Here is something remarkable: the parallax and magnitude measurement intervals are each improved using the information coming from the other. This is required in order for the system to be consistent.

Look at the apparent magnitude of Vega. The original measurement supplied from Bohlin and Gilliland was $m = 0.026 \pm 0.008$. This translates to the interval

```
(+->interval 0.026 0.008)
(interval .018 .034)
```

But now the value is a bit better—$[0.018, 0.028456]$:

```
(inquire Vega-apparent-magnitude)
((vega-apparent-magnitude)
 (has-value (interval 1.8e-2 2.8456e-2))
 (depends-on gatewood2008
             fvanleeuwen2007nov
             bohlin-gilliland2004))
```

The high end had to be pulled in to be consistent with the information from the parallax measurements. This is true for each measurable quantity. The absolute magnitude supplied by Gatewood 2008 (page 338) was:

```
(+->interval 0.582 0.014)
(interval .568 .596)
```

But now the low end is pulled in:

```
(inquire Vega-absolute-magnitude)
((vega-absolute-magnitude)
 (has-value (interval 5.8554e-1 5.96e-1))
 (depends-on gatewood2008
             fvanleeuwen2007nov
             bohlin-gilliland2004))
```

The parallax is also improved by information from the magnitude measurements:

```
(inquire Vega-parallax)
((vega-parallax)
 (has-value (interval 6.2963e-7 6.3267e-7))
 (depends-on fvanleeuwen2007nov
             gatewood2008
             bohlin-gilliland2004))
```

The fact that the computation propagates in all directions gives
us a powerful tool for understanding the implications of any new
information.

Exercise 7.1: Making writing propagator networks easier

In our propagator system it is pretty painful to write the code to build
even a simple network, because all internal nodes must be named. For
example, a constraint propagator that converts between Celsius and
Fahrenheit temperatures looks like:

```
(define-c:prop (celsius<->fahrenheit celsius fahrenheit)
  (let-cells (u v (nine 9) (five 5) (thirty-two 32))
    (c:* celsius nine u)
    (c:* v five u)
    (c:+ v thirty-two fahrenheit)))
```

It would be much nicer to be able to use expression syntax for some
propagators, so we could write:

```
(define-c:prop (celsius<->fahrenheit celsius fahrenheit)
  (c:+ (ce:* (ce:/ (constant 9) (constant 5))
             celsius)
       (constant 32)
       fahrenheit))
```

Here ce:* and ce:+ are propagator constructors that create the cell for
the value and return it to their caller. The procedure ce:+ could be
written:

```
(define (ce:+ x y)
  (let-cells (sum)
    (c:+ x y sum)
    sum))
```

Besides constraint propagators, there are also directional propagators
such as p:+. A nice name for the expression form of this is pe:+.

We have access to the names of all of the primitive arithmetic operators. Write a program that takes these names and installs both
directional- and constraint-expression forms for each operator.

Exercise 7.2: An electrical design problem

Note: You don't need to know electronics to do this problem.

Anna Logue is designing a transistor amplifier. As part of her plan she
needs to make a voltage divider to bias a transistor. The voltage divider

is made of two resistors, with resistance values R_1 and R_2. ρ is the ratio of output voltage V_{out} to power-supply voltage V_{in}. There is also Z, the output resistance of the divider.

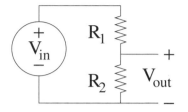

Here are the relevant equations:

$$\rho = \frac{V_{out}}{V_{in}}$$

$$\rho = \frac{R_2}{R_1 + R_2}$$

$$Z = R_1 \rho$$

Since Anna has many problems like this to solve, she makes a constraint network to help her:

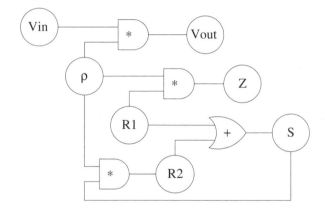

a. Make a propagator network that implements this diagram.

b. Anna has a power supply with a voltage between 14.5 and 15.5 volts, and she needs the output of the voltage divider to be between 3.5 and 4.0 volts: $V_{in} \in [14.5, 15.5]$ and $V_{out} \in [3.5, 4.0]$.

She has in stock a 47000-ohm resistor for R_2. What is the range of values from which she can select R_1? Can she choose a value for R_1 that satisfies her specification?

c. Anna also needs the output resistance of the divider to be between 20000 and 30000 ohms: $Z \in [20000, 30000]$.

So her real problem is to find appropriate ranges of values for the voltage-divider resistors R_1 and R_2 given the division ratio ρ required and the specification of Z.

If instead of choosing R_2 (remember to retract the support for this value!) she chooses to assert the Z specification, this should determine R_1 and R_2; but the network will not find the value of R_2! Why? Explain this problem.

d. If we now tell R_2 that it is somewhere in the range of 1000 ohms to 500000 ohms, the propagator network will converge to give a useful answer for the real range of R_2. Why? Explain this!

Exercise 7.3: Local consistency—a project

Propagation is a way of attacking local consistency problems. For example, the Waltz algorithm [125] is a propagation method for interpreting line drawings of solid polyhedra. Map coloring and similar problems can be successfully attacked using propagation.

The essential idea is that there is a graph with nodes that can be assigned one of a set of discrete labels, and that the nodes are interconnected by constraints that limit which labels are allowed based on the labels in neighboring nodes. For example, in the Waltz algorithm a line may have one of several labels. Each line connects two vertices. A vertex constrains the lines that terminate on it to be consistent with one of a set of possible geometric interpretations of the vertex. But the interpretation of a line must be the same at both ends of the line.

a. For these experiments you will need an "arithmetic" of discrete sets. You will need unions, intersections, and the complement of one set in another. Build such an arithmetic.

b. The set of possibilities for a node is partial information about the actual status of the node: the smaller the set of possibilities the more information we have about the node. If we represent the knowledge about the status of a node as a propagator cell, the merger of two sets is their intersection. This is consistent with the intersection of intervals for ranges of real values. Make intersection of discrete sets a handler for generic `merge`.

c. Build and demonstrate your solution to a local consistency problem using this organization.

d. Notice that in many graphs the assignment of a node depends only on a few of the constraints. Show how to use support tracking to give explanations for the assignment of a node.

7.2   The propagation mechanism

The essential propagation machinery consists of *cells*, *propagators*, and a *scheduler*. A *cell* accumulates information about a value. It must be able to say what information it has, and it must be able to accept updates to that information. It also must be able to alert propagators that are interested in its contents about changes to its contents. Each cell maintains a set of propagators that may be interested in its contents; these are called *neighbors*.

A *propagator* is a stateless (functional) procedure that is activated by changes in the value of any cell it is interested in. Cells that may activate a propagator are its *input* cells. An activated propagator gathers information from its input cells and may compute an update for one or more *output* cells. A cell may be both an input and an output for a propagator.

The *content* of a cell is the information it has accumulated about its value. When asked for its value, for example by a propagator, it responds with the *strongest* value it can provide. We have seen this in the use of intervals—a cell reports the tightest possible interval it knows about for its value. When a cell receives input it determines if the change in its contents makes a change in its strongest value. If the strongest value changes, the cell *alerts* its neighbors. This tells the scheduler to activate them. The *scheduler* is responsible for allocating computational resources to the activated propagators. It is intended that the computational result of propagation is independent of the details or order of scheduling.

Cells and propagators are elements organized in a hierarchy. Each cell or propagator has a *name*, a *parent*, and perhaps a set of *children*. These are used to construct unique path names for each cell or propagator in the hierarchy. The path name can be used to access the element and to identify it in printed output. A cell or propagator is made either by the user or by a compound propagator. The parameter *my-parent* is dynamically bound by the parent. This allows the new cell or propagator to attach itself to the family.

7.2.1   Cells

A cell is implemented as a message-accepting procedure, using the bundle macro. The cell maintains its information in the content variable, which is initialized to a value the-nothing (identified by the predicate nothing?) that represents the absence of any information about the value. The value that the cell reports, when asked, is the strongest value that it has at the moment. The cell also maintains a list of its neighbors, the propagators that need to be alerted when the strongest value of the cell changes. An auxiliary data structure relations is used to hold the cell's family relations.

Here is an outline of the constructor for cells. The interesting
parts are add-content! and test-content!, explained below.

```
(define (make-cell name)
  (let ((relations (make-relations name (*my-parent*)))
        (neighbors '())
        (content the-nothing)
        (strongest the-nothing))
    (define (get-relations) relations)
    (define (get-neighbors) neighbors)
    (define (get-content) content)
    (define (get-strongest) strongest)
    (define (add-neighbor! neighbor)
      (set! neighbors (lset-adjoin eq? neighbors neighbor)))
    (define (add-content! increment)
      (set! content (cell-merge content increment))
      (test-content!))
    (define (test-content!)
      See definition on page 345.)
    (define me
      (bundle cell? get-relations get-neighbors
              get-content get-strongest add-neighbor!
              add-content! test-content!))
    (add-child! me (*my-parent*))
    (set! *all-cells* (cons me *all-cells*))
    me))
```

A cell receives new information through a call to add-content!.
The new information, increment, must be merged with the existing information in content. In general, the merging process is
specific to the kind of information being merged, so the merging
mechanism for the cell must be specified. However, the-nothing,
which represents the absence of information, is special. Any information merged with the-nothing is returned unchanged.

The reason for merging rather than replacement is to use partial
information to refine our knowledge of the value.[9] For example, in
the computation of stellar distances described above, intervals are
merged to produce better estimates by intersection. In the type-
inference example (see section 4.4.2) we combined descriptions by

---

[9]This is an essential insight in Alexey Radul's PhD thesis [99, 100].

unification to get more specific information. We will examine the general problem of merging values in section 7.4.

In some cases it may not be possible to merge two pieces of information. For example, the value of an unknown number cannot be both zero and one. In this case `cell-merge` returns a *contradiction object*, which may carry information about the details of the conflict. If there is no extra information to be had, the contradiction object is the symbol `the-contradiction`, which satisfies the primitive predicate `contradiction?`. More complex contradictions are detected by the generic predicate procedure `general-contradiction?`. Contradictions are resolved, if possible, by `handle-cell-contradiction`, as explained in section 7.5.

If the cell's strongest value changes, the neighbors are alerted. But if an increment does not affect the strongest value, it provides no additional information; in that case it is important to avoid alerting the neighbors, to prevent useless loops. All this is implemented by the `test-content!` procedure, which is defined as an internal procedure in `make-cell`.

```
(define (test-content!)
  (let ((strongest* (strongest-value content)))
    (cond ((equivalent? strongest strongest*)
           (set! strongest strongest*)
           'content-unchanged)
          ((general-contradiction? strongest*)
           (set! strongest strongest*)
           (handle-cell-contradiction me)
           'contradiction)
          (else
           (set! strongest strongest*)
           (alert-propagators! neighbors)
           'content-changed))))
```

The procedure `test-content!` is also used to alert all cells when a premise changes its belief status. Each alerted cell checks if its `strongest` value has changed, requiring some action, like signaling a contradiction or alerting its propagator neighbors. See section 7.3.

To hide the implementation details of a cell we provide convenient access procedures:

```
(define (add-cell-neighbor! cell neighbor)
  (cell 'add-neighbor! neighbor))

(define (add-cell-content! cell increment)
  (parameterize ((current-reason-source cell))
    (cell 'add-content! increment)))

(define (cell-strongest cell)
  (cell 'get-strongest))
```

The `current-reason-source` parameter in `add-cell-content!` is part of the layer that gives a reason for every value, as described in footnote 3 on page 333. This useful feature will not be further elaborated here.

7.2.2 Propagators

To make a propagator we supply a list of input cells, a list of output cells, and a procedure `activate!` to execute when alerted. The constructor introduces the propagator to its input cells with `add-cell-neighbor!`. It also alerts the new propagator so that it will be run if needed.

```
(define (propagator inputs outputs activate! name)
  (let ((relations (make-relations name (*my-parent*))))
    (define (get-inputs) inputs)
    (define (get-outputs) outputs)
    (define (get-relations) relations)

    (define me
      (bundle propagator? activate!
              get-inputs get-outputs get-relations))
    (add-child! me (*my-parent*))
    (for-each (lambda (cell)
                (add-cell-neighbor! cell me))
              inputs)
    (alert-propagator! me)
    me))
```

Primitive propagators are directional in that their outputs do not overlap with their inputs. We make primitive propagators from Scheme procedures that produce a single output. By convention, we build a primitive propagator by passing the input cells and the output cell together, with the output last. We could make a primitive propagator that produced several outputs, such as integer divide with remainder, but we do not need this here.

```
(define (primitive-propagator f name)
  (lambda cells
    (let ((output (car (last-pair cells)))
          (inputs (except-last-pair cells)))
      (propagator inputs (list output)
        (lambda ()
          (let ((input-values (map cell-strongest inputs)))
            (if (any unusable-value? input-values)
                'do-nothing
                (add-cell-content! output
                  (apply f input-values)))))
        name))))
```

When activated, a propagator may choose to compute a result using f. The result of calling f on the input values is added to the output cell. We call this choice process the *activation policy*. Here we require all inputs to be *usable* values. By default, contradiction objects and the-nothing are unusable, though we may add others later. Other policies are possible.

Propagators may be constructed by combining other propagators. We make compound propagators by supplying a procedure to-build that builds the desired network from parts. A compound propagator is not built until it is needed to make a computation. But that need arises only when data arrives at one or more of its input cells to activate it. However, we do not want to rebuild the compound propagator network every time it gets new values in its input cells, so the constructor must make sure that it is built only once. This is arranged with a boolean flag built? that is set when the build is done.

```
(define (compound-propagator inputs outputs to-build name)
  (let ((built? #f))
    (define (maybe-build)
      (if (or built?
              (and (not (null? inputs))
                   (every unusable-value?
                          (map cell-strongest inputs))))
          'do-nothing
          (begin (parameterize ((*my-parent* me))
                   (to-build))
                 (set! built? #t)
                 'built)))
    (define me
      (propagator inputs outputs maybe-build name))
    me))
```

The activation policy for a compound propagator is different from
the activation policy for a primitive propagator. Here we build
the network if any input has a usable value. This is appropriate
because some part of the network may do some useful computation
even if not all of the inputs are available.

The `parameterize` machinery is in support of the hierarchical
organization of the propagator elements. It makes the compound
propagator the parent of any cells or propagators that are constructed in the building of the network.

As described in figure 7.4 on page 332, constraint propagators
are constructed by combining directional propagators. For example, we can make the propagator that enforces the constraint that
the product of the values in two cells is the value in the third as
follows:

```
(define-c:prop (c:* x y product)
  (p:* x y product)
  (p:/ product x y)
  (p:/ product y x))
```

Here we see that three directional propagators are combined to
make the constraint. This can work because we merge values
rather than replacing them, and equivalent values do not propagate. If equivalent values propagated, anything like the `c:*` propagator would be an infinite loop.[10]

The macro `define-c:prop` is just syntactic sugar. The actual
code produced by the macro is:

```
(define (c:* x y product)
  (constraint-propagator
   (list x y product)
   (lambda ()
     (p:* x y product)
     (p:/ product x y)
     (p:/ product y x))
   'c:*))
```

where `constraint-propagator` is just:

---

[10]We are glossing over the serious problem of determining the equivalence of
inexact quantities. No global notion of equivalence can represent the criteria
for equivalence without additional local information. To address this problem
we could provide a local equivalence predicate for each cell, with a default
value for exact quantities.

```
(define (constraint-propagator cells to-build name)
  (compound-propagator cells cells to-build name))
```

All the cells associated with a constraint propagator are both input and output cells.

7.3   Multiple alternative world views

In our stellar distances example we showed that each value carried the support set of premises used in its computation, and also the "reason" for the value (the propagator that made it and the values that it was made from). This was done using the layered-data mechanism we introduced in section 6.4. But some "facts" are mutually inconsistent. In our example we modulated the belief in the premises to obtain locally consistent world views, depending on which premises we chose to believe.

A premise is either `in` (believed) or `out` (not believed). The user in our example could `assert!` a premise to bring it `in` or `retract!` it to kick it `out`. The "magic" in the system is that the observable values in cells are always those that are *fully supported*—those for which the supporting premises are all `in`—even as the beliefs in the premises are changed.[11]

It is silly to recompute all of the values as the belief status of the support changes. We can do better by remembering values that are not currently fully supported. This allows us to reassert a premise, and recover the values that it supports without re-computing those values. When the state of belief in a premise changes, cells must check if their strongest value has changed. This is accomplished by calling the `test-content!` for every cell; each cell whose strongest value changes alerts the propagators that depend on that cell's value. Each of those propagators then gets the strongest values of the contents of its input cells and computes (or recomputes!) its output value. If that output value is equivalent to the strongest value already stored in the output cell, there will be no further action. If the belief status of the strongest

---

[11] There is a very bad idea in our implementaton. A change of the belief status of a premise is implemented as a global operation—this is never a good idea in a simulation of a parallel process! A better implementation would propagate the change of belief by local processes, similar to the way the values that they support are propagated. But we didn't do this—sorry!

value in the output cell changes, this will cause its neighboring propagators to recompute. But the strongest value in the output cell may have independent support, in which case the propagation will stop there.

To make this work, in each cell the content may hold a set of values (the *value set*) paired with the premises they depend upon. The cell extracts the strongest-value from the content and keeps it in the local variable strongest, which can be accessed using cell-strongest. The strongest value is the best choice of the fully supported values in the set,[12] or the-nothing if none of the values in the set are fully supported.

It remains to elucidate strongest-value, which must be able to operate on raw data, on layered data, and on value sets. Thus it is appropriate to make it a generic procedure. The strongest value of an unannotated data item is just that data item, so this provides the default.

```
(define strongest-value
  (simple-generic-procedure 'strongest-value 1
                            (lambda (object) object)))
```

If a layered data item is fully supported, then its strongest value is itself, otherwise its strongest value is no information.

```
(define-generic-procedure-handler strongest-value
  (match-args layered-datum?)
  (lambda (elt)
    (if (all-premises-in? (support-layer-value elt))
        elt
        the-nothing)))
```

The strongest value of a value set is the strongest consequence of the set:

```
(define-generic-procedure-handler strongest-value
  (match-args value-set?)
  (lambda (set) (strongest-consequence set)))
```

The procedure strongest-consequence just merges together the elements of a value set that are fully supported. It uses

---

[12]What is the best choice is actually a rather complex judgment. If one supported value is more specific than another, for example a narrower interval, this is a better choice. Also, if a value has fewer premises in its support set than an "equivalent" value, it is better because it requires fewer premises to be believed. This is implemented by the mechanism of merging value sets, which we will describe in section 7.4.3.

merge-layered to determine the "best choice" of the fully supported values in the value set (see section 7.4.2). If there are no
fully supported values there is no information, so the result is
the-nothing.

```
(define (strongest-consequence set)
  (fold (lambda (increment content)
          (merge-layered content increment))
        the-nothing
        (filter (lambda (elt)
                  (all-premises-in?
                    (support-layer-value elt)))
                (value-set-elements set))))
```

7.4 Merging values

We have not addressed what it means to merge values. This is a
complicated process, with three parts: merging base values, such
as numbers and intervals; merging supported values; and merging
value sets. The procedure cell-merge in add-content! must be
assigned to an appropriate merger for the data being propagated.
On page 366, setup-propagator-system initializes cell-merge to
merge-value-sets.

7.4.1 Merging base values

There are only a few base value types in our example propagator
system: the-nothing, the-contradiction, numbers, booleans,
and intervals. Numbers and booleans are simple in that only
equivalent values can be merged. If they cannot be merged it
is a contradiction. Anything merged with the-nothing is itself.
Anything merged with the-contradiction is the-contradiction.
The merge procedure is generic for base values, and the default
handler deals with all the simple cases—all except intervals.

```
(define merge
  (simple-generic-procedure 'merge 2
    (lambda (content increment)
      (cond ((nothing? content) increment)
            ((nothing? increment) content)
            ((contradiction? content) content)
            ((contradiction? increment) increment)
            ((equivalent? content increment) content)
            (else the-contradiction)))))
```

In the astronomy example we also have interval arithmetic, so we need to be able to merge intervals:

```
(define (merge-intervals content increment)
  (let ((new-range (intersect-intervals content increment)))
    (cond ((interval=? new-range content) content)
          ((interval=? new-range increment) increment)
          ((empty-interval? new-range) the-contradiction)
          (else new-range))))
```

We can merge a number with an interval. We get the number if it is contained in the interval, otherwise it is a contradiction:

```
(define (merge-interval-real int x)
  (if (within-interval? x int)
      x
      the-contradiction))
```

This all gets glued together as a generic procedure handler:

```
(define-generic-procedure-handler merge
  (any-arg 2 interval? real?)
  (lambda (x y)
    (cond ((not (interval? x)) (merge-interval-real y x))
          ((not (interval? y)) (merge-interval-real x y))
          (else (merge-intervals x y)))))
```

There are no other cases of base value merges.

7.4.2 Merging supported values

A supported value is implemented as a layered data item that has a support layer and the base value being propagated. So the merger for supported values must be a layered procedure:

```
(define merge-layered
  (make-layered-procedure 'merge 2 merge))
```

The support layer implements merge with support:merge, which is given three arguments: the merged value computed by the base layer, the current content, and the new increment. The job of support:merge is to deliver the support set appropriate for the merged value. If the merged value is the same as the value from the content or the value from the increment, we can use that argument's support. But if the merged value is different, we need to combine the supports.

```
(define (support:merge merged-value content increment)
  (cond ((equivalent? merged-value
                      (base-layer-value content))
         (support-layer-value content))
        ((equivalent? merged-value
                      (base-layer-value increment))
         (support-layer-value increment))
        (else
         (support-set-union
           (support-layer-value content)
           (support-layer-value increment))))))

(define-layered-procedure-handler merge-layered support-layer
  support:merge)
```

Here `define-layered-procedure-handler` is used to attach the
procedure `support:merge` to the layered procedure `merge-layered`
as its `support-layer` handler.

7.4.3   Merging value sets

To merge value sets, we just add the elements of the increment to
the content to make a new set. Note that `->value-set` coerces its
argument to a value set.

```
(define (merge-value-sets content increment)
  (if (nothing? increment)
      (->value-set content)
      (value-set-adjoin (->value-set content) increment)))
```

When adjoining a new element to the content, we do not add the
element if it is subsumed by any existing content element.

```
(define (value-set-adjoin set elt)
  (if (any (lambda (old-elt)
             (element-subsumes? old-elt elt))
           (value-set-elements set))
      set
      (make-value-set
        (lset-adjoin equivalent?
                     (value-set-elements set)
                     elt))))
```

The criteria for subsumption are a bit complicated. One element
subsumes another if its base value is at least as informative as
the other's base value and if its support is a subset of the other's.

(Note: A smaller support set is a stronger support set, because it depends on fewer premises.)

```
(define (element-subsumes? elt1 elt2)
  (and (value-implies? (base-layer-value elt1)
                       (base-layer-value elt2))
       (support-set<= (support-layer-value elt1)
                      (support-layer-value elt2))))
```

The procedure `value-implies?` is a generic procedure, because it must be able to work with many kinds of base data, including intervals.

Exercise 7.4: Merging with unification

We have seen how intervals that partially specify a numerical value can be merged to get more specific information about that value. Another kind of partial information is symbolic patterns, with holes for missing information. This kind of information can be merged using unification, as described in section 4.4. We used unification to implement a simple version of type inference, but it can be used more generally for combining partially specified symbolic expressions. The example of combining records about Ben Franklin in section 4.4 may be suggestive. One way to think about organizing a propagator system is that each cell is a small database restricted to information about some particular thing. The propagators interconnecting cells are ways that deductions can be made. For example, one promising domain is the classification of topological spaces in point-set topology. Another is the organization of your living group—for example, the adjacency relationships of rooms and the social relationships of the inhabitants. Pick a domain that you find interesting. Use your imagination!

a. Design a propagator network where each cell will hold some particular kind of symbolic information. For example, a cell may represent what is known about a student at MIT. The information may be name, address, telephone number, class year, major, birthday, best friends... This requires designing an extensible data structure that can hold this information and more. You will also need propagators that relate the people. So you may get information from one person, or from multiple people, about another. This may be a nice model of gossip. Make some primitive propagators that manipulate these symbolic quantities and wire up an interesting network.

b. Add unification as a generic procedure handler for **merge**, and show how it can be used to combine partial symbolic information coming in from multiple sources.

c. Discover some interesting compound symbolic propagators that can be used to represent the common combinations of connections of related subjects in your network.

7.5 Searching possible worlds

It would be nice if search were unnecessary. Unfortunately, for many kinds of real problems it is helpful to "assume for the sake of argument" something that may not be true. We then work out the consequences of that assumption. If the assumption leads to a contradiction, we retract it and try something else. But in any case, the assumption may enable other deductions that help solve the problem.

We started to explore this idea in section 5.4, where we introduced `amb` and used it in search problems. In those adventures with `amb` we were working in an expression-oriented language with an order of execution that was constrained by the way expressions are evaluated. We partly extracted ourselves from that constraint with the painful use of continuations, either structuring the evaluator to explicitly pass around continuation procedures (in section 5.4.2), or using Scheme's implicit continuations via `call/cc` (in section 5.5.3). But even with `call/cc` we do not have sufficient control of the search process.

In section 6.4 we showed how to associate each value with a support set, the set of premises that the value depends on. If each assumption is labeled with a new premise, we can know exactly the combination of assumptions that led to a contradiction. If we are clever, we can avoid asserting that combination of assumptions later in the search. But in the evaluation of expressions it is hard to isolate the assertion of assumptions from the flow of control.

The problem is that in an expression language, the choice decisions are made as expressions are evaluated, producing a branching decision tree. The decision tree is evaluated in some order, for example, depth first or breadth first. The consequences of any sequence of decisions are evaluated after the decisions are made. If a failure is encountered (a contradiction is noted), only the decisions on the evolved branch are possible culprits. But if only some of the decisions on the branch are at fault, there may be some innocent ones that were made later than the last culprit. Computations that depend only on the innocent decisions are lost in backing up to the last culprit. So retracting a branch to an earlier decision may require losing lots of useful deductions.

By contrast, in real problems the consequences of decisions are usually local and limited. For example, when solving a crossword puzzle we often get stuck—we are unable to fill in any blanks that we are sure of. But we can make progress by assuming that some box contains a particular letter, without very good evidence for that assumption. Positing that the box contains that letter allows deductions to follow, but eventually it may be found that the assumption was incorrect and must be retracted. However, many of the deductions made since the assumption are correct, because they did not depend on that assumption. We do not retract those correct deductions just to eliminate the consequences of the wrong assumption. We want the actual consequences of wrong assumptions to be retracted, leaving consequences of other assumptions believed. This is rather hard to arrange in an expression-oriented language system.

With propagators we have escaped the control structure based on evaluation of expressions, at the cost of thinking of the propagators as independent machines running in parallel. Because a propagator cell may contain a value set whose elements are layered values, we can associate a support set with each value. In the propagator system a value is believed only when all of the premises in its support set are believed; and only believed values are propagated. In this way we have the ability to switch world views by modulating the belief status of each premise independently.

Some combinations of premises are contradictory. A contradiction is discovered when the system tries to merge two incompatible fully supported values, thus deriving a contradiction object. The contradiction object has a support set with those premises that imply the contradiction.

To make this work we introduce an **amb**-like choice propagator, which makes assumptions about the value of a cell that it controls. Each assumption is supported by a *hypothetical premise* created by the choice propagator that it may assert or retract. The propagator network computes the consequences of alternative assignments of the values of the assumptions made by the choice propagators in the network until a consistent assignment is found.

An example: Pythagorean triples

Consider the problem of finding the Pythagorean triples for natural numbers up to ten. (We considered a similar problem on page 272. Here we are setting up an even dumber algorithm!). We can formulate this as a propagator problem:

```
(define (pythagorean)
  (let ((possibilities '(1 2 3 4 5 6 7 8 9 10)))
    (let-cells (x y z x2 y2 z2)
      (p:amb x possibilities)
      (p:amb y possibilities)
      (p:amb z possibilities)
      (p:* x x x2)
      (p:* y y y2)
      (p:* z z z2)
      (p:+ x2 y2 z2)
      (list x y z))))
```

This code constructs a propagator network with three multiplier propagators and an adder propagator that will be satisfied if the values in cells x, y, and z are a Pythagorean triple. Each of these cells is connected to a choice propagator, created by p:amb, that will choose an element from **possibilities**.

To run this we must first initialize the propagator system:

```
(initialize-scheduler)
```

We can now build the propagator network and extract all of the triples from it. The procedure **pythagorean** constructs the propagator network and returns a list of the three cells of interest. The procedure **run** turns on the scheduler, thus running the network. While running, the choice propagators propose values of x, y, and z until either an unresolvable contradiction is found or the network becomes quiescent. If no contradiction is found, **run** returns **done**, and the base values of the strongest values of each of the interesting cells are printed. Then that combination of values is rejected, and the loop is continued with a new call to **run**.

```
(let ((answers (pythagorean)))
  (let try-again ((result (run)))
    (if (eq? result 'done)
        (begin
          (pp (map (lambda (cell)
                     (get-base-value
                      (cell-strongest cell)))
                   answers))
          (force-failure! answers)
          (try-again (run)))
        result)))
(3 4 5)
(4 3 5)
(6 8 10)
(8 6 10)
(contradiction #[cell x])
```

7.5.1   Dependency-directed backtracking

Dependency-directed backtracking is a powerful technique that
optimizes a backtracking search by avoiding asserting a set of
premises that support any previously discovered contradiction.[13]
The dependency-directed backtracking strategy we use is based
on the concept of a *nogood set*—a set of premises that cannot all
be believed at the same time, because their conjunction has been
found to support a contradiction. When a cell contains two or
more contradictory values, the union of the support sets of those
values is a nogood set.

When a contradiction is detected, the nogood set for that contradiction is saved to let the backtracker know not to try that

---

[13]Dependency-directed backtracking was first introduced by Richard Stallman
and Gerald Jay Sussman in the context of electrical circuit analysis [114]. A
very similar technique, "clausal learning," was developed in the context of logic
by Karl Lieberherr [84]. Clausal learning is now used in the best SAT solvers.
Ramin Zabih, David McAllester, and David Chapman showed one way to build
this technique into Lisp code [132]. Guy Steele showed an elegant way to incorporate dependency-directed backtracking into a constraint language [116].
Building on the work of Jon Doyle [30] and David McAllester [88], Ken Forbus and Johan deKleer elaborated the theory and practice of dependencies and
"truth-maintenance systems" [36], a general way to think about dependencies
and backtracking. The way we implement dependency-directed backtracking
in this book was developed by Alexey Radul and Gerald Jay Sussman [99, 100].

combination again. To make it easy for the backtracking mechanism, the nogood set is not stored directly: it is distributed to each premise in the nogood set. Each premise gets a copy of the set with itself removed. For example, if the nogood set is {A B C ...}, then the premise A gets the set {B C ...}, the premise B gets the set {A C ...}, and so on. For any given premise, the list of all the partial nogood sets that have been accumulated from contradictions that the premise has participated in can be obtained with the `premise-nogoods` accessor.

Once the nogood set is saved, the backtracker chooses a hypothetical premise from the nogood set (if any) and retracts it. The retraction activates the propagators that are neighbors of cells with values previously supported by that hypothetical, including the propagator that originally asserted that hypothetical, causing that propagator to assert a different hypothetical, if possible. If there are no hypothetical premises in the nogood set, the backtracker has no options, so it returns a failure.

Of course there is a lot of bookkeeping that needs to be done to make this work. Let's understand how that can be implemented.

Hypotheticals are made and controlled by `binary-amb`

The simplest choice propagator is constructed by `binary-amb`. The result of calling `binary-amb` on a cell is a binary-amb propagator with the cell as both an input and an output. A binary-amb propagator modulates the value of the cell to be either true or false, until a consistent assignment is found.

The procedure `binary-amb` introduces two new premises, which are marked as hypothetical premises. A *hypothetical premise* is one whose belief is allowed to be automatically varied as needed. The `binary-amb` procedure initializes the cell with a contradiction: the procedure `make-hypotheticals` creates both a true value and a false value, each supported by a new hypothetical premise, and adds both values to the content of the cell. Adding these values activates the cell, calling its `test-content!` procedure, which starts the contradiction-handling mechanism, which ultimately alerts the binary-amb propagator of the unhappy cell. The contradiction will then be fixed by the binary-amb propagator's `activate!` procedure `amb-choose`:

```
(define (binary-amb cell)
  (let ((premises (make-hypotheticals cell '(#t #f))))
    (let ((true-premise (car premises))
          (false-premise (cadr premises)))
      (define (amb-choose)
        (let ((reasons-against-true
                (filter all-premises-in?
                        (premise-nogoods true-premise)))
               (reasons-against-false
                (filter all-premises-in?
                        (premise-nogoods false-premise))))
          (cond ((null? reasons-against-true)
                 (mark-premise-in! true-premise)
                 (mark-premise-out! false-premise))
                ((null? reasons-against-false)
                 (mark-premise-out! true-premise)
                 (mark-premise-in! false-premise))
                (else
                 (mark-premise-out! true-premise)
                 (mark-premise-out! false-premise)
                 (process-contradictions
                   (pairwise-union reasons-against-true
                                   reasons-against-false)
                   cell)))))
      (let ((me (propagator (list cell) (list cell)
                            amb-choose 'binary-amb)))
        (set! all-amb-propagators
              (cons me all-amb-propagators))
        me))))
```

The amb-choose procedure uses the premise nogoods to determine whether the premise supporting the true value or the premise supporting the false value may be believed. Each element of the premise-nogoods of a premise is a set of premises such that if they are all believed, the premise cannot be believed. So if amb-choose finds any fully supported premise nogood for a premise, that premise cannot be believed.

If the premise supporting the true value or the premise supporting the false value is believable, amb-choose asserts true or false respectively. If neither is believable, it defers to higher-level contradiction processing (process-contradictions) in the hope that after the beliefs in other premises are modulated, it may be possible to assert true or false when this propagator is reactivated.

The argument given to process-contradictions, constructed by pairwise-union, is a set of nogoods. Each of these nogoods is the union of a set of premises that rule out the choice of true and a set of premises that rule out a choice of false. Thus, any one of these nogoods would prevent the choice of either alternative.[14]

```
(define (pairwise-union nogoods1 nogoods2)
  (append-map (lambda (nogood1)
                (map (lambda (nogood2)
                       (support-set-union nogood1 nogood2))
                     nogoods2))
              nogoods1))
```

Learning from contradictions

The procedure `process-contradictions` saves all of the nogoods it received, distributing the information in the nogoods to the premise nogoods of the premises. It then chooses a nogood to disbelieve by retracting one of its hypothetical premises, if there are any.

```
(define (process-contradictions nogoods complaining-cell)
  (update-failure-count!)
  (for-each save-nogood! nogoods)
  (let-values (((to-disbelieve nogood)
                (choose-premise-to-disbelieve nogoods)))
    (maybe-kick-out to-disbelieve nogood complaining-cell)))
```

The procedure `save-nogood!` augments the `premise-nogoods` of each premise in the given `nogood` set with the set of other premises it is incompatible with. This is how the system learns from its past failures. The premise being updated is not included in its own premise nogood sets, because a premise may not be incompatible with itself.

```
(define (save-nogood! nogood)
  (for-each (lambda (premise)
              (set-premise-nogoods! premise
                (adjoin-support-with-subsumption
                  (support-set-remove nogood premise)
                  (premise-nogoods premise))))
            (support-set-elements nogood)))
```

---

[14]This use of the procedure `pairwise-union` implements the *cut* rule of logic, which is a generalization of *modus ponens*. In propositional logic the cut rule is written $(A \lor B) \land (\neg B \lor C) \vdash (A \lor C)$. This rule, combined with unification (section 4.4), is the basis of the famous resolution theorem proving algorithm invented by Robinson [104].

The new premise nogood may either subsume or be subsumed by one of the existing premise nogoods; minimal premise nogoods are most useful.

Resolving the contradiction

A contradiction is resolved by retracting one of the premises in the nogood set that supports the contradiction. The only premises that can be retracted are the hypotheticals, which are asserted "for the sake of argument." If there is more than one nogood set supporting a contradiction, we choose one with the smallest number of hypotheticals, because disbelieving a small nogood set rules out more possiblities than disbelieving a nogood set with a larger number of hypotheticals.

```
(define (choose-premise-to-disbelieve nogoods)
  (choose-first-hypothetical
   (car (sort-by nogoods
          (lambda (nogood)
            (count hypothetical?
                   (support-set-elements nogood)))))))
```

However, the choice of which hypothetical from the selected nogood set to reject is not apparent. Here we arbitrarily choose the first hypothetical premise available in the nogood set.

```
(define (choose-first-hypothetical nogood)
  (let ((hyps (support-set-filter hypothetical? nogood)))
    (values (and (not (support-set-empty? hyps))
                 (car (support-set-elements hyps)))
            nogood)))
```

The procedure `maybe-kick-out` finishes the job of resolving the contradiction. If the chooser was able to find a suitable hypothesis to disbelieve, then that hypothesis is retracted and propagation continues normally. Otherwise, the propagation process is stopped and the user is informed about the contradiction.

```
(define (maybe-kick-out to-disbelieve nogood cell)
  (if to-disbelieve
      (mark-premise-out! to-disbelieve)
      (abort-process (list 'contradiction cell))))
```

Contradictions discovered in a cell

If in the process of adding content to a cell a contradiction is discovered, the unhappy cell calls `handle-cell-contradiction` with itself as the argument. At that moment the strongest value in the cell is the contradiction object, and the support of the contradiction object is the irritating nogood set. This can be handed off to `process-contradictions` to deal with.

```
(define (handle-cell-contradiction cell)
  (let ((nogood (support-layer-value (cell-strongest cell))))
    (process-contradictions (list nogood) cell)))
```

This is all that needs to be done to support dependency-directed backtracking.

Non-binary `amb`

Although `binary-amb` can be used in the formulation of many problems, most choices are not binary. It is possible to construct an *n*-ary choice mechanism from `binary-amb` by building a circuit of conditional propagators controlled by cells whose true or false values are modulated by binary-amb propagators, but this is very inefficient and introduces lots of extra machinery. So we provide a native *n*-ary choice mechanism with `p:amb`. The procedure `p:amb` is analogous to `binary-amb`. For `binary-amb` there are exactly two choices, `#t` or `#f`, for the value in the cell, and each is supported by a hypothetical premise. When `p:amb` is applied to a cell and a list of possible values, the procedure `make-hypotheticals` adds those values to the cell, each supported by a new hypothetical premise.

When the propagator constructed by `p:amb` is activated, the procedure `amb-choose` is called. It first tries to find a hypothetical premise, among its hypotheticals, that is not ruled out by its `premise-nogoods`. If there is one, it marks that premise in and marks all of the other premises out, thus choosing the value associated with that premise as the value of the cell. If none of the hypothetical premises can be believed, it marks all of its premises out and makes a new set of nogoods to pass to `process-contradictions`, which will retract a hypothetical premise from one of those nogoods, if possible. The generalization of the procedure `pairwise-union` to take more than two sets is `cross-product-union`. As before, this is a resolution step.

```
(define (p:amb cell values)
  (let ((premises (make-hypotheticals cell values)))
    (define (amb-choose)
      (let ((to-choose
              (find (lambda (premise)
                      (not (any all-premises-in?
                                (premise-nogoods premise))))
                    premises)))
        (if to-choose
            (for-each (lambda (premise)
                        (if (eq? premise to-choose)
                            (mark-premise-in! premise)
                            (mark-premise-out! premise)))
                      premises)
            (let ((nogoods
                    (cross-product-union
                      (map (lambda (premise)
                             (filter all-premises-in?
                               (premise-nogoods premise)))
                           premises))))
              (for-each mark-premise-out! premises)
              (process-contradictions nogoods cell)))))
    (let ((me (propagator (list cell) (list cell)
                          amb-choose 'amb)))
      (set! all-amb-propagators
            (cons me all-amb-propagators))
      me)))
```

Choice propagators built with p:amb introduce only as many hypothetical premises as there are choices. Constructions for $n > 2$ choices based on binary-amb introduce about twice that many premises.

7.5.2 Solving combinatorial puzzles

To demonstrate the use of dependency-directed backtracking to solve combinatorial puzzles efficiently, consider the famous "multiple dwelling" puzzle:[29]

> Baker, Cooper, Fletcher, Miller, and Smith live on different floors of an apartment house that has only five floors. Baker does not live on the top floor. Cooper does not live on the bottom floor. Fletcher does not live on either the top or the

bottom floor. Miller lives on a higher floor than does Cooper. Smith does not live on a floor adjacent to Fletcher's. Fletcher does not live on a floor adjacent to Cooper's. Where does everyone live?

We can set this up as a propagator problem. Here is a very unsophisticated formulation of the problem:

```
(define (multiple-dwelling)
  (let-cells (baker cooper fletcher miller smith)
    (let ((floors '(1 2 3 4 5)))
      (p:amb baker floors)    (p:amb cooper floors)
      (p:amb fletcher floors) (p:amb miller floors)
      (p:amb smith floors)
      (require-distinct
       (list baker cooper fletcher miller smith))
      (let-cells ((b=5 #f)    (c=1 #f)    (f=5 #f)
                  (f=1 #f)    (m>c #t)    (sf #f)
                  (fc  #f)    (one 1)     (five 5)
                  s-f   as-f   f-c    af-c)
        (p:= five baker b=5)       ;Baker is not on 5.
        (p:= one cooper c=1)       ;Cooper is not on 1.
        (p:= five fletcher f=5)    ;Fletcher is not on 5.
        (p:= one fletcher f=1)     ;Fletcher is not on 1.
        (p:> miller cooper m>c)    ;Miller is above Cooper.
        (c:+ fletcher s-f smith)   ;Fletcher and Smith
        (c:abs s-f as-f)           ; are not on
        (p:= one as-f sf)          ; adjacent floors.
        (c:+ cooper f-c fletcher)  ;Cooper and Fletcher
        (c:abs f-c af-c)           ; are not on
        (p:= one af-c fc)          ; adjacent floors.
        (list baker cooper fletcher miller smith)))))) 
```

This says that Baker, Cooper, Fletcher, Miller, and Smith all choose to live on one of the five floors, and their choices must be distinct. We then see the constraints on their choices represented as a propagator circuit. Some cells, such as b=5, are initialized to a boolean value. Thus, the line (p:= five baker b=5) represents the constraint that Baker does not live on the fifth floor. The constraint that Cooper and Fletcher do not live on adjacent floors is implemented by the assignment of fc to #f and the last three constraints.

To use the propagator system we need to define all the primitive
propagators, with the appropriate layering of the data:

```
(define (setup-propagator-system arithmetic)
  (define layered-arith
    (extend-arithmetic layered-extender arithmetic))
  (install-arithmetic! layered-arith)
  (install-core-propagators! merge-value-sets
                             layered-arith
                             layered-propagator-projector))
```

This rather complicated setup procedure gives the information
required to build and install the propagators with an arithmetic,
layered with premises that can be tracked and reasons that are
available for debugging. The default setup, when the propagator
system is loaded, is for numerical data:

```
(setup-propagator-system numeric-arithmetic)
```

We are now in a position to run our puzzle example:

```
(initialize-scheduler)

(define answers (multiple-dwelling))
(run)
(map (lambda (cell)
       (get-base-value (cell-strongest cell)))
     answers)
;Value: (3 2 4 5 1)

*number-of-calls-to-fail*
;Value: 106
```

We see the (correct) result: the floor on which each protagonist
lives. We also see that it takes roughly 100 failed assignments to
find a correct assignment.[15] It turns out that this assignment is
unique: there are no other assignments consistent with the constraints given.

Notice that the total number of unconstrained assignments is
$5^5 = 3125$, but we are solving this with only about 100 trials. We

---

[15]The precise number of failed choices of assignments is very dependent on the
details of the computation. In this problem the number of failed choices can be
anywhere from about 60 to about 200, depending on the order of propagator
activations. But for this formulation of this problem the average number of
failures is about 110.

are able to do this because the system learns from its mistakes: For each failure it accumulates information about which sets of premises cannot be simultaneously believed. Correctly using this information prevents the investigation of paths that are hopeless given the results of previous experiments.

Exercise 7.5: Yacht name puzzle

Formulate and solve the following puzzle using propagators.[16]

Mary Ann Moore's father has a yacht and so has each of his four friends: Colonel Downing, Mr. Hall, Sir Barnacle Hood, and Dr. Parker. Each of the five also has one daughter and each has named his yacht after a daughter of one of the others. Sir Barnacle's yacht is the Gabrielle, Mr. Moore owns the Lorna; Mr. Hall the Rosalind. The Melissa, owned by Colonel Downing, is named after Sir Barnacle's daughter. Gabrielle's father owns the yacht that is named after Dr. Parker's daughter. Who is Lorna's father?

Exercise 7.6: Multiple-dwelling puzzle

It is easy to formulate the multiple-dwelling problem for the amb evaluator of chapter 5.4. In fact it is easier than for the propagator system, because we can think and write in terms of expressions. Indeed, you will be able to write constraints like the fact that Fletcher and Cooper do not live on adjacent floors as something like:

```
(require (not (= (abs (- fletcher cooper)) 1)))
```

rather than

```
(c:+ cooper f-c fletcher)
(c:abs f-c af-c)
(p:= one af-c fc)
```

where cells like f-c, af-c, and fc must be declared and one and fc are initialized. This is because the propagation system is a general wiring-diagram system rather than an expression system.

a. Formulate and solve the multiple-dwelling problem using the amb evaluator of section 5.4. Instrument the system to determine the number of failures. How many failures does it take?

b. Write a small compiler that converts constraints written as expressions into propagator diagram fragments. You will find that this is very easy. We made a first stab at this in exercise 7.1 on page 340. But here we really want to make a translator for code from section 5.4 to a

---

[16]This puzzle is taken from a booklet called *Problematical Recreations*, published in the 1960s by *Litton Industries*, where it is attributed to the *Kansas State Engineer*.

propagator target. Demonstrate that your compilation gets the correct answer.

c. How many failures are needed to solve the problem with the propagator diagram that you compiled into? If it takes more than about 200 failures you compiled into very bad code!

Exercise 7.7: Card game puzzle revisited

Redo exercise 5.17 using propagators.

Exercise 7.8: Type inference

In section 4.4.2 we built a type-inference engine as an example of the application of unification matching. In this exercise (which is really a substantial project) we implement type inference taking advantage of propagation.

a. Given a Scheme program, construct a propagation network with a cell for every locus that is useful to type. Each such cell will be the repository of the type information that will be accumulated about the type information at that locus in the program. Construct propagators that connect the cells and impose the type constraints implied by the program structure. Use unification match as the `cell-merge` operation. The unification may yield a contradiction if the program cannot be typed.

b. There may be some cells of a program where a type is not sufficiently constrained by the types of the neighboring cells. However, propagation can be stimulated by dropping a general type variable into such a cell and allowing that variable to accumulate constraints by propagation. This is called "plunking." Try it.

c. In hard cases a type inference may require making guesses (using hypotheticals) and backtracking on discovery of contradictions. Show cases where this is necessary.

d. Tracking of premises and reasons enables the construction of informative error comments, but to do this you must associate each program locus with its cell so that things that are learned by propagation can be related to the program being annotated. You may use any kind of "sticky note" you like to associate the locus bidirectionally with the cell. In any case, try to make good explanations about why a particular locus has the type that was determined, or why a program could not be consistently typed.

e. Is this implementation of type inference practical? Why or why not? If not, how can it be improved?

A moral of this story

Solving combinatorial puzzles is fun, but it is not the real value of what we have done. Indeed, "SAT solvers" are important for solving real-world problems of this kind. But there is a deeper message here for the design of computational systems. By generalizing our programming from expression structures to wiring diagrams (which can be inconvenient—but that can be mitigated with compiling) we have made it possible to smoothly integrate nondeterministic choice into programs in a natural and efficient way. We can introduce hypotheticals, which provide alternative values supported by propositions that may be discarded without pain. This gives us the freedom to treat things like quadratic equations correctly. They really have two solutions, and any computation based on a choice of one solution may decide to reject it, while the other solution may lead, after a long computation, to an acceptable outcome. For example, given that p:sqrt computes the traditional positive square root of a real number, we can build a directional propagator constructor p:honest-sqrt, with input cell x^2 and output cell x, that gives its users a (hidden) choice of square roots:

```
(define-p:prop (p:honest-sqrt (x^2) (x))
  (let-cells (mul +x)
    (p:amb mul '(-1 +1))
    (p:sqrt x^2 +x)
    (p:* mul +x x)))
```

What is important here is that such choices may be introduced without arranging that the enclosing machinery knows how to handle the ambiguity. For example, the constraint propagator that relates numbers to their squares can just use p:honest-sqrt:

```
(define-c:prop (c:square x x^2)
  (p:square x x^2)
  (p:honest-sqrt x^2 x)))
```

7.6   Propagation enables degeneracy

In the design of any significant system there are many implementation plans proposed for every component at every level of detail. However, in the system that is finally delivered this diversity of plans is lost, and usually only one unified plan is adopted and implemented. As in an ecological system, the loss of diversity in the traditional engineering process has serious consequences.

We rarely build degeneracy into programs, partly because it is expensive and partly because we traditionally have supplied no formal mechanisms for mediating its use. But the propagation idea provides a natural mechanism to incorporate degeneracy. The use of partial information structures in cells (introduced by Radul and Sussman [99]) allows multiple, perhaps overlapping, sources of information to be merged. We illustrated this with intervals in the stellar distance example in section 7.1. But there are many ways to merge partial information: partially specified symbolic expressions can be merged with unification, as shown in section 4.4.2. So the idea of partially specified information is not restricted to systems built with propagators, but if this is done in a propagator system, as proposed in exercise 7.8 on page 368, we have a paradigm for combining the contributions of multiple independent mechanisms.

Similarly, we considered another idea from the AI problem-solving world for degenerate designs: goal-directed invocation. The idea is that instead of specifying "how" we want a goal accomplished, by naming a procedure to accomplish it, we specify "what" we want to accomplish, and we link procedures that can accomplish that goal with the goal. This linkage is often done with pattern matching, but that is accidental rather than essential.[17] If there is more than one way to accomplish the goal, then the choice of an appropriate procedure is a choice point that can be registered for backtracking. But chronological backtracking, constrained by the control flow of an expression-oriented language, is extremely inefficient. We must break out of the expression-evaluation structure to make dependency-directed backtracking work well, and propagation is one way to go. We still have a potentially exponential search, but the combinatorics are significantly reduced by eliminating many bad choices using nogood sets learned from experience.

Of course, besides using a backtracking search for choosing a particular way to accomplish a goal, there are other ways that the goal can invoke degenerate methods. For example, we may want to run several possible ways to solve a problem in parallel, choosing the one that terminates first.

---

[17] *Pattern-directed invocation* was introduced by Carl Hewitt in PLAN-NER [56] and by Alain Colmerauer in Prolog [78]. This idea has spread to many other systems and languages.

Suppose we have several independently implemented procedures all designed to solve the same (imprecisely specified) general
class of problems. Assume for the moment that each design is reasonably competent and actually works correctly for most of the
problems that might be encountered in actual operation. We know
that we can make a more robust system by combining the given
procedures into a larger system that independently invokes each
of the given procedures and compares their results, choosing the
best answer on every problem. If the combination has independent ways of determining which answers are acceptable we are in
very good shape. But even if we are reduced to voting, we get
a system that can reliably cover a larger space of solutions. Furthermore, if such a system can automatically log all cases where
one of the designs fails, the operational feedback can be used to
improve the performance of the procedure that failed.

This degenerate design strategy can be used at every level of
detail. Every component of each subsystem can itself be degen-
erately designed. If the components are shared among the subsystems, we get a controlled redundancy that is quite powerful.
However, we can do even better. We can provide a mechanism for
consistency checking of the intermediate results of the independently designed subsystems, even when no particular value in one
subsystem exactly corresponds to a particular value in another
subsystem.

For a simple example, suppose we have two subsystems that are
intended to deliver the same result, but computed in completely
different ways. Assume that the designers agree that at some stage
in one of the designs, the product of two of the variables in that
design must be the same as the sum of two of the variables in
the other design.[18] There is no reason why this predicate should
not be computed as soon as all of the four values it depends upon
become available, thus providing consistency checking at run time
and powerful debugging information to the designers. This can be
arranged using a locally embedded constraint network.

---

[18]This is actually a real case. In variational mechanics the sum of a Lagrangian
for a system and the Hamiltonian related to it by a Legendre transformation
is the inner product of the generalized momentum 1-form and the generalized
velocity vector [121].

8
Epilogue

Serious engineering is only a few thousand years old. Our attempts at deliberately producing very complex robust systems are immature at best. We have yet to glean the lessons that biological evolution has learned over the last few billion years.

We have been more concerned with efficiency and correctness than with the kind of robustness of biological systems that comes from optimizing evolvability, flexibility, and resistance to attack. This is sensible for developing mission-critical systems that have barely enough resources to perform their function. However, the rapid advance of microelectronics has alleviated the resource problem for most applications. Our increasing dependence on computational and communications infrastructure, and the development of ever more sophisticated attacks on that infrastructure, make it imperative that we turn our attention to robustness.

We are not advocating biomimetics; but observations of biological systems give us hints about how to incorporate powerful principles of robustness into our engineering practice. Many of these principles are in direct conflict with the established practices of optimization of efficiency and of the ability to prove correctness. In this book we deliberately violate these established practices to explore the possibilities of optimizing for flexibility. A motivation of our approach is the observation that most systems that have survived the test of time are built as an assembly of domain-specific languages, each of which is appropriate to make some parts of the system easy to construct.

As part of the effort to build artificially intelligent symbolic systems, the AI community has incidentally developed technological tools that can be used to support principles of flexible and robust design. For example, rather than thinking of backtracking as a method of organizing search, we can employ it to increase the general applicability of components in a complex system that organizes itself to meet externally imposed constraints. We believe that by pursuing this new synthesis we will obtain better hardware and software systems.

We started out in chapter 2 with some rather unobjectionable techniques that are universally applicable. We introduced the strategy of building systems of combinators—libraries of parametric parts that have standardized interfaces. Such parts can be combined in many ways to meet a great variety of needs. We demonstrated how this idea can be used to simplify the construction of a language of regular-expression matchers. We introduced systems of wrappers that allow us to adapt parts to applications with different standards than the parts were built to, and we used this to make a language of unit-conversion wrappers. We progressed to build a rule interpreter for a language to express the rules of board games like checkers.

In chapter 3 we embarked on an exciting and dangerous adventure: we investigated what can be done if we are allowed to modulate the meanings of the primitive procedures of a language. We extended arithmetic to handle symbolic expressions and functions, as well as numbers. We created extensible generic procedures and used the extension mechanism to integrate forward-mode automatic differentiation into our arithmetic. This kind of extension is dangerous, but if we are careful, we can make old programs have new abilities without losing their old abilities. To make this strategy efficient and even more powerful, we proceeded to explore user-defined types, with declarable subtype relationships, and we used that to make a simple but easily extensible adventure game.

Pattern matching and pattern-directed invocation, introduced in chapter 4, are crucial techniques for erecting domain-specific languages. We started with term-rewriting rules for algebraic simplification. We then showed an elegant strategy for compiling patterns into a composition of elementary pattern matchers in a system of pattern-matching combinators. We then expanded our pattern-matching tools to allow pattern variables on both sides of a match, implementing unification, which we then used to make an elementary type-inference system. Finally, we built matchers that match arbitrary graphs, not just expression trees, and used graphs and graph matching to express the rules for moves in chess in an elegant manner.

Because all sane computer languages are universal, programmers do not have an excuse that a solution cannot be expressed in some language. If seriously pressed, good programmers can make an interpreter or compiler for any language they please in any language they are stuck with. This is not very hard, but it is probably the most powerful move a programmer can make. In chapter 5 we showed how to make increasingly powerful languages by interpretation and compilation. We started with a simple applicative-order interpreter for a Scheme-like language. For extensibility, the interpreter was built on generic procedures. We then extended it to allow procedure definitions to declare lazy formal parameters. Next we compiled the language to a combination of execution procedures—a system of combinators. We then added a model of nondeterministic evaluation, with the `amb` operator. Finally, we showed how by exposing the underlying continuations we could arrange to get the power of `amb` in the underlying Scheme system.

In chapter 6 we began to explore multilayer computations, based on a novel mechanism closely related to generic procedures. For example, we modified our arithmetic so that a program that computes numerical results from numerical arguments could be extended, without modification, to compute the same results, augmented with units. The units of the result are automatically derived from the units of the inputs, and combinations are checked for consistent units: adding 5 kilograms to 2 meters will signal an error. We used the same layering mechanism to augment programs to carry dependencies, so that a result automatically has reference to the sources of the ingredients that went into making that result.

The propagator model of chapter 7 is really a way of thinking about the plumbing of large systems. Although, in the examples we show in this chapter, the propagators are all simple arithmetic functions or relations, the idea is far more general. A propagator could be hardware or software. It could be a simple function or a huge computer doing an enormous crunch. If it is software, it could be written in any language. Indeed, a system of propagators does not have to be homogeneous. Different propagators may be constructed differently. Cells may be specialized to hold different kinds of information and they may merge information in their own favorite way. The communication between propagators and cells may be signals on a chip or on a global network. All that matters is the protocol for a propagator to query a cell and to add information to a cell.

In this book we introduced many programming ideas. It is now up to you to `evaluate` them and perhaps `apply` them.

A
Appendix: Supporting Software

All of the code shown in this book and the infrastructure code that supports it can be downloaded as an archive file from
http://groups.csail.mit.edu/mac/users/gjs/sdf.tgz
The archive is organized as a directory tree, where each subdirectory approximately corresponds with a section of this book. The software runs in MIT/GNU Scheme version 11.2 or later, which can be obtained from
http://www.gnu.org/software/mit-scheme
The software uses a number of features specific to the MIT/GNU implementation, so it won't work with other distributions. It should be possible to port it to another distribution, but we have not tried this and it is likely to require some work. Because this is free software (licensed under the GPL) you may modify it and distribute it to others.

The software archive is a `tar` file called `sdf.tgz`, which can be unpacked using the command

```
tar xf .../sdf.tgz
```

This `tar` command produces a directory `sdf` in whatever directory the tar command is executed in.

The primary interface to the software archive is a management program, which is distributed with the archive. To use this program, start MIT/GNU Scheme and load it like this:

```
(load ".../sdf/manager/load")
```

where `.../` refers to the directory in which the archive was unpacked. The manager creates a single definition in the global environment, called `manage`. Once loaded, it's not necessary to reload the manager unless a new instance of Scheme is started.

Suppose you are working on section 4.2 "Term rewriting," and you'd like to play with the software or work on an exercise. The loader for code in that section is stored in the subdirectory `.../sdf/term-rewriting`, along with files that are specific to that section. But you do not need to know how the loader works. (Of course, you may read the manager code. It is pretty interesting.)

The `manage` command

```
(manage 'new-environment 'term-rewriting)
```

will create a new top-level environment, load all of the necessary files for that section, and move the read-eval-print loop into that environment. After you are done with that section, you can use the `manage` command to load the software for another section by replacing `term-rewriting` with the name corresponding to the new section.

Usually, the name of a subdirectory can be used as an argument to (`manage 'new-environment ...`). When used in this context, the subdirectory name is called a *flavor*. However, some of the subdirectories have multiple flavors, and in those cases the available flavor names differ from the subdirectory names.

The correspondence between sections of the book and subdirectories/flavors in the archive can be found in the file

`.../sdf/manager/sections.scm`

In addition, there are two special subdirectories: `common` holds shared files that are used extensively; and `manager` holds the implementation of `manage`.

The software management program `manage` has many other useful abilities. Among them are managing working environments by name, finding the files that define a name and those that refer to it, and running unit tests. For more information refer to the documentation that is included in the `manager` subdirectory.

Using the software may require additional steps that are not spelled out in the book text, such as initialization. Every subdirectory contains tests: any file named `test-`*FOO*`.scm` is a "standard" test, using a testing framework similar to those of other programming languages. Additionally, the `load-spec` files in each subdirectory may contain references to tests, marked with the `inline-test?` symbol, that use a different testing framework that is similar to read-eval-print loop transcripts. Look there for examples of how to run the programs.

B
Appendix: Scheme

> Programming languages should be designed not by
> piling feature on top of feature, but by removing
> the weaknesses and restrictions that make
> additional features appear necessary. Scheme
> demonstrates that a very small number of rules for
> forming expressions, with no restrictions on how
> they are composed, suffice to form a practical and
> efficient programming language that is flexible
> enough to support most of the major programming
> paradigms in use today.
>
> *IEEE Standard for the Scheme Programming
> Language* [61], p. 3

Here we give an elementary introduction to the Scheme dialect of
Lisp. For a longer introduction see the textbook *Structure and
Interpretation of Computer Programs (SICP)* [1].

For a more precise explanation of the language see the IEEE
standard [61] and the Seventh *Revised Report on the Algorithmic
Language Scheme (R7RS)* [109]

Some of the programs in this book depend on nonstandard features in MIT/GNU Scheme; for documentation of this system see
the *MIT/GNU Scheme Reference Manual* [51]. Also, for Scheme
features that are documented elsewhere the index to the Reference
Manual provides pointers to the appropriate documents.

B.1   Essential Scheme

Scheme is a simple programming language based on expressions.
An expression names a value. For example, the numeral 3.14
names an approximation to a familiar number, and the numeral
22/7 names another approximation to it. There are primitive expressions, such as numerals, that we directly recognize, and there
are compound expressions of several kinds.

Compound expressions are delimited by parentheses. Those that start with distinguished keywords, such as if, are called *special forms*. Those that are not special forms, called *combinations*, denote applications of procedures to arguments.

Combinations

A *combination*—also called a *procedure application*—is a sequence of expressions delimited by parentheses:

(*operator operand-1* ... *operand-n*)

The first subexpression in a combination, called the *operator*, is taken to name a procedure, and the rest of the subexpressions, called the *operands*, are taken to name the arguments to that procedure. The value returned by the procedure when applied to the given arguments is the value named by the combination. For example,

```
(+ 1 2.14)
```
3.14

```
(+ 1 (* 2 1.07))
```
3.14

are both combinations that name the same number as the numeral 3.14.[1] In these cases the symbols + and * name procedures that add and multiply, respectively. If we replace any subexpression of any expression with an expression that names the same thing as the original subexpression, the thing named by the overall expression remains unchanged.

Note that in Scheme every parenthesis is essential: you cannot add extra parentheses or remove any.

Lambda expressions

Just as we use numerals to name numbers, we use lambda expressions to name procedures.[2] For example, the procedure that squares its input can be written:

---

[1] In examples we show the value that would be printed by the Scheme system using *slanted* characters following the input expression.

[2] The logician Alonzo Church [16] invented λ notation to allow the specification of an anonymous function of a named parameter: λx[expression in x]. This is read, "That function of one argument whose value is obtained by substituting the argument for x in the indicated expression."

```
(lambda (x) (* x x))
```

This expression can be read: "The procedure of one argument, x, that multiplies x by x." Of course, we can use this expression in any context where a procedure is needed. For example,

```
((lambda (x) (* x x)) 4)
16
```

The general form of a **lambda** expression is

```
(lambda formal-parameters body)
```

where *formal-parameters* is (usually) a parenthesized list of symbols that will be the names of the formal parameters of the procedure. When the procedure is applied to arguments, the formal parameters will have the arguments as their values. The *body* is an expression that may refer to the formal parameters. The value of a procedure application is the value of the body of the procedure with the arguments substituted for the formal parameters.[3]

In the example shown above, the symbol x is the only formal parameter of the procedure named by (lambda (x) (* x x)). That procedure is applied to the value of the numeral 4, so in the body, (* x x), the symbol x has the value 4, and the value of the combination ((lambda (x) (* x x)) 4) is 16.

We said "usually" above because there are exceptions. Some procedures, such as the procedure that multiplies numbers, named by the symbol *, can take an indefinite number of arguments. We will explain how to do that later (on page 389).

Definitions

We can use the **define** special form to give a name to any object. We say that the name identifies a *variable* whose value is the object. For example, if we make the definitions

```
(define pi 3.141592653589793)
```

```
(define square (lambda (x) (* x x)))
```

---

[3]We say that the formal parameters are *bound* to the arguments, and the *scope* of the binding is the body of the procedure.

we can then use the symbols `pi` and `square` wherever the numeral
or the `lambda` expression could appear. For example, the area of
the surface of a sphere of radius 5 is

```
(* 4 pi (square 5))
```
314.1592653589793

Procedure definitions may be expressed more conveniently using
"syntactic sugar." The squaring procedure may be defined

```
(define (square x) (* x x))
```

which we may read: "To square x multiply x by x."

In Scheme, procedures are *first-class* objects: they may be
passed as arguments, returned as values, and incorporated into
data structures. For example, it is possible to make a procedure
that implements the mathematical notion of the composition of
two functions:[4]

```
(define compose
  (lambda (f g)
    (lambda (x)
      (f (g x)))))
```

```
((compose square sin) 2)
```
.826821810431806

```
(square (sin 2))
```
.826821810431806

One thing to notice is that the values of `f` and `g` in the returned
procedure, `(lambda (x) (f (g x)))`, are the values of the formal
parameters of the outer procedure, `(lambda (f g) ...)`. This is
the essence of the lexical scoping discipline of Scheme. The value
of any variable is obtained by finding its binding in the lexically
apparent context. There is an implicit context for all the variables
defined globally by the system. (For example, `+` is globally bound
by the system to the procedure that adds numbers.)

Using the syntactic sugar shown above for `square`, we can write
the definition of `compose` more conveniently:

---

[4]The examples are indented to help with readability. Scheme does not care
about extra white space, so we may add as much as we please to make things
easier to read.

```
(define (compose f g)
  (lambda (x)
    (f (g x))))
```

In MIT/GNU Scheme we can use the sugar recursively, to write:

```
(define ((compose f g) x)
  (f (g x)))
```

Sometimes it is advantageous to make a definition local to another definition. For example, we may define `compose` as follows:

```
(define (compose f g)
  (define (fog x)
    (f (g x)))
  fog)
```

The name `fog` is not defined outside the definition of `compose`, so it is not particularly useful in this case, but larger chunks of code are often easier to read if internal pieces are given names. Internal definitions must always precede any expressions that are not definitions in the body of the procedure.

Conditionals

Conditional expressions may be used to choose among several expressions to produce a value. For example, a procedure that implements the absolute value function may be written:

```
(define (abs x)
  (cond ((< x 0) (- x))
        ((= x 0) x)
        ((> x 0) x)))
```

The conditional `cond` takes a number of *clauses*. Each clause has a *predicate expression*, which may be either true or false, and a *consequent expression*. The value of the `cond` expression is the value of the consequent expression of the first clause for which the corresponding predicate expression is true. The general form of a conditional expression is

```
(cond (predicate-1 consequent-1)
      ...
      (predicate-n consequent-n))
```

For convenience there is a special keyword `else` that can be used as the predicate in the last clause of a `cond`.

The `if` special form provides another way to make a conditional when there is only a binary choice to be made. For example, because we have to do something special only when the argument is negative, we could have defined `abs` as:

```
(define (abs x)
  (if (< x 0)
      (- x)
      x))
```

The general form of an `if` expression is

(`if` *predicate consequent alternative*)

If the *predicate* is true the value of the `if` expression is the value of the *consequent*, otherwise it is the value of the *alternative*.

Recursive procedures

Given conditionals and definitions, we can write recursive procedures. For example, to compute the nth factorial number we may write:

```
(define (factorial n)
  (if (= n 0)
      1
      (* n (factorial (- n 1)))))
```

```
(factorial 6)
```
720

```
(factorial 40)
```
815915283247897734345611269596115894272000000000

Local names

A `let` expression is used to give names to objects in a local context. For example,

```
(define (f radius)
  (let ((area (* 4 pi (square radius)))
        (volume (* 4/3 pi (cube radius))))
    (/ volume area)))
```

```
(f 3)
```
1

The general form of a `let` expression is

```
(let ((variable-1  expression-1)
      ...
      (variable-n  expression-n))
  body)
```

The value of the `let` expression is the value of the *body* expression in the context where the variables *variable-i* have the values of the expressions *expression-i*. The expressions *expression-i* may not refer to any of the variables *variable-j* given values in the `let` expression.

A `let*` expression is the same as a `let` expression except that an expression *expression-i* may refer to variables *variable-j* given values earlier in the `let*` expression.

A slight variant of the `let` expression provides a convenient way to write a loop. We can write a procedure that implements an alternative algorithm for computing factorials as follows:

```
(define (factorial n)
  (let factlp ((count 1) (answer 1))
    (if (> count n)
        answer
        (factlp (+ count 1) (* count answer)))))

(factorial 6)
720
```

Here, the symbol `factlp` following the `let` is locally defined to be a procedure that has the variables `count` and `answer` as its formal parameters. It is called the first time with 1 and 1 as arguments, initializing the loop. Whenever the procedure named `factlp` is called later, these variables get new values that are the values of the operand expressions (+ `count` 1) and (* `count` `answer`).

An equivalent way to express this procedure has an explicitly defined internal procedure:

```
(define (factorial n)
  (define (factlp count answer)
    (if (> count n)
        answer
        (factlp (+ count 1) (* count answer))))
  (factlp 1 1))
```

The procedure `factlp` is defined locally; it exists only in the body of `factorial`. Because `factlp` is lexically enclosed in the definition of `factorial`, the value of `n` in its body is the value of the formal parameter of `factorial`.

Compound data—lists, vectors, and records

Data can be glued together to form compound data structures. A *list* is a data structure in which the elements are linked sequentially. A *vector* is a data structure in which the elements are packed in a linear array. New elements can be added to lists, but to access the nth element of a list takes computing time proportional to n. By contrast, a vector is of fixed length, and its elements can be accessed in constant time. A *record* is similar to a vector, except that its fields are addressed by names rather than index numbers. Records also provide new data types, which are distinguishable by type predicates and are guaranteed to be different from other types.

Compound data objects are constructed from components by procedures called *constructors* and the components are accessed by *selectors*.

The procedure `list` is the constructor for lists. The predicate `list?` is true of any list, and false of all other types of data.[5]

For example,

```
(define a-list (list 6 946 8 356 12 620))

a-list
(6 946 8 356 12 620)

(list? a-list)
#t

(list? 3)
#f
```

Here `#t` and `#f` are the printed representations of the boolean values true and false.[6]

---

[5]A *predicate* is a procedure that returns true or false. By Scheme cultural convention, we usually give a predicate a name ending with a question mark (?), except for the elementary arithmetic comparison predicates: `=`, `<`, `>`, `<=`, and `>=`. This is just a stylistic convention. To Scheme the question mark is just an ordinary character.

[6]It is convenient, but irritating to some, that the conditional expressions (`if` and `cond`) treat any predicate value that is not explicitly `#f` as true.

Lists are built from pairs. A *pair* is made using the constructor cons. The selectors for the two components of the pair are car and cdr (pronounced "could-er").[7]

```
(define a-pair (cons 1 2))
```

```
a-pair
```
(1 . 2)

```
(car a-pair)
```
1
```
(cdr a-pair)
```
2

A list is a chain of pairs, such that the car of each pair is the list element and the cdr of each pair is the next pair, except for the last cdr, which is a distinguishable value called the empty list and written (). Thus,

```
(car a-list)
```
6

```
(cdr a-list)
```
(946 8 356 12 620)

```
(car (cdr a-list))
```
946

```
(define another-list
  (cons 32 (cdr a-list)))
```

```
another-list
```
(32 946 8 356 12 620)

```
(car (cdr another-list))
```
946

The lists a-list and another-list share their tail (their cdr).

The predicate pair? is true of pairs and false of all other types of data. The predicate null? is true only of the empty list.

---

[7]These names are accidents of history. They stand for "Contents of the Address part of Register" and "Contents of the Decrement part of Register" of the IBM 704 computer, which was used for the first implementation of Lisp in the late 1950s. Scheme is a dialect of Lisp.

Vectors are simpler than lists. There is a constructor `vector` that can be used to make vectors and a selector `vector-ref` for accessing the elements of a vector. In Scheme all selectors that use a numerical index are zero-based:

```
(define a-vector
  (vector 37 63 49 21 88 56))

a-vector
#(37 63 49 21 88 56)

(vector-ref a-vector 3)
21

(vector-ref a-vector 0)
37
```

The printed representation of a vector is distinguished from the printed representation of a list by the character `#` before the initial parenthesis.

There is a predicate `vector?` that is true of vectors and false for all other types of data.

Scheme provides a numerical selector for the elements of a list, `list-ref`, analogous to the selector for vectors:

```
(list-ref a-list 3)
356

(list-ref a-list 0)
6
```

Records are more involved, as they must be declared before they can be constructed. A simple record declaration might be

```
(define-record-type point
    (make-point x y)
    point?
  (x point-x)
  (y point-y))
```

After this declaration, we can make and use points:

```
(define p (make-point 1 2))

(point? p)
#t
```

```
(point-x p)
1
(point-y p)
2
```

The elements of lists, vectors, and records may be any kind of data, including numbers, procedures, lists, vectors, and records. Numerous other procedures for manipulating lists, vectors, and records can be found in the Scheme online documentation.

Procedures with an indefinite number of arguments

The procedures that we have seen are specified with a list of formal parameters that are bound to the arguments that the procedure is called with. However, there are many procedures that take an indefinite number of arguments. For example, the arithmetic procedure that multiplies numbers can take any number of arguments. To define such a procedure we specify the formal parameters as a single symbol rather than a list of symbols. The single symbol is then bound to a list of the arguments that the procedure is called with. For example, given a binary multiplier `*:binary` we can write

```
(define * (lambda args (accumulate *:binary 1 args)))
```

where `accumulate` is just

```
(define (accumulate proc initial lst)
  (if (null? lst)
      initial
      (proc (car lst)
            (accumulate proc initial (cdr lst)))))
```

Sometimes we want a procedure that takes some named arguments and an indefinite number of others. In a procedure definition a parameter list that has a dot before the last parameter name (called *dotted-tail notation*) indicates that the parameters before the dot will be bound to the initial arguments, and the final parameter will be bound to a list of any remaining arguments. In the example of `*` above there are no initial arguments, so the value of `args` is a list of all the arguments. Thus, alternatively, we could define `*` as:

```
(define (* . args) (accumulate *:binary 1 args))
```

The procedure named by – is more interesting, as it requires at least one argument: when given one argument – negates it; when given more than one argument it subtracts the rest from the first:

```
(define (- x . ys)
  (if (null? ys)           ; Only one argument?
      (-:unary x)
      (-:binary x (accumulate +:binary 0 ys))))
```

This can also be written

```
(define -
  (lambda (x . ys)
    (if (null? ys)
        (-:unary x)
        (-:binary x (accumulate +:binary 0 ys)))))
```

Parameters like `args` and `ys` in the examples above are called *rest parameters* because they are bound to the rest of the arguments.

Symbols

Symbols are a very important kind of primitive data type that we use to make programs and algebraic expressions. You probably have noticed that Scheme programs look just like lists. In fact, they *are* lists. Some of the elements of the lists that make up programs are symbols, such as + and `vector`.[8]

If we are to make programs that can manipulate programs, we need to be able to write an expression that names such a symbol. This is accomplished by the mechanism of *quotation*. The name of the symbol + is the expression '+, and in general the name of an expression is the expression preceded by a single quote character. Thus the name of the expression (+ 3 a) is '(+ 3 a).

We can test if two symbols are identical by using the predicate `eq?`. For example, we can write a program to determine if an expression is a sum:

---

[8]A symbol may have any number of characters. A symbol may not normally contain whitespace or delimiter characters, such as parentheses, brackets, quotation marks, comma, or #; but there are special notations that allow any characters to be included in a symbol's name.

```
(define (sum? expression)
  (and (pair? expression)
       (eq? (car expression) '+)))

(sum? '(+ 3 a))
#t

(sum? '(* 3 a))
#f
```

Consider what would happen if we left out the quote in the expression (sum? '(+ 3 a)). If the variable a had the value 4, we would be asking if 7 is a sum. But what we wanted to know was whether the expression (+ 3 a) is a sum. That is why we need the quote.

Backquote

To manipulate patterns and other forms of list-based syntax, it is often useful to intersperse quoted and evaluated parts in the same expression. Lisp systems provide a mechanism called *quasiquotation* that makes this easy.

Just as we use the apostrophe character to indicate regular quotation, we use the backquote character to indicate quasiquotation.[9] We specify such a partially quoted expression as a list in which the parts to be evaluated are prefixed with the comma character. For example,

```
`(a b ,(+ 20 3) d)
(a b 23 d)
```

The backquote mechanism also provides for "splicing" into a list expression: an evaluated subexpression produces a list, which is then spliced into the enclosing list. For example,

```
`(a b ,@(list (+ 20 3) (- 20 3)) d)
(a b 23 17 d)
```

Consult the Scheme Report [109] for a more detailed explanation of quasiquotation.

---

[9]On an American keyboard the backquote character "`" is the lowercase character on the key that has the tilde character "~" as the uppercase character.

Effects

Sometimes we need to perform an action, such as plotting a point or printing a value, in the process of a computation. Such an action is called an *effect*.[10] For example, to see in more detail how the factorial program computes its answer, we can interpolate a `write-line` statement in the body of the `factlp` internal procedure to print a list of the count and the answer for each iteration:

```
(define (factorial n)
  (let factlp ((count 1) (answer 1))
    (write-line (list count answer))
    (if (> count n)
        answer
        (factlp (+ count 1) (* count answer)))))
```

When we call the modified `factorial` procedure we can watch the counter being incremented and the answer being built:

```
(factorial 6)
(1 1)
(2 1)
(3 2)
(4 6)
(5 24)
(6 120)
(7 720)
720
```

The body of every procedure or `let`, as well as the consequent of every `cond` clause, allows statements that have effects to be used. The effect statement generally has no useful value. The final expression in the body or clause produces the value that is returned. In this example the `if` expression produces the value of the `factorial`.

Assignments

Effects like printing a value or plotting a point are pretty benign, but there are more powerful (and thus dangerous) effects, called *assignments*. An assignment *changes* the value of a variable or an entry in a data structure. Almost everything we are computing is a mathematical function: for a particular input it always produces the same result. However, with assignment we can make objects

---

[10]This is computer-science jargon. An effect is a change to something. For example, `write-line` changes the display by printing something to the display.

that change their behavior as they are used. For example, we can use `set!` to make a device that increments a count every time we call it:[11]

```
(define (make-counter)
  (let ((count 0))
    (lambda ()
      (set! count (+ count 1))
      count)))
```

Let's make two counters:

```
(define c1 (make-counter))
(define c2 (make-counter))
```

These two counters have independent local state. Calling a counter causes it to increment its local state variable, `count`, and return its value.

```
(c1)
```
1

```
(c1)
```
2

```
(c2)
```
1

```
(c1)
```
3

```
(c2)
```
2

For assigning to the elements of a data structure, such as a pair, a list, or a vector, Scheme provides:

```
(set-car! pair new-value)
(set-cdr! pair new-value)

(list-set! list index new-value)
(vector-set! vector index new-value)
```

---

[11]It is another cultural convention that we terminate the name of a procedure that has "side effects" with an exclamation point (!). This warns the reader that changing the order of effects may change the results of running the program.

A record may be defined to allow assignments to its fields (compare page 388:

```
(define-record-type point
    (make-point x y)
    point?
  (x point-x set-x!)
  (y point-y set-y!))

(define p (make-point 1 2))

(point-x p)
1
(point-y p)
2

(set-x! p 3)

(point-x p)
3
(point-y p)
2
```

In general, it is good practice to avoid assignments when possible, but if you need them they are available.[12]

B.2   More advanced stuff

Scheme provides many more powerful features, but we won't try to describe them here. For example, you will probably want to know about hash tables. In general, the best sources are the *Revised Report on the Algorithmic Language Scheme (R7RS)* [109] and the *MIT/GNU Scheme Reference Manual* [51]. But here are two fairly complex features that you may need to reference while reading this book:

Dynamic binding
We sometimes want to specify the way in which some evaluation or action will be accomplished—for example, to specify the radix

---

[12]The discipline of programming without assignments is called *functional programming*. Functional programs are generally easier to understand and have fewer bugs than *imperative programs*.

to use when printing a number. To do this we use an object called
a *parameter*.

For example, the Scheme procedure `number->string` produces
a character string that represents a number in a given radix:

```
(number->string 100 2)
"1100100"
(number->string 100 16)
"64"
```

Suppose we want to use `number->string` in many places in a complex program that we run by calling `myprog`, but we want to be
able to control the radix used when the program is run. We can
accomplish this by making a parameter `radix` with the default
value 10:

```
(define radix (make-parameter 10))
```

The value of a parameter is obtained by calling the parameter
with no arguments:

```
(radix)
10
```

We define a specialized version of `number->string` to use instead
of `number->string`:

```
(define (number->string-radix number)
  (number->string number (radix)))
```

In an execution of (`myprog`), every call to `number->string-radix`
will produce a decimal string, because the default value of (`radix`)
is 10. However, we can wrap our program with `parameterize` to
change the execution to use another radix:

```
(parameterize ((radix 2))
  (myprog))
```

The syntax of `parameterize` is the same as the syntax of `let`, but
it can be used only for parameters created by `make-parameter`.

Bundles

MIT/GNU Scheme provides a simple mechanism for building a
collection of related procedures with shared state: a *bundle*. A

bundle is a procedure that delegates to a collection of named procedures: the first argument to the bundle is the name of the delegate to use, and the rest of the arguments are passed to the specified delegate. This is similar to the way that some object-oriented languages work, but much simpler, and without classes or inheritance.

A bundle is sometimes called a *message-accepting procedure*, where the message type is the delegate name and the message body is the arguments.[13] This emphasizes that the bundle supports a message-passing protocol and can be thought of as a node in a communications network.

Here is a simple example:

```
(define (make-point x y)
   (define (get-x) x)
   (define (get-y) y)
   (define (set-x! new-x) (set! x new-x))
   (define (set-y! new-y) (set! y new-y))
   (bundle point? get-x get-y set-x! set-y!))
```

The procedure `make-point` defines four internal procedures, which share the state variables x and y. The `bundle` macro creates a bundle procedure, for which those procedures are the delegates.

The first argument to the `bundle` macro is a predicate, which is created with `make-bundle-predicate`. The bundle that is created will satisfy this predicate:

```
(define point? (make-bundle-predicate 'point))

(define p1 (make-point 3 4))
(define p2 (make-point -1 1))

(point? p1)
#t
(point? p2)
#t
(point? (lambda (x) x))
#f
```

The argument to `make-bundle-predicate` is a symbol that is used to identify the predicate when debugging.

---

[13]This terminology dates back to the ACTOR framework [58] and the Smalltalk programming language [46].

If a predicate is not needed, **bundle** alternatively accepts **#f** as a first argument. In that case there will be no way to distinguish the created bundle procedure from other procedures.

The remaining arguments to the **bundle** macro are the names of the delegate procedures: `get-x`, `get-y`, `set-x!`, and `set-y!`. These names are looked up in the lexical environment of the macro to get the corresponding delegate procedures. A bundle procedure is then created, containing an association from each name to its delegate procedure.

When the resulting bundle procedure is called, its first argument is a symbol that must be the name of one of the delegate procedures. The association is used to select the named delegate procedure, which is then called with the bundle procedure's remaining arguments as its arguments.

It is easier to use a bundle than to describe it:

```
(p1 'get-x)
```
3
```
(p1 'get-y)
```
4
```
(p2 'get-x)
```
−1
```
(p2 'get-y)
```
1

```
(p1 'set-x! 5)
```

```
(p1 'get-x)
```
5
```
(p2 'get-x)
```
−1

References

[1] Harold Abelson and Gerald Jay Sussman with Julie Sussman, *Structure and Interpretation of Computer Programs* (2nd ed.). Cambridge, MA: MIT Press, 1996.

[2] Harold Abelson, Don Allen, Daniel Coore, Chris Hanson, George Homsy, Thomas F. Knight Jr., Radhika Nagpal, Erik Rauch, Gerald Jay Sussman, and Ron Weiss; "Amorphous Computing," in *Communications of the ACM*, 43(5) (May 2000): 74–82.

[3] Lee Altenberg; "The Evolution of Evolvability in Genetic Programming," in *Advances in Genetic Programming*, ed. Kenneth E. Kinnear Jr., 47–74. Cambridge, MA: MIT Press, 1994.

[4] *The ARRL Handbook for Radio Amateurs*, American Radio Relay League, Newington, CT (annual).

[5] Jean-Paul Arcangeli and Christian Pomian; "Principles of Plasma Pattern and Alternative Structure Compilation," in *Theoretical Computer Science*, 71 (1990): 177–191.

[6] Franz Baader and Wayne Snyder; "Unification theory," in *Handbook of Automated Reasoning*, ed. Alan Robinson and Andrei Voronkov. Elsevier Science Publishers B.V., 2001.

[7] Jonathan B.L. Bard; *Morphogenesis*, Cambridge: Cambridge University Press, 1990.

[8] Alan Bawden and Jonathan Rees; "Syntactic closures," in *Proc. Lisp and Functional Programming* (1988).

[9] Jacob Beal; *Generating Communications Systems Through Shared Context*, S.M. thesis, MIT, also Artificial Intelligence Laboratory Technical Report 2002-002, January 2002.

[10] Jacob Beal; "Programming an Amorphous Computational Medium," in *Unconventional Programming Paradigms International Workshop* (September 2004). Updated version in Lecture Notes in Computer Science, 3566 (August 2005).

[11] M.R. Bernfield, S.D. Banerjee, J.E. Koda, and A.C. Rapraeger; "Remodelling of the basement membrane as a mechanism of morphogenic tissue interaction," in *The role of extracellular matrix in development*, ed. R.L. Trelstad, 542–572. New York: Alan R. Liss, 1984.

[12] Martin Berz; "Automatic differentiation as nonarchimedean analysis," in *Computer Arithmetic and Enclosure Methods*, ed. L. Atanassova and J. Herzberger. Elsevier Science Publishers B.V. (North-Holland), 1992.

[13]Philip L. Bewig; *Scheme Requests for Implementation 41: Streams* (2008). https://srfi.schemers.org/srfi-41/

[14]R.C. Bohlin and R.L. Gilliland; "Hubble Space Telescope Absolute Spectrophotometry of Vega from the Far-Ultraviolet to the Infrared," in *The Astronomical Journal*, 127(6) (June 2004): 3508–3515.

[15]J.P. Brocks; "Amphibian limb regeneration: rebuilding a complex structure," in *Science*, 276 (1997): 81–87.

[16]Alonzo Church; *The Calculi of Lambda-Conversion*. Princeton, NJ: Princeton University Press, 1941.

[17]Alonzo Church; "An Unsolvable Problem of Elementary Number Theory," *American Journal of Mathematics*, 58 (1936): 345–363.

[18]Alonzo Church; "A Note on the Entscheidungsproblem," in *Journal of Symbolic Logic*, 1 (1936): 40–41.

[19]Lauren Clement and Radhika Nagpal; "Self-Assembly and Self-Repairing Topologies," in *Workshop on Adaptability in Multi-Agent Systems*, RoboCup Australian Open, January 2003.

[20]William Kingdon Clifford; "Preliminary sketch of bi-quaternions," in *Proceedings of the London Mathematical Society*, 4 (1873): 381–395.

[21]William Clinger; "Nondeterministic Call by Need is Neither Lazy Nor by Name," in *Proceedings of the 1982 ACM symposium on LISP and functional programming*, 226–234 (August 1982).

[22]William Clinger and Jonathan Rees; "Macros that work," in *Proceedings of the 1991 ACM Conference on Principles of Programming Languages*, 155–162 (1991).

[23]A Colmerauer., H. Kanoui, R. Pasero, and P. Roussel; *Un système de communication homme-machine en français*, Technical report, Groupe Intelligence Artificielle, Université d'Aix Marseille, Luminy, 1973.

[24]*Constraints, An International Journal* ISSN: 1383-7133 (Print) 1572-9354 (Online).

[25]Wikipedia article on continuations. https://en.wikipedia.org/wiki/Continuation

[26]Haskell Brooks Curry; "Grundlagen der Kombinatorischen Logik," in *American Journal of Mathematics*. Baltimore: Johns Hopkins University Press, 1930.

[27]Johan deKleer, Jon Doyle, Guy Steele, and Gerald J. Sussman; "AMORD: Explicit control of reasoning," in *Proceedings of the ACM Symposium on Artificial Intelligence and Programming Languages*, 116–125 (1977).

[28]E.M. del Pino and R.P. Elinson; "A novel developmental pattern for frogs: gastrulation produces an embryonic disk," in *Nature*, 306 (1983): 589–591.

[29]Howard P. Dinesman; *Superior Mathematical Puzzles.* New York: Simon and Schuster, 1968.

[30]Jon Doyle; "A truth maintenance system," in *Artificial Intelligence,* 12 (1979): 231–272.

[31]K. Dybvig, R. Hieb, and C. Bruggerman; "Syntactic abstraction in Scheme," in *Proc. Lisp and Symbolic Computation* (1993).

[32]G.M. Edelman and J.A. Gally; "Degeneracy and complexity in biological systems," *Proceedings of the National Academy of Sciences,* 98 (2001): 13763–13768.

[33]M. D. Ernst, C. Kaplan, and C. Chambers; "Predicate Dispatching: A Unified Theory of Dispatch," in *ECOOP'98—Object-Oriented Programming: 12th European Conference, Proceedings,* ed. Eric Jul, 186–211, Lecture Notes in Computer Science, 1445. Berlin: Springer, 1998.

[34]Zsuzsa Farkas; "LISTLOG—A PROLOG extension for list processing," in *TAPSOFT 1987,* ed. Ehrig H., Kowalski R., Levi G., Montanari U., Lecture Notes in Computer Science, 250. Berlin: Springer, 1987.

[35]Robert Floyd; "Nondeterministic algorithms," in *Journal of the ACM,* 14(4) (1967): 636–644.

[36]Kenneth D. Forbus and Johan de Kleer; *Building Problem Solvers.* Cambridge, MA: MIT Press, 1993.

[37]Stefanie Forrest, Anil Somayaji, David H. Ackley; "Building Diverse Computer Systems," in *Proceedings of the 6th workshop on Hot Topics in Operating Systems,* 67–72. Los Alamitos, CA: IEEE Computer Society Press, 1997.

[38]Joseph Frankel; *Pattern Formation, Ciliate Studies and Models.* New York: Oxford University Press, 1989.

[39]Eugene C. Freuder; *Synthesizing Constraint Expressions.* AI Memo 370, MIT Artificial Intelligence Laboratory, July 1976.

[40]Daniel P. Friedman and David S. Wise; "Cons should not evaluate its arguments," in *Automata Languages and Programming;* Proc. Third International Colloquium at the University of Edinburgh, ed. S. Michaelson and R. Milner, 257–284 (July 1976).

[41]Daniel P. Friedman, Mitchell Wand, and Christopher T. Haynes; *Essentials of Programming Languages.* Cambridge, MA: MIT Press/McGraw-Hill, 1992.

[42]Richard P. Gabriel and Linda DeMichiel; "The Common Lisp Object System: An Overview," in *Proceedings of ECOOP'87. European Conference on Object-Oriented Programming,* ed. Jean Bezivin, Jean-Marie Hullot, Pierre Cointe, and Henry Lieberman, 151–170. Paris: Springer, 1987.

[43]George Gatewood and Joost Kiewiet de Jonge; "Map-based Trigonometric Parallaxes of Altair and Vega," in *The Astrophysical Journal,* 450 (September 1995): 364–368.

[44]George Gatewood; "Astrometric Studies of Aldebaran, Arcturus, Vega, the Hyades, and Other Regions," in *The Astronomical Journal*, 136(1) (2008): 452–460.

[45]Kurt Gödel; "On Undecidable Propositions of Formal Mathematical Systems," *Lecture notes taken by Kleene and Rosser at the Institute for Advanced Study* (1934), reprinted in Martin Davis *The Undecidable: Basic Papers on Undecidable Propositions, Unsolvable Problems and Computable Functions*, 39–74. New York: Raven, 1965.

[46]Adele Goldberg and David Robson; *Smalltalk-80: The Language and Its Implementation*. Reading, MA: Addison-Wesley, 1983.

[47]Michael Gordon, Robin Milner, and Christopher Wadsworth; *Edinburgh LCF*, Lecture Notes in Computer Science, 78. New York: Springer-Verlag, 1979.

[48]Cordell Green; "Application of theorem proving to problem solving," in *Proceedings of the International Joint Conference on Artificial Intelligence*, 219–240 (1969).

[49]Cordell Green and Bertram Raphael; "The use of theorem-proving techniques in question-answering systems," in *Proceedings of the ACM National Conference*, 169–181 (1968).

[50]John V. Guttag; "Abstract data types and the development of data structures," *Communications of the ACM*, 20(6) (1977): 397–404.

[51]Chris Hanson; *MIT/GNU Scheme Reference Manual*. https://www.gnu.org/software/mit-scheme/

[52]Chris Hanson; SOS software: Scheme Object System, 1993.

[53]Chris Hanson, Tim Berners-Lee, Lalana Kagal, Gerald Jay Sussman, and Daniel Weitzner; "Data-Purpose Algebra: Modeling Data Usage Policies," in *Eighth IEEE International Workshop on Policies for Distributed Systems and Networks (POLICY'07)*, (June 2007).

[54]Hyman Hartman and Temple F. Smith; "The Evolution of the Ribosome and the Genetic Code," in *Life*, 4 (2014): 227–249.

[55]Jacques Herbrand; "Sur la non-contradiction de larithmetique," *Journal fur die reine und angewandte Mathematik*, 166 (1932): 1–8.

[56]Carl E. Hewitt; "PLANNER: A language for proving theorems in robots," in *Proceedings of the International Joint Conference on Artificial Intelligence*, 295–301 (1969).

[57]Carl E. Hewitt; "Viewing control structures as patterns of passing messages," in *Journal of Artificial Intelligence*, 8(3) (1977): 323–364.

[58]Carl Hewitt, Peter Bishop, Richard Steiger; "A Universal Modular ACTOR Formalism for Artificial Intelligence," in *IJCAI-73: Proceedings of the Third International Joint Conference on Artificial Intelligence*, 235–245 (1973).

[59]Edwin Hewitt; "Rings of real-valued continuous functions. I," in *Transactions of the American Mathematical Society*, 64 (1948): 45–99.

[60]Paul Horowitz and Winfield Hill; *The Art of Electronics*. Cambridge: Cambridge University Press, 1980.

[61]IEEE Std 1178-1990, *IEEE Standard for the Scheme Programming Language*, Institute of Electrical and Electronic Engineers, Inc., 1991.

[62]Paul-Alan Johnson; *The Theory of Architecture: Concepts, Themes, & Practices*. New York: Van Nostrand Reinhold, 1994.

[63]Jerome H. Keisler; "The hyperreal line. Real numbers, generalizations of the reals, and theories of continua," in *Synthese Library*, 242, 207–237. Dordrecht: Kluwer Academic, 1994.

[64]Richard Kelsey, William Clinger, and Jonathan Rees (editors); *Revised^5 Report on the Algorithmic Language Scheme* (1998).

[65]Richard Kelsey; *Scheme Requests for Implementation 9: Defining Record types* (1999). https://srfi.schemers.org/srfi-9/

[66]Gregor Kiczales; Tiny CLOS software: Kernelized CLOS, with a metaobject protocol, 1992.

[67]Gregor Kiczales, John Lamping, Anurag Mendhekar, Chris Maeda, Cristina Videira Lopes, Jean-Marc Loingtier, and John Irwin; "Aspect-oriented programming," in *ECOOP'97: Proceedings of the 11th European Conference on Object-Oriented Programming*, 220–242 (1997).

[68]Gregor Kiczales, Jim des Rivieres, and Daniel G. Bobrow; *The Art of the Metaobject Protocol*. Cambridge, MA: MIT Press, 1991.

[69]Simon Kirby; *Language evolution without natural selection: From vocabulary to syntax in a population of learners.*, Edinburgh Occasional Paper in Linguistics EOPL-98-1, University of Edinburgh Department of Linguistics (1998).

[70]Marc W. Kirschner and John C. Gerhart; *The Plausibility of Life: Resolving Darwin's Dilemma*. New Haven: Yale University Press, 2005.

[71]Marc W. Kirschner, Tim Mitchison; "Beyond self-assembly: from microtubules to morphogenesis," in *Cell*, 45(3) (May 1986): 329–342.

[72]D. Knuth, P. Bendix; "Simple word problems in universal algebras," in *Computational Problems in Abstract Algebra*, ed. John Leech, 263–297. London: Pergamon Press, 1970.

[73]E. Kohlbecker, D. P. Friedman, M. Felleisen, and B. Duba; "Hygienic Macro Expansion," in *ACM Conference on LISP and Functional Programming* (1986).

[74]E. Kohlbecker and Mitchell Wand; "Macro-by-example: Deriving syntactic transformations from their specifications," in *Proc. Symposium on Principles of Programming Languages* (1987).

[75]Milos Konopasek and Sundaresan Jayaraman; *The TK!Solver Book: A Guide to Problem-Solving in Science, Engineering, Business, and Education.* Berkeley, CA: Osborne/McGraw-Hill, 1984.

[76]Robert Kowalski; *Predicate logic as a programming language,* Technical report 70, Department of Computational Logic, School of Artificial Intelligence, University of Edinburgh, 1973.

[77]Robert Kowalski; *Logic for Problem Solving.* New York: North-Holland, 1979.

[78]Robert M. Kowalski; "The Early Years of Logic Programming," in *Communications of the ACM,* 31(1) (January 1988): 38–43.

[79]Temur Kutsia; "Pattern Unification with Sequence Variables and Flexible Arity Symbols," in *Electronic Notes in Theoretical Computer Science,* 66(5) (2002): 52–69.

[80]Butler Lampson, J. J. Horning, R. London, J. G. Mitchell, and G. K. Popek; *Report on the programming language Euclid,* Technical report, Computer Systems Research Group, University of Toronto, 1981.

[81]Peter Landin; "A correspondence between Algol 60 and Church's lambda notation: Part I," *Communications of the ACM,* 8(2) (1965): 89–101.

[82]Henrietta S. Leavitt; "1777 variables in the Magellanic Clouds," in *Annals of Harvard College Observatory,* 60 (1908): 87–108.

[83]Floor Van Leeuwen; "Validation of the new Hipparcos reduction," in *Astronomy & Astrophysics,* 474(2) (2007): 653–664.

[84]Karl Lieberherr; *Informationsverdichtung von Modellen in der Aussagenlogik und das P=NP Problem,* ETH Dissertation, 1977.

[85]Barbara H. Liskov and Stephen N. Zilles; " Specification techniques for data abstractions," in *IEEE Transactions on Software Engineering,* 1(1) (1975): 7–19.

[86]Harvey Lodish, Arnold Berk, S Lawrence Zipursky, Paul Matsudaira, David Baltimore, and James E Darnell; *Molecular Cell Biology* (4th ed.). New York: W. H. Freeman & Co., 1999.

[87]Oleksandr Manzyuk, Barak A. Pearlmutter, Alexey Andreyevich Radul, David R. Rush, and Jeffrey Mark Siskind; "Confusion of Tagged Perturbations in Forward Automatic Differentiation of Higher-Order Functions," arxiv:1211.4892 (2012).

[88]David Allen McAllester; *A three-valued truth-maintenance system,* AI Memo 473, MIT Artificial Intelligence Laboratory, 1978.

[89]David Allen McAllester "An outlook on truth maintenance," AI Memo 551, MIT Artificial Intelligence Laboratory, 1980.

[90]John McCarthy; "A basis for a mathematical theory of computation," in *Computer Programming and Formal Systems,* ed. P. Braffort and D. Hirshberg, 33–70. Amsterdam: North-Holland, 1963.

[91]Wikipedia article on MDL.
https://en.wikipedia.org/wiki/MDL_(programming_language)

[92]Piotr Mitros; *Constraint-Satisfaction Modules: A Methodology for Analog Circuit Design*, PhD thesis, MIT, Department of Electrical Engineering and Computer Science, 2007.

[93]Paul Penfield Jr.; *MARTHA User's Manual*, MIT Research Laboratory of Electronics, Electrodynamics Memorandum No. 6 (1970).

[94]Barak A. Perlmutter and Jeffrey Mark Siskind; "Lazy Multivariate Higher-Order Forward-Mode AD," in *Proc. POPL'07*, 155–160. New York: ACM, 2007.

[95]Tim Peters; *PEP 20—The Zen of Python*.
http://www.python.org/dev/peps/pep-0020/

[96]*POSIX.1-2017*, "Base Definitions," Chapter 9, "Regular Expressions." http://pubs.opengroup.org/onlinepubs/9699919799/

[97]Jonathan Bruce Postel; *RFC 760: DoD standard Internet Protocol* (January 1980). http://www.rfc-editor.org/rfc/rfc760.txt

[98]W. H. Press, B. P. Flannery, S. A. Teukolsky, and W. T. Vetterling; "Richardson Extrapolation and the Bulirsch-Stoer Method," in *Numerical Recipes in C: The Art of Scientific Computing* (2nd ed.), 718–725. Cambridge: Cambridge University Press, 1992.

[99]Alexey Andreyevich Radul and Gerald Jay Sussman; "The Art of the Propagator," MIT CSAIL Technical Report MIT-CSAIL-TR-2009-002; Abridged version in *Proc. 2009 International Lisp Conference* (March 2009). http://hdl.handle.net/1721.1/44215

[100]Alexey Andreyevich Radul; *Propagation networks: a flexible and expressive substrate for computation*, PhD thesis, MIT, Department of Electrical Engineering and Computer Science, 2009.
http://hdl.handle.net/1721.1/54635

[101]Eric Raymond; *The New Hacker's Dictionary* (2nd ed.). Cambridge, MA: MIT Press, 1993.

[102]Jonathan A. Rees and Norman I. Adams IV; "T: A dialect of Lisp or, lambda: The ultimate software tool," in *Conference Record of the 1982 ACM Symposium on Lisp and Functional Programming*, 114–122 (1982).

[103]John C. Reynolds; "The discoveries of continuations," in *Proc. Lisp and Symbolic Computation*, 233–248 (1993).

[104]J.A. Robinson; "A Machine-Oriented Logic Based on the Resolution Principle," in *Journal of the ACM*, 12(1) (January 1965): 23–41.

[105]Guido van Rossum; *The Python Language Reference Manual*, ed. Fred L. Drake Jr., Network Theory Ltd, 2003.

[106]Jane L. Russell, George D. Gatewood, and Thaddeus F. Worek; "Parallax Studies of Four Selected Fields," in *The Astronomical Journal*, 87(2) (February 1982): 428–432.

[107]Erik Sandewall; "From systems to logic in the early development of nonmonotonic reasoning," in *Artificial Intelligence*, 175 (2011): 416–427.

[108]Moses Schönfinkel; "Uber die Bausteine der mathematischen Logik," in *Mathematische Annalen*, 92 (1924): 305–316.

[109]Alex Shinn, John Cowan, and Arthur Gleckler (editors); *Revised⁷ Report on the Algorithmic Language Scheme* (2013).
http://www.r7rs.org/

[110]Alex Shinn; *Scheme Requests for Implementation 115: Scheme Regular Expressions* (2014).
https://srfi.schemers.org/srfi-115/

[111]Jeffrey Mark Siskind and Barak A. Perlmutter; "Perturbation confusion and referential transparency: Correct functional implementation of forward-mode AD," in *Implementation and application of functional languages–17th international workshop*, ed. Andrew Butterfield, Trinity College Dublin Computer Science Department Technical Report TCD-CS-2005-60, 2005.

[112]Brian Cantwell Smith; *Procedural Reflection in Programming Languages*, PhD thesis, MIT, Department of Electrical Engineering and Computer Science, 1982.

[113]Richard Matthew Stallman; *EMACS: The Extensible, Customizable, Self-Documenting Display Editor*, AI Memo 519A, MIT Artificial Intelligence Laboratory, March 1981.

[114]Richard Matthew Stallman and Gerald Jay Sussman; "Forward Reasoning and Dependency-Directed Backtracking in a System for Computer-Aided Circuit Analysis," in *Artificial Intelligence*, 9 (1977): 135–196.

[115]Guy Lewis Steele Jr.; *Common Lisp the language*. Maynard, MA: Digital Equipment Corporation, 1990.

[116]Guy L. Steele Jr.; *The Definition and Implementation of a Computer Programming Language Based on Constraints*, PhD thesis, MIT, also Artificial Intelligence Laboratory Technical Report 595, August 1980.

[117]Guy Lewis Steele Jr., Donald R. Woods, Raphael A. Finkel, Mark R. Crispin, Richard M. Stallman, and Geoffrey S. Goodfellow; *The Hacker's Dictionary*. New York: Harper & Row, 1983.

[118]Patrick Suppes; *Introduction to Logic*. New York: D. Van Nostrand, 1957.

[119]Gerald Jay Sussman and Richard Matthew Stallman; "Heuristic Techniques in Computer-Aided Circuit Analysis," in *IEEE Transactions on Circuits and Systems*, 22(11) (November 1975): 857–865.

[120]Gerald Jay Sussman and Guy L. Steele Jr; "The First Report on Scheme Revisited," in *Higher-Order and Symbolic Computation*, 11(4) (December 1998): 399–404.

[121]Gerald Jay Sussman and Jack Wisdom; *Structure and Interpretation of Classical Mechanics*. Cambridge, MA: MIT Press, 2001/2014.

[122]Gerald Jay Sussman and Jack Wisdom with Will Farr; *Functional Differential Geometry*. Cambridge, MA: MIT Press, 2013.

[123] *The TTL Data Book for Design Engineers*, by the Engineering Staff of Texas Instruments Incorporated, Semiconductor Group.

[124]Alan M. Turing; "On Computable Numbers, with an Application to the Entscheidungsproblem," in *Proceedings of the London Mathematical Society (Series 2)*, 42 (1936): 230–265.

[125]David L. Waltz; *Generating Semantic Descriptions From Drawings of Scenes With Shadows*, PhD thesis, MIT, also Artificial Intelligence Laboratory Technical Report 271, November 1972. http://hdl.handle.net/1721.1/6911

[126]Stephen A. Ward and Robert H. Halstead Jr.; *Computation Structures*. Cambridge, MA: MIT Press, 1990.

[127]Stephen Webb; *Measuring the Universe: The Cosmological Distance Ladder*, Springer-Praxis Series in Astronomy and Astrophysics. Berlin: Springer, 1999.

[128]Daniel J. Weitzner, Hal Abelson, Tim Berners-Lee, Chris Hanson, Jim Hendler, Lalana Kagal, Deborah McGuinness, Gerald Jay Sussman, and K. Krasnow Waterman; *Transparent Accountable Data Mining: New Strategies for Privacy Protection*, MIT CSAIL Technical Report MIT-CSAIL-TR-2006-007, January 2006.

[129]Robert Edwin Wengert; "A simple automatic derivative evaluation program," in *Communications of the ACM*, 7(8) (1964): 463–464.

[130]Carter Wiseman; *Louis I. Kahn: Beyond Time and Style: A Life in Architecture*. New York: W.W. Norton, 2007.

[131]Lewis Wolpert, Rosa Beddington, Thomas Jessell, Peter Lawrence, Elliot Meyerowitz, and Jim Smith; *Principles of Development* (2nd ed.). Oxford: Oxford University Press, 2001.

[132]Ramin Zabih, David McAllester, and David Chapman; "Non-deterministic Lisp with dependency-directed backtracking," in *AAAI-87*. (1987): 59–64.

Index

Any inaccuracies in this index may be explained by the fact that it has been prepared with the help of a computer.

Donald E. Knuth, *Fundamental Algorithms* (Volume 1 of *The Art of Computer Programming*)

Page numbers for Scheme procedure definitions are in *italics*.
Page numbers followed by n indicate footnotes.

List of Exercises